To Mike Un[...]

who also had his
shoulder to the wheel
in making The Gantry's
programme a success.
All the best!
5/7/96
Malcolm

*Economic Recovery
in The Gambia:
Insights for Adjustment
in Sub-Saharan Africa*

Harvard Studies in International Development

Other volumes in the series include:

Reforming Economic Systems in Developing Countries
edited by Dwight H. Perkins and Michael Roemer, 1991

Markets in Developing Countries: Parallel, Fragmented, and Black
edited by Michael Roemer and Christine Jones, 1991*

Progress with Profits: The Development of Rural Banking in Indonesia
by Richard Patten and Jay K. Rosengard, 1991*

Green Markets: The Economics of Sustainable Development
by Theo Panayotou, 1993*

The Challenge of Reform in Indochina
edited by Börje Ljunggren, 1993

Africa and Asia: Legacies and Opportunities in Development
edited by David L. Lindauer and Michael Roemer, 1994*

Macroeconomic Policy and Adjustment in Korea, 1970-1990
by Stephan Haggard, Richard N. Cooper, Susan Collins, Choongsoo Kim, Sung-Tae Ro, 1994

Framing Questions, Constructing Answers: Linking Research with Education Policy for Developing Countries
by Noel F. McGinn and Allison M. Borden, 1995

Industrialization and the State: The Korean Heavy and Chemical Industry Drive
by Joseph J. Stern, Ji-hong Kim, Dwight H. Perkins, Jung-ho Yoo, 1995

*Jointly published by the International Center for Economic Growth.

Economic Recovery in The Gambia: Insights for Adjustment in Sub-Saharan Africa

Edited by
Malcolm F. McPherson
and
Steven C. Radelet

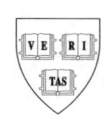

Harvard Institute for International Development
Distributed by Harvard University Press

Published by Harvard Institute for International Development
December 1995

Partially funded by the United States Agency for International Development
under the Consulting Assistance on Economic Reform Project, contract
no. PDC-0095-Z-00-9053-00

Distributed by Harvard University Press

Copyright © 1995, The President and Fellows of Harvard College.
All rights reserved.

Editorial management: Don Lippincott
Editorial assistance: Sarah Newberry
Proofreading and editorial assistance: Communications Development, Inc.;
HIID Staff Tamara Bond, Amy Cranley, Jen Ganem, and Dan Gilligan
Design and production: Editorial Services of New England, Inc.

Chapter 18 is largely a condensed version of an article that appeared in the *Journal of Policy Modeling*. The substance of that article is reprinted by permission of Elsevier Science, Inc., from "The Gambia's Economic Recovery: Policy Reforms, Foreign Aid, or Rain?" by Steven C. Radelet, *Journal of Policy Modeling*, Vol. 15 No. 3, pp. 251–276. Copyright 1993 by the Society for Policy Modeling.

Library of Congress Cataloging-in-Publication Data

Economic recovery in the Gambia : insights for adjustment in Sub-
   Saharan Africa / edited by Malcolm F. McPherson and Steven C.
   Radelet.
        p.   cm. — (Harvard studies in international development)
   Includes bibliographical references and index.
   ISBN 0-674-22975-4 (cloth)
        1. Structural adjustment (Economic policy)—Gambia. 2. Gambia—
   Economic conditions—1965–   I. McPherson, Malcolm F. II. Radelet,
   Steven C., 1957–   . III. Series.
   HC1070.E25   1995
   338.96651—dc20

Printed in the United States of America

95-36778
CIP

To the memory of
Sheriff Saikouba Sisay
Minister of Finance, The Gambia, 1982 to 1989

Contents

Contributors   *x*

Preface   *xiii*

Acronyms Used in the Text   *xvi*

I. Overview of the Economic Recovery Program

1
Introduction   *3*
Malcolm F. McPherson and Steven C. Radelet

2
The Economic Recovery Program: Background and Formulation   *19*
Malcolm F. McPherson and Steven C. Radelet

3
The Politics of Economic Reform   *33*
Steven C. Radelet and Malcolm F. McPherson

4
Donor Support for the Economic Recovery Program   *47*
Steven C. Radelet

II. Macroeconomic Reform

5
Exchange Rate Reform   *61*
Catherine J. McAuliffe and Malcolm F. McPherson

6
Monetary Policy and Financial Reform   77
James S. Duesenberry and Malcolm F. McPherson

7
Rural Credit and Savings   95
Paul E. McNamara and Parker Shipton

8
Budget Reform   111
Paul E. McNamara

9
Tax Reform   125
Clive S. Gray and Malcolm F. McPherson

10
Recurrent Costs and the Public Expenditure Program   145
Malcolm F. McPherson

11
External Debt Management   159
Steven C. Radelet, Clive S. Gray, and Paul E. McNamara

12
Rationalizing Domestic Debt   173
Catherine J. McAuliffe and Malcolm F. McPherson

III. Sectoral and Institutional Reform

13
Macroeconomic Reform and Agriculture   191
Malcolm F. McPherson

14
The Groundnut Sector   205
Christine Jones and Steven C. Radelet

15
Capacity Improvement in the Ministry of Finance   219
Clive S. Gray and Deborah A. Hoover

16
Parastatal Reform, Performance Contracts, and Privatization   235
Richard M. Hook, Richard D. Mallon, and Malcolm F. McPherson

17
Customs Reform   251
Paul E. McNamara and Malcolm F. McPherson

IV. What Can Be Learned?

18
Accounting for Growth under the Economic Recovery Program:
Results from a CGE Model   267
Steven C. Radelet

19
The Program for Sustained Development   281
Brendan M. Walsh

20
Insights from the Economic Recovery Program
for Sub-Saharan Africa   293
Merilee S. Grindle and Michael Roemer

Epilogue: The July 1994 Coup d'État   311
Steven C. Radelet and Malcolm F. McPherson

Select Bibliography   319

Index   333

Contributors

James S. Duesenberry is the William Joseph Maier Professor of Money and Banking Emeritus in the Department of Economics at Harvard University. As an HIID consultant in The Gambia, Professor Duesenberry advised on monetary policy, exchange rate policy, interest rate policy, and central bank independence. He received a Ph.D. in economics from the University of Michigan.

Clive S. Gray is an institute fellow at HIID and served most recently as senior advisor for HIID's Pricing Policy Project in Morocco. In The Gambia Dr. Gray worked on tax reform, computerization, and debt management. In 1983 he conducted a study for USAID/Banjul that led to the government's undertaking the Economic and Financial Policy Analyses Project in 1985. He received his Ph.D. in economics from Harvard University.

Merilee S. Grindle, faculty fellow at HIID, is also the Edward S. Mason Professor of International Development and the faculty advisor to the Edward S. Mason Program in Public Policy and Management. She is a specialist in the comparative analysis of policymaking, implementation, and public management in developing countries. Dr. Grindle earned a Ph.D. in political science from the Massachusetts Institute of Technology.

Richard M. Hook, former research associate at HIID, is now an independent consultant specializing in financial management. In The Gambia Mr. Hook worked on parastatal reform and privatization. He has an M.B.A. from Amos Tuck School of Business and has undertaken graduate work at Harvard University.

Deborah A. Hoover is former executive director of the Council on the Arts at the Massachusetts Institute of Technology. She currently is the administrator of HIID's Macroeconomic Technical Assistance Project in Zambia and an arts management consultant. As administrative consultant to the EFPA project, she was responsible for training, finance, and general administration. Ms. Hoover holds a master's degree from Cambridge University.

Christine Jones is a senior economist with the World Bank and was formerly an institute associate at HIID. Dr. Jones has worked extensively on rural development, women in development, and agricultural marketing issues. In The Gambia she studied groundnut pricing and marketing. She holds a Ph.D. in economics from Harvard University.

Richard D. Mallon is an institute fellow emeritus at HIID. He specializes in national development planning, structural adjustment and stabilization policies, trade and industrial policy reforms, and the reform and privatization of state-owned enterprises. In The Gambia he advised on privatization and parastatal reform and conducted workshops on these topics. Dr. Mallon received a Ph.D. in economics from Harvard University.

Catherine J. McAuliffe is with the Africa Department of the International Monetary Fund. As a consultant to the EFPA project, she worked on the rationalization of domestic debt, the monitoring of the IMF/World Bank programs, and customs reform. Ms. McAuliffe received her master's degree from the Fletcher School of Law and Diplomacy, where she is currently a Ph.D. candidate.

Paul E. McNamara is a former project assistant in the EFPA project in The Gambia. In that capacity he worked on debt management and customs reform issues, and the computerization of the budget. He was also a member of a special committee in 1988 that reviewed the customs administration. Mr. McNamara is currently a doctoral candidate in applied economics at the University of Minnesota.

Malcolm F. McPherson is a fellow of the institute at HIID. He served as a consultant to the Minister of Finance in The Gambia from 1983 to 1985 and then as director of the EFPA project until 1989. Dr. McPherson is currently the director of both the Macroeconomic Technical Assistance Project and the Tax Administration and Computerization Project in Zambia. He holds a Ph.D. in economics from Harvard University.

Steven C. Radelet is an institute associate at HIID and lecturer on economics at Harvard University. He specializes in stabilization, structural adjustment, and debt issues. He served as project assistant and project associate in The Gambia for HIID, where he conducted economic and financial policy analyses for the Ministry of Finance. He monitored the IMF structural adjustment program and helped computerize The Gambia's debt-reporting system. Dr. Radelet holds a Ph.D. in public policy from Harvard University.

Michael Roemer is an institute fellow at HIID and senior lecturer on economics at Harvard University. He specializes in macroeconomic reform, trade, and industrial policy. A former executive director of HIID, Dr. Roemer recently helped The Gambia begin developing an industrial policy. He holds a Ph.D. in economics from the Massachusetts Institute of Technology.

Parker Shipton is an associate professor of anthropology at Boston University and a faculty associate at HIID. His research interests include agrarian systems, land tenure, rural finance, small-scale enterprise, and general cultural and social anthropology. He has served as a consultant to the World Bank and other international agencies. Dr. Shipton earned his Ph.D. in social anthropology from Cambridge University.

Brendan M. Walsh is professor of national and applied economics at University College, Dublin. He was the director of the EFPA project from 1989 to 1991 and worked extensively on macroeconomic policy reform. He was a major contributor to the Program for Sustained Development, the successor to the ERP. Professor Walsh holds a Ph.D. in economics from Boston College.

Preface

In 1985 the Harvard Institute for International Development began working on a sustained basis with the Ministry of Finance of the Government of The Gambia. Mr. Sheriff Sisay, the leader of the ministry until his death in 1989, was an effective and dedicated minister, determined to reverse a decade of decline in the Gambian economy. It was our privilege to work with him, his successors, and the career staff of the ministry. Primarily through their efforts, the decade of decline was turned into eight years of growth and the beginnings of more fundamental institutional reform.

HIID left The Gambia in 1992 when our second contract financed by the United States Agency for International Development (USAID) came to an end. During the seven years in which HIID managed the Economic and Financial Policy Analyses (EFPA) Project, more than thirty HIID staff and consultants participated. Because the Gambians with whom we worked continually demonstrated their commitment to reform, they attracted to their country some of the ablest talent HIID has to offer. Many of those who participated in the project have contributed essays to this book. HIID's team leader for the first four years of this project was Malcolm McPherson, who continued as project backstopper on his return to Cambridge, Massachusetts. He was succeeded by Brendan Walsh and finally by Charles Mann. Working with the team leaders on a resident basis were Steven Radelet, Paul McNamara, and Andrew Adam, all of whom are graduates of the public policy program of the Kennedy School of Government at Harvard.

The July 1994 military coup and its aftermath have been sobering experiences for everyone involved in The Gambia's economic development efforts. As described in the epilogue to this volume, although the coup was not a response to the Jawara government's reform program, it underscores the fragility of the process of economic development in sub-Saharan Africa. The coup has made it all the more important that the salient lessons of the Economic Recovery Program (ERP) are not lost. This volume, then, provides insights not only into the successes and failures of the reform effort, but also the relationships between economic reform and the dynamics of the political process.

We believe that, in many ways, the reform effort in The Gambia between 1985 and the 1994 coup, and the technical assistance that contributed to it, was a model of how these types of programs *should* work but frequently do not. Leadership and all of the major decisions were taken by the Gambian government officials elected or appointed to that role. HIID's role was to strengthen the limited analytical skills of the Ministry of Finance to provide input into these decisions. We did so in two ways — by providing training for the Gambian civil servants in the ministry and by filling gaps with resident advisors and outside consultants. During the seven years, more than seventy-five Gambians were sent abroad for short- and long-term training. Others learned on the job. The long-term advisors brought in a range of macroeconomic, quantitative, and computer skills that helped The Gambia deal with such donors as the International Monetary Fund (IMF) on The Gambia's own terms rather than as supplicants. Short-term consultants provided international experience and special skills that no small developing country could reasonably expect to find within its own population.

This book, therefore, is really a comprehensive case study of substantive policy reform in sub-Saharan Africa and the ingredients that are required to make such reforms a reality. HIID's experience in The Gambia is one of the cornerstones of our expanding interest in assisting African countries to become part of, and to benefit from, the emerging global economy. Through advisory projects in other African countries, collaborative research on African development issues, and teaching and training African scholars and government officials, HIID seeks to assist African governments in designing and implementing improved economic policies. Drawing on its own internationally renowned staff and the faculty and students of Harvard University, HIID will help propose new approaches to the pressing problems of economic development and global economic integration in Africa.

HIID is grateful to all of those who contributed to the success of the Gambian project. We wish to thank the USAID mission personnel in Banjul who not only funded the project but helped us deal with the sometimes mystifying processes of the USAID bureaucracy. We are also grateful to the external reviewers who in 1987 and 1990 reviewed and praised the project and its contributions to The Gambia's economic recovery.

Most of all, however, our gratitude goes to the leaders and staff of the Ministry of Finance of The Gambia. It was they who ultimately decided on and carried out the reforms, often against considerable resistance. Despite the setback of the 1994 coup, we believe that the positive legacy of the economic reforms will remain a linchpin of The Gambia's future economic development.

Jeffrey D. Sachs
Director, HIID
December 1995

Acronyms Used in the Text

ACBI	Africa Capacity Building Initiative
ADP II	Agricultural Development Project II
AEPRP	African Economic Policy Reform Program
AG	attorney general
ARP	Administrative Reform Program
BICI	International Bank for Commerce and Industry
CFA	Communauté Financière Africaine
CGE	computable general equilibrium
CRD	Central Revenue Department
CTCS	Co-operative Thrift and Credit Societies
DOA	Department of Agriculture
ECOWAS	Economic Community of West African States
EEC	European Economic Community
EFPA	Economic and Financial Policy Analyses Project
ERP	Economic Recovery Program
ESAF	Enhanced Structural Adjustment Facility
GAMTEL	Gambia Telecommunication Company
GCDB	Gambia Commercial and Development Bank
GCU	Gambia Cooperatives Union
GEDRES	Gambia External Debt Reporting System
GNIC	Gambia National Insurance Corporation
GOTG	Government of The Gambia
GPA	Gambia Ports Authority
GPMB	Gambia Produce Marketing Board
GPTC	Gambia Public Transport Corporation
GUC	Gambia Utilities Corporation
HIID	Harvard Institute for International Development
IBAS	Indigenous Business Advisory Service

IDA	International Development Association
IDB	Islamic Development Bank
IMF	International Monetary
ITD	Income Tax Division
LMB	Livestock Marketing Board
MDI	Management Development Institute
MEPID	Ministry of Economic Planning and Industrial Development
MoA	Ministry of Agriculture
MoF	Ministry of Finance
NDL	National Development Levy
NIB	National Investment Board
NTC	National Trading Corporation
O&M	operations and maintenance
OAU	Organization of African Unity
OECD	Organization for Economic Cooperation and Development
PAYE	pay-as-you-earn
PE	public enterprise
PEP	public expenditure program
PIP	public investment program
POSB	Post Office Savings Bank
PPBS	planning and programming budgeting system
PPMU	Planning, Programming, and Monitoring Unit (of the DOA)
PPP	People's Progressive Party
PSD	Program for Sustained Development
PVO	private voluntary organization
RDP I	Rural Development Project I
SAC	Structural Adjustment Credit
SAF	Structural Adjustment Facility
SAL	Structural Adjustment Loan
SAP	Supplementary Appropriations
SBG	Standard Bank Gambia
SDR	Special Drawing Right
SSA	Sub-Saharan Africa
SSHFC	Social Security and Housing Finance Corporation
SSSU	Statistics and Special Studies Unit
UNDP	United Nations Development Programme
USAID	United States Agency for International Development
WACH	West African Clearing House

Part I

Overview of the Economic Recovery Program

1

Introduction

Malcolm F. McPherson and Steven C. Radelet

In mid-1985, The Gambia initiated one of the most comprehensive economic adjustment programs devised by any country in sub-Saharan Africa (SSA)—the Economic Recovery Program (ERP). The broad objectives of the ERP were twofold—to halt the deterioration of the economy and to lay the foundation for sustained economic growth. By mid-1986, just a year later, the revival of the Gambian economy had begun.

For the next eight years, the economy continued to expand, with real gross national product growing by more than 5 percent annually. Per capita income increased, inflation remained low, and the current account deficit of the balance of payments remained under control. The government reduced its budget deficit, increased its foreign exchange reserves, and eliminated its debt service arrears. Moreover, the austerity measures introduced under the ERP did not lead to civil strife.

How did The Gambia—widely regarded as a "basket case" in mid-1985—recover so dramatically? What lessons can other countries in SSA draw from both the success and failures of the ERP? What lessons have Gambians themselves learned? What additional measures are needed to transform the recovery into more sustained growth and development?

The essays in this volume respond to these questions by exploring the evolution and components of the ERP. Broadly, the essays examine:

- the underlying macroeconomic conditions that led the government to adopt wide-ranging policy changes;
- the immediate and longer-term impacts of the policies;
- the problems encountered as the policies were being implemented;
- the adjustments made to the policies as the ERP unfolded;
- the additional actions necessary to support sustainable, long-term economic growth.

These elements—why, how, and the success with which the ERP was implemented—provide a framework for examining not just the Gambian experience, but also how that experience relates to the broader patterns of economic adjustment throughout SSA.

Economic Decline and Adjustment in SSA[1]

Since the late 1970s economic deterioration has become widespread and even self-perpetuating in SSA. Most of the countries in the region have experienced declining real income, falling rates of investment, accelerating inflation, dwindling exports, a declining capacity to import, shrinking domestic savings, and mounting external debt. Many countries appear likely to continue to stagnate or even regress in the immediate future. Rectifying this macroeconomic environment has not been and will not be easy. Recovery efforts are being handicapped by the overhang of foreign debt, a deteriorating resource base, a limited supply of skilled personnel, and institutions that have found it difficult to achieve their stated objectives.

Country-specific data reveal the general pattern of economic disintegration and regression even more starkly. Examples include countries whose political and social climate has been relatively stable—Tanzania, Zambia, Ghana, and Senegal—as well as countries that have experienced civil war—Uganda, Angola, Sudan, Chad, Somalia, Liberia, and Ethiopia. The regression of their economies is evident in their extensive deindustrialization and by the fact that agriculture now contributes a larger share to gross domestic product (GDP) than it did two decades ago. Both trends are contrary to "normal" patterns of economic development.

To be sure, not all of the countries of SSA have exhibited these patterns. Botswana has recorded one of the highest sustained increases in per capita income of any country in the world during the last twenty-five years. Lesotho, Swaziland, Mauritius, and the Seychelles have also performed impressively. Moreover, several countries that earlier experienced difficulties have begun to recover. Ghana is the most oft-cited example; Burkina Faso, Tanzania, Zimbabwe, Uganda, as well as The Gambia, have all (to varying degrees) shown improved performance in recent years. The experiences of these countries indicate that economic deterioration is neither inevitable nor irreversible in the region.

Nevertheless, for many countries in the region, the pattern of decline has been so pronounced and widespread that a set of stylized facts can be identified. Common problems include:

Production
- low capital and labor productivity;
- declining output in key sectors, particularly agriculture;
- a bias against exports, and the domestic production of import substitutes due to an overvalued exchange rate;
- a deteriorating physical infrastructure, caused by disinvestment and the lack of maintenance;

Income
- a widening rural–urban income gap due to the explicit and implicit taxation of agriculture;
- a decline in rural welfare as public expenditures have become concentrated in urban areas;
- income redistribution to selected entrepreneurs and government officials through influence peddling and corruption;

Finance
- slow growth of public sector revenue due to tax evasion and price controls on public services;
- an accumulation of arrears on both internal and external payments;
- financial disintermediation because of low nominal interest rates and credit controls;
- the emergence of parallel and alternative markets to bypass official controls;
- high rates of credit creation due to excessive borrowing by the public sector to cover its deficit;
- a decline in domestic savings;
- a decline in foreign assets due to an overvalued exchange rate;
- currency substitution and capital flight.

An economy that exhibits even a few of these features would face serious difficulties. Many countries in SSA experience most of these conditions.

Economic Adjustment in SSA

Much research has been devoted to describing and understanding the pervasiveness of economic decline in SSA.[2] Both internal and external factors have been identified, although opinions about their relative importance vary. Yet the consensus is that remedies for economic decline require fundamental changes in economic policies, supported by technical and financial assistance from the donor community.

But consensus has not been reached in all areas—for example, how rapidly economic policies can and should be adjusted, the type of policy changes that are necessary, and the form of foreign assistance that is most appropriate. These divergent views were underscored when, with the assistance of the United Nations Economic Commission for Africa, the Organization of African Unity (OAU) published an "alternative structural adjustment program." (OAU, 1989). Specifically, the program advocated that the adjustment measures be adopted gradually, that multiple exchange rates be applied, and that government remain highly interventionist. It also argued that donor conditionality was not a useful mechanism for promoting adjustment. In contrast, the approximately thirty structural adjustment programs supported by the IMF and World Bank in SSA have called for broad-based adjustment, immediate measures to eliminate exchange-rate distortions, the removal of government from direct economic activity, and rigid conditionality.

Neither stance has met with unqualified success.[3] Too little time has passed to clearly distinguish their relative merits from the effects of other, non-policy-related changes. The deterioration in many countries has been so extensive that economic recovery, by whatever means, will take a long time. Perhaps the most comprehensive and careful study completed so far is the World Bank's *Adjustment in Africa: Reforms, Results, and the Road Ahead.* (World Bank, 1994). It reviews the policies and performance of twenty-nine SSA countries between 1981 and 1991 and concludes that where reforms have been implemented, economic performance has improved. But policy reform has been uneven in many countries, and important policy changes have not always been sustained. The report also argues that sustained development requires much more than good macroeconomic policies; it requires investment in human capital and infrastructure, strong institutions, and good governance.

Indeed, institutional problems have been far more serious than originally anticipated by the advocates of economic reform. Overcoming them will be difficult. Some have attributed institutional problems to "mediocre leadership" (Mwaipaya, 1980; Mazrui, 1980; Obasanjo, 1987); some believe that they stem from the absence of "agencies of constraint" (Collier, 1991); and still others associate them with a general lack of accountability, due to cronyism, nepotism, opportunism, and corruption.[4]

The recent focus on governance and political reform may provide some useful insights. However, much work must still be done.[5] Donor agencies, for example, are only now defining an agenda for improving governance. Political reform to return SSA countries to systems of responsible government is just beginning. The recent elections in South Africa, Zambia, and Eritrea were encouraging, but these events have been overshadowed by political chaos in Rwanda, Somalia, Angola, and Liberia.

The Gambian Economy

Background and Economic Structure

The Gambia is the smallest country in Africa. With only 11,000 square kilometers, it is roughly the size of the state of Connecticut. It lies on the banks of The Gambia River in the westernmost part of Africa, completely surrounded by Senegal except on its narrow Atlantic coast. Its 1992 population of 990,000 is the fifth smallest on the continent.

Despite its tiny size the population is diverse. There are five major ethnic groups (and several minor ones), each with its own distinct language.[6] Approximately 85 percent of the population are Moslem, 8 percent are Christian (mainly in the capital city Banjul), and the remainder follow traditional beliefs. Incomes vary as well: average income in the modern urban sector was about four times the average rural income in the early 1980s. (World Bank, 1985b, p. 3).

Until a July 1994 coup (discussed later in this chapter), The Gambia was one of the few multiparty democracies in Africa. Gambians enjoyed constitutionally guaranteed freedoms of speech, religion, and the press. These traditions notwithstanding, one party—the People's Progressive Party (PPP)—completely dominated politics between The Gambia's independence from the United Kingdom in 1965 and the 1994 coup. Sir Dawda Jawara of the PPP was the country's only leader. During this time The Gambia enjoyed political stability, with one exception: a July 1981 attempted coup d'état that left an estimated 1,000 Gambians dead. The eight-day uprising was finally put down by 1,500 Senegalese troops called in by Jawara under a mutual defense treaty. In the wake of the coup attempt, The Gambia and Senegal formed the Senegambia Confederation, which lasted until 1989. The Gambia's proximity to and relationship with Senegal affect economic activity and government policy in both countries (see Chapter 3).

The Gambian economy depends heavily on agriculture (small-scale farming, groundnut production, livestock, forestry, and fishing), which employs three-quarters of the population and accounts for 30 percent of GDP. Most farmers rely on groundnut production for their cash income. Groundnut production, processing, and trade together account for approximately 15 percent of GDP, and groundnut products constitute about 75 percent of domestically produced merchandise exports.

Outside of agriculture the major activity is trade. The Gambia imports about half of its food supplies, all of its fuel, and most of its capital and manufactured goods. Mainly because of the river, entrepôt trade with other countries in the region has been an important activity for generations. The reexport trade grew rapidly in the 1970s as The Gambia kept its tariffs low while neighboring countries increased tariffs and introduced quotas in an attempt to protect domestic industries. Reexports have surpassed groundnuts as the largest net foreign-exchange-earning activity. Manufacturing activities are limited, accounting for only about 6 percent of GDP (about half of which is groundnut processing). Although there are a growing number of hotels and restaurants, tourism accounts for less than 4 percent of GDP.

Economic Circumstances in 1985

Many of the stylized facts about SSA described earlier can be identified in the Gambian experience. By mid-1985 The Gambia's economy was in deep trouble. Relative to GDP:

- External arrears exceeded 50 percent.
- Foreign debt was approaching 250 percent.
- The current account deficit on the balance of payments was more than 30 percent.
- The public sector (government and public enterprise) budget deficit was around 25 percent.

Furthermore, The Gambia was beset by a host of other economic difficulties.

- Inflation was accelerating.
- Real per capita income was declining.
- Capital flight had reached major proportions.
- Currency substitution was well advanced.
- Agricultural production was falling.
- Real investment was declining.
- The physical infrastructure (roads, bridges, and schools) was deteriorating.

- Shortages of basic commodities (fuel, rice, and spare parts) were common.
- Business confidence was low.
- The country's international creditworthiness had evaporated.
- Donors had suspended all aid except for humanitarian assistance.

However, while the problems The Gambia faced were similar to those facing other SSA countries, the outcome of the reform efforts was very different. As described in Chapter 2, the economy quickly stabilized, with a reduction in both the rate of inflation and the current account deficit of the balance of payments. Gross domestic product grew sufficiently to provide a small, but welcome, increase in per capita income. And, as the foreign exchange market stabilized, shortages of imported commodities eased. The program was not universally successful—many institutional reforms failed to take hold—but it led to a dramatic reversal in the direction in which the economy was moving.

The crisis in The Gambia evolved over several years. Many of the fundamental problems were well known to the government and its advisors, but action was delayed. Why did the government wait so long to act constructively? Why, like so many other countries, did The Gambia for several years choose merely to "muddle through" with halfhearted efforts at adjustment? What happened to encourage—perhaps even force—the government to break so dramatically with this pattern?

The answers to these questions provide the basis for the story of The Gambia's recovery. They also provide many helpful insights into some of the choices and pressures confronting other governments facing similar circumstances. In particular, the Gambian experience shows that economies can recover relatively quickly, despite massive internal and external imbalances. Yet it also shows that success is predicated on a mutually reinforcing set of policy changes, leaders who remain committed to implementing the policies, and a donor community that provides adequate support. Still another message is that recovery can be achieved without undermining established democratic traditions or compromising basic freedoms and individual rights.

Although the macroeconomic crisis in The Gambia has ended and modest growth has ensued, The Gambia is not yet on a path of sustained development. Thus, the Gambian experience also shows how difficult it is for a small, open, aid-dependent country to move beyond the stabilization and adjustment phases of recovery to long-term growth and development. In The Gambia and elsewhere, changes in leadership, less vigilant donors, and/or concerted resistance to specific policy changes often impede policy implementation. Fundamental reforms of important public sector institutions have proved to be much more difficult than macroeconomic policy reforms, so scarce resources continue to be poorly allocated and misused. And as soon as recovery is underway, recollections of economic difficulties begin to dim, political priorities shift, resistance to reform becomes more entrenched, and donor conditions that were accepted during the crisis no longer appear to be reasonable. Corruption can reemerge, and efforts to increase accountability can lapse. As successful as The Gambia has been in stabilizing the economy, it will need to meet these challenges if it is to succeed in laying the foundation for sustained growth and development.

The Gambia's future became even more uncertain following a successful coup d'etat in July 1994, when four junior military officers led by 29-year-old Lieutenant Yaya Jammeh overthrew President Jawara's government (see the Epilogue for more details). The soldiers had several grievances, including resentment over the presence of Nigerian advisers within the army (especially the Nigerian commander of the Gambian army), late payment of soldier's allowances, and alleged corruption within the army's senior ranks. Since the coup, there have been reports of newspaper shutdowns and arbitrary arrests and detentions. The United States, Britain, Japan, and the European Union all suspended economic and military aid; the World Bank initially did so, but resumed relations when the military council announced it would hold elections in 1998. Five months after the coup, an attempted countercoup led by more senior members of the military failed. Following this event, Nordic tour groups, which were a major source of foreign exchange earnings, evacuated nine hundred tourists and canceled future trips. After the attempted countercoup, the election timetable was moved up to 1996. A second attempted countercoup in January 1995 also failed.[7]

The coup itself was rooted in internal army problems and issues of national security, and had little to do with economic policy. Indeed, the new government claimed that it planned to continue with the basic macroeconomic policies that formed the backbone of the ERP and PSD. However, the widespread initial public support for the coup apparently resulted from perceived failings in both economic policy and the political system. The public was unhappy about the government's failure to achieve sustained development since independence and Jawara's apparent unwillingness to step down after nearly thirty years in power. But they seemed even more annoyed about the apparent increase in corruption in the early 1990s. Farmers were angered by revelations of an embezzlement scheme at the Gambia Cooperatives Union (GCU), customs corruption had increased (yet again), and the privatization of the Gambia Commercial and Development Bank (GCDB) had revealed many large and nonperforming loans to politically well-connected individuals. It was apparent that once the economic crisis of the 1980s had passed, government oversight and control again weakened. A good example of this lapse is customs administration. As is pointed out in Chapter 17, the government failed on several occasions to root out widespread corruption in the customs department, and each time the immediate budgetary need for customs revenues disappeared, corruption reappeared. Although the ERP successfully stabilized the macroeconomy and revived economic growth, it failed to reform public sector institutions, improve public management, and reduce the scope for corruption.

The coup diminishes the prospects for sustained economic development in The Gambia. Africa's experience with military leaders promising to root out corruption does not bode well. Major aid donors have withdrawn support, tourists are leaving, and the reexport trade is shrinking (because of both tightened security on the Senegalese border and trade liberalization in the franc zone). As a result, foreign exchange inflows have fallen sharply. It is possible that, over time, the new government can solidify the gains from the ERP and address the areas in which it was unsuccessful. But it is more likely that many of the successes of the ERP will be reversed. The Gambia easily could slide into economic regression similar to that of the early 1980s. These events make it all the more important that the salient lessons of the ERP are not lost.

Organization of the Essays

We have prepared the essays to address the basic themes of the ERP—exchange rate reform, the promotion of agriculture and other productive sectors, civil service reform, the reform of monetary and fiscal policy, parastatal reform, improved public investment, and debt management. The first part of the volume provides background for the ERP policy measures, focusing on the prevailing economic climate that led to the ERP. The main body of the text examines each of the major macroeconomic and sectoral reforms. The concluding part rounds out the technical components of reform by reviewing the results, lessons, and future direction of reform. Each chapter also contains concluding observations and insights that, taken as a whole, can provide valuable direction for other SSA countries in the midst of economic reform.

This approach, we feel, will be of the greatest assistance to African policymakers and advisers who are in the process of formulating or reformulating programs to revive their economies. It should also be useful to those members of the donor and academic communities who are interested in the specific aspects of economic adjustment and reform. Students of comparative economic and political systems may find the final chapters of some relevance.

Review of the Essays

Part I: Overview of the Economic Recovery Program

The Economic Recovery Program: Background and Formulation. The degree to which the Gambian economy had deteriorated was quite extraordinary. This essay provides some perspective on the size and nature of the economic imbalances that existed and the various pressures and limited options facing the government when it decided to formulate and implement the ERP. An important aspect of the ERP implementation process was its openness. The main provisions were discussed widely and shared publicly with policymakers, thus avoiding major policy surprises.

The Politics of Economic Reform. Political factors played a major role in the dynamics of The Gambia's economic difficulties. Formulating and implementing the ERP required that many of those factors be neutralized. In the face of concerted local resistance, the ERP was implemented successfully. Key elements in its success were leadership by Minister of Finance Sisay and the vigilance of donors to ensure that the conditions they imposed were met.

Donor Support for the Economic Recovery Program. Given the fragile state of the government's finances and its limited technical capacity, the success of the ERP depended heavily on timely and generous support from the donor community. The support took a variety of forms—commodity aid, project support, technical assistance, and balance of payments finance. Commodity aid (food and fuel) was crucial to easing key constraints in the first three years of the ERP. Project support helped build and maintain important infrastructure. Technical assistance allowed the government to deal with the complex policy and monitoring problems associated with the ERP. The balance of payments support helped The Gambia service its foreign debt and rationalize its external arrears.

Part II: Macroeconomic Reform

Exchange Rate Reform. The exchange rate became progressively overvalued from the mid-1970s onward. The government was unwilling to devalue, and the situation got out of hand. Foreign debt grew rapidly, foreign arrears mounted, and a parallel exchange market began to flourish. Capital flight and currency substitution were common. The official exchange rate became largely irrelevant. Under the ERP the government floated the dalasi and removed all restrictions on foreign exchange transactions. With an appropriate set of supporting policies—notably, market-determined interest rates and a reduction in the budget deficit, together with balance of payments support from the donors—the exchange rate stabilized.

Monetary Policy and Financial Reform. With a budget deficit that averaged 10 percent of GDP between 1965–1966 and 1985–1986, the government had been a large borrower, both domestically and abroad. Moreover, in an attempt to promote development, the government established its own central bank and commercial bank. Both of these organizations pursued highly expansionary credit policies. With a fixed exchange rate, declining export revenue, and limits on the level of foreign aid, serious pressures built up on the financial system. Inflation accelerated, the exchange rate became increasingly overvalued, and capital flight and currency substitution became the norm. Financial reform under the ERP entailed liberalizing interest rates and rehabilitating the public financial institutions. Interest rate reform proved to be far easier than reform of the financial institutions.

Rural Credit and Savings. The government directed large amounts of subsidized credit to the farming community, encouraged by the notion that poor farmers needed cheap credit. Little of it was repaid. Ultimately, the institutions involved—the Gambia Cooperatives Union and the Gambia Commercial and Development Bank—became insolvent. Reorganizing these institutions has taken much time and effort. If institutional credit is to serve a useful role in agriculture, the financial behavior of and constraints facing rural producers have to be better understood and addressed.

Budget Reform. One of the government's most important achievements during the ERP was to reduce the budget deficit dramatically. This step was critical in stabilizing the economy. However, the government made very little progress in reforming the underlying budget process. Many chronic budgetary problems were not addressed. Ironically, the success in reducing the deficit may have hampered efforts to improve the budget process because it diverted attention from the need for improved allocation within the budget. This episode illustrates the difficulties in promoting institutional change in the context of a macroeconomic adjustment program.

Tax Reform. Even prior to introducing the ERP, The Gambia had undertaken some important initiatives to reform the system of direct and indirect taxes. The Gambia has always been, and remains, heavily dependent on taxes on international trade. Senior government officials have appreciated the risks of that dependency and sought measures to broaden the tax base. The reform of the direct tax system focused on efforts to improve tax compliance, reduce the administrative burden, and make the system more equitable. Indirect tax reform sought to broaden the domestic tax base. Finally, the reform of the investment tax incentives sought to make the system more transparent and to reduce leakages. Although progress was made, tax compliance remained low, administration remained weak, and investment incentives continued to reduce revenue without encouraging productive investment.

Recurrent Costs and the Public Expenditure Program. Following the dramatic expansion in public investment after the mid-1970s, serious problems arose in providing the resources necessary to operate and maintain the capital created by that investment. An acute recurrent cost problem emerged. The economic difficulties of the 1980s simply accentuated the problem. The ERP focused attention on funding operations and maintenance expenditures for rehabilitating the public-sector capital stock, an effort that was only partially successful.

External Debt Management. Until the mid-1970s, The Gambia made few external commitments, but by the early 1980s the volume of debt had grown rapidly. Due to a foreign exchange shortage, the debt could not be serviced. Restructuring and reorganizing the external obligations necessitated developing a debt management system. This task was time-intensive. Many records were missing, many debts were unrecorded, and few government officials had the motivation to improve the debt data. Debt was considered to be "someone else's problem." But with the macroeconomic policy changes of the ERP and the support of the donors, the debt burden eased considerably in the late 1980s.

Rationalizing Domestic Debt. The rapid expansion of the public sector could not be financed. Taxation receipts and domestic borrowing from the nonbank public were inadequate. Over time the government and its agencies began to borrow at increasingly larger rates from the banking system. Eventually, the government simply failed to pay its obligations. Domestic arrears reached major proportions and took considerable effort and several years to unravel.

Part III: Sectoral and Institutional Reform

Macroeconomic Reform and Agriculture. A major reason for the poor economic performance of the Gambian economy was the collapse of agriculture. Drought and fluctuating prices for exports were important factors. Inappropriate policies were also significant. Government-determined producer prices were too low, the exchange rate was overvalued, public investment in agriculture was inadequate and misdirected, and the public enterprises associated with agriculture taxed rather than supported the sector. The ERP focused heavily on revitalizing agriculture. Groundnut production was subsidized, prices were decontrolled, and measures were adopted to reduce the costs imposed on farmers by public enterprises. Agriculture began to respond, but its longer-term growth has been limited by serious resource constraints.

The Groundnut Sector. The Gambia's principal domestic export has been groundnuts. In the early 1970s both production and revenue in the sector increased rapidly. That situation changed dramatically in the late 1970s and early 1980s. In order to give the agricultural sector a boost and to stimulate exports, the government agreed to subsidize the price of groundnuts as part of the IMF/World Bank structural adjustment programs. In 1986 the subsidy represented more than 8 percent of GDP. The subsidy could not be sustained, and groundnut prices fell substantially over the next three years.

Capacity Improvement in the Ministry of Finance. Throughout the 1970s the Gambian civil service expanded rapidly and its efficiency deteriorated. A major thrust of the ERP was to rationalize the size of the civil service and improve its organization. A program for the systematic restructuring of all ministries was formulated. The Ministry of Finance was basically untouched by the reorganization, which compromised its role in the economy. However, a major effort was made to improve the skills of the ministry staff. This took the form of short- and long-term training programs, computerization, and on-the-job training by visiting consultants.

Parastatal Reform, Performance Contracts, and Privatization. With the collapse of the groundnut sector, an important source of fiscal revenue—namely, revenue generated by the Gambia Produce Market Board—disappeared. Because the government was running large deficits and most public enterprises (PEs) were making losses, the entire public sector became a major drain on the economy. The ERP emphasized two measures for rationalizing the operations of PEs. One was a system of performance contracts that delineated the separate responsibilities of the government and each PE; the other was privatization. These activities took considerably longer than anticipated. Both measures encountered considerable local resistance, which was overcome only partly with pressure from donors. Many parastatals continued to be a drag on the economy.

Customs Reform. Although the ERP involved a comprehensive set of policy changes, some measures were not anticipated. Customs reform is an example. In response to a sharp drop in revenue collection, Minister of Finance Sisay ordered an investigation, which revealed widespread customs fraud. The actions taken to reduce fraud significantly reduced both the government budget deficit and domestic credit creation. Inflation declined and the exchange rate stabilized. Indeed, without the reduction in customs fraud, the ERP could not have succeeded. Nonetheless, it has been exceedingly difficult to prevent its resurgence.

Part IV: What Can Be Learned?

Accounting for Growth under the Economic Recovery Program: Results from a CGE Model. One of the most important determinants of the success of the ERP was the comprehensive nature of the policies implemented by the government. There were fortuitous external developments, such as an end to the Sahelian drought. Donor support was important as well. A macroeconomic model was used to determine the relative contribution of each of these factors—policies, luck, and aid—to the success of economic reform.

The Program for Sustained Development. The ERP was a four-year program. Its objectives were to turn the economy around and lay the foundation for sustained growth. It achieved the first objective and made some progress toward the second. The government recognized that more had to be done. It thus prepared the successor for the ERP—the Program for Sustained Development (PSD). To build on the success of the ERP, its primary challenge is to push ahead with the policy initiatives of the ERP and sustain the momentum achieved so far. Mobilizing more resources domestically and using them productively will be vital to this effort.

Lessons from the Economic Recovery Program for Sub-Saharan Africa. Many SSA countries have begun to address their structural problems. The Gambia has been more successful than most. The final chapter of the study draws lessons and insights from the ERP that may be useful to other African countries.

NOTES

1. This and the next sections draw on McPherson and Zinnes (1991) and McPherson (1992).
2. World Bank, 1981a, 1984, 1986, 1989a, and 1994; Organization of African Unity, 1980 and 1989; United Nations, 1986; Ravenhill, 1986; Loutfi, 1989; McPherson and Zinnes, 1991.
3. World Bank, 1988a; World Bank/United Nations Development Program, 1989; Gallagher, 1991; Radelet, 1992b.

4. Dumont, 1969; Hyden, 1983; Sandbrook, 1987 and 1990; Parfitt and Riley, 1989; Klitgaard, 1988; Hyden and Barrett, 1991.

5. For example, there is a major gap in our understanding of what must be done—and how, when, and with and by whom—to redress the basic weaknesses of the *permanent* institutions of government, such as the Central Bank and the Ministries of Finance, Justice, and Public Works. Improving the performance of these institutions will be critical in any reform effort. A double bind exists. Economic reform is required due largely to institutional failures; promoting economic reform, however, requires functional and effective institutions.

6. Mandinkas make up 37 percent of the population, and Fulas, Wolofs, Jolas, and Serahulis make up 17, 13, 7, and 6 percent, respectively. In addition to local languages, English (the official language), French, and Arabic are spoken.

7. See *New York Times,* July 24, 1994, and August 28, 1994; Reuters news services, October 28, 1994; *International Herald Tribune,* November 12–13, 1994; Associated Press news services, November 30, 1994; and *West Africa,* February 6, 1995.

2

The Economic Recovery Program: Background and Formulation

Malcolm F. McPherson and Steven C. Radelet

The evolution of economic policy in The Gambia in the past two decades largely reflects domestic reaction to external developments. In principle, the country's small size and its reliance on trade leave little room for the government to pursue policies that are inconsistent with broad movements in international pricing and the priorities of international donors. Yet, in practice, policymakers have had much discretion over when and how they react to external developments. As noted in Chapter 1, the government was slow to react to adverse shifts in the external economic setting. As a result, economic performance suffered.

When in 1985 the government finally responded by introducing the Economic Recovery Program, the turnaround was remarkable. Within eighteen months the economy had stabilized and was growing.

The Gambia's reform effort has been unusual both because rapid improvements were made and because the government implemented the program without overt public opposition. President Sir Dawda Jawara was reelected with a 60 percent majority just nineteen months after the ERP began. The People's Progressive Party was returned to Parliament with an enhanced majority.

This chapter provides the background to and discusses the implementation and impacts of the ERP. It addresses several questions that broadly set the stage for the chapters that follow. How and why was the government prompted to formulate the ERP? What economic events preceded its introduction, and what types of pressures affected economic policy? How was the ERP then formulated, and what was the rationale for the mix of policies recommended, as well as some of the actions

This chapter draws heavily from McPherson and Radelet (1991).

taken? Finally, what was the initial impact of the ERP, and what factors were responsible for its success?

Background to Reform: Economic Conditions Prior to the ERP

Many factors, both external and internal, had led to economic deterioration in The Gambia prior to the ERP. Sharp increases in the price of imports (including petroleum products), the long Sahelian drought, low world prices for groundnuts, declining foreign aid flows, high international interest rates, poor planning, mismanagement, and inappropriate fiscal and monetary policies—all contributed to growing internal and external imbalances. The adverse effects of some factors, such as the overvalued exchange rate and the government budget deficit, were evident in the late 1970s. (see McPherson, 1979, especially Appendix III). However, not until early 1982, when foreign payment arrears began to accumulate rapidly, did the full extent of The Gambia's difficulties emerge. From that point onward economic deterioration accelerated.

The change in The Gambia's economic circumstances can best be illustrated by a comparison of the country's economic performance during the first and second decades after independence—from fiscal years 1965–1966 to 1974–1975 and from 1975–1976 to 1985–1986. Using 1975–1976 as the starting point of the second decade is useful because it coincides with several important structural changes in the economy. The external factors included the first oil shock, a sharp increase in aid from international donors, and the increasingly erratic pattern of rainfall in the Sahel.[1] Internally, the introduction of the first five-year plan dramatically changed the government's role in the economy. (GOTG, 1975b). The comparison ends with fiscal year 1985–1986 because some of the measures introduced under the ERP (particularly exchange rate reform, the liberalization of rice marketing, and improved budgetary discipline) were taking effect by then. It was also when the international financial standing of The Gambia began to improve after it paid its arrears to the International Monetary Fund.

Economic performance diverged markedly over the two decades (see the second and third columns of Table 2-1). In the first decade aggregate real income increased substantially, average per capita income rose, inflation was moderate, and the foreign exchange rate was stable—indeed, the dalasi was revalued by 20 percent in 1973.[2] Other positive economic indicators included an accumulation of foreign exchange

Table 2-1. Basic Economic Data, The Gambia

Economic Indicators	Pre-ERP 1965–66 to 1974–75	Pre-ERP 1975–76 to 1985–87	ERP 1985–86 to 1988–89
Real GDP (% per annum)	4.9	2.7	3.8
Real GDP per capita (% per annum)	2.3	-0.3	0.6
Agriculture growth per capita (% per annum)	0	-1.2	0.4
Agricultural output (% of GDP)	37.8	29.2	29.1
Inflation (% increase per annum)	5.0	12.1	15.0
Exchange rate (dalasi per US$) (% of devaluation per annum)	-2.0	-6.4	-12.9
External debt (increase per annum)	US$.9m	US$44.4m	US$46.5m
External arrears (increase per annum)	0	US$9.2m	-US$22.5m
Government recurrent expenditures (% of GDP)	13.6	20.7	29.1[a]
Government budget deficit (% of GDP)	2.6	13.2	13.8[a]
Development expenditures (% of GDP)	3.9	12.8	12.6
Net foreign assets (average change per annum)	D4.7m	-D59.3m	D108.7m
Net domestic credit (average change per annum)	D3.7m	D42.7m	-D64.9m
Net credit to government (average change per annum)	D1.0m	D9.2m	-D53.9m
Money supply (% increase per annum)	14.0	11.7	17.1
Food imports (% of GDP)	7.1	15.2	18.6
BoP current account deficit (% of GDP)	8.3	35.9	25.5
Domestic exports (annual average)	D3.8m	D6.2m	D19.4m
Exports (including reexports) (annual average)	D3.9m	D12.7m	D132.8m
Imports (annual average)	D5.2m	D24.8m	D178.0m
BoP current account deficit	D1.5m	D17.1m	D69.4m
Groundnut sales (1000 metric tons per annum)	122.9	8.5	51.3
Rainfall (millimeters per annum) Basse (East Gambia)	919	822	867

[a]These data are inflated by extraordinary transfers to parastatals of 5.1 percent of GDP.
Source: Ministry of Finance and Economic Affairs, Macro Policy Analysis Unit.

reserves, little foreign debt, a balanced recurrent budget, high and rising groundnut production, and a balance between imports and exports. In the second decade the growth of aggregate real income slowed (after 1981–1982 real income declined), average per capita income fell, inflation accelerated, the foreign exchange rate depreciated, foreign debt increased sharply, and, by mid-1986, foreign payment arrears reached US$105 million (equivalent to 53 percent of GDP). The government budget became unbalanced, development expenditures expanded rapidly without stimulating a major increase in aggregate output, foreign exchange reserves were depleted, average groundnut production declined, and imports increased well beyond the country's capacity to export.

Whereas the Gambian economy was in basic balance during the first decade after independence, unsustainable imbalances in both the domestic budget and the balance of payments emerged during the second decade. Several factors led to economic deterioration.[3] Externally, the petroleum price increases of 1973 and 1979 sharply raised the foreign exchange cost of fuel; the prolonged Sahelian drought reduced agricultural production, simultaneously lowering agricultural exports and increasing imports of staple foods; international inflation increased the costs of manufactured imports; and foreign aid and soft loans, which had increased dramatically in the second half of the 1970s, declined in the early 1980s as industrialized countries reoriented their aid programs. International prices for agricultural products (especially groundnuts) fell as the agricultural surpluses generated by subsidies from the European Economic Community, the United States, and Japan depressed prices in the world oilseeds market; and international interest rates rose as the major industrialized countries tightened their monetary policies in order to control inflation and as the United States increased its borrowing to cover its budget deficit.

Inappropriate economic policies and administrative weaknesses aggravated the impact of these external events in the second decade. The expenditures included in the first five-year plan (1975) were too large and were managed too poorly to have a long-term positive effect on economic growth and development. Subsidies for rice, fertilizer, electricity, and transport services increased parastatal financial losses and diverted resources from productive investment.

Government budgetary discipline eroded as supplementary appropriations became a regular feature of government budgeting, revenue collection procedures broke down, and public employment expanded sharply. The number of civil service posts expanded by 70 percent in 1977–1978 alone, and nearly doubled between 1975–1976 and 1985–1986. In 1975–1976 the government wage bill was equivalent to 30 percent of the value of groundnut production; by 1985–1986 it had grown to 140 percent.

At the same time price controls on staples, such as rice, cooking oil, and meat, eroded the income of farmers. The overvalued exchange rate and the export tax on groundnuts depressed revenue from and investment in agriculture. The prolonged drought damaged agricultural production further. Thus agriculture output as a percentage of GDP declined by 8.6 percentage points between the first and second decades (see Table 2-1).

Despite the massive increase in foreign borrowing and investment relative to GDP, productive capacity per worker declined. To provide the anticipated impetus to development, the government increased its involvement in the economy by creating public enterprises and by providing investment incentives such as tax abatements, guaranteed loans, and subsidized credit. The attempt failed. Administered prices, unproductive investment, mismanagement, and poor cost recovery prevented the PEs from making a net positive financial contribution to the economy. Thus the entire public sector (both government and PEs) became a financial drain on the economy.[4]

Many developing countries have sustained internal imbalances for extended periods by adopting policies that insulate them from the rest of the world. Given The Gambia's limited productive base and openness to trade, it had few mechanisms for insulating itself. Many of the adverse trends, such as declining exports relative to imports, higher rates of inflation, mounting pressure on the budget, and the depletion of foreign exchange reserves, were evident as early as 1977–1978. But for several years the economy was cushioned from these difficulties by the availability of foreign exchange reserves (which had reached the equivalent of ten months of imports in 1974–1975), the country's ability to borrow abroad, and the low levels of debt service (because most of the loans contracted in the 1970s had grace periods of six to ten years).

Pressure on the economy increased in phases. In 1979 foreign assets became negative, the government began to have difficulty in discharging some overseas debts, and traders began to hold foreign exchange offshore. By mid-1982 payment arrears had begun to accumulate rapidly. Open evidence of a parallel foreign exchange market emerged in 1983, and capital flight, which had long been a concern of the Central Bank, accelerated. In response to IMF pressure to increase incentives to farmers, the government attempted to raise groundnut producer prices in 1982–1983. When world prices fell sharply in that year, the Gambia Produce Marketing Board (GPMB) effectively went bankrupt. The 25 percent devaluation of the dalasi in February 1984 merely postponed more decisive action. The large food imports necessary to cover the shortfalls in the 1983–1984 harvest aggravated the foreign exchange position further. By late 1984 the cumulative effect of these factors was a serious erosion in business confidence. Private-sector investment virtually ceased, and currency substitution into Communauté Financière Africaine (CFA) francs, pounds, and dollars was widespread.[5]

A serious situation became untenable when The Gambia fell into arrears with the IMF, which then canceled the stand-by program that had been negotiated in mid-1984. The foreign exchange situation continued to deteriorate. Gross foreign exchange reserves fell to the equivalent of two weeks of imports, and arrears to the IMF and other international creditors mounted rapidly. By mid-1985 they were approximately 58.5 million Special Drawing Rights (SDRs), equivalent to US$75 million. Disbursements for many development projects were suspended, normal short-term credit facilities were withdrawn, and shortages of rice and petrol became commonplace. The premium for foreign exchange in the parallel market reached 50 percent. A general sense of malaise was evident. The pressure intensified when the managing director of the IMF moved to have The Gambia declared ineligible for borrowing. Other donors exerted more pressure when they indicated that, unless the government changed its economic policies, they would, or could, do little to assist.[6] Time had run out for The Gambia in international financial circles.

Formulating the ERP

When it became evident that the international community had no intention of rescuing The Gambia financially, the government was forced to act. The minister of finance, Sheriff Sisay, assembled a task force of senior officials in June 1985 to develop a reform program. Sisay assigned staff from the Ministry of Finance (MoF), the Ministry of Economic Planning, and the Central Bank to the task force. He also asked two expatriates to participate—an economic adviser in the MoF and a World Bank economist. Minister Sisay instructed the task force to design a program that was as comprehensive as necessary to reverse The Gambia's economic decline and return it to sustainable growth. He told them not to be concerned with the political consequences of reform measures. Minister Sisay wanted a sound economic program; others would deal with its political acceptability.

The Economic Recovery Program: Background and Formulation 25

After meeting continuously for a week, the task force produced an action plan that formed the basis of the ERP. The minister's 1985–1986 budget speech described the seven major components of this program: exchange rate reform, the promotion of agriculture, the promotion of other productive sectors, civil service and parastatal reform, monetary and fiscal policy measures to reduce the budget deficit, the reorientation of the public investment program (PIP), and the rationalization of the external debt.

What the ERP task force intended, and ultimately what it achieved, was an adjustment program that built on and enhanced the complementarities and interdependencies that already existed within the Gambian economy. The following were the medium-term objectives of the ERP (later to become part of the series of policy framework papers developed by the IMF and World Bank):

- to reform the exchange rate system
- to revitalize the productive sectors, especially agriculture
- to curtail government activity in the economy to a level consistent with its resource base
- to rationalize the relationship between the activities in which the government can and should be involved and those that can be directed most effectively by the private sector
- to restructure the financial system whereby it forms a solid foundation for sustained financial development
- to strengthen existing public-sector institutions by rationalizing, redeploying, and training staff
- to improve the effectiveness with which existing capital facilities are maintained and used
- to reorient public-sector investment toward complementing the expansion of productive activity throughout the economy
- to restore The Gambia's international creditworthiness

Exchange rate reform was essential to removing the main distortions from the system of payments and exchange. Because the parallel market had effectively undercut the official exchange rate and because the accumulation of foreign arrears had reached such major proportions, anything less than a full-blown market-oriented solution that exposed the exchange rate to all economic pressures would have been inadequate. Exchange rate reform also was designed to promote and sustain a major real devaluation of the dalasi. That element would be the key to restoring the attractiveness of agriculture and reversing the decline in rural real income that had been exacerbated by production declines (due to drought) and low farmgate prices (due to price controls and the misaligned exchange rate).

Revitalizing agriculture was essential to the success of the ERP. Other productive activities, such as fisheries, tourism, business services, and small manufacturing, had to be promoted as well, especially if a solid basis for future growth were to be created. As shown clearly by the data in Table 2-1, agriculture had been particularly hard hit in the decade prior to the ERP. Given the poor performance of aggregate GDP, other productive activity also had fared poorly. That situation had to be dealt with decisively.

Important to that task was a *complete rationalization of the public sector* in terms of both its size and its relation to economic activity. As already noted, the public sector had expanded too far, too fast. It had become a major drain on the economy.[7] Public-sector reform had several components. The civil service had to be reduced, reorganized, and redirected. Public enterprises had to be restrained from engaging in socially unproductive activities. The efficiency and effectiveness of public-sector programs had to be enhanced; the key element was to *reorient the public investment program* from new capital projects to rehabilitation and reconstruction. With external and internal debt at levels that could not be serviced, the overall efficiency of all public-sector resources in The Gambia had to be raised. Accordingly, a major thrust of the ERP was to reduce waste. Physical resources had to be maintained adequately, unproductive workers had to be retrenched, loss-making activities had to be discontinued, and welfare-reducing activities had to be abandoned. In effect, the public sector's claims on the economy's resources had to decline, and its contribution to income and welfare had to increase.

The keystone was to *reduce the budget deficit* substantially. Notwithstanding the fact that external events had made economic management more difficult during the late 1970s, the economic imbalances in The Gambia had been perpetrated by poor public-sector spending policies. The Gambia's economic imbalances would not have become so extreme had the government pursued a more prudent fiscal policy. Consequently, economic adjustment would be impossible without a major change in the public-sector budget. That change would also have important repercussions for monetary policy and the financial system.

Because the government had essentially run a Ponzi scheme immediately prior to the ERP—that is, issuing new debt to cover its debt service—the financial system had become severely strained. A compliant Central Bank had exacerbated the fiscal pressure by allowing real interest rates on loans and deposits to become highly negative and by failing to supervise the local financial system adequately. The government then added to the problem by effectively using the state-owned Gambia Commercial and Development Bank (GCDB) as a grant-making organization.

The final measure was to *rationalize The Gambia's external debt*. With its arrears threatening its eligibility to borrow from the IMF, The Gambia was risking the prospect of losing all credibility in international financial circles. The sheer volume of debt was overwhelming and could not be serviced. It had to be rescheduled and refinanced.

All of these measures were mutually complementary. For instance, the success of the exchange rate reform depended on whether an appropriate interest rate policy was adopted and the public-sector deficit reduced. The latter depended on whether the civil service could be made more efficient and public enterprises could be disengaged from loss-making and welfare-reducing activities.

Implementing the ERP

Implementation of the ERP began with Minister Sisay's 1985 budget speech. He announced that the government immediately would liberalize the importation and marketing of rice, sharply increase the producer price of groundnuts, and eliminate the fish export tax. He also affirmed the government's previously adopted ban on creating new civil service posts and the freeze on civil service wages.

In September the Central Bank raised interest rates. In December the Gambia Public Transport Corporation (GPTC) increased public transportation fares, the MoF raised the prices of petroleum products, and the government adopted a moratorium on contracting or guaranteeing new nonconcessional medium-term debt. In January the Gambia Utilities Corporation (GUC) raised both water and electricity charges, and the government liberalized the fertilizer market. Also in January the MoF floated the dalasi by establishing an interbank market for foreign exchange and lifted all restrictions on capital flows. The government initiated a crackdown on customs fraud in February; and in May it laid off 1,644 temporary employees and abolished 280 vacant civil service posts, reducing the number of civil servants by nearly 10 percent.

In the second year of the ERP, the government sharply raised the producer price of groundnuts for the second successive year, this time to well above world-market levels in order to obtain support from the IMF. It also raised taxes on petroleum and rice and lowered import duties on many other items. The Central Bank established a treasury bill tender system for determining market interest rates; the MoF and Central Bank rescheduled debts with the Paris Club; the government laid off an additional 291 temporary employees and 922 established staff, and abolished 816 vacant civil service posts, reducing the number of government employees by another 8 percent; and the Ministry of Economic Planning attached stricter investment criteria to the public investment program. The government divested its shares in a bank and a trading company and took over D72.6 million of government-guaranteed, and primarily nonperforming, debts from the GCDB. In order to cover their costs more effectively, the GUC and GPTC again raised their interest rates.

New initiatives continued in 1987–1988: the MoF introduced a national sales tax and restructured the income tax system; the Central Bank refinanced its London Club debts; and the government paid off D80 million in debts that the GPMB had accumulated with the Central Bank. President Jawara signed performance contracts with three public enterprises; the government reorganized the Ministry of Agriculture and began to reshape the GCDB; and Parliament passed a revised Development Act.

The breadth of the reforms was striking; most were introduced in a relatively short (eighteen-month) period of time. They affected nearly all areas of economic activity. At the same time other important external changes were influencing the economy. First, rainfall increased by nearly 30 percent over the drought levels of the early 1980s. Second, the world price of rice (the largely imported urban staple food) fell sharply just after the dalasi was floated, briefly reducing the domestic price to below the prefloat level. Third, to support the adjustment program, donors and commercial banks provided financing that averaged the equivalent of 43 percent of GDP between 1986 and 1989, almost double the level of the early 1980s. Although this amount of resources was huge, most of the aid was *not* used to finance the current account deficit. About two-thirds was used to retire debt service arrears and increase reserves, rationalizing the implicit borrowing undertaken by The Gambia in the early 1980s. Foreign financing for current investment and consumption actually *declined* during the period, as reflected by a decline in the current account deficit after 1987.

Progress of the Recovery Effort

As the foreign exchange market stabilized in mid-1986 and the government tightened its control over the budget and monetary policy, the Gambian economy began to recover. The extent of the recovery after 1985–1986 is shown in column (3) of Table 2-1.

Aggregate real income increased significantly, providing a welcome increase in per capita real income. The annual rate of inflation fell to below 10 percent, the government budget deficit narrowed to more sustainable levels, net credit from the banking system to the government contracted sharply, and exports increased by more than imports. After initially increasing, the current account of the balance of payments declined steadily. The overall balance of payments was positive in 1987–1988 for the first time in fourteen years, allowing the government to repay some of its debt service arrears and to increase its gross foreign exchange reserves (to the equivalent of eleven weeks of imports). Groundnut and livestock production increased, tourism expanded, construction activity surged, the range of financial services broadened, the transport and communications sectors expanded, and wholesale and retail activity was buoyant.

Of all the changes that occurred, perhaps the most welcome was the increase in per capita income. Real GDP increased by approximately 5 percent in both 1986–1987 and 1987–1988. Particularly noteworthy is that the sharpest increases occurred in rural areas, where the poorest Gambians live. GDP in agriculture grew by nearly 20 percent during the first three years of the ERP. After years of poor harvests, low producer prices, and the relative neglect of agriculture in the national development effort, improvement in this sector vindicated the measures adopted under the ERP. More importantly, because the ERP redirected income to the poorest members of Gambian society, it was one of the most potent forces for economic development in The Gambia since its independence.

Although it is important to highlight the improvements, the hardships created by the ERP should not be overlooked or minimized.

- The devaluation of the dalasi eroded the incomes of civil servants and those on fixed incomes.
- High interest rates raised the cost of institutional finance for individuals and enterprises.
- The contraction of government employment and the retargeting of government expenditures required some painful adjustments, particularly among the urban population.
- The reorganization of the parastatal sector increased the costs of such basic services as transport, ferries, electricity, and water.
- Higher user charges and commodity prices, particularly for petrol, raised costs for businesses and individuals.

These difficulties, however, must be weighed against the hardships that would have been felt in the absence of an adjustment program. The severity and duration of shortages of basic commodities would have increased; parallel-market foreign exchange rates, commodity prices, and interest rates would have risen; more development projects would have been canceled in the face of mounting debt service arrears; both inflation and unemployment would have increased; and the quality of basic services would have continued to deteriorate.

Not all of the reform measures were successful. In particular, many of the institutional reforms envisaged under the ERP did not take place or were only partially introduced under extreme pressure from the donors. For example, although some of the parastatals introduced reforms, once the immediate pressure to reform eased, backsliding occurred, and reforms that had been planned for other parastatals never developed. Customs administration initially improved, forced by the need for dramatic increases in revenues at the outset of the ERP. But by the time the ERP ended, many of the original problems had resurfaced. Similarly, although the government successfully reduced the budget deficit, the budgeting process remained virtually unchanged, so that programs went ahead without evaluation, monitoring, or oversight. And although the tax structure was improved substantially, administration remained weak, and tax holidays continued for many questionable investment projects.

Despite these shortfalls the government achieved the first goal of the ERP—stabilizing the economy—and made some progress toward the second—sustained economic growth. Several broad factors contributed to its success. First, The Gambia benefited from adopting a comprehensive adjustment program. By 1985 most aspects of the economy had deteriorated seriously. Because no single policy change or adjustment measure could have reversed the situation, the government was forced to implement a wide range of changes. But in doing so, it was able to spread the costs of adjustment more widely and overcome resistance to individual reforms. Moreover, the mutually reinforcing effects of many of the reforms enhanced the general effectiveness of the overall program.

Second, The Gambia benefited from designing and implementing its own reform program. Although donors influenced the program, the government maintained control over its content and timing. This sense of "ownership" helped minimize resistance and mobilize support for the reforms, easing their implementation.

Third, the level of donor assistance was large enough to make a major difference to the economy. It eased the process of adjustment by sustaining both consumption and investment during the adjustment period. It also helped The Gambia repay its debt service arrears and replenish its foreign exchange reserves.

Fourth, the political climate helped promote economic reform. The rural power base of the ruling People's Progressive Party, its weak political opposition, and the rapid, visible economic improvement for many people reduced public opposition and, in so doing, helped the PPP achieve its electoral victory nineteen months after introducing the ERP. Moreover, The Gambia's relationship with Senegal helps explain both the government's decision to introduce reforms and the weak public opposition to the reforms as they were introduced (see Chapter 3).

Finally, individual personalities were decisive. Minister Sisay was probably the only one in the government able to marshal the resources necessary to introduce and implement the ERP fully. His background, professional record, academic training, and relationship with donors equipped him to head the effort and enabled him to gain the trust of President Jawara, the public, and the donors all at once.

Although the ERP helped bring about an end to the macroeconomic crisis and a modest amount of economic growth, The Gambia is not yet on a path of sustained economic development. For the economy to continue to grow, two elements are essential. First, the government must continue its commitment to the basic macroeconomic policies of the ERP. Second, the government has to bring about some of the institutional changes that did not occur under the ERP or its successor, the Program for Sustained Development (Chapter 19). Both of these steps are necessary in order to mobilize additional resources for development and to use those resources as efficiently as possible. The July 1994 coup, although nominally aimed at eliminating the corruption that the ERP failed to address, makes the future path of development even more uncertain. It remains to be seen whether the new government can capitalize on the gains made from the ERP and make greater progress in areas where it was unsuccessful, or whether the gains that were made will be lost.

NOTES

1. The Sahel is not known for a consistent pattern of rainfall. However, from the mid-1940s to the late 1960s, rainfall was higher than average, without major disruptive droughts (see World Bank, 1985b, Table 8.1).
2. Before March 1973 the dalasi was fixed at D5 = £1. It was then revalued to D4 = £1 and devalued to D5 = £1 in February 1984. The dalasi was floated in January 1986 and quickly depreciated to about D10 = £1. By the end of the ERP (June 1989), the exchange rate was D12.1 = £1. In June 1994 it was D14.5 = £1.

3. The factors associated with the decline of the Gambian economy have been examined widely (McPherson, 1983; USAID, 1984, Annex K; World Bank, 1985b; GOTG, 1987).

4. From 1975–1976 to 1985–1986, the government ran a deficit (excluding grants) that averaged 10 percent of GDP. The profits of the Gambia Produce Marketing Board from groundnut operations averaged only 1.7 percent of GDP during the same period. Corresponding data for the 1965–1966 to 1974–1975 decade are 2.1 percent and 5.5 percent, respectively.

5. The CFA franc is the currency unit used in most former French African colonies. During the period covered by this volume it stood in a fixed ratio of 50 to the French franc.

6. Donors made this point at a conference sponsored by the United Nations Development Program in November 1984, which, far from generating support for the government's proposed D1.15 billion four-year public investment program, ended with calls for major cuts in it.

7. The August 3, 1985, memorandum to Cabinet on the ERP noted that "(t)he public sector no longer acts as a buffer against adverse climatic factors or exogenous shocks, but, instead has become an additional source of disequilibrium."

3

The Politics of Economic Reform

Steven C. Radelet and Malcolm F. McPherson

Perhaps the most intriguing aspect of the ERP was the absence of overt public resistance to the reforms. Despite massive civil service layoffs, a rapid exchange rate depreciation, and large price increases, there were no strikes, rallies, or marches. The stability of the government was never challenged during the program.[1] The government did not have to ban public gatherings, use force to dissuade opponents, jail members of the opposition, or declare a state of emergency. Although the public was skeptical about the reforms, it did not express much outright opposition. Moreover, in March 1987, nineteen months after Cabinet approved the ERP and just fourteen months after the float of the dalasi, President Jawara was reelected to a fifth term with a 60 percent majority. His party, the People's Progressive Party, increased its majority in Parliament by two seats. He was again reelected in 1992.

The unusual political success of the ERP raises several questions. Why did the government postpone reform for so long in the face of major economic deterioration? Why did the government decide to introduce major reforms in 1985? Why was there so little protest in The Gambia to reforms that in other countries engender strong, often violent reaction? This chapter explores these questions.[2]

Reform Postponed: 1975 to 1985

By the mid-1970s the ruling PPP had a comfortable hold on power. President Jawara and his party had easily won the three elections that had been held since independence, with its strongest support coming from the rural areas. Economic performance had been robust in the early

1970s, as high world groundnut prices had led to steady growth, large foreign exchange reserves, and essentially no foreign debt.

As mentioned in Chapter 2, the first five-year plan in 1975 dramatically expanded the role of the public sector. Rather than provide a solid foundation for economic expansion and improved social welfare, the plan politicized most aspects of economic decision making. Special interest groups, bureaucrats, and politicians found greater opportunities for manipulating public resources for their own benefit. The PPP was comfortable with its rural political base and used government institutions to maintain its support and extract resources for its own benefit. The government established several urban-based parastatals, increased public investment dramatically, and doubled the size of the civil service. Urban-based businesses—particularly tourist hotels—reaped the benefits of loan guarantees and "development certificates" that gave generous tax breaks. Urban residents also benefited from low-interest loans from the government, an overvalued exchange rate, and subsidies for rice, utilities, and transport.

One source of financing for this system was groundnut receipts. The profits of the Gambia Produce Marketing Board per tonne of groundnuts averaged 47 percent of the farmgate price between 1974 and 1978. Most of these funds were transferred to the central government to help cover its burgeoning deficits. The deficits that were not covered by groundnut receipts were financed with grants and loans from donors and with loans from the banking system.

Despite the massive transfers from groundnut farmers, the PPP was able to keep its rural support largely through the activities of The Gambia Cooperatives Union, which became the party's conduit between rural areas and the government. The GCU gave its membership the benefits of its virtual monopsony in domestic groundnut marketing, as well as priority access to seed, fertilizer, and subsidized loans. Along with the GCU, a small number of well-placed rural roads, river wharfs, schools, and health clinics ensured the support of important rural leaders. Finally, the government mitigated the threat of the urban policy bias to rural political support by financing a large part of public-sector expansion with foreign borrowing. Loans imposed few immediate costs on any one group. The burden of foreign debt would become evident only over time, and even then would be spread out among taxpayers. However, the political benefits to the government from these loans were large and immediate.

An attempted coup d'état in 1981 provided surprisingly little immediate impetus for changing the existing system. The eight-day uprising, which left an estimated 1,000 Gambians dead, was finally suppressed by 1,500 Senegalese troops called in by President Jawara under a mutual defense treaty. The prevailing view was that the rebels were a small group, perhaps supported by Libya, with only limited popular support. Policymakers who believed that the rebellion did not reflect widespread dissatisfaction had little reason to advocate changing government policy. Indeed, the unrest may have helped buttress the existing system: donors quickly expanded their financial support, and the government increased public-sector wages in an attempt to garner more support from the civil service.

Despite the rapid economic deterioration in the early 1980s, government economic and financial analysis did not recommend changing the basic policy thrust. The few major economic analyses that were generated domestically during the period largely ignored the growing public-sector deficits, diminishing foreign exchange reserves, and emerging parallel markets, attributing the economic difficulties to continued drought, low world groundnut prices, oil shocks, and the attempted coup.

Donors also did not advocate major reform in The Gambia, at least until early 1984. Indeed, a 1981 World Bank study concluded that "the economic policies of the government, including producer prices, have been quite satisfactory . . . [and] the poor growth record of the 1970s was almost exclusively attributable to unfavorable weather conditions" (World Bank, 1981b, p. i). Although some individual consultants financed by aid agencies called for reform as early as 1979 (McPherson, 1979), the international community continued to provide substantial financial support without exerting pressure for policy reform. Thus, because neither government policymakers and analysts nor donors urged economic reform, economic policy stagnated, and the economy continued to deteriorate into 1985.

But the situation facing Gambian policymakers began to change in 1984 and 1985, as foreign exchange problems surfaced. Reserves were depleted, debt service arrears were mounting, and export earnings remained low. The country was essentially bankrupt. When shortages of imported goods began emerging, the government made an emergency appeal to the United Kingdom for financial assistance, but was refused. The British government said that it was unwilling to continue aid flows in the absence of major reform. Other donors adopted a similar stance. If the donors were truly serious about withholding assistance, the government would no longer be able to finance such a large current account deficit. Without aid, the question was not *whether* reforms should be implemented, but *how*.

Government Deliberations

The Economic Options

As shortages became more acute, pressure on the government to take action mounted. As described in Chapter 2, Minister of Finance Sisay assembled a task force to develop a program for economic reform.

Minister Sisay submitted the task force report to President Jawara and Cabinet without any guarantee that they would approve the program. Cabinet had three options. The first was to do nothing. If it chose this option, and the donors continued to withhold aid, the economy would collapse. Yet if the donors decided that the political costs of allowing one of the few democracies in Africa to founder were too high, they might have decided to provide emergency support. Aid would have continued to bolster the system, enabling the economy to sputter along as it had in the early 1980s. A vital question for the president and Cabinet was whether the donors were serious about withholding aid.

The second option was to adopt some of the recommendations and negotiate with the IMF for a stand-by program—in effect, implementing as few changes as possible, but enough of them to obtain support from the IMF and other donors. But The Gambia was in arrears to the IMF, and the IMF Board of Directors was moving toward declaring The Gambia ineligible for further borrowing. The arrears would have to be paid before an agreement could be signed, and the government did not have the foreign exchange to do so. Financing would first have to be found from another source. It was not clear that the promise of a stabilization program on its own would have been enough to convince other lenders of The Gambia's sincerity or creditworthiness.

The third option was to accept the task force's recommendations. The program offered some prospect for renewed economic growth, an end to the shortages, and financial support from the donor community. But the program did not guarantee renewed growth, as was being recognized by other countries undergoing structural adjustment at the time. Indeed, the economy might have continued to stagnate, particularly during the initial stages of reform. Comprehensive changes also meant greater administrative difficulties—a concern in a country with so few well-trained managers and technical specialists. Moreover, because the proposals would effect a redistribution of income and would wrest from the government its control over access to domestic resources, they would face strong political opposition. Accepting the task force recommendations was effectively a decision to change the system on which the Gambian political economy had been based since independence.

The President's Role

In choosing among these options, only one vote really mattered: the president's. President Jawara had been the country's leader since independence, and little could be accomplished without his support. This view has been expressed succinctly by opposition political leaders: "In The Gambia the Parliament does not matter, the political party does not matter, the civil service does not matter; the only person who matters is the President of the Republic." (*West Africa*, December 15, 1980).

While subject to some poetic license, that statement reflected the influence wielded by the president. He had come to the forefront of the PPP in the late 1950s by forging a consensus among the most powerful rural chiefs, and he has been the leader of the PPP ever since. With the extension of universal suffrage to the rural areas in 1963, the PPP gained a strong majority in the pre-independence Legislative Assembly, with Jawara as prime minister. He led The Gambia to independence in 1965, and many consider him to be the father of the country. He was not seriously challenged in any of his six bids for reelection prior to the 1994 coup. The Gambia's democratic institutions and strong human rights record since independence have enhanced his stature both domestically and internationally.

Trained as a veterinarian, the president had always relied on his advisers to determine economic policy. Most of those who advised him in 1985 were poorly trained in economics, and their earlier economic advice had proved to be ineffective and even detrimental. While there was some dissent about specific aspects of the proposed program—for example, the Central Bank was opposed to adjusting the exchange rate—none of the president's advisers, nor anyone else inside or outside of government, presented any credible alternative to the ERP. And then there was Minister Sisay, who had been minister of finance during a period of relative economic prosperity in the early 1960s, was the first governor of the Central Bank, and held a graduate degree in economics. Early on he held leadership positions in the PPP and was one of the few remaining active original members of the party other than the president. His background undoubtedly strengthened his position in influencing the president's decision about the program. Eventually, Minister Sisay's leadership would prove critical to the success of the ERP.

Despite the deteriorating economy, political groups, citizens' groups, and private businesses all exerted strong pressures against reform. Representatives of the Chamber of Commerce and Industry and the commercial banks opposed the ERP when they met with Minister Sisay. The Central Bank resisted any exchange rate reform, arguing that the 25 percent devaluation in 1984 had been ineffective. Civil servants were against the wage freeze and the proposed staff reductions. Parastatal managers opposed credit restrictions and the notion of performance contracts. The groundnut marketing board, while favoring a higher groundnut price, was uncomfortable about having its financial performance closely scrutinized by the MoF and the IMF. Finally, the rest of Cabinet initially opposed the reforms. Few, if any, seriously believed the donors' threat to suspend aid completely, and they viewed the crisis as Minister Sisay's problem, not theirs.

Finally, and perhaps most importantly, the president had to be concerned about the possibility of another coup attempt and about the elections scheduled for early 1987, just eighteen months away. However, it was unclear whether the greater political threat was posed by inaction or reform. Inaction could easily have led to political discontent. Shortages of some imported commodities were already severe, and prices were rising rapidly in parallel markets. If the donors continued to withhold aid, these problems would have intensified, further undermining the tax base and weakening the government's position. Reforms obviously carried their own political risks from major protests, strikes, or violence, as in other African countries. The same dilemma confronting all reform-oriented governments was evident in The Gambia: urban pressure groups did not want the continued economic deterioration associated with current policies, or the medicine of reform. What they wanted—high levels of public spending and low prices—could no longer be provided by the government.

In one very important respect, the risks in The Gambia, whatever the choice, were greater than in other African countries. Whereas many African governments risk losing power from political unrest, many Gambians perceived that they were confronting the possibility that the country itself would disappear. A major disturbance in The Gambia—either due to continued economic deterioration or in protest of reforms—could have led to the overthrow of the Jawara government and the incorporation of The Gambia into its neighbor, Senegal.

The Gambia's Relationship with Senegal

The existence of The Gambia has long created economic and political difficulties for Senegal. The Gambia is a tiny sliver of land, completely surrounded on three sides—north, east, and south—by its much larger neighbor. The Gambia effectively divides Senegal into two regions, making the transport of goods from the north (where the capital, Dakar, is located) to the south expensive and inconvenient. The two regions of Senegal differ ethnically, economically, and politically, and a secessionist movement has been active in the southern region.

The attempted coup in The Gambia in 1981 permanently changed the relationship between the two countries. As mentioned previously, Senegalese troops were brought in to put down the rebellion. Most of the troops left shortly afterwards; however, some Senegalese troops remained in The Gambia until 1989.

In December 1981, five months after the attempted coup and with The Gambia's security clearly dependent on Senegal, the two countries agreed to form the Senegambia Confederation. Throughout the 1980s a Confederal Parliament met regularly, and protocols were signed in defense, transportation, communications, and cultural exchange. Negotiations were also held on a free-trade area, a monetary union, and other issues. Fearing complete domination by its larger neighbor, The Gambia moved slowly and cautiously in negotiating these agreements. Conversely, Senegal was interested in moving toward complete integration as quickly as possible.[3]

Given this historical background, many people both inside and outside The Gambia believe Senegal might use another major disturbance in The Gambia as a pretext for taking over the country.

The Gambia's relationship with Senegal was a factor in the donors' refusal to provide emergency aid in 1985. Several donor officials recounted in private interviews that some members of their respective organizations were leaning toward withdrawing support in order to allow the Gambian government to fall. Although they were reluctant to see a Western-style democracy disappear, the fact that Senegal would assume power (as opposed to some unknown group) softened the risks associated with the potential downfall of the Gambian government. The Senegalese (and the French) would welcome it, the "problem" of The Gambia would be resolved, and the outcome would be a warning to other countries reluctant to undertake adjustment measures that the donors would not necessarily bail them out.

Donors and diplomats felt that this pressure was critical in the president's decision to adopt the ERP. As one diplomat put it, continuing economic decline without donor support probably would have "eventually forced President Jawara to go hat in hand to President Diouf" of Senegal. Minister Sisay was clearly aware of this possibility. He later observed that "in assessing the impact of the ERP it is also relevant to consider whether The Gambia's integrity as a nation would have long withstood an IMF declaration of ineligibility and the regional pressures this would have generated" (GOTG, 1987, p. 20).

Thus while both technical analysis and international pressures were pushing the president toward adopting the ERP, bureaucratic and institutional factors were pressing him in the opposite direction. The fact that Minister Sisay supported the ERP and that the president eventually agreed suggests that these two concluded that economic reform posed less political threat. By mid-1986 it was clear that they had been correct.

Political Acceptance

The Absence of Strong Opposition

Perhaps the most striking and puzzling aspect of the ERP was the absence of strong public opposition. Why were there no demonstrations, marches, strikes, riots, or other disturbances? How did the PPP win reelection with such ease so soon after initiating the ERP?

There were several reasons. One important factor was the nature of the political system and the political power base in The Gambia. The Gambia was (until 1994) a democracy—a rarity in Africa. There was universal adult suffrage, and it was widely acknowledged that voting in the six general elections since independence was free and fair. The Constitution guarantees the freedom of speech, religion, and the press. Political parties did not have to register and were free to campaign actively.

These political freedoms notwithstanding, the PPP totally dominated politics in The Gambia for nineteen years following independence. The 75 percent of the population living in rural areas, primarily Mandinka and Fula farmers, formed the backbone of the party's constituency. The country's small size and the accessibility of rural villages also contributed to the rural power base. Essentially all villages are linked by roads, and even the most distant village is only an eight-hour bus ride from Banjul. Consequently, rural dwellers are not geographically (and thus not politically) isolated.

Combined with the specific impact of the policy reforms, the rural political power base (also rare in Africa) helps explain the PPP's easy electoral victory so soon after the ERP was introduced. The reforms that tended primarily to hurt urban dwellers—the float of the dalasi; higher interest rates, petroleum prices, utility rates, and transport fares; and the retrenchment of civil servants—did little to erode the party's historic base of support. Other reforms—the liberalization of the rice trade and, most importantly, the increased groundnut producer price—directly benefited the party's rural constituents. Those policy changes and the end of the drought helped increase per capita real income in rural areas by approximately 12 percent between 1985 and 1988.

Although these factors contributed to the electoral victory of 1987, they do not fully explain why there was so little overt *urban* opposition to the reforms. One reason was the perception of urban dwellers that the government was both legitimate and stable. The crisis the government faced was economic, not political.

Another reason was the absence of a strong group that might have become a focal point for active opposition to the reforms. Opposition parties were small and unable to mount a credible challenge to the PPP, despite the economic crisis. The few labor unions that existed were small and politically weak. Moreover, because The Gambia does not have a university, the political opposition that is often sparked by students was absent. The military was small, apolitical, and conscious of how the larger army in Senegal (with troops stationed in Banjul) might react to trouble in The Gambia. Civil servants were not organized, and the possibility that troublemakers might be the first to lose their jobs during retrenchment helped dampen protest. Civil servants contributed significantly to institutional resistance to some of the reform measures, such as tax, budget, and customs reform. But this institutional opposition was not strong enough to be transformed into open political challenge. Thus none of these urban groups was able to fuel public opposition into outright protest.

Finally, while urban dwellers clearly bore the brunt of the costs of reform, the impact on urban dwellers was not as great as it might have been. This was in part due to how the policy package was designed. The reforms were comprehensive and many were mutually reinforcing, easing the negative economic impact on any one group. For example, the liberalization of interest rates, the crackdown on customs fraud, the reduction in government expenditures, and limits on domestic credit—all reduced the extent to which the exchange rate depreciated. Thus real income declined by less than many had initially feared.

There clearly was opposition—in some cases very strong opposition—to the ERP. Traders who had benefited from the weak customs administration, businessmen who had previously enjoyed government protection or special incentives, managers of state-owned enterprises that had not been closely supervised, and civil servants in several ministries all resisted or tried to undermine different measures implemented under the ERP. In some cases they were successful. But what made the Gambian case different, and what helped it to be successful, is that these pockets of resistance did not coalesce into broad-based public opposition to the program.

Government Leadership
The government helped mitigate resistance by the way in which it introduced the ERP. It took several steps to make information available to and to receive feedback from the public about the program. The

contents of the daily task force meetings, while officially confidential, were discussed publicly each evening. President Jawara and Minister Sisay presented the details of the program in a series of speeches, and the government made full written descriptions available to the public. Minister Sisay discussed the reform measures in several meetings with representatives of local businesses, commercial banks, traders, and the Chamber of Commerce. President Jawara made a special point of discussing the ERP in rural areas during his annual "meet the farmers" tour. These government actions made the public more aware of the problems they faced, the options that were available, and the prospects for improvement under the ERP, thereby allaying public opposition.

Aid and Luck
The burden on urban dwellers was eased further by the resources made available by donors. Foreign aid supported the exchange rate and allowed higher levels of both consumption and investment than would have been the case otherwise during the adjustment period. Many of the civil servants who lost their jobs were absorbed into the growing sectors or joined relatives on farms to take advantage of the high returns offered to groundnut producers. The fact that displaced urban workers found employment opportunities helped minimize public opposition to the program.

Fortuitous events, particularly in the world price of rice and the amount of rainfall, also defused potential opposition. The end of the drought enhanced rural income, increasing the demand for urban-based products and services. Moreover, the dalasi price of rice (the urban staple food), which more than doubled just after the float, quickly fell to below its prefloat level as world prices fell and domestic production increased. The lower rice prices were critical to the acceptance of reforms in urban areas. One diplomat called it "the lucky break The Gambia needed." In addition, the world price of oil fell. Domestic prices remained fixed, but the price drop reduced foreign exchange requirements and raised government revenues.

Possibly the most important factor mitigating public opposition was the legacy of the 1981 attempted coup—only four years prior to the ERP—and The Gambia's relationship with Senegal. Gambian citizens had more to worry about than the immediate economic impact of the ERP—the very existence of their nation was at stake. Although urban residents were not particularly happy about the ERP, they did not want a repeat of the violence and bloodshed of the coup attempt.

Insights from the Politics of Economic Reform

Several political lessons emerge from the Gambian experience. First, democratically elected governments *can* implement strong stabilization programs. The Gambia is one of a growing number of democracies that contradict the notion that popularly elected governments cannot implement comprehensive reform programs.[4] The more crucial ingredients for success, as shown in The Gambia and elsewhere, are the strength and autonomy of the government (Nelson, 1990). The PPP's large majority in Parliament, President Jawara's long tenure in office, the perceived legitimacy of the government (both domestically and internationally), and the weakness of opposition allowed the government to introduce a broad and comprehensive reform program.

Second, The Gambia provides an interesting counterpoint to the conventional wisdom that political leaders cannot introduce austerity measures just before an election (see Nelson, 1990). The government floated the currency, laid off 20 percent of its work force, sharply raised interest rates, and increased utility, petroleum, and transport prices—all within fourteen months before the election. Yet it was reelected by a comfortable margin.

Third, the Gambian experience shows that governments can actively manage potential opposition, implying that political reaction may be at least partially endogenous to economic reform (Grindle and Thomas, 1991). To design the ERP, Minister of Finance Sisay established a task force consisting primarily of Gambian technicians, immediately giving the government some measure of control that it would not have captured had the program been designed by the IMF and the World Bank. Thus the ERP was perceived to be a Gambian program, enhancing its acceptance both within Cabinet and among the general public. The government also eased opposition to the program by keeping the public well informed. There was still strong opposition to specific measures of the ERP, from within and outside the government. But these steps helped mollify that resistance so that the bulk of the most important measures could be introduced in a timely matter.

Fourth, opposition to reform can be overshadowed by more pressing issues. Gambians were concerned not only with their short-term economic interests but also with their national sovereignty. The government's decision to undertake reform and the absence of strong public opposition were in part an acknowledgment that political unrest—either from progressive economic deterioration or in response to reform measures—could eventually lead to the demise of The Gambia as a nation.

Fifth, the leadership of specific individuals can be decisive. Minister of Finance Sisay was probably the only person in the government able to introduce and implement a comprehensive reform program successfully. His reputation, professional record, and academic training equipped him to head the effort and enabled him to gain the trust of the president, the public, and the donors. Similarly, President Jawara's long tenure in office made his authority and influence forceful. His support was critical for gaining initial acceptance of the ERP and for ensuring that the individual reforms were implemented subsequently.

Sixth, the international community can play a vital role in reform. In The Gambia, the donors' refusal to continue financing the current account deficit was critical to the government's decision to adopt the ERP. The substantial aid flow and technical assistance provided by donors after the reforms were implemented bolstered the quick economic turnaround, thereby easing opposition, particularly in urban areas.

Seventh, factors external to government actions can help gain acceptance of reform measures. The end of the drought provided immediate economic relief throughout the economy. In addition, the fall in the world price of rice just after the float of the dalasi helped stabilize its price, easing the economic cost of the reforms to urban residents. In addition, the fall in world oil prices helped reduce foreign exchange requirements and increase government revenues.

Finally, the Gambian experience highlights the link between economic and political success in economic reform programs. The economic recovery in rural areas helped the PPP gain reelection, while the moderate negative impact on urban consumers minimized opposition to the ERP. At the same time, the political success of the program made investors and consumers more confident, helping to reverse capital flight and stabilize the economy.

NOTES

1. At least the government was unchallenged until the July 1994 coup. As discussed in the introduction, the coup took place almost nine years after Minister Sisay introduced the ERP and was not directly related to it. It may, however, have been related to government corruption, which the ERP was unable to reduce significantly. The coup occurred just as this volume was being completed, so a full analysis of its origins and consequences is not possible here.
2. For more detailed analyses of the politics of reform in The Gambia, see McPherson (1991) and Radelet (1992a).

3. The Confederation was dissolved on unfriendly terms in September 1989.
4. Haggard and Kaufman (1989) discuss types of regimes and the success of their economic reform.

4

Donor Support for the Economic Recovery Program

Steven C. Radelet

The donor community initially became actively involved in The Gambia in the early 1970s. Many aid agencies strongly supported the government's first five-year plan, providing loans and grants to finance the rapid expansion of the public sector under that plan. But in the late 1970s and early 1980s, the donors failed to pay adequate attention to the Gambian economy's dynamically unsustainable growth path. It was not until 1983, when debt service arrears began to mount rapidly and creditors were no longer being repaid, that they became concerned about the direction of the economy. Over the next two years, the donors gradually withdrew their financial support. The cessation of aid was key to forcing the government to initiate the ERP in 1985.

With the government's commitment to implementing the reforms, the donors began to provide generous financial and technical support. Between 1986 and 1989 aid agencies and commercial banks provided financing that averaged the equivalent of 43 percent of GDP. About one-third of these resources was used to finance investment and consumption. The other two-thirds were used to build up foreign exchange reserves and pay current and overdue debt service. The conditions attached to these aid flows sometimes hindered but usually facilitated the implementation of the ERP.

This chapter examines the role of the donor community in the ERP. It begins by recounting international support for public-sector expansion in the late 1970s, and explaining why that support was withdrawn in the early 1980s. It then examines the role of the International Monetary Fund, the World Bank, and other international agencies in formulating and implementing the ERP, and analyzes the economic and political impact of their financial support. It concludes with several lessons about the role of donors in economic reform.

Donor Support Before the Economic Recovery Program

Financing the Public-Sector Expansion, 1975 to 1983

International agencies first began providing substantial support for The Gambia in the early 1970s. In 1975 the government introduced its first five-year plan, which, as discussed in Chapter 2, quickly fueled an expansion of the public sector. The government dramatically increased spending for development projects, civil service wages (primarily by increasing the number of employees), and subsidies for rice, fertilizer, electricity, and transport. Public investment increased by 700 percent in six years, and many new parastatals were established. By 1983 the public sector accounted for two-thirds of all employment in the modern sector.

This expansion was funded primarily by the donor community. During this period almost all of the increase in the current account deficit from 2 percent to 21 percent of GDP was financed with grants and loans from multilateral and bilateral agencies. Between 1975 and 1985 foreign aid averaged US$80 per capita/per year, one of the highest levels in Africa, and 67 percent higher than foreign aid to neighboring Senegal (World Bank, 1985b). Aid flows were particularly high in 1980 and 1981 (US$120 per capita) because of the drought and the attempted coup. About half of the aid (equivalent to 10 percent of GDP) consisted of grants. The other half was loans, and from 1975 to 1985 The Gambia's indebtedness to multilateral and bilateral creditors increased from US$13 million to US$139 million.

On the plus side, the foreign assistance shielded The Gambia from the impact of increases in world oil prices and the decline in world groundnut prices. The Gambia's external terms of trade fell by 60 percent between 1976 and 1981. Although the terms of trade improved between 1981 and 1985, they declined 20 percent over the full ten-year period. Nevertheless, the increase in grant financing was more than *twice* as large as the foreign exchange losses from the deteriorating terms of trade (Radelet, 1990, p. 49).

Using foreign aid to shield The Gambia from the severe terms of trade shocks was a double-edged sword. While donor support financed investment that would not have been possible otherwise, the government's choice of investment projects and its management of them were poor at best. But donor oversight was no better, and they continued to finance many development projects that made little net contribution to national income.

Moreover, aid flow permitted The Gambia to avoid the policy adjustments that should have been made in response to the terms of trade shocks. Donors continued to finance an unsustainable situation for several years, even after the IMF and other observers called for fundamental policy change

(McPherson, 1979). When the donors finally began to press the government for reform in 1983, the magnitude of the necessary changes was much larger, and The Gambia's external debts had become unserviceable.

The Withdrawal of Donor Support, 1983 to 1985

The international community began to rethink its support when The Gambia fell into arrears on its debt service obligations. Creditors reduced loan disbursements dramatically in 1983 and began to call for reform. With the reduction in disbursements, foreign exchange reserves declined sharply, forcing The Gambia to negotiate a stand-by agreement with the IMF. The agreement, signed in February 1984, required a 25 percent devaluation and established limits on domestic credit expansion and government expenditures. But these changes were too little and too late to halt the economic deterioration.

Despite the poor state of the economy and the withdrawal of external support, most government officials had not yet recognized that fundamental change was necessary. The government convened a donor conference in November 1984 to seek financing for a four-year D1.15 billion investment program (170 percent of 1984–1985 GDP). The proposed program did not include any policy changes to address the basic macroeconomic imbalances. The program did not gain financial support; instead, most observers suggested that it be cut drastically and refocused to deal with the economy's basic problems (World Bank, 1985b).

By January 1985 the government was in arrears to the IMF, and it had breached the expenditure targets in the stand-by agreement. The IMF canceled the program, and its board began the process of declaring The Gambia ineligible for further drawings. Without an IMF program the government was unable to attract additional financial support. It made special appeals for balance-of-payments assistance to the governments of the United Kingdom, the United States, and Saudi Arabia. Each appeal was denied. The World Bank also indicated that it would not provide assistance until The Gambia reached a new agreement with the IMF. The government's normal channels of foreign support had completely evaporated. Meanwhile, foreign exchange reserves had dwindled to less than one week's import coverage, and shortages of rice, fuel, and other imported products were widespread.

Donor Support for the Economic Recovery Program

The donors played an important role in the formation of the ERP. The catalyst for action was the World Bank's draft *Country Economic*

Memorandum of May 1985. It bluntly described the nature and origins of The Gambia's economic crisis and recommended that the government introduce a wide range of organizational and policy reforms as part of a stabilization and structural adjustment program. Shortly after the World Bank released the report, Minister of Finance Sisay assembled his task force of Gambian economists and others to develop an economic reform program.

Soon after Cabinet approved the ERP, the government outlined the program and the country's resource requirements at a Special Donor's Conference in London. Initial reaction was favorable. The donors generally agreed that the ERP was bold and comprehensive. Nevertheless, they were not willing to pledge support based only on the government's *intention* to initiate reform.

When the government floated the dalasi, raised interest rates, and retrenched nearly 3,000 government employees in early 1986, the international community began to recognize the depth of the government's commitment. Initial support consisted of fuel grants from the United Kingdom and the Netherlands. However, donors made it clear that more substantial support would not be forthcoming until The Gambia reached a new stand-by agreement with the IMF. And agreement would not be reached until The Gambia repaid its arrears to the IMF.

The IMF Programs

After the IMF reacted favorably to the ERP in late 1985, senior government officials began hoping that an IMF mission in February 1986 would be the impetus for negotiations for a stand-by agreement. But the mission did not share the government's view that the new policies adopted under the ERP had generated results that justified an agreement. Specifically, the mission highlighted what it saw as two major problems. First, it claimed that the float of the dalasi had failed (only three weeks after it was introduced) because liquidity had been allowed to increase sharply. Second, it found what it thought were large (unprogrammed) increases in development spending.

The government saw the situation differently. Indeed, as subsequent events showed, the IMF mission's response to the float was premature. The increased liquidity came from an abnormally early peak in groundnut purchases that was accentuated by a sharp increase in the groundnut price (from D640 per tonne to D1,100 per tonne); and the increased development spending identified by the IMF was later found to be due to an arithmetical error made by the mission staff when it converted Norwegian kroner into SDRs. Despite the merits of the government's case, the damage had been done: the departure of the IMF mission delayed any prospect for new donor support.

However, both the U.K. high commissioner and the USAID resident representative in Banjul sought to limit the damage done by the IMF's assessment. Both made a special effort to convey The Gambia's point of view to their superiors, giving a much more positive assessment than had the IMF mission. Due in part to their support, the IMF team was sent back to Banjul in May 1986 to design a stand-by program.

The IMF team found that the economy had stabilized and a solid recovery was underway, and so negotiations for a stand-by agreement began. But The Gambia's arrears to the IMF remained an obstacle to an agreement. The IMF board decided to review these arrears on August 2, and, if they were not settled, to declare The Gambia ineligible for borrowing. The problem had thus become critical.

The government approached Standard Chartered Merchant Bank (London) for bridging finance to pay its IMF arrears. With assurance from the IMF and the World Bank that they would provide assistance to The Gambia as soon as it settled its arrears, Standard Chartered loaned the government SDR15.3 million. The government used SDR11.1 million to pay the IMF arrears, designated SDR1.9 million to pay obligations that would fall due to the IMF between August and October 1986, and targeted SDR2.3 million to repaying government debt service obligations overdue to Standard Chartered Merchant Bank. After clearing its arrears to the IMF, the government was able to sign an agreement for SDR18 million[1] on August 1—one day before the IMF board was scheduled to meet to determine whether The Gambia should be declared ineligible for borrowing.

The conditions imposed by the IMF under the stand-by program were consistent with the broad thrust of the ERP, allowing discussions between the government and the IMF to focus on the details and timing of policy implementation rather than on the general direction of policy. The agreement imposed limits on bank credit to the government, bank credit to the Gambia Produce Marketing Board, the stock of net domestic assets, the stock of outstanding external arrears, and the amount of short-term external debt owed by the GPMB and the Central Bank. They also included a moratorium on publicly guaranteed nonconcessional foreign borrowing in the one- to twelve-year maturity range.

The one area of disagreement was the producer price of groundnuts. As discussed fully in Chapter 14, the IMF advocated a 50 percent subsidy for groundnut producers, requiring a transfer equivalent to 8 percent of GDP to the GPMB. Minister Sisay, while supporting the idea of a subsidy, wanted it to be much smaller (17 percent). The IMF's position prevailed.

The agreement with the IMF was critical, because it paved the way for additional financing from other donors. It also imposed strong discipline on fiscal and monetary policies, ensuring a package of stabilization measures necessary to support the float of the dalasi. The government met all of the performance criteria under the program (with one exception, for technical reasons). Based on the success of the stand-by agreement and the accompanying three-year Structural Adjustment Facility (SAF), the government negotiated a three-year Extended Structural Adjustment Facility (ESAF) loan for SDR21 million in September 1988. During the entire five-year period when these programs were in place, the government met essentially all performance targets and regularly received positive reviews from IMF missions. When the ESAF ended in 1991, the IMF no longer considered a program necessary, and The Gambia became the first African country to "graduate" from an IMF ESAF program.

The World Bank Structural Adjustment Program
The World Bank has been closely associated with the ERP from its inception. A Bank staff member was part of the ERP task force, and numerous missions indicated their support for the government's adjustment efforts. Nevertheless, the World Bank required that the government sign an IMF stand-by agreement before it would agree to a Structural Adjustment Credit (SAC). In 1985–1986 frequent consultation was held among the IMF, the World Bank, and the government, and discussions about a SAC proceeded concurrently (and often simultaneously) with discussions about an IMF stand-by agreement. Final discussions on the SAC were held during the last week of July 1986, concurrently with IMF negotiations. The total amount available under the SAC was SDR29 million. Of this amount, SDR14 million came from the World Bank, SDR10 million from the African Development Bank, £3 million from the U.K. government (as a grant), and SR12 million from the Saudi Arabian government.

The conditions of the SAC reflected the Bank's relative emphasis on structural adjustment (rather than stabilization) and thus did not focus as heavily as the IMF on exchange rate and monetary policy. They mandated reorganizing and streamlining the civil service, improving the quality of the public investment program, reforming the agricultural credit system, eliminating the groundnut subsidy over a period of three years, implementing performance contracts with several parastatals, and establishing a managed fund of D72 million in loans to be made as government guarantees by the Gambia Commercial and Development Bank.

Measuring the government's progress under the World Bank loans proved to be more difficult than under the IMF programs. Almost all of the IMF targets were established as numerical limits, making performance relatively easy to measure. By contrast, the World Bank conditions were much more subjective, including such phrases as "adopting programs" and "reviewing the feasibility of" new systems. Whether they were completed successfully was subject to some debate.

Under the first SAC, the World Bank agreed that the government met all of the conditions. However, negotiations on the second SAC were delayed, for two reasons. First, the World Bank itself was in the midst of reorganization, which slowed decision making in Washington. Second, and later, the two parties disagreed on the timetable for introducing reforms in the GCDB. The second SAC was finally signed in June 1989, providing US$41 million from the World Bank, the African Development Bank, and the governments of the Netherlands, Switzerland, and Norway. The second tranche of SAC II was originally scheduled for early 1991 but was delayed because the World Bank was dissatisfied about progress toward reforming groundnut marketing, reorganizing the GCDB, and preparing the public expenditure program.

Whereas the government's agreement with the IMF was important because it provided a signal to the international community, the World Bank programs were critical because they provided a vast amount of resources. With such large funding The Gambia was able to repay all of its arrears and replenish its foreign exchange reserves (as discussed later in the chapter).

Assistance from Other Donors

Three other sources of foreign aid were important to the success of the ERP: fuel grants from the United Kingdom and the Netherlands, STABEX[2] grants from the European Economic Community (EEC), and U.S. rice and African Economic Policy Reform Program (AEPRP) grants.

The Dutch government donated a total of 20 million guilders in fuel between 1984 and 1987, and the U.K. government donated £10.5 million in fuel between 1986 and 1989. These grants were important for two reasons. First, they were the only substantial support provided by the donors before the IMF agreement, and they were crucial to stabilizing the dalasi after the float. Second, they helped bring a quick end to the shortage of fuel that had emerged in 1985, easing potential political opposition to the reform program.

The EEC provided a total of SDR13 million in STABEX grants to The Gambia from 1986 to 1988. Although these grants were not explicitly connected with the ERP, they helped build up foreign exchange reserves and finance the groundnut subsidy. These relatively large grants, which arrived at crucial times and without any explicit conditions attached, were particularly effective at promoting the goals of the ERP.

Between 1983 and 1985 the U.S. government helped cover drought-induced shortfalls in domestic food production with emergency food shipments. After 1985, in an effort to regularize this support and encourage the expansion of agricultural production through appropriate price policy, USAID agreed to supply The Gambia with 24,000 tons of rice (worth US$4 million) over three years. The rice, which was used as a buffer stock to ensure against shortages in the local market, was tendered to private traders for resale in The Gambia. The dalasi proceeds were used to finance the groundnut subsidy.

The rice grants differed from both the fuel grants and the STABEX funds in that they were highly conditional. The conditions required that the government liberalize the rice and fertilizer markets, reform the indirect tax system, and introduce a series of measures to work toward privatizing the GPMB.

The rice grants had three effects. They eased pressure on the balance of payments by reducing the amount of foreign exchange required to import rice, they provided counterpart funds to help finance the groundnut subsidy, and they enabled the government to enhance national food security through a buffer stock.

The U.S. government also provided US$6 million over three years as an AEPRP grant. The Gambia used these grants to discharge specified external debt payments. The funds were conditional on whether the government implemented financial-sector reforms, most of which were targeted at improving the performance of the GCDB.

Debt relief was another important source of support for the balance of payments. Refinancing and rescheduling agreements worth US$65 million were reached with the Paris Club, the London Club, the Islamic Development Bank, and the West African Clearing House (see Chapter 11). The debts with the French government were later forgiven.

Finally, several donors provided technical assistance to the government during the ERP. The U.K. government provided assistance in the accountant general's office, the Central Bank, and the president's office; the U.S. government provided assistance to the MoF; the IMF sent two advisers to the Central Bank; and the United Nations provided assistance in the MoF and the Ministry of Economic Planning. This assistance eased the administrative and technical burden on the government during the adjustment program, freeing up time for senior officials to concentrate more fully on reformulating and implementing policy.

The Economic and Political Effects of Foreign Aid

Taken together, the international community provided The Gambia with resources equivalent to SDR38 million in 1985–1986 (24 percent of

GDP), SDR84 million in 1986–1987 (74 percent of GDP), SDR59 million in 1987–1988 (43 percent of GDP), and SDR51 million (34 percent of GDP) in 1988–1989. Slightly more than half of these amounts were grants, and most of the rest were concessional loans.

By almost any measure this amount of foreign financing was huge. About one-third of the aid was used to finance current consumption and investment, both of which showed a small real increase during the adjustment period (Figure 4-1).[3] The increased investment was key to providing a foundation for long-term growth, while the small increase in consumption helped ease political opposition to the reforms. In addition, the aid flow was critical to stabilizing the exchange rate and reducing the extent of the depreciation necessary during the ERP. The bulk of the aid went to paying current debt service obligations, repaying arrears, and increasing the government's depleted foreign exchange reserves. The government completely paid off its arrears of SDR89 million between 1986 and 1990 and increased its foreign exchange reserves from the equivalent of one week of imports to the equivalent of twelve weeks of imports in just two years. In effect, the aid flow rationalized the implicit borrowing The Gambia had undertaken in the early 1980s, when it failed to service its debts. The donors not only financed current economic activities but also effectively released the aid flow they had been withholding in previous years.

The largest single source of this financing was the World Bank. The SAC was primarily a refinancing package. The government was able to borrow

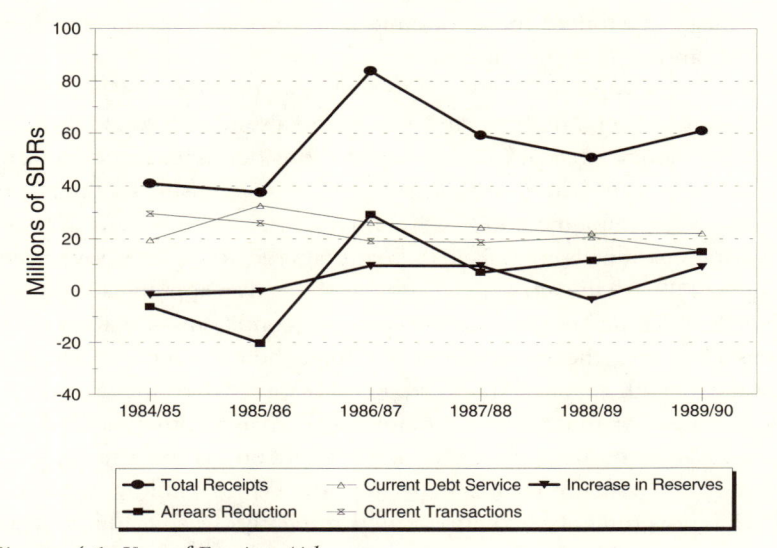

Figure 4-1. Uses of Foreign Aid

new money on soft terms (a forty-year repayment period with a ten-year grace period and 0.75 percent interest) to repay all of its overdue loans.

Chapter 18 analyzes the impact of this aid flow on The Gambia's economic growth after the ERP was introduced. The analysis indicates that about one-third of the renewed growth can be traced to the impact of the foreign aid flow. The aid flow also helped ease political opposition to the ERP (see Chapter 3).

The timely fuel grants from the U.K. and Dutch governments, received just before the government floated the dalasi, helped ease the fuel shortages and mitigate the immediate pressures on the exchange rate. In turn, the price increases faced by urban consumers for imported goods were minimized, preventing an erosion of real income. The resumption of aid-financed investment projects created a large number of urban jobs, particularly in construction and small manufacturing, both of which grew rapidly during the ERP.

Concluding Observations

The Gambia exemplifies both the failure and the success of foreign aid. Despite the massive amount of resources provided by the donors to The Gambia in the late 1970s, the economy did not progress toward a path of sustained growth. While much of the blame for this failure can be attributed to the government itself, as well as to a series of external shocks, the donors share some responsibility. Project selection often did not realistically reflect the economic and physical constraints of The Gambia, and project oversight was lax.

Yet donor support for the ERP was highly effective. To begin with, by refusing to continue financing The Gambia's imbalances, the international community forced the government to consider fundamental reforms. Foreign aid also provided the necessary leverage to ensure that important reforms were implemented. The conditions attached to the aid were broadly consistent with policies already agreed to by the government under the ERP. For the most part the donors showed an appropriate combination of flexibility and resolve in establishing the conditions—flexibility when it was clear that the government had breached a condition for good reasons (as with several IMF targets) and resolve when the government tried to renege on important commitments (such as reforming the GCDB).

Moreover, the aid agencies tended to maintain a consistent approach. The staff of the major donors—the IMF, the World Bank, and the U.K. and U.S. governments—communicated regularly. Despite different orientations they were careful not to work at cross-purposes.

Finally, the international community provided funding that was large enough to stabilize the economy and to spur economic growth. Donor resources helped The Gambia rationalize its debts and replenish its reserves without unduly compressing investment and consumption.

The future direction of aid programs will have an important bearing on economic progress in The Gambia. While the IMF was pleased to graduate an African country from its ESAF program, it is not clear whether the government by itself can maintain the fiscal and monetary discipline initiated under the ERP. With the government's arrears cleared, a comfortable stock of foreign reserves, and a growing economy, donor support is much less critical than in 1985. But following the 1994 coup and the new government's announcement that elections would not be held until 1998, several donors (including the United States and the United Kingdom) cut off their support. An unanswered question is whether the new government will strengthen or reverse the earlier reforms, especially as donor influence wanes. Early indications are that a policy reversal is the more likely outcome.

NOTES

1. The agreement included a three-year Structural Adjustment Facility worth SDR8 million, a thirteen-month stand-by agreement for SDR5.1 million, and SDR4.7 million from the Compensatory Financing Facility.
2. The EEC STABEX program provides grants to developing countries that suffer shortfalls in export earnings due to drought or sharp declines in world prices for their export products. The STABEX grants provided to The Gambia were to cover export shortfalls in 1981, 1985, and 1986.
3. The graph shows that the amount of aid used for current transactions declined during the period. Yet total current consumption and investment rose slightly. The difference was financed by private capital inflows, which grew sharply during the period.

Part II

Macroeconomic Reform

5

Exchange Rate Reform

Catherine J. McAuliffe and Malcolm F. McPherson

In January 1986 The Gambia floated the dalasi by introducing an interbank market for foreign exchange. The move eliminated a price distortion that had created serious economic difficulties since the mid-1970s.[1] The float had an immediate positive effect on the economy and substantially improved The Gambia's relations with donors, since it demonstrated the government's commitment to structural adjustment. As discussed in Part I, the subsequent financial support of donors was critical to the success of the ERP. For more than nine years after the float, exchange rate reform has continued to serve its intended purposes. The foreign exchange market has proved to be surprisingly robust.

Exchange rate reform has been both a central and a controversial part of adjustment programs throughout sub-Saharan Africa. A wide range of observers agrees on the importance of a competitive real exchange rate. The major issues that continue to be debated are the optimal transition path, the appropriate supporting policies, and the most suitable long-term policy regime. Analysts disagree about how quickly countries should move to a competitive rate, whether all capital controls ultimately should be relaxed, whether a unified rate or multiple rates should be established, and whether the rate should be fixed or flexible.[2]

The Gambia's experience in moving quickly from a fixed to a floating regime and in maintaining a successful float despite the relatively thin market for foreign exchange provides useful insights for other SSA countries considering exchange rate reform. This chapter examines the conditions that led to the decision to float the dalasi, the complementary measures that supported exchange rate reform, and the economic response to the float. The chapter ends with some concluding observations that provide more general insights on exchange rate reform.

The Exchange Rate and Economic Performance

Background

The Gambia floated the dalasi in 1986 in response to balance-of-payments difficulties. Starting in the mid-1970s, imports increased sharply and domestic exports stagnated. The government's efforts to promote diversification failed to generate a significant additional net flow of foreign exchange, and despite price controls domestic prices increased rapidly. Consequently, foreign exchange reserves declined, the real exchange rate became increasingly overvalued, the current account deficit on the balance of payments rose significantly, and external debt service arrears emerged.

A structural change in the pattern of foreign trade occurred in 1974–1975 (Table 5-1). Imports increased by 44.7 percent as the government began to promote development through its first five-year plan (GOTG, 1975b);[3] in the following year, imports increased by 55.5 percent. Corresponding changes in exports were 25.4 percent in 1974–1975 and –11 percent in 1975–1976. Domestic exports continued to perform poorly for the rest of the decade due to drought, production disincentives, and fluctuations in the world price of groundnuts.[4] For several years the adverse effects of the imbalance between imports and exports were disguised by a reduction in official reserves and an increase in foreign debt.

The exchange rate had become overvalued for several reasons. The gap between Gambian interest rates and those prevailing in international markets began to widen. The Gambia also began to experience significantly higher rates of inflation than its major trading partners, primarily because it turned to expansionary monetary and fiscal policies after 1975–1976. And as the fiscal deficit increased sharply (averaging 8.2 percent of GDP between 1974–1975 and 1984–1985), both credit and money grew rapidly (Table 5-1). With this further impetus for inflation, downward pressure on the real exchange rate became exaggerated.[5]

These developments were reflected in changes in the real exchange rate (Table 5-2). The nominal and real exchange rate (for exporters) appreciated significantly between 1976–1977 and 1980–1981. The balance of payments deteriorated because movements in the real exchange rate encouraged imports and discouraged the production of exports and import substitutes.

With the current account deficit on the balance of payments exceeding 40 percent of GDP in the early 1980s, the need for exchange rate action intensified. But by the time The Gambia devalued the exchange rate in February 1984, it was already too late. Foreign exchange reserves had been depleted, external payment arrears were increasing, and a

Table 5-1. The Gambia: Trade, Debt, and Monetary Indicators

| | Millions of Dalasis ||||||| Millions of SDRs ||
Year	Imports (f.o.b.)	Exports (f.o.b.)	Current Account Balance[a]	Gross Official Reserves	Total External Debt	Debt/ GDP	Real Domestic Credit	Real Money Supply[b]
1965–66	−29.1	25.0	−5.8	15.3	7.0	0.07	−4.8	5.6
1966–67	−35.4	29.6	−7.8	21.0	0.8	0.01	−3.2	4.9
1967–68	−37.6	26.2	−15.3	16.2	3.7	0.04	−1.5	6.1
1968–69	−46.7	36.1	−12.9	18.1	7.8	0.07	−0.7	6.3
1969–70	−35.1	32.1	−8.0	25.7	10.3	0.09	−1.1	6.5
1970–71	−42.7	30.2	−19.1	32.9	10.0	0.07	−0.1	6.6
1971–72	−46.2	34.9	−14.9	44.5	12.4	0.08	−9.2	8.3
1972–73	−54.3	33.7	−18.8	44.8	13.2	0.09	1.8	10.6
1973–74	−63.5	67.6	7.2	48.7	16.9	0.08	5.5	13.2
1974–75	−91.9	84.8	−6.6	81.3	21.6	0.10	5.5	17.0
1975–76	−142.9	75.5	−72.7	58.7	26.5	0.10	11.8	19.0
1976–77	−169.1	106.7	−67.8	67.1	56.0	0.16	22.2	24.9
1977–78	−208.1	80.2	−161.1	42.8	91.9	0.27	33.6	29.1
1978–79	−221.0	88.4	−165.3	20.1	87.4	0.21	53.8	30.8
1979–80	−290.4	83.1	−244.2	11.7	118.2	0.28	85.5	34.0
1980–81	−263.4	55.9	−257.4	48.3	153.0	0.37	86.2	35.3
1981–82	−240.6	82.6	−228.7	11.8	224.1	0.49	88.6	36.1
1982–83	−262.1	156.8	−171.3	7.5	508.9	0.96	114.6	45.8
1983–84	−346.7	235.9	−195.1	16.6	778.4	1.30	104.0	38.5
1984–85	−358.7	251.1	−183.5	13.0	767.5	1.14	94.0	45.4
1985–86	−432.6	321.7	−269.6	7.1	1287.5	1.50	91.8	41.7
1986–87	−752.3	526.6	−373.4	100.3	2310.9	2.14	35.6	35.7
1987–88	−760.0	546.8	−294.1	193.8	2332.8	1.86[c]	28.4	43.8
1988–89	−902.2	727.4	−257.1	160.8	2486.9	1.65[c]	26.4	46.6
1989–90	−1142.5	899.5	−379.8	255.5	2057.8	1.15[c]	7.5	47.5
1990–91	−1319.7	1003.6	−362.4	467.3	2204.4	1.07[c]	1.1	53.0

[a] These data differ from those reported by IMF, particularly for the period from 1977–1978 to 1981–1982. The IMF data show a lower deficit due to higher estimated tourism receipts.
[b] Money plus quasi money.
[c] Reflects Paris/London Club rescheduling and other bilateral debt relief.

Sources: *Central Bank of The Gambia Quarterly Bulletins*, various editions; *Estimates of Recurrent Revenue and Expenditures*, various editions; GEDRES File and GDATA89 File, Ministry of Finance and Trade; IMF, *International Financial Statistics*, various editions; and International Monetary Fund, SM/92/111, June 2, 1992.

Table 5-2. The Gambia: Real Exchange Rates for Imports and Exports

Year	Average Duties Imports	Average Duties Exports	Nominal Exchange Rate (D/US$)	Real Exchange Rate[a] Imports[b]	Real Exchange Rate[a] Exports[c]
1965–1966	0.28	0.03	1.79	0.75	0.48
1966–1967	0.29	0.02	1.79	0.75	0.53
1967–1968	0.24	0.01	2.08	0.75	0.44
1968–1969	0.26	0.02	2.08	0.82	0.70
1969–1970	0.26	0.07	2.08	0.81	0.56
1970–1971	0.27	0.07	2.08	0.71	0.55
1971–1972	0.28	0.08	1.96	0.81	0.58
1972–1973	0.29	0.04	1.54	0.75	0.45
1973–1974	0.21	0.04	1.67	0.79	0.94
1974–1975	0.18	0.05	1.85	1.07	1.30
1975–1976	0.19	0.06	2.22	0.98	0.85
1976–1977	0.22	0.05	2.32	1.00	1.00
1977–1978	0.17	0.09	2.13	1.03	0.59
1978–1979	0.21	0.07	1.88	1.17	0.68
1979–1980	0.19	0.13	1.72	1.23	0.63
1980–1981	0.18	0.02	1.97	1.25	0.44
1981–1982	0.24	0.10	2.39	1.48	0.70
1982–1983	0.24	0.00	2.55	1.55	0.96
1983–1984	0.23	0.15	3.04	1.61	0.96
1984–1985	0.25	0.00	3.71	1.64	1.17
1985–1986	0.28	0.15	4.41	1.42	1.16
1986–1987	0.27	0.00	7.33	2.00	1.59
1987–1988	0.26	0.00	6.89	1.75	1.34
1988–1989	0.31	0.00	7.30	1.52	1.21
1989–1990	0.23	0.00	8.13	1.79	1.21
1990–1991	0.23	0.00	7.94	1.68	1.27

[a] 1976–1977 = 1
[b] One plus the import duty multiplied by the ratio of the dalasi import price index and the domestic price index (GDP deflator for 1976–1977 = 100).
[c] One minus the export duty multiplied by the ratio of the dalasi export price index and the domestic price index (GDP deflator for 1976–1977 = 100).
Sources: Central Bank of The Gambia Quarterly Bulletins, 1965–1991 editions; Central Statistics Department, The Gambia; IMF, International Financial Statistics, various editions; International Monetary Fund, SM/92/111, June 2, 1992; and GDATA90.WK1 spreadsheet.

parallel market for foreign exchange was flourishing. The devaluation had little impact on the economy. Confidence in the dalasi continued to erode, and the differential between the official and parallel market exchange rates increased to more than 80 percent by the end of 1985. A major adjustment to the official exchange rate could no longer be avoided.

Exchange Rate Reform and the Economic Recovery Program

Many government officials were not convinced that the exchange rate system should be reformed.[6] Much of the resistance stemmed from the perceived disadvantages of devaluation—higher import costs, cuts in real income, and accelerated inflation. But some resistance came from the notion that The Gambia's problems (as in most developing countries) were due to external factors such as drought, declining terms of trade, lower levels of aid, and increases in international interest rates. In particular, members of Cabinet, the Ministry of Economic Planning, and the Central Bank claimed that nothing could be done locally to rectify the situation; solutions had to be external. One such solution was additional support from the donor community.[7]

Thus even in mid-1985, when the economy was falling apart around them, few government officials believed that changing the exchange rate would be a viable strategy for economic revitalization. The Central Bank argued that more time was required to assess the effects of the February 1984 devaluation. Its position was curious, since Central Bank staff were better placed than most to recognize the ineffectiveness of the devaluation. In the sixteen months between the devaluation and the formulation of the ERP, official reserves had declined further, and external debt and payments arrears continued to accumulate. Indeed, the devaluation, because it was too small and had not been supported with other policies, had the negative effect of demonstrating that the government was not prepared to act decisively on the exchange rate.

In the end the government had little room to maneuver, and formal devaluation seemed inevitable. Foreign exchange reserves had fallen to the equivalent of one week of imports, aid flow had disappeared, and shortages of many imported commodities had emerged. The parallel market had undermined the official exchange rate, and the small amount of foreign exchange that continued to flow was being traded through alternative channels. The advantages of devaluation as one element of a policy package could no longer be ignored. Thus the MoF switched its attention from arguing about the relative merits of a devaluation to debating the appropriate timing of and method for achieving it.

The most important and immediate objective in The Gambia was to remedy the balance-of-payments crisis. Price stability and economic growth were issues of secondary importance. Thus a large and immediate change in the exchange rate was called for. A more gradual approach, which may have been more appropriate in other circumstances, simply would have lengthened the time frame necessary for alleviating the balance-of-payments situation.

Three options for a long-term regime were available—a series of programmed devaluations, a foreign exchange auction, or a float. A large and well-known body of literature exists on the relative merits of fixed versus floating exchange rates (see, for example, Aghevli et al., 1991;

Edwards, 1988; Quirk et al., 1987). The literature does not provide unambiguous guidelines about whether a small open economy is better off with one or the other. The optimal system depends on the structure of the economy, the sources of likely external shocks, and the administrative capabilities of the relevant government agencies.

In The Gambia the ineffectiveness of the fixed-rate system during the late 1970s and early 1980s in general, and the failure of the 1984 devaluation in particular, undermined the attractiveness of continuing with a fixed rate. The absence of financial discipline in the government was likely to undermine any new fixed rate, leading to a cycle of continued devaluations and a loss of credibility. Concern was also expressed about whether the Central Bank was capable of determining the appropriate size and frequency of any devaluations. Because waning confidence in the dalasi had led to widespread disintermediation, predicting the size of a potentially sustainable devaluation posed serious problems. The parallel exchange rate provided a guide, but adverse expectations could continue to exert downward pressure on the dalasi. Few officials believed that a preannounced series of devaluations (as had been attempted in Ghana) would succeed under such circumstances.

The Gambia could also have tried to join the CFA zone. Indeed, The Gambia had agreed with Senegal in principle to work toward unifying the exchange rate within the context of the Senegambia Confederation. Although joining the zone would have forced The Gambia to undertake some of the necessary financial and monetary discipline, the country would have surrendered significant economic, and eventually political, independence. This move would have been considered a first step toward a potential merger with Senegal (see Chapter 3). Due primarily to its political implications, this option was never seriously considered.

A foreign exchange auction was also unattractive, primarily because the absence of foreign exchange would preclude the initiation of the process. But senior ministry officials also lacked confidence in the capacity of the Central Bank to organize and sustain an auction. Auctions require significant government involvement in making frequent decisions about the timing of auctions, the amount to be auctioned, and the Central Bank's cutoff price. The administrative and managerial difficulties encountered by Uganda with its auction reinforced these views (see Quirk et al., 1987). Government officials were also concerned that large traders would attempt to corner the market, as had occurred in Sierra Leone. Indeed, the primary reason for rejecting an auction was the fear that Senegalese traders would take advantage of the situation and attempt to disrupt the market.

In contrast, a floating exchange rate system would automatically eliminate currency overvaluation. A float could be initiated without a build-up of official resources. Because it could be operated with relative ease, administrative weaknesses at the Central Bank probably would not be a deterrent, and it would build on parallel market activity with which Gambians were already familiar. It would also deflect political criticism away from the government, because the rate would be determined by market forces and not by government decision. Of course, a float carried many risks. Developing countries had relatively little experience with a floating rate from which The Gambia could learn. In Africa only Uganda and Zaire had attempted a float prior to The Gambia—and Uganda only after its auction system had failed. There were concerns that the market was too thin (only three commercial banks would be participating) and that the financial system was too underdeveloped to support a float. Concern was also expressed that, with the large backlog of debt service arrears, extensive intervention by the Central Bank could lead to a dramatic depreciation. However, this problem could be addressed with a gradual, programmed reduction in arrears.

Due primarily to its administrative simplicity and its effectiveness at eliminating market distortions quickly, the government decided to float the currency. Accordingly, an interbank market for foreign exchange was introduced on January 20, 1986, and the dalasi was officially allowed to float freely.

The Float and Its Consequences

The float led to a major real depreciation of the dalasi (see Table 5-2). The demand of both official and nonofficial sources for foreign exchange declined sharply. As confidence in the government's commitment to economic reform began to rise, additional foreign exchange was supplied to the official market. After agreements were reached with the IMF, World Bank, African Development Bank, and bilateral donors in August 1986, a large inflow of foreign aid also helped stabilize the exchange rate.

Although the float has not always operated smoothly, the system has proved to be robust. Comprehensive supporting policies, debt relief, and higher levels of aid from donors were crucial to stabilizing the market. Developing a consistent set of monetary and fiscal policies was a primary focus. These measures helped stabilize the foreign exchange rate, reduce the risks of short-term fluctuations, and restore confidence in the domestic economy.

As mentioned previously, an argument against floating exchange rates in developing countries is the absence of well-functioning foreign exchange and financial markets. Since those markets were thin in The Gambia, the government focused on the structure of the interbank market, its operating rules, and measures that would insulate it from potentially disruptive changes in supply and demand conditions. Commercial banks were required to participate in a weekly "fixing session," chaired by the Central Bank. The purpose of the session was to allow the commercial banks and the Central Bank to trade among themselves, to consult about market developments, and to determine the weekly "fixing rate," the rate at which official transactions were valued for the following week.[8]

Although fixed once each week for official transactions, the exchange rate was free to vary at the commercial banks on a daily or even hourly basis in response to market forces. To strengthen the system, the government removed all restrictions on private payments and transfers for current international transactions, established foreign exchange surrender requirements for public enterprises, and set limits on the foreign exchange balances of the commercial banks.[9] The government also obtained technical assistance to improve Central Bank management and sought continued donor support for fuel grants. By insulating the foreign exchange market from the large irregular demands associated with petroleum imports, the grants had an important stabilizing influence. Finally, the government began to sell treasury bills aggressively in order to absorb excess liquidity in the economy.[10]

Despite the precautions some difficulties had to be overcome. Initially, the commercial banks would not compete actively for foreign exchange. Their management was antagonistic toward the float and skeptical about its benefits. As the parallel exchange rate moved well beyond the rate at which they were prepared to trade, the banks were quickly cut out of the foreign exchange market. The situation changed in mid-February 1986, when pressure was applied by the MoF. When the banks began to make a market for foreign exchange, the official and parallel rates converged (see Table 5-3). The dalasi depreciated sharply in the first eight weeks of the float, falling from D/£7.45 in late January to D/£10 in March. By April the banks began to dominate the foreign exchange market, volumes traded through official channels increased sharply, and the exchange rate stabilized. Between April and July the D/£ rate changed only slightly, and the premium for foreign exchange in the parallel market was just 2 percent.

Table 5-3. The Gambia, Commercial Bank, and Parallel Exchange Rates: January to July 1986 (Dalasis per Pound)

Date	Bank Rate	Parallel Rate	Official Fixing Rate[a]
1/17/86	5.00	8.50–9.00	5.00
1/24/86	7.50	9.75–10.00	7.45
1/31/86	7.50	10.25–10.75	7.56
2/7/86	7.50	10.75–11.25	7.61
2/14/86	7.55	7.50–8.50	7.64
2/21/86	7.50–7.55	7.50–11.00	7.64
2/28/86	7.50–9.05	8.25–10.25	7.90
3/7/86	9.00–9.08	9.50–10.50	9.00
3/14/86	10.00	9.75–10.50	10.00
3/21/86	10.00	10.50	10.00
3/28/86	10.00	10.50	10.00
4/4/86	10.00	10.25–10.50	10.00
4/11/86	10.00	10.75	10.10
4/18/86	10.00	10.75	10.10
4/25/86	10.00	10.50–10.80	10.15
5/2/86	10.00	10.50–10.75	10.15
5/9/86	10.50	10.75–10.80	10.60
5/16/86	10.50	11.00	11.00
5/23/86	10.90	11.05	11.00
5/30/86	10.90	11.05	11.00
6/6/86	10.90	11.45	11.00
6/13/86	10.90	11.50	11.00
6/20/86	10.90	11.50	11.10
6/27/86	11.05	11.75	11.10
7/4/86	11.05	11.75	11.45
7/11/86	11.40	11.80	11.45
7/18/86	11.40	11.80	11.25
7/25/86	11.20	11.75	11.25

[a]Set on a weekly basis.
Source: Central Bank of The Gambia.

Supporting Policies

The exchange rate change in February 1984 had shown clearly that devaluation alone was ineffective. The ERP did not repeat that mistake, and it encompassed numerous changes to ensure that appropriate, timely, and complementary policies would be implemented. The government explicitly recognized that it had to minimize the potential for major macroeconomic disturbances.[11]

In order to ensure that the exchange rate adjustment led to the necessary expenditure-reducing and expenditure-switching changes, the ERP sought to remove price controls to allow for a complete pass-through of exchange rate changes on domestic prices. In one of the first steps taken, the government decontrolled the retail price of rice and removed all restrictions on rice imports. It then introduced a flexible pricing system for other key commodities. The producer price of groundnuts was raised on three occasions during the 1985–1986 season. After January 1986 numerous adjustments were made to other administered prices—petroleum, public utilities, and transport—to reflect movements in costs, including those associated with fluctuations in the exchange rate. These prices were subsequently decontrolled.

Demand management policies were critical to reducing the inflationary effects of the exchange rate depreciation after the float. The main focus was on the budget deficit. To contain government expenditures, the government retrenched 20 percent of the civil service, froze wages and salaries, and implemented a program to rationalize the operations of the major public enterprises (see Chapter 16). These actions were reinforced with measures to control the expansion of credit in the economy. The government set limits on public-sector borrowing and reached agreement with the IMF on a general ceiling on bank lending. The government also agreed to a moratorium on government guarantees and the contracting of new nonconcessional medium-term debt (see Chapter 11). These actions substantially reduced credit growth, thereby providing a nominal anchor for the economy.[12]

The flexible interest rate policy supported the new exchange rate system. Interest rates were raised administratively in September 1985, but the treasury bill tender introduced in July 1986 allowed market forces to determine their level (see Chapter 6). These high-yielding dalasi-denominated assets gave asset holders an incentive to substitute away from foreign exchange, further reducing the pressure on the exchange rate.

The float was crucial to reengaging donors. Although they had been impressed with the intentions behind the ERP, the donors wanted an explicit demonstration of the government's commitment to economic reform. The float demonstrated its commitment. The generous support that ensued was instrumental in stabilizing the exchange rate and in accentuating the effects of other ERP reforms. Finally, as The Gambia's international creditworthiness improved, it rescheduled its external debts and began rationalizing its arrears situation. The reduction in the debt overhang also took pressure off the foreign exchange market.

Economic Response and Recent Developments

Exchange rate reform and its supporting measures had a positive effect on the economy. Output and trade grew, inflation and external payments arrears fell, and foreign reserves began to accumulate. The improvements provided a foundation for sustained growth.

An essential element of the improved economic performance was the significant real depreciation of the dalasi. The initial nominal depreciation against the U.S. dollar was approximately 40 percent; the real depreciation was on the order of 30 percent. Without this real depreciation none of the benefits of the float for resource allocation, the structure of demand, income distribution, and the balance of payments could have occurred.

Exchange rate reform helped reintegrate parallel and official market activity. The initial benefit was an increase in demand for dalasi-denominated assets. By the time the parallel and official exchange rates converged in mid-1986, the bulk of exchange market activity was being channeled through the banks.

By reducing excess demand for foreign exchange, the float also enabled the Central Bank to accumulate reserves. The reabsorption of parallel market activity, the increase in donor support, the reduced budget deficit, and the increase in customs revenue after the crackdown on customs fraud (see Chapter 17) freed up a large amount of resources. Gross official reserves grew from SDR1.3 million in mid-1986 to SDR16.4 million in mid-1989 (or from the equivalent of four days of imports to 1.7 months of imports). As The Gambia's external financial relations were normalized and external payments arrears were eliminated (in July 1990), those reserves greatly strengthened the exchange rate system. In contrast to the period prior to the ERP, some scope existed to protect the economy from external shocks, as demonstrated by the departure of Mauritanian traders in April 1989 and by the Gulf War in 1991. Whether the exchange rate system will continue to be robust following the 1994 coup remains to be seen.

The exchange rate has fluctuated since 1986, both appreciating and depreciating periodically. Notwithstanding other measures to support the float, rigidities have emerged, with adverse consequences. The Central Bank's ill-advised attempt to refix the dalasi created difficulties. For most of 1988–1989 there was a de facto fix of the dalasi against the pound sterling (see Walsh, 1990, for a discussion). The D/£ exchange rate remained virtually stable from June 1988 to June 1989. At the same time the real effective exchange rate appreciated by approximately 13 percent. To prevent the dalasi from depreciating, the Central Bank withdrew from the interbank market. Taking their cue from the Central Bank, the commercial banks did not adjust their buying and selling rates in response to market pressures. Excess demand for foreign exchange led to rationing rather than to changes in the exchange rate. The commercial bank "pipeline"[13] reemerged, parallel market activity increased, and a premium of approximately 10 percent was being paid for foreign exchange by June 1989.

Unwilling to compete for foreign exchange during 1989, the Central Bank missed its reserve accumulation target under the IMF program. Furthermore, in order to clear the commercial pipeline, the Central Bank had to sell some of its reserves.

Under pressure from the donors, primarily the IMF, the Central Bank aggressively reentered the foreign exchange market in early 1990. Its main tasks were to clear the commercial pipeline, rebuild official reserves, and restore confidence in the interbank market. The exchange rate responded appropriately. The dalasi depreciated by 10.4 percent against the pound in nominal terms between August and December 1989, and by another 6.4 percent by April 1990. The real effective exchange rate depreciated by 10.8 percent during 1989–1990.[14] The parallel market premium was virtually eliminated by mid-September 1989. To enhance competition in the foreign exchange market, the authorities allowed foreign exchange bureaus to operate from April 1990 onward.

Insights from The Gambia's Exchange Rate Reform

Floating the dalasi was crucial to the success of the ERP because it removed a major distortion that had undermined the performance of the Gambian economy. The experience provides several lessons.

First, the success of a flexible exchange rate depends on whether it is part of a comprehensive and consistent package of policy changes. In particular, budget deficits must be reduced, and money and credit growth must be curtailed. Measures to liberalize interest rates and limit the growth of public-sector debt are also important. Without strong supporting policies the Gambian float of the dalasi would not have succeeded.

Second, holders of financial assets need to be assured that the new policies will be sustained. If not, they will seek other outlets for their resources. This element of a flexible rate is one advantage over a fixed rate, since the latter would likely be subject to frequent changes, eroding confidence. In The Gambia the support of the donor community was crucial to strengthening the confidence of the private sector in the sustainability of the float.

Third, shocks in the foreign exchange market must be minimized. In The Gambia reductions in debt service payments (through debt relief), a schedule for the gradual repayment of debt service arrears, and special arrangements for "large ticket" items (such as fuel) proved to be vital.

Fourth, increased competition in the foreign exchange market was crucial to success. For example, The Gambia encouraged independent foreign exchange dealers and gave the Central Bank direct oversight of the commercial banks.

Fifth, the Central Bank should operate regularly and openly on both sides of the market. The bank must establish a presence in the market to deflect any potentially adverse expectation effects fostered by irregular, behind-the-scenes operations. This action is obviously difficult in the early stages, when foreign exchange reserves are limited, but foreign exchange sales (as well as purchases) should be a normal aspect of Central Bank operations after a minimum level of foreign exchange reserves has been accumulated.

Sixth, the capacity of the Central Bank should be enhanced before exchange rate reform is introduced. Gaps may be filled initially with technical assistance. Nonetheless, additional staff must be hired and trained. This component is critical even with a flexible rate, which requires substantially less administration and management than either an auction or a crawling peg.

Finally, the Gambian experience shows that the advantages of a fixed exchange rate tend to be overblown. Contrary to some influential opinions,[15] a small, open, developing country can shift successfully to a flexible exchange rate to address its internal and external imbalances. What is required is appropriate and timely management from the central bank to ensure a competitive environment, as well as a strong set of supporting macroeconomic policies.

NOTES

1. The Gambian dalasi, created in 1971, was D5 = £1 until March 1973, when it was revalued to D4 = £1. In February 1984 it was devalued to D5 = £1, the level it retained until the float in January 1986.
2. For discussions of these and other related issues, see Duesenberry et al. (1994); Cornia et al. (1992); Aghevli et al. (1991); World Bank (1989a); UNECA (1989); Edwards (1988); Dornbusch (1988); and Quirk et al. (1987). A separate set of issues pertain to the countries of the CFA zone, which face the task of altering their real exchange rates without changing their nominal rate.
3. The surge in import demand coincided with a shift in formal sector employment and urbanization. Because the average propensity to import is higher and the average propensity to export is lower among the urban

population, the redistribution of population and income from rural to urban areas led to a major structural shift in the pattern of merchandise trade (and hence the current account on the balance of payments).

4. The decline in groundnut production from 1977–1978 to 1980–1981, when world prices reached unprecedented levels, was costly to The Gambia. Over that four-year period, purchases by the Gambia Produce Marketing Board averaged 79.2 thousand tonnes annually. The world price averaged US$502.4 per tonne. In contrast, for the five years before 1977–1978, average GPMB purchases had been 127.7 thousand tonnes, and the world price was US$404 per tonne. The experience led many Gambian officials to attribute the country's subsequent economic difficulties (when groundnut prices fell) to declining terms of trade.

5. Uncovered interest parity implies that the exchange rate would increase as the interest rate spread on equivalent financial instruments widened. Letting e^* be the expected change in the exchange rate, i_w a relevant "world" interest rate (such as the U.K. treasury bill rate), and i_g the comparable Gambian interest rate, then:

$$e^* = f(i_g - i_w) \quad f' > 0$$

Similarly, purchasing power parity implies that:

$$e^* = g(dp_w - dp_g) \quad g' < 0,$$

where dp_w and dp_g are, respectively, the rate of inflation in the rest of the world and in The Gambia.

Both sources exerted significant pressures on the exchange rate. Between 1975 and 1985 the average spread between the bill rates in The Gambia and the United Kingdom was 2.7 percentage points. For the same period consumer prices in The Gambia increased by 377 percent, while prices in the United Kingdom increased by 177 percent, in the United States by 100 percent, in West Germany by 48 percent, in France by 159 percent, and in Japan by 31 percent. (All data come from *International Financial Statistics Yearbook 1991*.)

6. Even as late as April 1984, the minister of finance was not convinced that the exchange rate was a significant determinant of The Gambia's economic decline. Minister Sisay made his views known during the 1983 Article IV consultations. For a discussion of the official view, see IMF, 1983, p. 11.

7. That reasoning was reflected in the *Mid-Term Review of the Second Development Plan* (GOTG, 1984) prepared by consultants from the United Nations Development Program and by staff from the Ministry of Economic Planning.

8. The "fixing rate" was derived from a weighted average of the transactions of the previous week, unless transactions occurred during the fixing session, which then set the rate. Despite its inappropriate connotations in a floating exchange rate system, the "fixing rate" was adopted from the IMF (IMF, 1985). The name persisted until early 1990, when it was changed to the "customs valuation rate."

9. At the end of each week, the commercial banks were required to sell in the interbank market any foreign exchange in excess of established working balances. The export earnings of public enterprises (primarily the GPMB) had to be repatriated and sold through the interbank market. All other restrictions on capital movements were removed when the government suspended the relevant provisions of the Exchange Control Act (Cap. 64).

10. As the balance of payments improved, treasury bills provided a useful way to sterilize foreign inflows. The T-bills have been a highly effective mechanism for enabling the government to build up its foreign exchange reserves.

11. Professor James Duesenberry, as an adviser to the MoF in the period immediately before the float, emphasized that with a floating exchange rate, all macroeconomic disturbances are reflected in the rate. Special measures were necessary to minimize those disturbances (GOTG, 1986, p. 21).

12. The freeze on public-sector wages was key to reducing the growth of government expenditures. Wage payments encompassed 31 percent of government current expenditures in 1985–1986; they were 14 percent of current expenditures in 1987–1988. In real terms the wage bill declined by 16.5 percent in the first three years of the ERP.

13. The "commercial pipeline" was a series of deposit accounts established at commercial banks that allowed private businesses with outstanding foreign exchange obligations to deposit the dalasi equivalent while awaiting foreign exchange availability. When such deposits were made, the government took over the foreign exchange liability.

14. The Central Bank action had been associated with other policy slippages. For instance, excessive monetary expansion in the first half of 1989–1990 accelerated inflation from 7.7 percent in the previous year to 13.4 percent.

15. According to Dornbusch (1988, p. 104), "flexible exchange rates may be appropriate for major currency blocks, but they are certainly a poor idea for an individual developing country."

6

Monetary Policy and Financial Reform

James S. Duesenberry and Malcolm F. McPherson

At the time the ERP was being formulated, monetary policy was in disarray: inflation was accelerating, interest rates were highly negative in real terms, currency substitution and capital flight were major problems, foreign arrears were mounting, financial disintermediation was increasing, and the parallel foreign exchange had largely displaced the official market. Worse, the government had no effective way to conduct monetary policy because long lags in data reporting meant that it did not know the levels of the major monetary aggregates until several months after the fact.

In response to these problems, The Gambia implemented a series of remarkably constructive changes in monetary and financial policy. The government raised interest rates to positive real levels, floated the exchange rate, and introduced market-based mechanisms to control reserves and the money supply. It substantially reduced the government budget deficit and took major steps toward rehabilitating financial institutions.

The monetary policy and financial sector problems faced by The Gambia are common to many countries in sub-Saharan Africa. In general, improved monetary management requires moving the government away from direct credit allocation and controls and toward market-based financial instruments as the primary tools of monetary policy. There is now a large literature on the adverse effects of excessive direct financial controls.[1] The general conclusion from these studies is that direct financial controls have failed because they create disincentives to hold assets and because the public loses confidence that the government and Central Bank can ultimately withstand the inflationary and balance-of-payments pressures created by direct controls. Asset holders find that existing formal financial channels are too expensive or too risky, so they turn to either informal or overseas markets. The former leads to the development of local parallel markets and currency substitution; the latter leads to capital flight. Both choices indicate that the government and the central bank are losing (or, indeed, have lost) control over the local monetary system. Governments often react to these worsening problems by introducing even more controls, but this strategy almost always fails. The basic lesson is that the government and the central bank can begin to regain some influence over the financial system only when they begin to exercise restraint and to operate in ways consistent with market developments.

The experiences of other countries suggest that to improve monetary management, governments must strengthen financial markets; improve the data monitoring, policy making, and supervisory capacities of the central bank; introduce market-based monetary instruments; and exercise fiscal restraint. Indirect monetary control can be enhanced by introducing financial programming and planning, which include growth targets for the principal monetary aggregates and predetermined strategies for responding to changes in balance of payments and local credit conditions.

This chapter describes The Gambia's experiences in monetary policy and financial sector reform. It begins by briefly reviewing the monetary and financial systems and institutions in The Gambia and examining the changes in monetary and financial management under the ERP. It then reviews some of the issues that have to be addressed if improvements in monetary management are to be sustained, and concludes with observations about monetary policy reform.

The Monetary and Financial Setting

Because The Gambia is a small, open economy, monetary and financial developments domestically and abroad are crucial to its economic performance (McPherson, 1979, Appendix 3). On the positive side, access to international financial markets has opened up a rich array of high-yield, secure financial instruments. On the negative side, adverse changes in the external financial climate require an appropriate response from Gambian policymakers to minimize damage to the domestic economy.

Many of The Gambia's monetary difficulties arose because important government policies ran counter to financial stability. Two policy actions were particularly destabilizing: extensive government intervention to promote economic development, and monetary accommodation of external shocks—a policy that became more pronounced as the 1970s progressed.

Active government intervention in promoting economic development evolved over several years. It began when the government established the Central Bank in 1971 and the Gambia Commercial and Development Bank in 1972. It intensified when the government introduced the first five-year plan in 1975. Under the plan the objectives of the government's monetary and financial policies were twofold: to maintain financial stability and to provide credit to promote development (GOTG, 1975b, Chapter 7). The plan did not provide guidance about how the potential trade-offs between these two goals could be resolved.

The government could pursue an accommodating monetary policy only after it established the Central Bank. The predecessor to the Central Bank was the Gambia Currency Board, whose operating procedures were rigidly enforced. Its currency issue was backed by foreign assets, its lending to the government was strictly limited, and loans from the board had to be repaid within a specified period.[2] These procedures enabled the Gambian pound to be fully convertible into sterling and imposed consistency on economic management—specifically, the monetary authorities could not attempt to control both the exchange rate and the money supply.[3] These strictures were not subsequently imposed on the Central Bank.

The Gambia's Financial System

Given its low real income and uncomplicated economic structure, The Gambia has a simple financial system. In the mid-1980s it consisted of several financial institutions: the Central Bank; three commercial banks—the GCDB, Standard Bank Gambia (SBG), and the International Bank for Commerce and Industry (BICI); a thrift institution, the Government Savings Bank, commonly referred to as the Post Office Savings Bank (POSB); four insurance companies; and the Social Security and Housing Finance Corporation (SSHFC). Various financial services are also provided by two parastatals—the Gambia Produce Marketing Board and the Gambia Cooperatives Union—and by three government entities—the Indigenous Business Advisory Service (IBAS), the National Investment Board (NIB), and the Gambia Women's Finance Corporation. Several nongovernmental organizations, such as Action Aid, also engage in financial activities. More recently, several *bureaux de change* have been established.

Little competition exists among the banks. BICI has a select clientele. Because its loans and advances comprise less than 5 percent of the national total, it does not affect the volume and pattern of lending. The GCDB has been in financial trouble for so long that it no longer has the resources to be competitive. The SBG also has a select clientele and is selective about the terms on which it agrees to conduct business on their behalf.

In contrast, competition for foreign exchange business has been intense. Since the dalasi was floated in 1986, the rates quoted by the banks have ranged within a few points and, with one exception (discussed later), are at levels that undercut the parallel market. The entry of *bureaux de change* in 1990 intensified the competition.

Financial Markets in The Gambia

The Gambia has two formal financial markets: the interbank market for foreign exchange (established in January 1986) and the treasury bill tender (established in July 1986). The parallel market for foreign exchange now operates semiformally. Informal financial arrangements are discussed in Chapter 7.

In the interbank market, foreign exchange is bought and sold at prices determined by each of the banks and their customers or by the banks and the Central Bank. With one major exception—when in 1989 and 1990 the Central Bank attempted to resist further depreciation of the dalasi—this market has functioned well (see Chapter 5).

The treasury bill tender has two purposes. It gives financial institutions and individuals access to high-quality government paper in order to absorb excess liquidity (Duesenberry, 1986) and establishes a market-determined rate of interest that serves as a benchmark rate for the entire economy.

A formal money market does not exist. None of the large firms or the banks has endeavored to lend their cash surpluses on a short-term basis. Some one-off transactions have been brokered by the Central Bank, but firms and individuals do not have a formal mechanism for trading financial assets. Most large operators find it easier to place their spare resources in offshore banking facilities. Active formal markets in bonds or equities also do not exist (Ladd, 1989).

The Central Bank and the Ministry of Finance

In The Gambia the Central Bank and the Ministry of Finance have always had a close formal relationship. The first governor of the Central Bank, Sheriff Sisay, had been minister of finance from 1962 until 1968. When he moved from the Central Bank to reassume the position of minister of finance in 1982, the permanent secretary of finance was appointed governor.

For several years after its founding, the Central Bank had some autonomy. Gradually, however, the views and requirements of the MoF began to prevail. The first indications of this shift appeared in the Central Bank *Annual Reports* of 1975–1976 and 1976–1977, when it became clear that the government had not repaid its short-term ways and means advances to the Central Bank in the legally specified time frame. The government also turned to the Central Bank for the first of several "temporary" advances to fund specific development projects. Although they were classified as "bridge finance" so that projects could proceed while awaiting donors to disburse the funds,[4] the loans became permanent when some donors did not disburse the loans as expected and when some of the funds were diverted to other uses. In effect, the government began using the Central Bank for permanent rather than temporary financing.

The Impact of the ERP on the Financial System

Despite the evident breakdown in the financial system and a deteriorating economy, the government was reluctant to change its policy stance. However, as the ERP was introduced, the government began to regain control over the budget. The Central Bank curtailed credit growth and the dalasi stabilized, helping the economy recover on a broad front.

With the return of financial stability, the Gambian financial system began the process of reintermediation. The treasury bill tender system became well established; demand for T-bills and T-notes emerged among nonbank customers; the volume of time and savings deposits grew faster than GDP; the bulk of foreign exchange trading shifted to the formal financial sector; and new financial institutions commenced operations. These developments were encouraged by the payment of positive real interest rates on deposits, the attractive yields offered on T-bills and T-notes, competition in the foreign exchange market, and the government's progress toward improving the performance of the major financial parastatals.

Notwithstanding these improvements, asset holders continued to hedge their bets. Despite the sharp drop in inflation and the relative stability of the dalasi, most financial activity had a very short time horizon. Private investment in long-term ventures was minimal. The bulk of private investment in The Gambia continued to be devoted to wholesale trade and tourism, both of which are short-term. Even the more recent expansion of specialty agricultural products required little long-term investment, especially given the tax breaks and duty waivers provided by the government. With nearly 20 percent yields on short-term assets such as T-bills, inflation at roughly half that level, and no major gyrations in the exchange rate, few investors needed to run the risks associated with long-term investment in real assets.

Monetary and Financial Management Since the Economic Recovery Program

The Objectives of Monetary Management

Prior to the ERP, the Central Bank and the government had numerous, sometimes conflicting monetary and financial objectives. The ERP forced consistency on the operational objectives of monetary management. The government's compliance with the IMF's approach to financial stabilization ensured this consistency. The strategy called for:

- a realistic (market-determined) exchange rate;
- positive real interest rates;
- control over public-sector borrowing;
- a moratorium on new loan guarantees and nonconcessional external borrowing;
- the decontrol of prices;
- improvements in the efficiency of public investment.

These measures sought to reduce the rate of inflation, accumulate foreign reserves, reestablish the international creditworthiness of The Gambia, and promote financial reintermediation. In general, the government pursued these measures with only a few slippages.

Notably absent from this strategy was the use of credit and finance to promote development. Under the ERP this objective would have been redundant. Indeed, by stabilizing the economy with prudent monetary and fiscal policies, the government and the Central Bank did more to promote economic development than they had in their decade-long experiment with financial intervention. Major monetary aggregates clearly showed the renewed stability (see Table 6-1 and Figure 6-1). During the ERP, net foreign assets grew markedly, and net credit to the government fell sharply. M2 grew at an average annual rate of 16 percent between 1986–1987 and 1990–1991, after growing 21 percent annually from 1980–1981 to 1985–1986. Private-sector credit growth increased from an average of 3 percent to an average of 14 percent during the same period.

Interest Rate Policy under the Economic Recovery Program

Although Central Bank policies have been reoriented along several dimensions, perhaps the most dramatic shift has been the change in interest rate policy. After many years of arbitrarily low interest rates, government policy changed with the adoption of the ERP. Despite the potential inflationary pressures exerted by floating the exchange rate, eliminating

Table 6-1. Monetary Aggregates in The Gambia: 1980–1981 to 1990–1991 (Millions of Dalasis; End of Period)

	Pre-ERP					ERP				Post-ERP	
	1980–81	1981–82	1982–83	1983–84	1984–85	1985–86	1986–87	1987–88	1988–89	1989–90	1990–91
Net Foreign Assets	-48	-102	-161	-255	-255	-585	-313	-176	-150	-146	143
Monetary authorities	-32	-94	-135	-238	-258	-595	-333	-192	-156	-167	115
Foreign assets						11	98	256	232	282	553
Foreign liabilities						-607	-431	-448	-388	-449	-438
Commercial banks	-17	-8	-26	-18	3	11	20	16	6	21	28
Net Domestic Assets						596	295	225	192	112	-67
Domestic credit	210	242	331	370	378	501	326	256	242	175	58
Government (net)	51	78	165	196	179	100	-65	-37	-115	-115	-297
Public enterprises						217	217	101	133	39	48
of which GPMB						133	156	56	75	28	38
Private sector	159	164	166	174	199	184	174	192	225	251	290
Revaluation Account						237	393	392	433	590	564
SDR Allocation	-9	-13	-14	-20	-34	-19	-47	-47	-48	-57	-57
Money and Quasi Money	86	99	132	137	183	227	327	394	427	500	584
Money (cash & demand deposits)	57	59	80	77	96	130	192	222	235	282	334
Quasi money (savings & time deposits)	30	40	52	60	86	98	135	172	192	218	250
Other Items (Net)	76	42	38	-22	-60	-311	-315	-314	-335	-471	-428
Reserve Money						60	123	145	165	192	225
Currency outside banks						60	96	108	119	155	169
Liabilities to commercial banks						-0	27	37	46	38	56
Liquidity of Commercial Banks											
Liquid assets							102	151	145	182	218
Treasury bills							47	90	103	143	116
Excess liquidity							28	63	48	78	93

Sources: *Central Bank of The Gambia Quarterly Bulletins*, various editions; *International Financial Statistics*, various editions; and International Monetary Fund, SM/92/111, June 2, 1992.

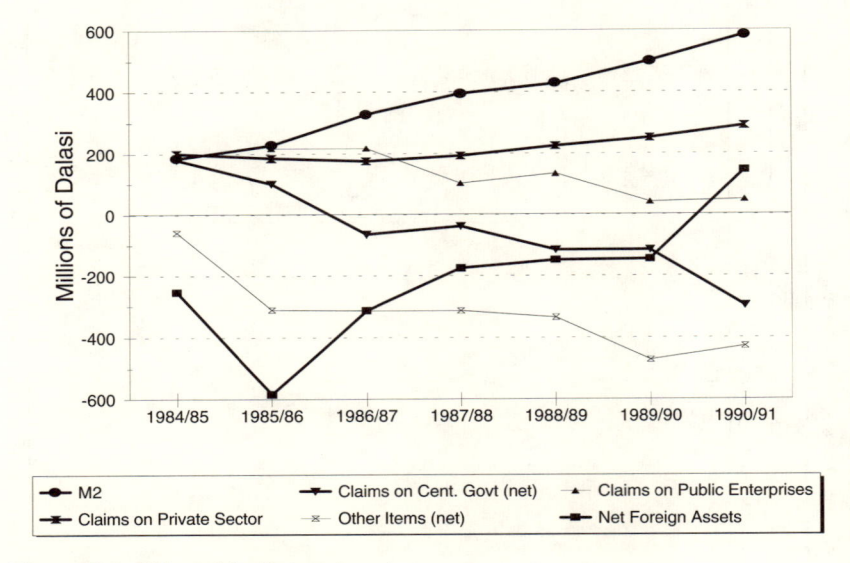

Figure 6-1. M2 and Its Determinants

price controls, and reducing subsidies for key commodities, the dalasi stabilized and inflation began to slow in less than a year. An important reason for the progress toward stabilization was the Central Bank's efforts to restrain monetary growth and its move toward a "market-determined" interest rate.

Under such circumstances it is not surprising that the treasury bill rate rose to 20 percent during the stabilization process. Although it later declined to 17.5 percent, the inflation rate also declined, so the *real* interest rate on treasury bills rose significantly. The treasury bill rate was the benchmark interest rate in the system. The discount rate was set at 2 percentage points above the bill rate, while the minimum deposit rate was set at 3 percentage points below the bill rate. With deposit rates of around 12.5 percent, the real rate was slightly positive.

Banks could of course pay more than minimum. Although they paid the minimum rate to most customers for three-month deposits, they posted higher rates for longer-term deposits. Customers with large balances could negotiate higher rates. In particular, the GCDB often found it necessary to offer a deposit rate equal to its reserve deficiency penalties to the Central Bank. Thus the treasury bill rate was set at the marginal cost of funds to the GCDB and at the opportunity cost of funds to the private banks that would have excess reserves if they did not buy treasury bills.

The Central Bank used the bill tender to absorb the excess reserves of the commercial banks, equivalent to an open-market operation. The large volume of bills outstanding since 1986 served to mop up the excess reserves created earlier by the government.

Intermediate Targets and the Transmission Mechanism

Starting with the ERP, the government's principal intermediate targets were domestic demand and the exchange rate. By setting limits on the sectoral and aggregate allocation of credit and by providing a profitable outlet for excess liquidity in the form of T-bills, the government systematically lowered the growth of domestic demand. For instance, from 1980 to 1985 domestic credit increased by 106 percent, and domestic demand increased by 19 percent. From 1985 to 1990 they grew 39 percent and 154 percent, respectively. In turn, the relative reduction in domestic credit eased inflationary pressures.

The Central Bank influenced the exchange rate both directly and indirectly. Its direct influence came from buying and selling foreign exchange. Given the government's commitment to servicing all of its non-rescheduable debt fully and to accumulating official reserves, the Central Bank became a large net buyer of foreign exchange.

But to avoid major shifts in the exchange rate, the Central Bank also relied on indirect measures. Interest rate policy was crucial in this regard. By continuing to offer more T-bills than the market could absorb, the Central Bank kept upward pressure on the discount rate. As a guide, it attempted to maintain a spread of 5 to 7 percentage points between the Gambian T-bill rate and the equivalent rate in the United Kingdom. The policy sterilized resources that might otherwise have been used to expand domestic demand. The policy also diverted resources into domestic assets, thereby reducing pressure on the balance of payments. These manipulations enabled the Central Bank to achieve its reserve accumulation objectives without causing major fluctuations in the exchange rate.

Because the Gambian economy is so open, the mechanism for transmitting credit policy was simple and direct. As the economy unraveled before the ERP, two alternative channels of monetary leakage emerged: a growing volume of local transactions were being made with foreign currency, and the bulk of foreign exchange began to be traded on the parallel market. These developments changed how credit policy affected the economy. Credit expansion raised the demand for local and imported goods and services. But because foreign exchange was in short supply, the excess demand led to a depreciation of the parallel exchange rate, raising import prices. The prices of domestically produced commodities also increased, and commodities whose prices were controlled (cooking oil, bread, and meat) were rationed more intensely. Higher prices reduced real income and aggregate demand. As the supply of foreign exchange declined, many traders and individuals began to shift away from local currency. It became more convenient and less risky to use CFA francs or some other hard currency (usually U.S. dollars) for transactions.

The ERP changed how credit policy was transmitted. Interest rate liberalization made domestic financial assets more attractive, taking pressure off the exchange rate. Moreover, in order to mitigate fluctuations in the exchange rate, the government took steps to avoid domestic credit shocks. In effect, the ERP provided a framework for allowing market forces to determine the demand for and supply of credit. It also gave the government an incentive to ensure that public-sector activities would not lead to sharp changes on either side of the credit market.

Credit Controls and Monetary Programming

Credit controls were the primary monetary policy instrument from June 1980 to September 1990, when the Central Bank shifted to a policy of reserve management. However, before the ERP, credit controls had been ineffective, for three reasons. First, the Central Bank was unable to control its lending to the GCDB. Second, no effective limits had been placed on the level of government borrowing. Third, Central Bank data were incomplete and out-of-date, making it difficult to monitor movements in money and credit.

After 1979 the only two banks that expanded their lending were the Central Bank and the GCDB. The SBG and BICI essentially stopped lending. In June 1979 their loans were D31.8 million; by June 1985 they were D29.1 million, which represented a real contraction of approximately 38 percent. During the same period the GCDB increased its loans and advances from D65 million to D135.5 million, a real increase of 42 percent (Ladd, 1989, Exhibit 6). That expansion was financed with a D51.2 million increase in deposits and D45.6 million in credit from the Central Bank.[5]

Thus any controls on SBG and BICI lending were irrelevant. Moreover, ceilings on GCDB's lending were ineffective, since most of its credit came from the Central Bank. But even so, the credit granted to the GCDB was significantly less than that granted to the government. Controls on bank lending to the government were imposed only after the ERP was implemented.

Another problem was that, in general, the Central Bank and the government did not know the aggregate level and sectoral breakdown of bank credit. Without up-to-date information it was impossible to adhere to a credit plan. Two constraints were prevalent. First, data on credit and money were regularly several months out-of-date. That situation changed only toward the end of 1986, when with donor support the government developed a monitoring system for staying abreast of the data. Monetary programming in any meaningful sense was not undertaken. Second, under the ERP, credit ceilings were typically derived by and agreed upon with the IMF. Any adjustments to those ceilings were ad hoc. Ceilings for individual banks were based on previous levels of lending.

The change in 1990 to indirect monetary control required the Central Bank staff to become proficient in monetary programming. Guidance was still provided by IMF staff during their regular visits to The Gambia, but monetary programming, though rudimentary and mechanical in many respects, became an essential aspect of reserves management.

Seasonal and Cyclical Patterns of Credit

As an agriculturally based economy in a subregion whose seasonal trading patterns are pronounced, The Gambia has always experienced seasonal variations in its volume of credit and money. The Central Bank, and the Currency Board before it, developed a variety of procedures for accommodating these seasonal movements. Two key concerns were associated with managing the seasonal patterns of finance—that the credit be used for its intended purpose and that the advances be retired in a regular manner.

Problems emerged in the late 1970s when a large amount of crop financing was diverted to other uses.[6] In order to improve its control over seasonal credit, the Central Bank introduced an "imprest system" in 1980. Organizations that relied on seasonal credit were required to retire their advances fortnightly. Collection rates increased dramatically, without placing additional strain on crop marketing. In the four years before the imprest system, less than half of crop financing had been retired.

Improving Monetary Management: Pending Issues

The Gambia clearly made progress toward a more market-oriented system of monetary management. The transition to a fully rationalized market-based system will be time-consuming.[7] In the meantime further actions are needed to improve data collection and monitoring procedures, introduce new financial instruments, and strengthen financial supervision and the capacity of existing institutions. Perhaps the most important requirement is to keep the economy on a stable growth trajectory.

Public-Sector Borrowing

Significant reductions in public-sector borrowing occurred under the ERP. Price decontrol allowed several parastatals to generate substantial profits, including the Gambia Ports Authority (GPA) and the Gambia Public Transport Corporation. Restrictions on the activities of others (for example, the GCDB and GPMB) prevented them from going deeper into debt. Moreover, the government substantially reduced its budget deficit (excluding grants and special provisions) from an average of 11 percent of GDP in the early 1980s to 2.5 percent of GDP in 1990–1991 (see Chapter 8). In aggregate terms the public sector is now less of a drain on national savings than it used to be. That change will have to be sustained to ensure a stable economy.

Alternative Instruments

In the post-ERP financial environment, any attempt by the Central Bank to influence the exchange rate or the interest rate, especially on the downside, would undermine confidence.[8] For practical purposes both the exchange rate and interest rate have to remain at or close to levels determined in the foreign exchange and treasury bill markets. Some discretion can be exercised in Central Bank advances, especially since the parastatal reform program has enabled the Central Bank to curtail its lending to cover public-sector losses through the GCDB.

However, that discretion is limited by the continued existence of excess liquidity in the commercial banks. A review of the level and trends of other components of the Central Bank's balance sheet indicates that, under current conditions, it has little discretion over any of them.

To change the level of bank reserves in the economy systematically, the Central Bank must use the purchase and sale of treasury bills as its main policy instrument. These bills have a direct effect on the government's deposits. Indeed, for the foreseeable future the Central Bank will rely on the T-bill market to influence liquidity. Any unfortunate experience with the G-bill issue will make it difficult to issue other debt instruments.[9]

Appropriate Supporting Policies

In order to encourage financial development—that is, a steady accumulation of a wider variety of financial assets with progressively longer maturities—confidence is a must in The Gambia. As with creditworthiness and trust, confidence is a mercurial concept. The objective facts provide reason to be optimistic. The most obvious has been the solid economic recovery since early 1986. Yet a deep-rooted suspicion exists that, despite improved economic conditions and changes in government policies, the situation could unravel. The 1994 coup almost certainly will set back the confidence that has been built up.

An important way to build confidence is to emphasize the reintegration of parallel markets. The rapidity with which the gap between the parallel and formal foreign exchange markets closed in 1986 was a practical demonstration of the potency of price decontrol as an equilibrating mechanism. Yet the reemergence of the gap in 1989, when the Central Bank attempted to refix the dalasi, was a warning that the financial channels that appeared during the period of dislocation before the ERP have not disappeared. The same applies to any shift in the external deposits held abroad and the willingness of farmers to move their produce into Senegal (and the ease with which they can) in response to price differentials.

The continued integration of official and parallel markets will depend on the incentives created by government policies. Donor conditionality has been crucial to sustaining these incentives. For instance, wage costs were limited by the IMF program, a moratorium was placed on external nonconcessional borrowing, and the government's ability to provide subsidies was limited. To continue these initiatives, the government and the Central Bank have to move from donor-imposed constraints to a policy of self-restraint.

The Potential for New Institutions

As the Gambian economy has improved, some new financial institutions have been established. A private insurance company was set up in 1986, and in 1990 several *bureaux de change* began operations.

The potential for other institutions has been explored. They include an organized stock market, one or more additional commercial banks, finance houses, and facilities for offshore banking. Although domestic savings are too low and the legal and institutional framework too fragile and unpredictable to support a stock market (see Ladd, 1989), some potential may exist for a finance house (or an investment bank).

The success of any new financial initiative will depend on the demand for and the quality of the services offered. Previous experience has shown that government sponsorship of financial activities does not create viable institutions. Yet recent experience suggests that government initiatives based on market-oriented policies—for example, the T-bill market—can be successful.

Supporting Legal Framework

The legal system in The Gambia offers little support for the financial sector (Deloitte and Touche, 1990). Both the government and the public enterprises have cut many legal and procedural corners. Although some laws are outdated and could be revamped, the problem is not the law as such. Rather, the challenge is to ensure compliance with the laws.

In its present form the legal system is a serious impediment to additional financial instruments, such as bonds, mortgages, and debentures. Potential participants realize that the courts are unlikely to enforce contracts effectively, thus increasing the risks of long-term transactions. In the interim, asset holders maintain a short planning horizon and provide credit only on the basis of long-standing relationships and/or readily recoverable collateral (such as compensating balances or goods in transit).

Increasing the Autonomy of the Central Bank

The primary cause of the financial imbalances before the ERP was the public-sector deficits. But with increasing accountability over the past several years, attention has now shifted to how a recurrence of the deficits can be prevented. One suggestion is that the Central Bank be granted more autonomy, if not be made independent.

Thinking on the issue goes both ways. On the one hand, because central banks gain their status through special legislation, governments can readily change that legislation if the bank attempts to exercise too much independence. Under those circumstances it may be impossible for central banks in sub-Saharan Africa to be truly autonomous.

On the other hand, the Central Bank of The Gambia also was responsible for policy actions that contributed to the country's economic difficulties. Its belated action on interest rates (and then only under pressure from the IMF) and its resistance to devaluing the dalasi—even when it was clear that foreign debt was out of control—were major mistakes. It also made a serious error when it allowed its accounting system to collapse in 1988.[10]

To become an effective policy-making body, the Central Bank's management and operations need to be improved significantly. Some progress has been made in the past few years, but more has to be done to ensure consistent and prudent economic policy.

Financial Supervision and Bank Examination

The Financial Institutions Act of 1974 made financial supervision a formal responsibility of the Central Bank. Since then, the bank examination units have generated high-quality reports, identifying major problems and including useful recommendations. Yet bank examinations will become a meaningful activity only when the reports are seriously considered and acted upon. For instance, in 1983 a report that highlighted the GCDB's difficulties and recommended numerous measures for dealing with them was ignored by Central Bank management. Central Bank examiners also recommended that the Agricultural Development Bank not be granted a license; nevertheless, the license was approved.

Increasing the Rewards for Investment

In his midterm review of the ERP, Minister of Finance Sisay noted that perhaps the most important challenge facing The Gambia was to improve productivity (GOTG, 1987). Given the continuing low level of productivity, sustained economic growth will require much more efficient use of The Gambia's resources.

Several changes in financial policy under the ERP have helped. First, higher interest rates discouraged low-productivity investments. Second, as part of its public investment program, the government began to apply specific criteria for raising the returns on its investment. Third, both funding agents and the government began to focus more heavily on how development projects were managed. Fourth, the reorganization of the civil service had some positive effect on the performance of the public sector.

Nonetheless, the ERP was criticized because the interest rates necessary for stabilizing the economy greatly exceed the rates that were perceived to be needed to promote long-term investment. This imbalance will become less pronounced as more resources are mobilized and their allocation is improved. In the short run, little can be done to force interest rates down.

Nevertheless, government and Central Bank officials continued to call for measures to reduce long-term interest rates.[11] The emphasis on long-term investment takes attention from the overriding need to enhance the efficiency of resource use. Economic growth can be promoted just as effectively with a series of high-productivity short-term investments. In view of the financial disruptions of the last two decades, that option may be the best available. Private long-term investment in The Gambia is simply too risky at present to attract capital. In fact, to promote growth, in the 1970s The Gambia attempted to use subsidized long-term investment financed with cheap foreign aid. The costs of that failure will take decades to work off.

Evidence from The Gambia and elsewhere shows that cheap credit policies do not work. If the government wants to subsidize particular activities, it should do so through the budget, not the financial system.

Dealing with Contingencies

By controlling bank reserves in an attempt to influence the path of money and credit, The Gambia has to determine what measures it should use to deal with external and internal developments that could disrupt the financial system. For example, a drought may lead to a sharp drop in export receipts and increase the demand for imported food. The consequent pressures on the balance of payments and exchange rate may fuel inflation and reduce reserves. Both could affect confidence. Alternatively, wage adjustments, higher levels of recurrent expenditures, or a collapse of revenue may increase the budget deficit sharply.

To prepare for such disruptions, the MoF and the Central Bank should jointly consider some alternative policy responses. When a crisis is underway, it is often too late to do so. Potential disputes about appropriate policy responses should be foreseen and their resolution dealt with in advance. Although all contingencies cannot be anticipated in advance, the idea is to have a mechanism in place for cooperatively dealing with problems when they arise.

Concluding Observations about Monetary Policy and Financial Reform

Major improvements have been made in the financial arena. Institutions have been rehabilitated, market processes are now used to control reserves and money supply, and interest rate policy has been improving the efficiency of resource allocation. Overall, the major financial and economic imbalances have been reduced, and a coherent framework now exists for continued economic growth.

Nonetheless, the rate of improvement has been constrained because few people are confident that the changes made thus far represent *reforms*, in the sense that both policies and behavior have been fundamentally transformed. Given the extent and sources of the financial disruptions in The Gambia in the past two decades, it may take years for that perception to change.

In the meantime, the government's only option is to persevere with a purposeful program of strengthening economic management and the institutions through which monetary policy is implemented. To do otherwise risks a return to the economic retrogression of the early 1980s.

In the period of economic collapse, Gambian policymakers saw that financial imprudence and economic growth were incompatible. With the introduction of the ERP, they began to understand that prudent financial policies do not guarantee sustained economic growth. With the ERP behind them, they have to find ways to sustain the momentum of financial reform. Improving monetary management by exerting market-based control over bank reserves is a useful start.

The overriding question is whether the transformation in The Gambia's financial policies is permanent. The ERP successfully halted the economic decline and enabled foreign arrears to be cleared. But it did so only with massive foreign aid. That so many resources have been required to turn the country around reflects the depths to which the economy had sunk. But it also reflects the fact that Gambians were unable, or unwilling, to supply many of the resources necessary to rehabilitate and develop the economy. Successful long-term development will depend on the extent to which the government can maintain financial stability and mobilize additional Gambian resources for economic development.

NOTES

1. Dooley and Mathieson, 1987; Chand, 1989; Long, 1990; Callier, 1991; Caprio and Honohan, 1991; McKinnon, 1991; Killick, 1993, Chapter 6; Stiglitz, 1993.
2. The board also maintained a 50 percent ratio of external reserves to currency and demand liabilities, discounted and rediscounted bills and promissory notes against prescribed security for a maximum of 120 days, limited outstanding advances to the government to less than 10 percent of the estimated current revenue, and limited government advances to a single fiscal year (*The Gambia Currency Board Final Report*, 1971, pp. 4–5).
3. With a fixed exchange rate, the money supply is endogenous (Niehans, 1984, pp. 267–271; Gleske, 1987, p. 19). An economy that is structured similarly to The Gambia's cannot fix its exchange rate and sustain an independent monetary policy. Although Central Bank staff understood this point (see, for example, Bajo, 1978, p. 106), they attempted to do both nonetheless.
4. These Central Bank advances went mainly to supporting the expansion of the Yundum airport. The "temporary" advances, which began in 1976, were eventually repaid by the government in 1987 with counterpart funds sterilized under the IMF program.
5. A common perception among senior Gambian officials was that the behavior of the SBG and BICI had been exploitative. They based their perception on the high profits earned by the two banks, their loan

concentration by sector, the short-term nature of their portfolios, and the selection criteria they applied to determine the types of customers and ventures they considered "bankable." A major reason for setting up the GCDB and the Agriculture Development Bank was to break out of this "colonial" pattern of lending. One of the goals was to provide long-term finance in order to promote development. When this finance was not repaid, the GCDB became, in effect, a grant-making organization, not a bank.

6. One of the reasons that the financial system unraveled initially in The Gambia was a major reversal of seasonal patterns in credit. Between March 1978 and September 1979, the pattern of bank loans and advances ran contrary to the normal seasonal flow, generating a major, unprecedented, real increase in bank credit.

7. The case of Australia is instructive. Its financial liberalization was as rapid as has occurred anywhere. Yet despite its already solid institutional base, the liberalization program required approximately five years to prepare and implement (Johnson, 1985).

8. The Central Bank could always choose to raise interest rates above market-clearing levels in order to force the mobilization of savings. It could also push the dalasi to the point at which it was undervalued in order to enhance The Gambia's competitiveness and to accumulate foreign exchange. This break with past behavior in The Gambia is unlikely.

9. G-bills were an attempt to develop a seasonal financing facility for groundnut marketing. However, when they were first issued in 1990, the GPMB could not redeem them in full. In effect, G-bills became an indirect vehicle for Central Bank financing of the GPMB.

10. The problem arose when two parts of the Bank recorded different values for foreign assets. The data were critical to the IMF program, since the accumulation of reserves was a performance criterion. The problem was resolved after the governor of the Central Bank was replaced and the MoF helped the Central Bank staff examine its accounts to find the accounting errors.

11. In doing so, the officials overlook the point that real interest rates in the informal sector of the economy have always been above the levels that were considered to be too high for the formal sector.

7

Rural Credit and Savings

Paul E. McNamara and Parker Shipton

The Gambia's economic difficulties were exacerbated by the government's rural credit policies. The Gambia Cooperatives Union, which was the government's primary institution for disbursing credit in rural areas, engaged almost exclusively in providing low-interest loans to farmers. The GCU paid little attention to collecting its outstanding loans and even less attention to mobilizing savings.

Over the years the government has devoted a large amount of national resources to subsidizing rural credit. Yet despite its significant investment few formal studies of rural credit and savings have been undertaken. Those few have typically approached the topic from the standpoint of formal, urban-based institutions exclusively. To overcome the biases associated with this approach, Shipton made a concerted effort to understand rural finance from farmers' and other rural people's points of view.[1]

The shift in orientation yielded information that suggested that many of the presumptions of policy makers about the credit needs and sources of credit and savings in rural Gambia were false. Many farmers have indeed needed credit and have not been averse to accepting it from government agencies. But those needs are part of a broader pattern of social and economic relationships that do not give much priority to the continued viability of the government agencies that provide the credit.

This chapter discusses how the reforms introduced under the ERP influenced rural finance. It begins by describing the cultural economy of rural credit and savings in The Gambia. It then examines the role of the GCU in providing financing and the ways the ERP affected its role. The following section analyzes rural financial policy reform, drawing lessons for policymakers. The chapter concludes with observations on rural credit and savings in The Gambia.

The Cultural Economy of Rural Credit and Savings in The Gambia

Most economic transactions in rural Gambia are only partly economic in nature, being enmeshed in activities and relationships that may have more to do with kinship, friendship, political power, religion, healing, entertainment, or other purposes. Money slides in and out of all these spheres. Attempts to review or quantify the "financial sector," then, are always somewhat artificial and arbitrary in definitions, and numbers in them should never be taken at face value. Gambians living in rural settings lend and borrow just about everything—including land, animals, human labor, tools, money, and in some ways even humans themselves—but not always as mere loans, with quantitative calculation, or with reciprocation in the same form. They borrow, lend, and save by entrusting each other cash, by protracting marriage payments, by circulating gifts at celebrations, by contributing to villager associations (in Mandinka, *kafo* groups),[2] by investing in relatives' labor migration in hopes of gaining remittances, and by all sorts of other transfers that remain hidden from official tallies. Most of this activity has little directly to do with organizations like banks and state cooperatives. Nor is much of it done by specialized moneylenders. In the weave of rural life, finance is largely submerged. In this subtle credit economy, where most loans are enmeshed in noneconomic meanings, formal contractual obligations do not always have much personal significance, and creditors who are least known and farthest away are likely to be the last to get repaid. Kin, neighbors, friends, and local merchants usually edge them out.

Rural Lending

Loans and quasi-loans stretch resources over time, and over distance. Rural Gambians' entrustments and obligations vary greatly in duration, sometimes lasting longer than a generation in matters like land loans or marriage payments. But most local lending of money, outside the cooperatives, occurs for durations of less than a year; and some, for instance, loans to market traders, is repaid in days or only hours. Similarly, in spatial terms, while one can certainly find "informal" loans occurring between city and country and between The Gambia and overseas, most Gambians tend to do their main borrowing and lending right in and around their own villages. Longer term, longer distance loans for major farm machinery, tree farming, and so forth, are hard for Gambians to come by without finance from international institutions. This is an invitation for foreign aid agencies and banks, but a caveat too.

It is a caveat because the credit systems that Gambians and other West Africans have designed for themselves tend to rely on both the lenders' and borrowers' knowledge of each others' characters, and the actual or potential involvement of third parties mutually acquainted with both. The members of a rotating contribution club, for instance, know each other intimately and have myriad ways (and not just financial) of sanctioning those who don't play by the group's rules and understandings. Aid agencies, commercial banks, and state cooperatives without local branch offices do not have that advantage.

As farmers and other rural dwellers design their own credits and debts, or entrustments and obligations, flexibility is of the essence. Lenders usually leave borrowers (once they are satisfied with their characters) to decide for themselves what they will do with their loans. Unlike institutional finance that is expected to be used within a particular "sector" of the economy, such as farm loans or housing loans, local loans flow from one activity into another according to the borrower's needs. Whereas institutional lenders are often surprised to learn that their borrowers have "diverted" fertilizer for one crop to another, used groundnut sacks to stuff their mattresses, or sold them to pay a marabout for a medicinal prayer, local lenders expect such occurrences as a matter of course. They know that real people do not live in sectors. Farmers' needs and capacities change. By initial agreement or by renegotiation, borrowers may repay local cash loans with groundnuts, seed loans with labor, or labor with cooked food or perhaps political protection. Lenders may indeed insist on switching the commodity between loan and repayment, to obfuscate interest charges deemed sinful in Islam. Repayment schedules and interest charges, where they apply, are adjustable in the event of poor harvests or family emergencies: things local lenders can readily assess and verify but distant institutions cannot.

By concentrating lately on loans for production and not for consumption, the state cooperatives have specialized their ostensible purposes more than local lenders do. But try as they might, they cannot control how their cash and inputs will be used, or who will use them. Farmers relend and resell borrowed inputs as they wish. They know, however, that if they fail to repay official loans in cash or kind, they may be expected to repay them in political support. Credit means debt, but not economic debt alone. Having stated that "formal" and "informal" loans often interconnect, that loans merge with other kinds of transactions, and that these are not always just economic in nature, we now touch upon several kinds of resources in turn to see how farming people actually borrow and lend them. The following information comes from Shipton's 1988 survey.

With respect to money, of the men who said they remembered the last time they had borrowed money (67 percent of the total), most had done so within the previous twelve months. About 59 percent had borrowed mainly for consumption of one kind or another; 51 percent of those who remembered borrowing cash had done so mainly in July and August, the hungriest months before the annual harvests. Informants reported amounts from under 25 dalasis to over D880, the median being about D140, and the most common amount being D100, followed by D150. As their main lenders, cash borrowers cited the cooperatives (33 percent), other farmers (31 percent), shopkeepers or other traders (21 percent), and others (15 percent). No ethnic group predominated in lending or in borrowing. Twenty-seven percent of the borrowers obtained their main cash loans within their own villages; 94 percent did so less than 50 kilometers away. Some 65 percent of the borrowers cited nonkin as their lenders (41 percent cited friends); 27 percent cited kin outside their immediate conjugal or natal families. (Doubtless some lending between close kin went unreported.) About 94 percent said no collateral had been required, and most, to judge by the amounts borrowed and lent, were charged no interest (though reporting on this was often open to doubt). Most borrowers did their repaying mainly in the "trade season" following the groundnut harvest, in January and February. Cash borrowers repaid mainly in cash. Some 16 percent of the borrowers said they had relent some of what they had borrowed; 23 percent claimed to have given some away.

Women, for their part, appeared to have borrowed money about as often as men (62 percent as against 67 percent reported remembering the last time they had done so), but in much smaller amounts (the median being about D40 as against about D140, and the maximum about D300 as against D880 or more). Women borrowed from June to August, leading their menfolk slightly in timing, perhaps because their more meager resources were exhausted first in this lean time of year. Women borrowed mostly from other farmers or from shopkeepers or other traders. Only 14 percent of female cash borrowers, as against 33 percent of men, cited cooperatives as their main lenders, reflecting the prevalent feeling that this is male domain, and probably also privileged male access. About 74 percent of women, as against only 27 percent of men, did their cash borrowing mainly within their own villages. The men searched more widely, took advantage of their contacts, and brought home the bigger loans—and thus the bigger debts.

Harder to quantify, but no less important, are loans of land, labor, and animals. The very personal nature of these transactions, and the fact of overlapping claims of different parties to the resources, mean that economic terms cannot capture the essence of these dealings. Land swapping, labor sharing, and seed lending can be part of kinship, friendship, or the asymmetric patron-client bond between host and "strange farmer." Men and women customarily place their animals in the stewardship of domestic compound heads. Men also entrust them to good friends living apart or to itinerant hired herdsmen; doing so reduces risks of herd losses to theft or disease, among other things. Farm tools like ox-drawn ploughs and hoes are widely lent around within families and villages after their owners finish using them. The cooperatives and some private organizations have also issued such implements on credit. Farmers' vocal demands for these and for larger machinery on credit has often surpassed their ability to repay them in this region of unreliable rains and vanishing soils. Credit always sounds better than debt, and it always looks best at the front end. Demand for it should not be taken at face value, or even treated as a single concept.

Groundnut seed lending is a contested activity in flux. The state cooperatives have made this their main business in recent years as they have tried to switch away from lending for immediate consumption. They have gradually crowded private, urban-based groundnut traders and their rural agents out of the market.[3] But erratic lending policies have led to dramatic swings in the annual percentages of farmers who are issued loans. In 1987, for instance, 94 percent of men surveyed who took seeds on loan obtained them from the cooperatives, but in 1988, after austerity cuts, only about 18 percent of male seed borrowers obtained them this way, most having to resort to other farmers instead. Migrant "strange farmers" who depend on their hosts for seed may suffer when cooperatives unpredictably deny expected loans to the latter. When or whether private traders would reenter the groundnut credit market was unclear in the late 1980s. Farmers who borrowed chemical fertilizers by the late 1980s did so almost exclusively for groundnuts, and from the cooperatives.[4] Interviews suggested that few would have bought these chemicals for cash, given their rising costs and the risks of Gambian agriculture. By pushing fertilizer into the countryside on credit, albeit at subsidized rates of interest, the cooperatives may well have been raising yields and deepening rural indebtedness at the same time.

Rural Savings

Rural Gambians save in many ways, just as they borrow and lend. Though foreign financiers have sometimes accused them of improvidence, Gambians do save wealth from month to month, from year to year, and indeed from generation to generation. Much of their saving activity, taking nonfinancial forms, remains hidden from official view. As with borrowing and lending, saving is submerged within social life that is not just economic in nature; and anyone who becomes financially involved with rural Gambians is likely to be getting involved at the same time with their relatives and neighbors.

Several factors underlie the diversity and complexity of rural saving, but one overriding rationale is currency instability. Keeping their assets in nonmonetary forms helps farming people avoid political and regulatory control and the ravages of currency inflation. The choice of cattle, sheep, and goats in particular as a favorite form of wealth carries numerous advantages. Live animals in the field multiply faster than money in banks, and they provide milk, manure, and traction along the way, to say nothing of the prestige and intangible satisfactions that many derive from herd ownership. Animal breeding is subject to none of the moral opprobrium that surrounds bank interest in a Muslim country. Being indivisible while living, animal wealth cannot be begged or frittered away as easily as cash. Rural Gambians can entrust it to kin and friends of their own choosing, whereas saving in a bank can mean entrusting total strangers in an institution that may collapse any time. The drawbacks of animal ownership—the labor and the risks of disease and theft—have so far seemed to pale by comparison with the advantages. For women, gold jewelry is a favorite form of saving as well as of ornamentation. This too carries the advantage of indivisibility, protecting personal wealth from grasping husbands, neighbors, or petty creditors.

None of this means, however, that rural Gambians do not need or want to save money. They do, and they have devised and or borrowed numerous strategies for so doing: *kondaneh* (condamnée) boxes,[5] interpersonal cash entrustment, voluntary deferral of wage collection, and contribution clubs like rotating saving and credit associations are just a few. While money hoarding is deemed unsociable, particularly in the hungry season, saving through a group like a contribution club is not. Individual savers with small notes try to convert them to large. Rather than a liquidity preference that many economists have assumed, these strategies suggest an *il*liquidity preference. Though they want access to their money in emergencies, rural Gambians don't want it too accessible from day to day, to others or to themselves.

Large and small aid agencies entering the Gambian financial scene have typically led with credit and considered mobilizing savings only as an afterthought, if at all. Starting on the credit foot has been a prescription for failure, allowing rural Gambians to feel little pride, commitment, or responsibility toward projects or programs. The loan schemes always seemed to belong to someone else. However sweet at the start, such credit always sours into resented debt.

Indigenous West African financial institutions, by combining saving with credit, point toward better ways. Contribution clubs like the rotating saving and credit association, known to Gambians as *osusu,* again provide lessons. An *osusu* begins by local initiative, in town or country. All members contribute regularly and one withdraws the total on each occasion, until each has taken a turn. Transactions that are savings to some are credit to others, depending on their places in the cycle. The group screens its own members by character and enforces repayment by peer pressure. Members consider an *osusu* group their own. Some *osusu* groups last over a decade; and as they dissolve, new ones form. While the *osusu* best serves nonagricultural purposes, the lessons of tying credit to saving, and to borrowers' own acquaintances, make sense in agricultural programs too.

Whether, and how, official financial institutions can emulate the lessons of local, indigenous ones on a large scale remains to be seen. Whether credit and savings are linked or not, farmers clearly feel they need some of each. They seek to balance liquidity and illiquidity, and they strive to make their financial dealings not just individual but also group actions. Unfortunately, national financial programs have not provided these kinds of balance. If anything, they have worsened the imbalances.

Government-Sponsored Rural Credit Programs

Since the mid-1970s, when the government began subsidizing rural credit on a large scale, its programs have been a succession of failures—primarily because they have been conceived of and implemented as external interventions. They have focused little on the factors that influence the financial behavior of farmers or the motivations for and constraints on credit and savings activities.

When functioning optimally in economic ferms, financial markets can, in conventional theory, serve several useful purposes (Johnson, 1967; Meier, 1983, Chapter 2). With or without governmental help, they can:

- ration financing according to the borrower's willingness to pay;
- allocate financing to its most productive use(s);
- allocate demand among financial instruments;
- stimulate the release of real savings in financial form;
- reward the factors employed in financial intermediation;
- provide a systematic basis for evaluating risk and transforming risk-bearing activity over time.

By using quantity controls rather than price (interest rates) to ration the supply of credit, institutions such as the GCU have undermined the long-term development of rural financial markets. The ultimate cost is less efficiency and lower rural welfare. The more immediate cost is the dearth of resources on which farmers and the institutions can rely when subsidized credit programs are eventually abandoned.

None of the government's initiatives in the area of rural finance, whether through the Agriculture Development Bank, the GCU, or the GCDB, has addressed these basic requirements in terms familiar to farmers. Institutions have provided financing to farmers primarily as a response to the prevailing view that farmers need it and that only the government can provide it on nonusurious terms. But politicians and program sponsors have also been aware of the political advantages of having farmers depend on the government for finance.

Because the focus on credit needs has placed little emphasis on finance and credit as economic resources, government-sponsored loan programs have been mismanaged and, in numerous cases, subject to fraud. The credit programs of the GCU were unsustainable interventions that continued to have a negative effect on the economy throughout the ERP.

The GCDB has never attracted significant deposits from rural people or undertaken an important loan program with villagers. The GCU links the GCDB with rural finance. By mid-1985 many donors and government policymakers had realized that the relationship between the GCDB and the GCU was a primary determinant of economic instability. The GCU repeatedly borrowed funds from the GCDB without repaying them, adding to the sharp expansion of credit in the economy. But more important, credit markets became politicized, and, given its access to GCDB funds, the GCU became dominant in groundnut marketing and input distribution.

The Gambia Cooperatives Union

The Gambia's cooperatives have taken over a large part of the country's rural lending and crop marketing since their inception under British rule in 1955 and their incorporation into a national union in 1959. By the late 1980s, as noted above, they had become the nation's largest lender of groundnut seeds and about the only way for farmers to buy or borrow chemical fertilizer. They lent money and sold animal-drawn farm machines also on credit.[6]

The GCU illustrates the main problem facing a government-controlled credit organization in The Gambia—political interference in its management and operations. Although it is technically a member-owned cooperative, the GCU has been controlled by the government since the mid-1970s. The GCU became insolvent when in 1979 and 1980 a blanket forgiveness was applied to subsistence credit loans (Clark, 1987). Throughout the 1980s the GCU used its overdraft account at the GCDB and financing from the GPMB, as well as project financing from the Rural Development Project I (RDP I) and the Agricultural Development Project II (ADP II),[7] to extend credit to its members (and to nonmembers under the RDP I and ADP II). Borrowers repaid little of this credit. By early 1988 the Cooperative Primary Marketing Societies (the village-level units) owed D76 million to the GCU (Demissie et al., 1989, p. 52). In effect, the GCU's credit program became an off-budget transfer to selected members of the rural population.

Yet from 1956 to 1970 the GCU was a viable enterprise. The GCU's credit program operated smoothly, with an average repayment rate of 97 percent for its subsistence loans (Clark, 1987). Subsistence loans were primarily small amounts of credit that went to food purchases during the "hungry season." The success of the GCU in that period can be attributed to the small, focused nature of its lending operations: seasonal loans secured with groundnut sales; the unwillingness of the government to interfere with the GCU's operations; and the generally high standards to which the GCU's management was held.

Credit discipline began to deteriorate significantly in the late 1970s, due to drought-imposed hardships and the GCU's introduction of medium- and long-term loans for farm machinery and input purchases under the RDP I. The RDP I credit program provided D4.75 million (equivalent to US$2.4 million) in credit for seasonal crop inputs, oxen for draft power, and animal-powered implements. Credit problems in the RDP I began when the project's Socio-Economic Survey and Monitoring Unit ignored established loan disbursement procedures by lending directly to farmers, many of whom were not GCU members or already had outstanding balances owed to the GCU (Clark, 1987). Furthermore, as

Table 7-1. RDP I and ADP II Loan Recoveries (as of March 1989)

Project Loan Category	Amount Due (D mill)	Amount Received (D mill)	Rate of Recovery (%)
RDP I Short-term	1.4	0.5	26
RDP I Medium-term	3.9	0.9	19
ADP II Pre-1987–1988	1.4	0.07	5
ADP II 1987–1988, 1988–89	4.3	2.0	32

Source: GCU, as reported in Demissie et al. (1990, p. 56).

a Commission of Enquiry later found, the GCU credit staff embezzled some of the RDP I funds. The ADP II also contained a large agricultural credit component for on-lending through the GCU; members were to receive US$2.7 million of farm inputs such as draft animals, animal-drawn machinery, coos mills, seed, and chemicals, either in cash or in credit. The ADP II credit program had a slightly higher level of repayment than the RDP I program, but it was still poor (see Table 7-1).

GCU Reform

In 1988 the GCU began to implement new credit control measures. These changes came in response to reports undertaken at the insistence of the donors as well as pressure for the GCDB to rationalize its relationship with the GCU. The GCU took steps to reduce its operating costs and to increase the interest rates it charged its members to market levels. The government absorbed many of its debts as well. The GCU began to obtain its crop-purchase financing on commercial terms; and in 1990–1991, the GCU borrowed from the Standard Bank and repaid the loan in full and on time.

The GCU had a heavy financial impact on the GCDB. In March 1988 the GCU accounted for 25 percent of the GCDB's loan portfolio, or D53 million in outstanding credit. (D19 million was for crop credit, D23 million was an overdraft account, and D11 million was a transport account.) GCDB management judged that these loans were unlikely to be repaid. (In March 1988 the GCU paid a small portion of its crop credit outstanding, and in 1989 and 1990 the government assumed the remaining crop credit obligations.) The GCDB's exposure to the GCU at one time had been higher: the government absorbed D33 million of GCU debts in the Managed Fund Agreement of 1987 (see Chapter 12). Lending to the GCU played a large role in the GCDB's insolvency.

The Economic Impacts of the GCU
The GCU had three main impacts on the economy:

1. The *financial impact*: diminished financial intermediation
2. The *welfare effect*: transfers rather than loans
3. The *macroeconomic effect*: pressure on prices and the exchange rate

The government's involvement in allocating credit dampened the mobilization of savings and allowed noncommercial criteria to be applied to the allocation of loans. The credit programs often failed to reach their targeted beneficiaries. And many of those who obtained credit received it as a transfer rather than as a loan. Politically connected borrowers benefited disproportionately. The unsustainable nature of these programs meant that, although benefiting from cheap credit for a while, borrowers were left without access to credit when the programs closed down. Agricultural producers, taxpayers, holders of dalasi assets, and donors bore the costs of these failed credit programs.

The macroeconomic impacts of the GCU's policies originated from its substantial contribution to the overall expansion of credit. In the context of a fixed exchange rate, interest rate ceilings, and a budget deficit, the increase in the supply of credit undermined confidence in the Gambian financial market.

Farmers and Cooperatives During the Economic Recovery Program

The cooperatives posed problems similar to those posed by many other state agricultural cooperatives across the continent. They were expensive to run, they delivered inputs late, they sometimes delayed paying farmers for their crops, they suffered transport blockages and storage incapacities, they collected scant and falling repayments, their accounting was often lax, and they were victims of theft (Ramamurthy 1986, Clark 1987).

Most farmers seemed to feel very little personal attachment or responsibility toward their cooperatives, though many did feel dependent upon them and to a degree may have grown dependent upon their loan subsidies. Few farmers trusted their local cooperative officers to weigh their inputs and crops honestly. Some commented that a main reason why they repaid any part of their loans, when they did, was to avoid the public embarrassment of being hounded by official creditors—they feared it might make other local people less willing to lend to them. In all, farmers expressed very mixed feelings toward the cooperatives, but alienation seemed to be the main theme.

Part of what bothered farmers about the coops was the inconsistency of their policies. It was always hard for farmers to know in advance whether loans would be issued for production or consumption; in cash, in kind, or both; and with or without tools. Few had any way to know even whether their local cooperative branch offices would be open or closed. Debts for some years had been forgiven, for others not. Few farmers had access to much information about the political pressures behind the frequent policy changes, or still less, ways to fathom the rather capricious dictates of shuffled officials who flew in and out from the World Bank and other international funding agencies. All that farmers could know for sure was that the rules of the game would keep shifting.

The Cooperative Societies and Other Social Units

The cooperatives have always had an anomalous place in Gambian society and political life. As an arm of government ostensibly relying on local participation and support, they are tools of political influence, subtle or overt, as well as of economic action. But they are a tool that does not always fit together with others. They are, to begin with, unique in scale. The primary cooperative societies, known to Gambians as *secco* units, are larger than villages but smaller than districts. In the late 1980s the average *secco* covered about 15 villages. But the territory covered by a *secco* was on average less than a third of a district.[8] Being anomalous in their compass, the cooperatives cannot benefit much from familiar or customary responsibilities between rural people. Life within a Gambian village is not always friendly, but it is always intimate; links between villages need not be either. One of the reasons why intravillage contribution clubs like rotating saving and credit associations work, where they do, is that members have many ways to ensure each other's cooperation through means outside the clubs themselves. Members of a village have ties of kinship, sport, worship, exchange, or political party with other members of their village. When one member borrows and fails to repay, others have many ways to get even. By contrast, ties between villages are much less dense. They may take many forms—a trade link, a single marriage alliance, a friendship, a healer-patient tie, a wrestling partnership, a friendship or livestock entrusting partnership—but interpersonal links between villages tend to be single- rather than multi-stranded, and less rich in history and meaning. These are the kinds of links, if any, that conjoin members of a cooperative society. There simply is not the sense of entangled lives and responsibilities among members that one finds within villages.[9] Moves to reduce the scale of the smallest unit responsible for loan payments, from the multivillage *secco* unit to the village, intravillage ward, or smaller lineage- or family-based units, are likely to heighten fiduciary cooperation between members. They would do so not by heightening their warmth or altruism, but by making use of their own, self-defined mutual responsibilities.

Relending Borrowed Resources: Strategies Beyond Official Control

Rural people who borrow money or farm inputs from the cooperatives do so not just on their own behalf, but also on behalf of kin and neighbors. Sometimes they do so as voluntary, free conduits, but sometimes not. By brokering between the official and unofficial exchange circuits, they can alter the possible risks and rewards for both the borrowers and lenders they tie together.

Nearly all members of the cooperative societies—probably over 97 percent—were male in the late 1980s, but women did much of the country's farm work and had taken over a good share of the production of groundnuts, the country's main cash crop and the one for which farmers engaged in most of their dealings with the cooperatives. Husbands who borrowed from coops on behalf of entire domestic groups or family work groups occasionally, but we think only rarely, levied their own interest surcharges on their wives. Some may, on the other hand, have helped cover for their wives' defaults. Those who relent to other neighbors, including migrant share contractors ("strange farmers"), added surcharges more commonly, sometimes exacting two bags for one while themselves paying the cooperatives only 10 to 15 percent interest for the growing season. Some farmers pooled their resources in small groups to repay one man's debts to the state coop, so that all could have access to animal-drawn farm tools obtained on further credit from the coops. In effect, they were forming their own mini-cooperatives for specific purposes. While, from the cooperative societies' perspective, unofficial relending may have raised risks of default by including more kinds of ostensibly uncreditworthy individuals in the pool of borrowers, members wishing to stay in the good graces of their local cooperative societies did have some incentive not to relend to just anyone over whom they had no control. "Strange farmers" tend to return to the same hosts year after year, and hosts-as-relenders thus have some leverage over their repayments. Whatever role unofficial relending plays in perpetuating the annual migrations of share contractors for the groundnut crop, the patron-client ties involved are likely always to involve a complex mix of reciprocal aid and exploitation.

Just as one cannot analyze a cooperative credit system without regard to its political uses and abuses, it is a mistake to try to analyze it in isolation from the older and broader systems of borrowing, lending, saving, and investment that farmers have devised partly to accommodate that very system. The ever shifting terms and conditions of cooperative lending under international policy pressures—with its stops and starts, its shifts in interest rates, and its surprises about crop purchases—would seem to require farmers to keep their own financial networks plugged into it just to lessen the shocks.

Concluding Observations about Rural Credit and Savings

The GCU's operations over the decade 1978–1988 confirm the well-known lesson that heavily subsidized credit delivered by a weak or politicized institution simply transfers resources to loan recipients, leaving the costs to be borne by the entire society. While the impact of the new measures on the GCU's future as a financial institution has yet to emerge, it is clear that the GCU will contribute to sustained development of the rural population in The Gambia only if it seeks to generate a financial surplus.

In addition to its large fiscal impact, the subsidized credit provided by the GCU distorted important rural markets. Private traders were driven out of the groundnut sector, inhibiting competition and lowering service quality (see Chapter 14 and Jones, 1986). Marginal producers, without connections to easy credit, were at a disadvantage. It is taking years to rehabilitate the credit and output markets distorted by the failed interventions.[10] The credit programs also distorted incentives within the government bureaucracy by providing numerous opportunities for rent seeking by civil servants and credit program operators.

Credit by itself, however heavily subsidized, has not proved a happy solution to rural poverty in The Gambia or elsewhere in Africa. People who depend heavily on rainfed agriculture do need to borrow at times, from each other or from outsiders, to smooth out seasonal shortfalls and longer term privations, but distant and unfamiliar lenders cannot sense these easily or accurately enough for loan programs to be of much help.

Rural Gambians need, and want, to save and invest resources of their own, and it is these that will allow them pride, participation, and a sense of possession. Credit needs to be linked to saving, and rural people themselves provide clues about how that can be done. Their financial institutions will, and should, remain largely their own. People already dependent on poor soils and an unreliable climate do not wish their livelihoods to depend ever more deeply on patronage from political regimes that may—as Gambians have lately been reminded—blow away at any time. National and international institutions that continually lend rural people more than they can ever save for themselves or repay are likely to render them poorer, not richer; to diminish their political autonomy; and to damage the morale that would seem at times to be about the only thing keeping Gambians going.

NOTES

1. Shipton's research methods included participant-observation, open-ended interviewing, and structured and semi-structured surveys carried out with trained local assistance. Open-ended interviewing was conducted mainly in two villages, randomly chosen within Upper River Division and Western Division, where he resided for parts of 1987 and 1988. The surveys included a 1987 survey of five randomly chosen villages including these, on both sides of the river, in Upper River Division, MacCarthy Island Division, and Western Division. In this survey, 138 farmers, one man and one woman per compound visited, were interviewed. A restudy of the same farmers and others in the same villages, totalling 167 after discarding doubtful information, was carried out in 1988. Again one man and one woman per compound were interviewed, each more than once. The ethnolinguistic composition of the samples approximated that of the nation as a whole as enumerated in the 1983 national census, the largest groups being Manding, Fula (Peul), Wolof, and Jola (Diola), in descending order of size. The authors acknowledge with gratitude the many people who helped with the surveys and other parts of the research.
2. Though the term referred in the past to men's or women's age-grade organizations, and usually still does, it can refer more generically to various types of interest groups in a village.
3. By one estimate in the 1980s, of the 14,000 tons of undecorticated seednuts required annually in The Gambia, 50 percent were saved in village

seed stores and 14 percent on the farms, while 36 percent were provided by the cooperatives (Clark, 1987, p. 32). However, these proportions were likely to vary according to the size of the previous harvest.

4. A PPMU survey of 537 Gambian domestic or family work groups (in Mandinka, *dabada* groups) found that 421 procured fertilizer in 1985–1986. Of these, 47 percent took it on loan from the cooperatives, 45 percent procured it with their own cash, and 8 percent received it through private lending channels (PPMU, 1985).

5. A *kondaneh* box resembles the Western-style "piggy bank." Built by a carpenter, it must be broken to be opened.

6. With 12 nominal interest rates of 24 to 26 percent per annum, and given 12 percent inflation in 1987–1988, the real interest rate was 12 to 14 percent. Based on groundnut prices, which fell by 17 percent that year, real interest rates were higher.

7. The RDP I was funded by a consortium of donors led by the World Bank. The ADP II was funded by the World Bank.

8. Some of the districts were based on and named after older political units, which precolonial travelers sometimes called kingdoms, but the size and nature of these units varied greatly, and they are no longer officially recognized.

9. Cooperative society committee members are chosen as representatives of individual villages. In public announcements about loan arrears, the names of villages (but not individuals) are mentioned.

10. The greatest damage may have been in the area of "lender credibility." The GCU's lax credit procedures created the impression that developmental projects provide agricultural inputs for free.

8

Budget Reform

Paul E. McNamara

The ERP left a mixed legacy with respect to fiscal policy. The government dramatically reduced the budget deficit, helping to stabilize the economy. But it made very little progress in changing the underlying budgeting *process*, and many chronic budgetary problems were not addressed. Ironically, the success in reducing the deficit may have hampered efforts to reform the budget process. The story of the attempted budget reform during the ERP illustrates how difficult it is to obtain the institutional and policy-making support necessary to improve the quality of the government's expenditure decisions.

Budget reform encompasses both global and partial changes in a government's system and procedures for developing and implementing public expenditure decisions. Global reforms include such changes as introducing a three-year rolling budget; partial reforms might include rehabilitating government accounting functions, introducing expenditure analysis through selected applications of cost/benefit or cost-effectiveness analysis, or introducing microcomputers to automate the operations of the budget and to facilitate budget comparisons.

One of the most common budgeting techniques in developing countries is "repetitive budgeting".[1] Finance ministries tend to respond to their uncertain fiscal environment by centralizing control and withholding payment voucher approvals until absolutely necessary to ensure that priority expenditures are made. Repetitive or continuous budgeting tends to shift administrative resources from implementing projects and programs to attempting to influence expenditure approval (Lee, 1992). Repetitive budgeting also undermines the legitimacy and authority of the formal budget process, thereby reducing the perceived importance of in-depth analyses of public spending.

Attempts at reforming budget processes have generally been disappointing (Lacey, 1989). The experiences of Sri Lanka, India, Malaysia, the Philippines, and Singapore suggest that while the outward forms of performance budgeting are sometimes adopted, the anticipated improvements in analysis and spending decisions generally do not materialize (Dean, 1989). Attempts to adopt new budgeting systems, such as the planning and programming budgeting system (PPBS) or performance budgeting, positively influenced public management by introducing concepts such as cost/benefit analysis (Premchand, 1980). But entire new budgeting systems only rarely replace the line-item budget. Thus many observers recommend an incrementalist approach to budget reform, beginning with strengthening accounting systems and applying basic economic analysis (Lacey, 1989; World Bank, 1991b). In Kenya partial reforms, including improved communication between the Ministry of Agriculture (MoA) and the Ministry of Finance and greater utilization of microcomputers for financial and economic analysis, led to better resource management in the MoA (World Bank, 1991b).

This chapter reviews the attempts made throughout the ERP to improve fiscal policy and promote budget reform. It begins by discussing why budget reform was a key element of the ERP and recounts the government's success in reducing the budget deficit. It then describes the budgeting system used by the government and its shortcomings, as well as the budget reforms considered by the MoF during the ERP. It examines the difficulties encountered in implementing budget reform and concludes with some observations about the budget reform process in The Gambia.

Budget Reform and the Economic Recovery Program

At the outset of the ERP there were many weaknesses in the government's budgeting system. Slow accounting procedures led to missed payments and arrears to foreign creditors. Insufficient economic analysis resulted in projects with little or no social return. The separation of the development budget from the recurrent budget created problems in funding materials and supplies for completed projects. Furthermore, many essential programs were underfinanced, with insufficient funds for petrol, textbooks, medicines, and health supplies. These problems and others contributed to budget deficits that averaged 11 percent of GDP from 1982–1983 to 1985–1986.

The ERP made changes in budgetary policy a high priority. Measures to "reduce fiscal deficits, improve the efficiency of public administration, and rationalize the external debt situation" were immediate needs (GOTG, 1985). The ERP recommended that expenditures be curtailed and adjusted, and proposed measures for increasing the productivity of public-sector investment. Three ERP commitments would hinder the government's efforts to reduce the deficit—paying all of its debt service on time, repaying all of its arrears, and including in the budget all transfers and subsidies. With such pressure on the budget, one goal was to "stretch" resources by improving the operational efficiency of the government.

The public-sector initiatives were to be broad-based. An embargo was to be imposed on creating new posts and regradings from 1986 to 1989. A staff audit of all vacant and temporary posts was to identify redundant positions in order to support the necessary retrenchments. A more comprehensive staff audit was to be undertaken in order to assess whether each civil service position was necessary for the current level of services being provided, as well as the training and support expenditures necessary to enable staff to provide those services efficiently. Remuneration levels were to be assessed according to whether they were sufficient to retain qualified individuals. The result of the study would be a five-year plan to streamline the civil service.

The ERP proposed that expenditures be shifted from wages to materials and supplies for maintaining and rehabilitating government assets. The ERP also called for a study of recurrent funding requirements, especially in the Ministries of Health, Education, and Agriculture, as well as for the rationalization of the government's vehicle fleet, with an audit "to review the justification, allocation, and maintenance requirements of all government vehicles." Other expenditure measures called for commercializing the workshop of the Public Works Department and improving the efficiency of vehicle maintenance.

The Budget Deficit

The fiscal situation at the outset of the ERP was the major impetus for budget reform. The IMF stand-by arrangement specified a target for the government's net credit position with the Central Bank that could only be achieved with strict budget austerity. Meeting this target was essential both to ensure continued donor support and to limit monetary growth and stabilize the economy.

To reduce expenditures, the government limited budget allocations, centralized the authority to approve spending, delayed spending authorizations whenever possible, and minimized supplementary (nonbudgeted) appropriations (see Table 8-1). Its most dramatic and difficult expenditure move was laying off a total of 1,935 temporary government employees and 922 established staff and eliminating 1,096 vacant civil service posts in two steps in 1986. This action reduced the number of government employees by 20 percent.[2] The retrenchment was in response to the 57 percent increase in the government wage bill between 1975 and 1985. In 1975 the government wage bill was approximately 30 percent of value added from groundnuts; by 1985 it had grown to 140 percent (Radelet, 1993). Despite these steps, reducing aggregate expenditures was made difficult by the increase in debt service payments from D28 million in 1984–1985 to D154 million in 1986–1987, which was due partly to the depreciation of the dalasi and partly to the commitment to pay arrears. The D83 million transfer to the Gambia Produce Marketing Board to finance the groundnut subsidy in 1986–1987 also added to the deficit. Donors relieved some of the pressure by financing the bulk of these extraordinary expenditures. Excluding debt service and special provisions (mainly the groundnut subsidy), aggregate government recurrent expenditures increased only 2 percent in real terms between 1985 and 1988. The most important revenue measure was the increase in customs duties from D81 million in 1985 to D203 million in 1987 (see Chapter 17). Other receipts increased as well, especially after the reform of the sales tax in 1988.

The combination of these expenditure and revenue measures dramatically reduced the budget deficit (excluding foreign grants and special provisions such as the groundnut subsidy and the liquidation of parastatal debt) from an average of 11 percent of GDP between 1982–1983 and 1985–1986 to 4.8 percent of GDP between 1986–1987 and 1990–1991 (see Figure 8-1). In 1990–1991 the deficit was only 2.5 percent of GDP. The smaller budget deficit combined with increased donor financing allowed a change in the banking system's net claims on the government from a net credit position of D100 million in 1985–1986 to a net deposit position of D115 million in 1988–1989. This change helped slow the growth of the money supply, ease inflation, and reduce pressure on the nominal exchange rate. Very few SSA countries have been as successful as The Gambia in reducing its budget deficit.

The Budget Process

Ironically, the government's success in reducing the deficit probably made more fundamental reform of the budget system more difficult. Although the

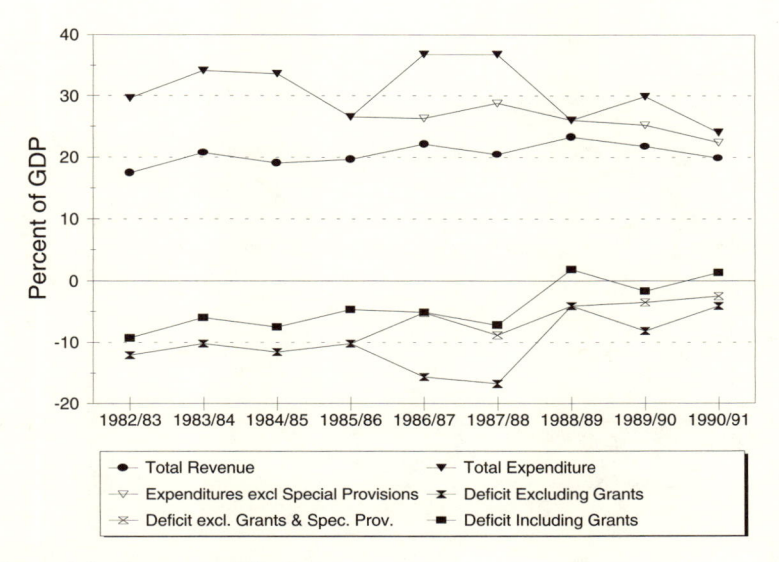

Figure 8-1. Government Budget

ERP called for improving the quality of public investment, it did not call directly for reforming the underlying process that created the inefficient spending plans and public deficits. Yet as specific measures began to be implemented—for example, reducing staff and implementing the vehicle audit—it became clear that changes in the budget process were essential. The most important changes called for introducing more rational analysis into spending plans, improving communications, ranking expenditure priorities more effectively, and using a longer time horizon in the budgeting exercise.

Some members of the government and most donor officials felt that the budget process in The Gambia undermined the effectiveness of public spending. The Gambia had retained its line-item budgeting system from colonial times. That system emphasized institutional control and the process of matching expenditures with budget categories rather than analysis of activities or program outputs. Over time the control orientation had allowed the budget to be used for influencing decisions and for graft. Officials responsible for approving payment vouchers were in a position to require a cut of the purchases they approved or to extract favors by delaying a voucher's approval.[3] More senior officials gained control by selecting vendors for government contracts and by allocating funds to the various spending ministries.

Donors also played an important role in the budget process at the outset of the ERP. As part of the stand-by agreement, the IMF required that the government reduce the fiscal deficit and pay all debt service in full and on time. These two requirements reduced the resources available for civil

Table 8-1. GOTG Recurrent Expenditures, Fiscal Years 1984–1985 to 1987–1988 (Millions of Dalasis)

Budget Head	1984–85	1985–86	1986–87	1987–88	Nominal	Real[a]
President's office	10.6	11.1	10.5	22.0	108	32
Legislature	0.5	0.5	0.4	0.6	20	-24
Public Service Commission	0.1	0.1	0.1	0.1	33	-15
Audit	0.3	0.3	0.3	0.4	33	-15
Ministries of:						
Defense	5.0	6.0	8.6	11.1	122	41
Interior	7.7	8.5	9.5	12.0	56	-1
Information and Tourism	4.3	3.9	3.8	6.8	58	1
External Affairs	5.7	6.9	13.2	19.3	239	115
Justice	1.2	1.8	1.7	1.9	58	1
Finance and Trade	7.0	7.7	12.4	17.9	156	63
Local Government and Lands	3.7	3.9	4.6	5.0	35	-14
Agriculture	11.2	10.7	9.4	13.3	19	-24
Water Resources[b]	3.6	4.1	3.7	4.8	33	-15
Works[c]	12.5	11.2	10.2	15.0	20	-24
Planning[d]	1.5	1.5	6.1	2.0	33	-15
Education	23.4	24.2	24.8	28.4	21	-23
Health	15.1	14.7	17.9	20.7	37	-13
Pensions and gratuities	5.0	6.5	9.0	8.0	60	2
Subtotal	118.3	123.5	146.0	189.1	60	2
Debt service charges[e]	27.9	102.7	153.8	136.2	388	211
Transfers to parastatals	10.2	16.3	91.4	163.9	1,507	923
Net lending[f] and unallocated	1.9	11.6	66.7	-13.3	—	—
Total	158.3	254.1	457.9	475.9	247	121

[a] Deflated by the GDP deflator, which increased 57 percent between 1985 and 1988.
[b] Ministry of Water Resources, Fisheries, and Forestry.
[c] Ministry of Works and Communications.
[d] Ministry of Economic Planning and Industrial Development.
[e] Includes current interest, amortization, and arrears payments. Note that in the IMF presentation of the budget, amortization and arrears are classified as financing items, not recurrent expenditure.
[f] Includes payments to the Managed Fund, discussed in Chapter 12.

Source: *Estimates of Recurrent Revenue and Expenditure*, various issues.

service salaries and programs for health, education, public works, and agriculture. The World Bank added more requirements in the context of its Structural Adjustment Credit—a three-year rolling budget (a public expenditure program) and a shift in spending away from salaries toward supplies and equipment maintenance. While the IMF focused on the overall level of spending, the World Bank became more involved in how spending was allocated among ministries and across sectors. USAID's African Economic Policy Reform Program grant to The Gambia required that the government make transfers to parastatals transparent in the budget.[4]

The Gambia prepares two separate budgets: a development (capital) budget and a recurrent budget. In 1987 the MoF was responsible for preparing the recurrent budget. The development budget was the responsibility of the Ministry of Economic Planning and Industrial Development (MEPID).[5] In interviews, senior officials in the Ministries of Finance, Planning, Agriculture, Education, and Health identified two types of problems in the budget process—those that required fundamental changes to the budget system and those that could be resolved by improving the current system (Gordon, 1986). The issues that could be resolved by improving the current system included:

- late and inaccurate submission of budget forms;
- insufficient consultation with the operating ministries and the noninvolvement of some key operating and administrative personnel
- unclear instructions;
- the absence of penalties or rewards to spur performance;
- MoF decisions about detailed budget items that caused imbalances within an activity and hampered its implementation;
- tardy expenditure reporting, which interfered with effective budgeting and the allocation of funds;
- an inadequate knowledge of and control over the implementation plans and the progress of foreign-aided development projects, making it difficult to prepare accurate development estimates;
- the inactivity of ministry personnel responsible for implementing programs and of some senior administrative officers responsible for formulating and reviewing program budget proposals;
- an understaffed MoF finance division (with only three full-time officers).

Other problems with the budget system required more fundamental changes. The major weakness was the failure to analyze activities or to assess trade-offs among alternative spending options. Budget officials did not pay much attention to ranking activities, largely because guidance for preparing the budget estimates did not call for justifying priorities. The limited number of staff devoted most of their time to preparing the personnel rolls and related details. The goals, achievements, and efficiency of those personnel were generally ignored.

Preparing budgetary estimates for a longer time horizon would have required major changes in the budget process. Because budget projections were made only for one year into the future, they did not capture important linkages between development projects and the future recurrent spending necessary for maintenance and operation. By failing to analyze the future cost of the proposed activities to which it was committed, the government assumed obligations for recurrent and local contributions to development projects that it could not ultimately meet (Chapter 10 discusses recurrent costs in greater detail).

Proposed Reforms

The MoF considered several proposals that would have begun the budget reform process, but very little action was ever taken. One proposal recommended that a task force be assembled to work on pressing budgetary issues, including the determination of spending priorities, and options for developing a three-year rolling budget. The proposed task force would consist of government officers in the operating ministries who were responsible for program management, administration, and finance as well as budget and treasury officials. The officials were to be convened after the budget session, so that discussion would center on the overall process and not on specific budgetary allocations. The MoF did not take any action on this proposal.

A second opportunity for reforming the budget system came in early 1987, when several incremental changes were proposed (Gordon, 1987). The proposals called for improving the guidance that ministries were to receive on budget submissions, as well as for changing the budget hearing process. The MoF was also to request that ministries submit two alternative budget proposals in addition to the one that matched the revised estimates for the current year. The alternative budgets were to be 10 percent less and 10 percent more than the current year. Ministries were to specify the alternative budgets only down to the subhead level. The alternatives were to be used to elicit the spending priorities of each ministry and to give each ministry room for making budgetary trade-offs.

The budget submissions were to include a statement of purpose for each subhead and a description of the targets expected to be achieved during the year. Changes in the budget hearings were also proposed that would place more emphasis on organizational and operational issues. The most important issues would be broached with senior decisionmakers. A computer located in the hearing room would facilitate analysis of budget options.

Following these recommendations, a seminar on budgeting was held for those responsible for preparing each ministry's submission. Initially, the permanent secretary of the MoF attempted to impose more structure on the hearing process. However, the seminar did not substantively change budget behavior, and the hearing process quickly lost its new structure. Otherwise, the new proposals were not implemented.

Finally, in an effort that had some impact, USAID provided microcomputers to the MoF for preparing and analyzing the budget. A software program was also developed to facilitate budgetary revisions and analysis. Called the MinFin budget system and based on a Lotus 1-2-3 spreadsheet, the program supported an examination of changes in budgetary allocations and their aggregate budgetary effects. Finance division personnel were trained in using the microcomputers and the Lotus 1-2-3 budget system. Several ministry personnel were also sent for short-term budget training in the United States. A parallel effort was undertaken for the development budget.

Why Did Budget Reform Fail to Materialize?

With the exception of the MinFin computer program, no significant changes in the budget process emerged from these proposals or the training of MoF officials. The government's budget process continued to lack an analytical component. Why was change so difficult?

There are several explanations. A more open and rational budget process would have taken some discretionary power and control away from MoF officials. On one level, budget reform threatened to reduce income from graft. On a policy level, a more rational budget process would have undercut the discretionary power of Cabinet to allocate extrabudgetary expenditures. Cabinet frequently increased expenditures or reduced revenues in the midst of the budget cycle—for example, to meet the unbudgeted expenses of official entourages or to waive duties on an investment project. The minister of finance would have faced serious opposition had he sought to limit the discretionary privileges of his colleagues.

For the Ministry of Economic Planning, an analytic approach to budgeting would have sharply reduced the number of development projects, since it would have necessitated bringing development spending into line with available recurrent cost funding. Budgeting in The Gambia never formally linked the development budget with the recurrent budget. The MoF and the Ministry of Economic Planning tended to respect each other's turf by not raising issues that cut across their separate agendas. For instance, the MoF did not ask whether the funding necessary to staff and equip the planned new capital project was likely to be available in the future. The MoF had already irked other ministries by centralizing expenditure control in order to meet the deficit targets agreed to with the IMF. Although officials in line ministries complained about aspects of the existing budget process, a reformed budget process that gave greater weight to the outcomes of ministry programs would have put the activities of line ministries under greater scrutiny. The permanent secretary of the MoF was reluctant to antagonize other ministries in this way.

Moreover, donors also did not initially push for substantive budget reform. As a condition for its Structural Adjustment Credit, the World Bank called for developing a public expenditure program that linked the development budget with the recurrent budget. However, other donors avoided the issue of budget reform.[6] In particular, the IMF was more concerned about keeping expenditures in line with overall deficit targets. One result of the IMF's focus was the erosion of budgetary discipline within the fiscal year. Line ministries dealt with "emergencies" simply by delaying payments. Thus line ministries with funds budgeted to buy petrol or other operating materials could not purchase the inputs necessary to support their programs. None of the other donors promoted budget reform. Yet they continued to fund development projects, even though the government was unlikely to be able to contribute significantly to their future operating costs.

The introduction of the MinFin computer program faced little opposition, primarily because it did not threaten the discretionary power of officials in the budget process. The MinFin software simply put the existing budget on a personal computer, greatly expediting budget preparation. It facilitated aggregate budget analysis, reduced the drudgery of budget preparation, and reduced the time needed to produce draft budgets. The ability to adapt to proposed modifications of fiscal targets in the budget negotiations with donors proved beneficial. However, the MinFin program did not introduce more rational analysis into the budget process, nor was it used for monitoring expenditures, a task for which it was ideally suited.

Concluding Observations about Budget Reform

One of the government's most significant achievements during the ERP was to reduce the budget deficit substantially. This success was mainly due to the civil service retrenchment, the tight controls on recurrent spending, and the crackdown on customs fraud. The reduction of the deficit from 11 percent of GDP in 1984–1985 to 2.5 percent of GDP in 1990–1991 was critical to reducing inflation, stabilizing the economy, and reducing pressure on the exchange rate.

But reforming the budget process proved to be much more difficult. Garnering support for complex administrative reform measures, whose benefits cannot be seen immediately and which create conflicts within the bureaucracy, is difficult. As Grindle and Thomas (1991, p. 177) hypothesize in their analysis of this type of organizational reform:

> When the response to a reform takes place in the bureaucratic arena, the political stakes for the leadership and for the regime are relatively low. The real issues are whether government capacity exists to implement the reform and whether there is support for the reform that will cause the bureaucracy to comply with the intention of the decision.

In The Gambia training and technical assistance helped improve the institutional capacity of the MoF, but top government officials did not press staff for the information and policy analyses that could be generated by a reformed budget system. Rather, most government officials preferred to avoid explicit analysis of government programs and expenditures.

The attempts at budget reform under the ERP did not improve the efficiency of public expenditures. Indeed, budgetary control diminished as the government moved further away from the crisis atmosphere of 1985—supplementary appropriations increased from D1.7 million in 1986–1987 to D13.6 million in 1987–1988 and to D38.8 million in 1988–1989. An IMF team in 1991 noted:

> The expenditure controls that have been introduced [during the ERP] rely heavily on centralized control over voucher processing, tendering, and the payments process. These have been effective in maintaining aggregate control over cash outlays and meeting quarterly credit targets, but the operation of the system has greatly reduced the

decision-making authority of the spending ministries, has allowed resources to shift between budget heads during budget implementation, has made suppliers unwilling to supply to government on credit, and has impeded the quality of service in some areas. (Allan, Woolley, and Rumbaugh, 1991)

The control exercised to meet macroeconomic targets undercut the budgeting and financial planning process. Tight controls were necessary because strong ministries and agencies (for example, the president's office) were able to press their contingency funding requests at the expense of budgeted spending. Until supplementary appropriations are controlled, efforts to strengthen the budget process will be unlikely to succeed.

Ironically, the fiscal austerity of the ERP probably contributed to the weak support for meaningful budget reform. The MoF centralized its control and delayed payments to ensure that scarce discretionary funds remained available for politically important contingencies. Moreover, with economic stabilization its main objective, the MoF dedicated its scarce staff resources to meeting the fiscal targets agreed to with the IMF. As in other countries, this approach probably had a negative effect on the budgeting process.[7] In The Gambia, as the IMF team suggested, the stabilization program actually encouraged a greater reliance on repetitive budgeting, thereby inhibiting the proposed reforms of the budget system.

NOTES

1. Caiden and Wildavsky, 1974; Bird, 1982; Roe, 1986; Omolehinwa and Roe, 1989.
2. Most of the retrenched workers found employment either in the rejuvenated groundnut sector or as day laborers in construction or petty trade. The government-run Indigenous Business Advisory Service established a loan facility for retrenched government employees in 1987, but only 125 people borrowed money under the scheme.
3. This is based on information provided by merchants in Banjul and other government officials.
4. This requirement was also part of the performance contracts between the government and the public enterprises (see Chapter 16).
5. In a reorganization in September 1990, MEPID was absorbed within the Ministry of Finance and Economics.
6. The World Bank's 1985 country memorandum called for a public expenditure program (PEP), and the 1986 SAC included a condition on

creating the PEP. That condition was not met during the ERP. The lack of progress on the PEP led to delays in disbursing the World Bank's Structural Adjustment Loan II (SAL-II). In the end, the PEP was developed by a team of World Bank-financed consultants (see Chapter 19).

7. In the Philippines Dean observed that the austerity program contributed to difficulties in implementing budget reforms (Dean, 1989).

9

Tax Reform

Clive S. Gray and Malcolm F. McPherson

The structure of The Gambia's tax system changed little between the colonial period and the mid-1980s. Beginning in the late 1970s and early 1980s, analysts began to highlight several deficiencies in the tax structure, including a heavy reliance on trade taxes, very high rates of personal income tax, and widespread tax evasion (Latham, 1970; Cnossen et al., 1976; Abdel-Rahman et al., 1982). The first concerted response to these issues came in 1983, when Minister of Finance Sisay established a committee to review personal and company taxes. During the next five years, separate reviews were undertaken on investment incentives, customs fraud, a proposed national sales tax, and taxes collected outside the Ministry of Finance. Beginning in 1988, the government introduced several tax policy reforms that significantly changed both the tax structure and tax administration. Although there were many difficulties in the process, the reforms resulted in a much simpler, easier-to-administer tax system that generates far more government revenue than the previous system.

Tax reform has been a key component of stabilization and structural adjustment programs in many countries because it affects both government revenues and market prices, and therefore the allocation of resources and the level of investment. A large and growing literature has begun to distill many of the basic principles and lessons learned from tax reform efforts.[1] In most countries the primary goal of tax reform has been to generate revenues on a sustained basis in order to finance public expenditures and reduce budget deficits. Secondary goals include improving efficiency and equity and simplifying tax administration. Revenue goals usually are addressed by introducing a broad-based consumption tax (either a value-added tax or a sales tax). In sub-Saharan Africa introducing consumption taxes implies relying much less on trade taxes, which have been the leading source of revenue in the past (Shalizi and

Squire, 1988). Most tax reform efforts also have aimed at broadening the tax base by increasing coverage and significantly reducing exemptions, and at rationalizing the rate structure by reducing both the top marginal rates and the number and the dispersion of rates (World Bank, 1991a). Equity goals are achieved by exempting certain goods (for example, unprocessed foods) from the consumption tax, by increasing the basic income tax exemption to exclude more low-income earners from income tax liability, and by introducing luxury taxes on a small set of goods. In conjunction with these structural reforms, most governments attempt to reform tax administration in order to simplify the process of tax collection and enforcement (Bird, 1989).

Tax reform in The Gambia followed many of these general principles. The characteristics of the tax structure changed from heavy reliance on trade taxes, high tax rates applied to a small base, and many exemptions, to lower rates, a wider base, and a heavier reliance on consumption taxes. The Gambia's experiences in making this shift provide several insights for other African countries attempting similar reforms. This chapter examines the process of tax reform in The Gambia, analyzing both its accomplishments and the areas in which progress has been slow. It begins by examining the imperatives for tax reform and then discusses reforms of both direct and indirect taxes. The concluding section highlights lessons from the Gambian experience.

Imperatives for Tax Reform in The Gambia

The major impetus for tax reform in The Gambia, as in many other countries, was extreme fiscal pressure. A budget deficit that averaged 2.7 percent of GDP in the two fiscal years ending in mid-1976 rose to 7.5 percent in fiscal year 1977 and averaged 9.5 percent in fiscal years 1978 and 1979.[2]

Beginning with the capital gains tax in 1978, several new taxes (and variations of existing taxes) were introduced in an effort to reduce the deficit. However, the revenue response was small: in 1982–1983 the new taxes produced only 1.2 percent of recurrent revenue (Gray et al., 1992). Exacerbating the shortfall was the abortive coup attempt in July 1981 (see Chapter 3), which led to major property destruction and compressed the income and trade tax bases.

Several factors persuaded Minister Sisay to take a broader look at the tax system. The first was the persistent budget deficit. With the general decline in groundnut prices and output, the surpluses that The Gambia

Produce Marketing Board had regularly turned over to the treasury or allocated to extrabudgetary expenditures had disappeared,[3] forcing a scramble for new sources of revenues.

Second, even at its peak before the 1981 coup attempt, the personal income tax was generating less than 10 percent of recurrent revenue. The income tax for low-income employees was not cost-effective, as the administrative costs were larger than the small amount of additional revenue collected. The progression of tax rates, culminating in a marginal rate of 75 percent at a taxable income of D50,000 (equivalent to US$19,000 at the average official exchange rate during 1983), led to widespread tax evasion among upper-income groups.

Third, Sisay recognized that relying heavily on revenue from taxes on international trade—which was 70 percent of total revenue in 1982–1983—would leave The Gambia highly vulnerable if under the existing protocols of the Senegambia Confederation a customs union was established. Finally, customs fraud had become a major drain on government revenue.

Table 9-1 provides data on the structure of the Gambian tax system in 1965–1966, 1975–1976, 1980–1981, 1985–1986, and 1988–1989, showing its dependence on international trade taxes, as well as the mounting imbalance between revenue and expenditures. International trade taxes accounted for between 60 and 70 percent of total revenue (excluding grants) through 1985–1986. Direct taxes grew to 22 percent of total revenue before the coup in 1980–1981 but declined to 15 percent in 1985–1986. Other domestic taxes were tiny until the introduction of the sales tax in 1988. Revenues (excluding grants) increased steadily from 13.6 percent of GDP in 1965–1966 to 25.1 percent of GDP in 1985–1986. But expenditures grew even more rapidly, so that the budget deficit grew from 4.9 percent of GDP in 1965–1966 to 19.2 percent of GDP in 1980–1981, before declining somewhat to 10.4 percent of GDP in 1985–1986.

MoF staff work on tax reform proceeded along several fronts:

- As noted earlier, a staff committee was established to examine the income tax. A revised version of the report originally drafted in 1985 was submitted to Cabinet in December 1987 and became the basis for the 1988 law.
- A review of several minor taxes and charges collected outside the MoF was undertaken, with a view toward rationalizing tax collection and revenue monitoring. Follow-up work culminated in recommendations for establishing a Central Revenue Department and a

Table 9-1. Tax Revenues in The Gambia, Selected Fiscal Years (Millions of Dalasis)

	1965–1966	1975–1976	1980–1981	1985–1986	1988–1989
Direct taxes	.4	4.8	17.4	32.1	57.2
Company	.2	2.4	8.9	15.0	31.5
Personal income	.2	1.9	7.7	11.6	18.2
Other	—	.4	.9	5.5	6.0
International trade	8.7	31.6	48.4	147.3	215.6
Import duties	8.0	27.1	47.6	138.1	214.0
Groundnut tax	.7	4.6	.1	8.1	—
Domestic taxes	—	1.0	3.7	13.1	125.0
Excise duties	—	—	1.0	6.2	1.2
Sales tax	—	—	—	—	113.3
Other	.1	—	.5	1.6	.6
Total tax revenue	9.2	37.4	70.1	194.1	398.4
Nontax revenue	4.4	8.6	9.9	21.6	41.7
Grants	7.2	1.9	24.3	59.1	135.6
Total revenue[a]	20.8	48.0	104.2	274.9	575.7
Percent of GDP					
Revenue (including grants)	21.0%	17.6%	25.5%	25.3%	29.7%
Revenue (excluding grants)	13.6%	16.9%	19.5%	19.9%	22.6%
Budget deficit (excluding grants)[b]	4.9%	3.4%	19.2%	8.2%	5.2%

[a]Totals may not correspond due to rounding.
[b]Fiscal year 1985–1986 excludes an increase in arrears of 3 percent of GDP. Fiscal year 1988–1989 includes a reduction in government arrears of 1.7 percent of GDP.
Source: *Estimates of Recurrent Revenue and Expenditures,* various issues.

Statistics and Special Studies Unit within the ministry to analyze and monitor all aspects of taxation in The Gambia (McPherson, 1984).

- Special studies were undertaken to assess whether a value-added tax or general sales tax should be introduced (Perry, 1985; Vincze, 1987).
- Extensive investigations of customs fraud were undertaken in 1986, 1988, and 1989.
- The Development Act (1973) was revised in an attempt to limit the revenue loss from tax holidays.
- Finally, numerous issues were raised about how the transit trade was administered, duty waivers were handled, and taxes were collected by public enterprises on behalf of the government.

The Reform of Direct Taxes

Under the Income Tax Act (1966), individuals were assessed according to either Schedule I or Schedule IV. Schedule I covered the majority of taxpayers. Schedule IV was used for a very limited number of low-income taxpayers, who were assessed according to either Schedule I or IV, whichever resulted in the greater liability.

Personal income tax should have been an elastic source of revenue, because Schedule I was very progressive, the underlying inflation rate was about 8 to 10 percent during the 1970s, and a major expansion of urban-based, government-controlled economic activity had occurred. In fact, the tax was elastic during the first fifteen years of independence, when personal income tax receipts grew fourteen times faster than GDP. But starting in 1980–1981, they rose more slowly than GDP. Indeed, reflecting the aftermath of the attempted coup, receipts declined in both 1981–1982 and 1982–1983. The declining elasticity of the personal income tax—from 4.9 between 1973–1974 and 1980–1981 to 0.4 between 1980–1981 and 1987–1988—can be explained partly by the special dispensations granted by the president (under section 3.2 of the Income Tax Act) in the aftermath of the coup attempt. Yet most of it can be attributed to growing tax evasion.

As mentioned earlier, the Income Tax (Amendment) Act of 1988 was the culmination of five years of work by the staff committee established in 1983. The committee's work took so long both because other policy issues were more pressing during the ERP and because the committee members could not reach full consensus on several questions. The committee addressed the following issues:

Personal Income Tax
- personal and spousal allowances;
- child and educational allowances;
- Schedule I rates;
- Schedule IV rates;
- National Development Levy;
- the taxation of in-kind perquisites;
- the introduction of comprehensive withholding;
- enforcement and penalties;

Company Income Tax
- capital allowances;
- capital gains taxation;

- turnover or minimum tax;
- system for accelerated collection.

Prior to the reforms the personal tax system suffered from three major problems. First, it was inequitable, both because low-income earners were subject to tax and because the rates were steeply progressive. Second, it led to economic inefficiencies, because skilled manpower was diverted from producing goods and services to devising ways to avoid (and evade) taxes. Third, the system was ineffective, because collections were substantially below what was owed. To begin to address these issues, the committee examined Schedules IV and I in turn.

Schedule IV
The committee noted that the 1980 assessments of 4,400 low-income Schedule IV taxpayers averaged only D26.6 per person, equivalent to approximately 1.2 percent of their declared income. Although these accounted for 63 percent of all those assessed under both Schedules I and IV, they contributed only around 2 percent of the total personal income tax collected in that year (IMF, 1982, p. 44). In a separate estimate based on 1985 records, a random sample of 2,300 assessments of self-employed Schedule IV taxpayers averaged D29.6 per taxpayer; these individuals owed *seven times as much in arrears* from previous years (Gray, 1985, p. 7).

The Income Tax Division (ITD) was manually preparing and mailing out around 3,000 assessments per year, virtually without follow-up. But even if the legal authorities had attempted to pursue defaulters, it would not have been cost-effective. Based on these considerations, the committee recommended that the schedule be abolished outright.

Schedule I
The committee saw immediately that, as with Schedule IV, the lower Schedule I income brackets were not cost-effective. The first four brackets, whose rates ranged from 2.5 percent to 6.25 percent and whose income bands were D4,000 or less, yielded the equivalent of only US$2,300 in 1980 at the prevailing average exchange rate. Based on 1980 tax year data, the 52 percent of Schedule I taxpayers whose income was below D5,000 owed only 3 percent of total personal income tax (IMF, 1982, p. 42). The committee soon concurred that the zero bracket should be raised and the lowest rates should be eliminated.

The committee also favored reducing the number of brackets and income bands under Schedule I, which numbered twelve in the 1966 act.

This measure would also improve horizontal equity by treating broad groups of income earners similarly.

Based on the same 1980 tax data, the bulk of personal tax revenue was being collected from persons who were being subjected to extremely high marginal tax rates. Eighty-five percent of the tax due under Schedule I was assessed against the 13 percent of taxpayers (331 individuals) who fell within the three highest marginal tax brackets—50 percent, 62.5 percent, and 75 percent. As shown in Table 9-2, the 50 percent bracket started at a chargeable income of D12,500, equivalent to US$7,300 in 1980 and only US$3,200 in 1985.

The same taxpayers declared 57 percent of total chargeable income in The Gambia under Schedule I. The committee did not dispute the principle of progressivity—that taxpayers who accounted for more than half of chargeable income should pay an even higher proportion of personal tax. But they noted that the bulk of the 85 percent of assessments came from the salaries of a small set of expatriate and Gambian employees (as declared by foreign and multinational employers) whose interests would prompt them to be relatively transparent in dealing with the government.[4]

On the flip side, even without attempting to quantify undeclared income, the committee noted that the majority of taxpayers whose true income exceeded D11,000 (the lower threshold of the 37.5 percent bracket) were probably so repelled by the 37.5 percent to 75 percent rates that they would endeavor to hide marginal income that could be taxed at those rates. In order to broaden the tax base, the committee believed that, at a minimum, the rate structure would have to be revamped.

One reason for broadening the tax base was to induce taxpayers to declare sources of income that had traditionally been poorly documented. One example was the rental of premises. A review of tax returns indicated that only a handful of landlords were declaring rental income.

The committee also had to consider the fact that the political commitment shown by the government in implementing strong measures under the ERP did not yet apply to prosecuting tax evaders. It had been many years since the courts had handed down a judgment against a tax offender. At most, a few individuals pursued by the tax authorities had chosen to pay—normally less than their true liability—rather than face continuing administrative harassment. Accordingly, the commissioner of income tax was skeptical that adopting stiffer penalties in an amended law, including "seizure and sale" powers, would broaden the tax base and improve compliance.

The committee engaged in lengthy debate about the extent to which voluntary compliance would increase if rates were lowered.

Table 9-2. Brackets and Income Bands of Personal Income Tax: Schedules I and IV

Schedule I Income Bands

Marginal Tax Rates	Dalasis	U.S. Dollar Equivalent of Threshold at 1980 rate = D1.719	U.S. Dollar Equivalent of Threshold at 1985 rate = D3.857
2.5%	≤1,000	0	0
3.3%	1,000 to 2,000	$582	$259
5.0%	2,000 to 3,000	$1,163	$519
6.5%	3,000 to 4,000	$1,745	$778
12.5%	4,000 to 5,000	$2,326	$1,037
17.5%	5,000 to 6,000	$2,908	$1,296
22.5%	6,000 to 8,500	$3,490	$1,556
27.5%	8,500 to 11,000	$4,944	$2,204
37.5%	11,000 to 12,500	$6,398	$2,852
50.0%	12,500 to 40,000	$7,270	$3,241
62.5%	40,000 to 50,000	$23,264	$10,372
75.0%	≥50,000	≥$29,080	≥$12,965

Schedule IV Income Bands

Dalasis	Tax	U.S. Dollar Equivalent of Threshold at 1980 rate = D1.719	U.S. Dollar Equivalent of Threshold at 1985 rate = D3.857
1,000 to 1,250	D 8.75	$582	$324
1,251 to 1,500	D12.50	$728	$389
1,501 to 1,750	D18.75	$873	$454
>1,751	D18.75 + 1.67%		

The commissioner expressed concern about losing revenue from reducing the rates for the few captive high-income earners. The weight of this consideration led the committee in November 1985 to agree initially to a rate structure that reduced the top marginal rate only from 75 percent to 65 percent. After accounting for inflation, the proposed structure would have imposed a greater overall burden on most Schedule I taxpayers than did the structure established in 1966.

The Committee's 1987 Report

As the committee continued its deliberations over the next two years, the weaknesses of the income tax system became increasingly obvious. The growing opinion was that since personal income tax accounted for less than 10 percent of recurrent revenue, relatively little would be lost in experimenting with the effect of substantial rate reductions on the tax base.

The committee submitted its report to Minister Sisay, who forwarded the provisions to Cabinet in December 1987; in May 1988 all but one of the provisions were adopted by Parliament. The report contained the following recommendations:

1. the introduction of a zero tax bracket of up to D5,000
2. the elimination of Schedule IV
3. the incorporation of the National Development Levy (NDL) into the income tax (not adopted)
4. the elimination of all personal allowances for education, wives, and children, in effect replacing them with the zero tax band
5. a reduction in the number of brackets from twelve to five, comprising 10, 15, 20, 25, and 35 percent
6. the inclusion of in-kind income—such as the value of cars, houses, and servants—in taxable income
7. the introduction of a pay-as-you-earn (PAYE) scheme for all individual taxpayers
8. efforts to strengthen the powers of the commissioner of income tax to improve compliance

The following are comments on each of these provisions and their implementation effects:

Provisions 1 and 2. The D5,000 zero tax bracket and the elimination of Schedule IV removed more than half of the taxpayers from the rolls, simplifying administration and freeing up resources to improve compliance, with minimal forgone revenue.

Provision 3. The National Development Levy had been introduced as a temporary measure to support the first five-year plan; taxpayers were told they were contributing directly to development expenditures. In practice, the revenue was consolidated with other tax receipts, and no direct link was ever established between NDL collections and development expenditures. Had the levy in fact been temporary as originally intended, it should have been either rescinded or incorporated into the income tax. To soften the revenue impact of the reforms, the government postponed the repeal of the NDL until 1990.

Provision 4. Eliminating all personal and family deductions and replacing them with a minimum threshold of D5,000 for each taxpayer served two purposes: it eliminated the incentive for high-income earners to exaggerate deductions, and it eliminated the administrative burden of verifying each taxpayer's deductions.

Provision 5. Table 9-3 shows the new tax schedule and the dollar equivalents for chargeable income thresholds (at the average exchange rates for 1988 and June 1992). While the new schedule sharply reduced tax rates for upper-income brackets, it was still progressive. At the same time it increased the liability of some lower-income bracket taxpayers by applying a marginal rate of 10 percent to income of more than D5,000, now calculated in the absence of personal or family deductions.[5] The larger a taxpayer's deductions under the previous system, the greater the relative increase in tax liability.

The effect of the proposed tax structure on tax liability was estimated based on a random sample of 1985 assessments of two groups of taxpayers: nongovernment employees, and traders and other self-employed persons (see Table 9-4). These estimates suggested that the liability of nearly three-fourths of these taxpayers would be lower. The 27 percent whose liability would be greater would have been assessed an average of only D23, or 5 percent, more than their actual 1985 assessments.

Table 9-3. Brackets and Income Bands under the 1988 Amendment

Marginal Tax Rates	Income Bands (Dalasis)	U.S. Dollar Equivalent of Threshold 1988	U.S. Dollar Equivalent of Threshold 1992
0%	< 5,000	0	0
10%	5,000 to 15,000	745	569
15%	15,000 to 25,000	2,236	1,706
20%	25,000 to 35,000	3,726	2,844
25%	35,000 to 45,000	5,217	3,982
35%	> 45,000	6,707	5,119

Note: The 1988 and 1992 average exchange rates against the dollar were D6.71 and D8.79, respectively.

Table 9-4. Estimated Impact of the 1988 Personal Income Tax Schedule on 1985 Taxpayers

Percentage of Taxpayers with:	Nongovernment Employees (A)	Traders and Other Self-Employed (B)	(A) + (B)
1. Reduced liability	93%	64%	73%
2. Increased liability	7%	36%	27%
Average increase (dalasi)	D130	NA	D23
Average increase (percent)	35%	NA	5%

Provision 6. Taxing in-kind income was meant to eliminate a major loophole in the law. Fifty percent of the value of expense accounts is now counted as taxable income. Items such as electricity and water, servants, and transport allowances are now included on a cost basis. Housing is valued at 25 percent of the base salary level[6] and cars at 10 percent, and the law requires all lease agreements to be registered with the commissioner of income tax.

Provision 7. The pay-as-you-earn system of tax collection once covered only civil servants, parastatal employees, and some large private enterprises. Other individual taxpayers were taxed on their assessed income for the previous year. PAYE now applies to all taxpayers. To discourage the underdeduction of tax due, the law assesses an interest penalty at 2 percentage points above the prevailing bank rate whenever the additional tax assessment exceeds 20 percent of the preceding year's deductions.

Provision 8. A new "seizure and sale" procedure was passed to empower the commissioner to appoint a government agent to seize a defaulting taxpayer's movable or immovable property and offer it for public sale to recover the amount of tax and penalties due. Moreover, tax clearance certificates are required before taxpayers are allowed to clear goods through customs, license private and commercial vehicles, obtain building permits, or register a property sale.

Impact on Revenue

An estimate based on a mechanical application of the new rate schedule on 1985 income data suggested that revenues would drop 25 percent, or about D3.7 million, assuming no change in compliance. The commissioner of income tax estimated that implementation of the new package would cut revenue by D4 million in the first year (1988) and D2 million the following year. But instead, collections *increased* steadily during the three years following enactment of the new law, from D14.1

million in 1987–1988 to D21.2 million in 1988–1989, D26.0 million in 1989–1990, and D29.3 million in 1990–1991. Speaking to a reorganized tax reform committee in late 1991, the commissioner made the following points about the increase in revenues:

- The Income Tax Division felt initially that government's drastic lowering of the rate schedule pushed it into a corner. It reacted by increasing collection targets and taking a stricter approach toward known tax evaders, such as raising its estimates of undeclared income and bringing more people into the net. According to the commissioner, the division "changed its way of working."
- The commissioner noted that one striking outcome was that "I now get peace—there are many fewer complaints." The dual implication is that taxpayers are less resentful of the new (lower) rates and more respectful of the division's administration of the law.
- The commissioner believed that the net would continue to widen and that revenues would continue to increase.

Reform of Indirect Taxes

The reform of the indirect tax system encompassed several separate activities. Three are examined here: the rationalization of revenue collection outside the MoF; the introduction of a general sales tax; and changes in the tax incentives used to promote development.

Revenue Collected Outside the MoF
By the early 1980s The Gambia's system of taxes, charges, and fees had proliferated into a patchwork of revenue items without clear direction and purpose. New taxes had been added as the government searched for ways to cover its deficit. The system had not been analyzed in any detail, because the MoF staff lacked the capacity to determine how and whether the structure of taxes and charges promoted the government's fiscal objectives.

Because no single government agency was responsible for monitoring the collection of all the revenue items, it was difficult to determine their economic impact. Furthermore, many of the agencies treated revenue generation as a peripheral activity. Indeed, some agencies, such as the Ministry of Tourism, were in the anomalous position of trying to promote the activities they were required to tax.

To begin to analyze the situation, the minister of finance requested a review of all of the various taxes and fees collected by twenty-one separate ministries and departments outside the MoF (McPherson, 1984). The report concluded that the revenue system had been extremely unwieldy. Numerous opportunities for rationalization and simplification were evident. For example, as noted later, several taxes were effectively sales taxes that could be administered more effectively by a single agency at a single rate. The report also revealed widespread evasion and underperformance. In some cases revenue was not being collected at all (for example, land rent); in other cases revenue was being diverted after it was collected (for example, the airport departure tax).

The report recommended that the government create a central revenue department (CRD) consisting of the existing income tax department and two new units—the Internal Revenue Division and the Statistics and Special Studies Unit (SSSU). The CRD would be responsible for all revenue collected by all departments and ministries outside the MoF. The commissioner of income tax was to be the director of the CRD.

But shifting revenue oversight to the CRD did not necessarily mean shifting collection as well. Other agencies were better positioned to undertake that task. For instance, the police were in the best position to collect motor vehicle license fees and the road tax. But the collection of some other taxes needed to be reassigned. Authority for collecting the airport departure tax was transferred to the customs administration, and authority for collecting the hotel bed-night tax was shifted from the Ministry of Tourism (which preferred not to have to collect the tax in the first place) to the Internal Revenue Division.

As a first step, the Statistics and Special Studies Unit within the CRD would monitor tax performance and assess the impact of particular taxes on specific activities, groups, or industries. The idea was to begin with relatively simple analyses of tax buoyancies, tax elasticities, and tax incidence and work progressively toward more detailed studies of the tax system. As experience accumulated, SSSU staff could turn their attention to issues associated with compliance costs, equity, effectiveness, and efficiency.

The minister endorsed the report, Cabinet approved it, legislation was drafted, and the Taxes Act (1984) was passed by Parliament. The entire process took six months. Among other things the report provided a useful example to senior policymakers of the benefits of undertaking economic analyses of alternative tax policies. Though the analysis was simple and straightforward, it was clear evidence of the value of regular systematic reviews of the impact and performance of revenue items.

The National Sales Tax

Based on work initiated as the ERP was being formulated, a national sales tax act was passed in 1988 and implemented in 1989 (Perry, 1985; Vincze, 1987). The purpose of the sales tax was twofold—to rationalize and simplify the revenue system by eliminating more than a dozen special taxes and to broaden the tax base. The impetus for the change was the realization that The Gambia had depended too heavily for too long on taxes on international trade. It was made more urgent by the progress of multilateral trade negotiations within the Economic Community of West African States (ECOWAS) and the bilateral negotiations under the Senegambia Confederation. Agreements in these areas would have required that The Gambia reduce its external taxes for goods originating in ECOWAS countries and in Senegal in exchange for having goods originating in The Gambia taxed similarly.

The government considered several options. One was a *value-added tax* (VAT). A VAT is advantageous because its wide tax base can raise a large amount of revenue from its low rate and because it taxes different levels of production similarly (that is, it is neutral). The disadvantage is that a VAT requires all producers, processors, and retailers to keep accurate and detailed records of their purchases and sales. The amount of information required can be reduced if certain goods and services are exempted from the tax. For those goods and services that are not exempt, the recordkeeping requirements are burdensome and, for The Gambia, unrealistic.

A second option was a *consumption tax*, which would directly encourage saving and investment and (if food were exempted) would have a positive effect on equity. Yet it is difficult to administer because it requires that all consumption transactions be taxed, most of which occur at the retail level.

The third option considered was a *general sales tax*, to be applied to as many goods and services as the government deemed administratively and politically feasible at the wholesale level. As with the VAT, its base is large. It is also easy to administer, particularly when applied at the wholesaler/manufacturer level. Its main disadvantage is that, with a flat rate, it becomes regressive when applied to staple items; also, the tax cascades when retailers pay tax on commodities that have already been taxed at the wholesale level. Yet regressivity can be overcome by exempting particular goods from the tax—for example, domestically produced food and clothing—and by adding excise taxes to goods and services, such as jewelry, perfume, liquor, or restaurant meals. Cascading can be minimized by reducing the scope of the retail tax.

The MoF recommended that a general sales tax be adopted at the wholesaler/manufacturer level. The following were the specific provisions of the enabling legislation:

- The sales tax rate was 10 percent.
- The customs and excise administration would administer the tax.
- Some items were exempt from the tax: specified educational, technical, cultural, religious, and literary material; domestically produced food; some capital equipment; and medicines and health items.
- The import tax of 6 percent was abolished, and the government made compensating reductions in all tariff levels to contain the general level of taxation.
- The sales tax replaced the telephone/telex surcharge (10 percent); the insurance premium tax (10 percent); the airline ticket surcharge (10 percent); the ad valorem tax on hotel bills (5 percent); and the service charge on domestic tours (10 percent). The hotel bed tax of D3 per bed daily was rescinded.
- The sales tax was applied to the domestic production of soft drinks and beer, and the existing excise tax on these items was reduced by 10 percentage points.
- The requirements for registering taxpayers were clarified, and the penalties for evasion and fraud were strengthened.

Administration was simplified by using a single uniform rate, applied at the wholesaler/importer level. The customs administration would collect the bulk of sales tax revenue at the point of import. Import clearance could be withheld until sales tax arrears were cleared. This arrangement significantly lowered the compliance costs of the new tax.

To reduce the regressivity of the tax, the act did not tax domestically produced food. But it did tax imported food, consistent with the government's efforts to promote domestic food production, to encourage a switch in consumption from imported rice to local cereals, and to ensure that tourists would bear more of the cost of the imported food they consumed. Customs was given the authority to administer all indirect taxes on the hotels. This arrangement improved compliance, as the hotels would not be allowed to clear their imports while sales tax arrears persisted.

The sales tax has become a major source of government revenue. From 1988–1989 to 1990–1991, sales tax receipts increased by 74 percent in nominal terms, or from 5.8 percent to 7.3 percent of GDP (Table 9-5).

Table 9-5. Sales Tax Receipts, 1988–89 to 1990–91 (Millions of Dalasis)

Source	1988–89	1989–90	1990–91
Imports	97.5	126.7	161.0
Manufacturers	3.6	6.7	7.6
Hotels	3.6	10.3	13.0
Tourist enterprises	.3	.5	.6
Telecommunications	3.2	4.6	5.2
Insurance	.9	1.7	1.6
Air services	3.0	5.5	4.9
Other	.3	1.0	1.2
Total receipts	112.4	156.9	195.2
Percentage of GDP	5.8	6.7	7.3
Internal sales tax (% of total)	13	19	16

Source: Ministry of Finance and Economic Affairs, Macro Policy Analysis Unit.

The Revised Development Act

One aspect of tax reform that was unsuccessful was the revision of the Development Act. The Development Acts of 1964 and 1973 had provided several types of tax exemptions and holidays nominally aimed at encouraging investment and developing the country. Despite the large amounts of forgone revenue involved, the government never undertook a detailed assessment of the relative costs and benefits of these incentives.

There were several indications that the costs of these incentives far outweighed any gains. Many of the loans guaranteed by the government under the act ended up as bad debts that the government had to service either through the managed fund, the Paris Club, or the London Club (see Chapters 11 and 12). In addition, many who held development certificates appeared to be taking advantage of them by evading taxes, diverting duty-exempt imported materials to other uses, diluting shares, and using transfer pricing mechanisms. Moreover, it was not clear that the act was achieving its objectives of increasing investment. Although the government gave up millions of dalasi in forgone revenue between 1975–1976 and 1985–1986 under the act, investment had declined and the economy had nearly collapsed.

Many of these problems could have been minimized by limiting the extent of the tax holidays, by increasing the penalties for malfeasance, and by strengthening enforcement. For example, one possibility would have been to introduce a penalty for default equal to the full value of the benefits received plus interest. Oversight and transparency could have been strengthened by requiring regular reports to Parliament on the costs incurred by the government in granting incentives and a breakdown of the support given to each enterprise.

However, when the act was revised in 1988, no analysis was undertaken of its benefits and costs. As a result, the revised act included only marginal changes that did little to increase penalties, strengthen enforcement, or improve transparency. The continuation of the tax exemptions that were included in the act undermined the income tax reform that the government enacted the same year.

Four years later, the incentives provided under the act were examined more thoroughly (Gray et al., 1992, Section 4, Appendix 3). The analysis suggested both widespread abuse of the incentives and indifferent government oversight. It examined the ten enterprises that had been granted development certificates under the 1988 act and found that none had complied with the provisions for reporting, monitoring, and economic performance. Yet the government had not applied any sanctions. It concluded that the main impact of the 1988 act, like its predecessors, had been to reduce government tax revenues.

Computerization of Tax Administration

Tax reform efforts worldwide have shown that computerization of tax records can simplify administration and improve compliance significantly. But introducing new computerized systems has proved to be difficult, and it has been resisted by tax officials who would prefer that the system not be changed (Jenkins, 1991). This was the pattern in The Gambia.

As part of the tax reform effort, tax officials received computer training that included learning several analytic techniques that could easily be applied with simple spreadsheet programs using tax return data. These included grouping returns and sorting them by various criteria (for example, chronologically by taxpayer); calculating tax liability and discrepancies vis-à-vis manual assessments; cash accounting; and estimating the impact of alternative rate schedules on individual liability and aggregate collections. Computer training also was included as part of a yearlong U.S. training program of a senior divisional officer. But management was unenthusiastic about introducing new routines and systems. This lack of enthusiasm was partly due to their understandable reluctance in giving up long-established reporting patterns and routines and their recognition that major institutional changes should never be undertaken lightly. But it also appeared to be due to their understanding that improved information flows might shift the existing relationships of power and influence within the ministry. For example, staff under their direction might have access to important information before management, and that situation might affect at least some of management's discretionary decision-making power on tax liability issues. Within a relatively short period of time, most of those who had received computer training were assigned to new posts, and their computer skills were not passed on to other colleagues.

Seven years after the initial demonstrations, the Income Tax Division acquired a personal computer for word processing. In late 1991 the intervening records were entered on the computer for analysis as part of a new tax study. But the professional staff was still reluctant to use the computer for regular assessment or tax analysis, and there was little sign that tax administration would be computerized in the foreseeable future.

Concluding Observations about Tax Reform

The Gambia's tax reform efforts resulted in several major improvements to the tax system. Income tax rates were lowered, the number of bands was reduced, and the exemption for low-income taxpayers was raised. Several other exemptions were eliminated, widening the base. The new sales tax replaced a plethora of small, difficult-to-administer, and sometimes conflicting taxes with a single tax administered across the board at the wholesaler/retailer level. In both cases the result was a significant increase in revenue, simplified administration, fewer taxpayer complaints, and improved equity. Sales tax revenues made up for the decline in international trade tax revenues (following the elimination of export taxes and the reduction in import tariff rates). As a percentage of GDP, total domestic revenues remained fairly constant (Figure 9-1).

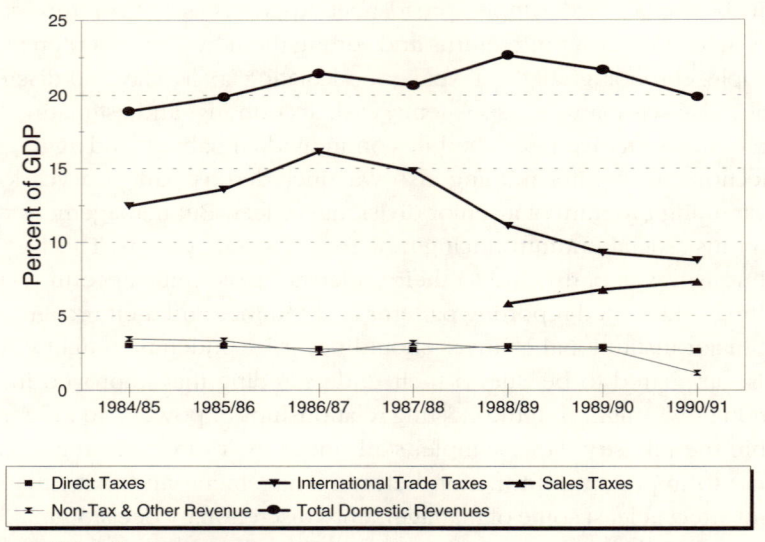

Figure 9-1. Government Revenues

The reform effort emphasized administrative efficiency by simplifying the laws and eliminating ministerial and administrative discretion. As a result, compliance improved. For the personal income tax, compliance was largely an endogenous response to the lower rates and the changed posture of the Income Tax Division.

Despite these improvements introducing the reforms was difficult. Tax reform aroused significant and concerted resistance from the beneficiaries of tax exemptions and at times from tax officials themselves. In many areas the pace of reform was sluggish; in others there was essentially no progress. It took several years to introduce the major policy changes on the income tax and the sales tax. The revision of the National Development Act failed to eliminate many wasteful exemptions. Computerization has yet to take hold, despite its promise for improved analysis and increased revenue. Moreover, enforcement of the tax laws and the penalties for evasion remains weak. This problem is partly due to weaknesses in the tax administration office and partly due to the broader issue of the weakness of the judicial system.

Tax reform in The Gambia has had a solid start. If enforcement and compliance can be improved and the basic principles of the reform can be applied more broadly, The Gambia will be in a strong position to raise the resources it needs to support government expenditure and more effectively finance its economic development.

NOTES

1. World Bank, 1991a; Jenkins, 1991; Harberger, 1990; Bird and Oldman, 1990; Gillis, 1989; Shalizi and Squire, 1988.
2. Calculated from the budget deficit and GDP series in World Bank, 1991d, p. 260.
3. As of 1978 the GPMB had reserves of D106.5 million (equivalent to US$52 million, or 31 percent of GDP). By 1981–1982 they had fallen to D15.3 million; the next year, the reserve account was overdrawn by D23 million.
4. That said, it is difficult to believe that none of these foreign and multinational employers were making undeclared payments to their high-level employees through foreign bank accounts or that the employees were declaring all of their foreign property income to the Gambian authorities.
5. For example, a taxpayer whose gross income is D8,000 and whose former deductions were D3,000—close to the average proportion in that bracket (see IMF, 1982, p. 42)—used to pay D298 on chargeable income of D5,000; he or she now pays 10 percent × (D8,000 − D5,000) = D300.

6. Under the existing law employer-provided housing was valued at a uniform D3,000 annually. Needless to say, this amount had long since been eroded by inflation.

10

Recurrent Costs and the Public Expenditure Program

Malcolm F. McPherson

The ERP gave special prominence to reorienting the public investment program for two reasons. First, the government could no longer postpone dealing with the public sector's acute recurrent cost problem. Second, public investment activity had to be made more efficient. Without action in both areas, the objective of sustained economic growth could not be achieved.

This chapter examines how the ERP sought to redress the recurrent cost problem and improve the efficiency of public investment. It begins by discussing the recurrent cost problem and then examines trends in public investment. It also reviews attempts to implement public expenditure programming. The concluding section draws some lessons from The Gambia's experience.

The Recurrent Cost Problem

General Dimensions of the Problem

The recurrent cost problem refers to the chronic underfunding of operations and maintenance (O&M) expenditures.[1] Although it can occur in either the private or public sectors, it has received far more attention as a public-sector problem. In the private sector the problem generally is seen as one dimension of inefficient resource allocation. When it occurs in the public sector, the macroeconomic consequences can be more widespread.

Recognition of the recurrent cost problem dates back to analyses of socialist economies in the 1940s that focused on the problems arising from the different allocation mechanisms and incentives associated with capital and recurrent expenditure. Because of bureaucratic pressures and inadequate pricing mechanisms, major imbalances emerged in the supply of recurrent and capital resources. Managers within socialist systems typically were judged by total output and therefore had little incentive to maintain their physical equipment adequately, especially in the short run. Planners were judged on the growth of investment and so had an incentive to inflate the expansion of the capital stock. Thus the expansion of the capital stock (to promote growth) was not matched by adequate recurrent resources to ensure that newly installed capital would be maintained and operated economically.

The recurrent cost problem gained more prominence in its applications to developing countries.[2] These analyses have focused on the misallocation of recurrent resources, both within a particular budget year and over time. Within a given year the misallocation of resources affects government operational efficiency but has only a limited impact on the productive capacity of the existing capital stock. However, if continued over time, it can create serious distortions. Roads, bridges, schools, hospitals, railways, and so on fall into disrepair. Equipment breakdowns become longer and more frequent. The supply of materials for schools, hospitals, and government ministries is reduced. And public-sector productivity declines due to the shortage of petrol, spare parts, and other materials. This deterioration also directly affects private-sector productivity. Costs increase as private operators provide additional maintenance, install backup capital to prevent operating delays (for example, electricity generators), and provide substitute services (mail, telephone, security, and so on).

The problem can arise in two ways. First, although adequate resources may be available, they are not allocated efficiently enough to ensure that O&M expenditures are sufficient. Second, all public resources may be in short supply, including those devoted to O&M.

The solutions to both cases differ. In the first case the problem is to improve the allocation of public resources. A well-known result in welfare economics is that the allocation of public resources is efficient when the marginal contribution to social welfare across expenditure categories is equalized. In practice that criterion is widely ignored. Moving toward this ideal in a country with a recurrent cost problem would require cutting other public expenditures (such as salaries) and reallocating them to O&M. Implementing this type of change is difficult. Vocal lobbies exist to defend expenditures on salaries. No such lobby exists to defend O&M.

In the second case the problem is due directly to the country's low income or the government's unwillingness to tax. The solution calls for improving the efficiency with which *all* public resources are used. Borrowing and/or foreign aid can be a temporary solution at best. Over the longer term the problem can be resolved only by increasing public-sector revenue based on sustained economic growth.

In general, however, solutions to the recurrent cost problem will involve both the expenditure and revenue sides of the public-sector budget.[3] Thus ways must be found to improve resource allocation *and* raise additional resources.

The Recurrent Cost Problem in The Gambia

The Gambia has had a serious recurrent cost problem since the mid-1970s. The first five-year plan led to a sharp increase in the scope and volume of public investment. The recurrent resources necessary to support that investment did not increase commensurately. During the expansion phase adequate resources were available for a wide range of activities—creating employment, establishing public enterprises, lending to public-sector employees, providing consumer subsidies, and making public investment. The availability of resources was not the problem; using them efficiently was.

The data in Table 10-1 provide some perspective. They are estimates of recurrent cost ratios for the entire public sector, as well as for agriculture, transport and communications, and social services (health and education). The ratios are calculated as annual expenditures on O&M in each sector relative to the capital stock in the preceding period.[4] The most notable feature of the data is the sharp decline in the ratios after the mid-1970s. The decline reflects the rapid increase in capital expenditures and the underfunding of recurrent costs.

The recurrent cost problem became evident in two ways. First, public-sector capital, such as roads, bridges, buildings, and drainage systems, deteriorated. Second, public-sector employees frequently had difficulty in obtaining the supplies, fuel, and spare parts necessary to complete their work. The effects of these two problems are difficult to measure.

In The Gambia capital expenditures were frequently substituted for recurrent expenditures because deteriorating public-sector capital was commonly just replaced or rebuilt. For example, the lack of maintenance at the Gambia Utilities Corporation led to the periodic breakdown of generating equipment. The generators had to be replaced. The Gambia River Transport Company's fleet of tugs and barges was in such poor shape that it became impossible to use the river to transport the groundnut crop. The system of roads and drains in and around Banjul had deteriorated so badly from 1979 to 1987 that the major roads had to be rebuilt and alternative drainage systems constructed. The airport was

Table 10-1. Government Capital Expenditures and Recurrent Cost Ratios

	1965–66	1970–71	1975–76	1980–81	1981–82	1982–83	1983–84	1984–85	1985–86	1986–87	1987–88	1988–89	1989–90	1990–91
Government Capital Expenditures	(Millions of dalasis: current prices)													
Government investment	6.3	3.1	11.3	69.8	68.8	43.8	70.1	109.1	91.3	153.3	188.2	141.1	160.5	177.7
Agriculture and natural resources	0.5	0.4	1.9	7.2	5.7	1.6	16.8	12.1	40.8	60.3	45.1	19.0	14.0	27.9
Industry and mining	0.5	0.3	0.3	1.0	0.1	0.7	1.7	17.0	4.8	9.3	0.0	0.2	0.2	0.0
Tourism, trade, and finance	0.0	0.0	0.0	1.4	0.9	1.4	5.3	1.3	10.3	0.5	0.9	0.3	1.7	2.7
Public utilities	0.5	1.0	0.6	3.1	6.6	4.2	7.7	1.9	24.6	16.4	5.1	19.1	37.0	33.7
Transport and communications	2.0	0.5	3.8	34.0	22.8	18.8	35.3	52.3	0.2	45.1	61.0	69.7	63.5	61.3
Social structure	0.0	0.3	2.2	14.4	26.6	14.5	3.0	21.1	1.3	16.0	66.6	23.7	31.5	37.3
Administration, security, and justice	2.5	0.5	2.5	4.2	6.2	2.6	0.3	3.5	4.2	5.6	9.5	9.1	12.6	14.8
Other	0.3	0.0	0.0	4.6	0.0	0.0	0.0	0.0	5.1	0.2	0.0	0.0	0.1	0.0
Government Capital Stock (10% Depr.)	(Millions of dalasis: constant 1976–1977 prices)													
Agriculture and natural resources	5.1	5.6	10.1	42.9	43.4	40.4	48.2	51.2	66.7	85.6	94.3	91.3	86.4	85.1
Transport and communications	20.4	26.1	36.4	125.2	132.1	134.6	146.1	165.3	148.8	153.1	161.2	168.6	170.7	169.9
Health and education	9.0	7.3	11.2	37.4	56.3	62.8	58.6	66.4	60.4	61.2	80.6	80.6	81.9	83.6
Other capital	30.2	35.9	40.1	89.3	95.9	97.9	103.2	112.8	131.2	136.9	135.3	138.0	146.0	151.5
Aggregate capital	64.7	74.8	97.9	294.8	327.6	335.8	356.1	395.8	407.2	436.8	471.5	478.6	485.0	490.2
Recurrent Cost Indicators[a]														
Public sector	0.34	0.54	0.50	0.26	0.34	0.24	0.22	0.19	0.14	0.17	0.24	0.16	0.18	0.15
Agriculture	0.48	0.57	0.66	0.29	0.18	0.20	0.19	0.15	0.11	0.06	0.06	0.05	0.06	0.05
Transport and communications	0.32	0.32	0.38	0.11	0.11	0.09	0.07	0.06	0.03	0.03	0.04	0.04	0.03	0.03
Health and education	0.48	0.97	1.11	0.78	0.67	0.47	0.40	0.43	0.30	0.30	0.31	0.29	0.38	0.34

[a] [Recurrent expenditures (t)/Implicit GDP deflator (t)]/Capital stock (t–1).
Sources: Ministry of Finance and Economic Affairs, Macro Policy Analysis Unit, GDATA91 spreadsheet; Central Statistics Department, Republic of The Gambia; and International Monetary Fund, SM/92/111, June 2, 1992.

maintained so poorly that its international accreditation was almost withdrawn on several occasions.

Nonetheless, the public-sector capital stock was not uniformly neglected. Some facilities and capital items were well maintained. The State House and its surroundings, the head offices of the largest parastatals, and the government printing press are examples.

The Consequences of Underfunding Recurrent Costs

The underfunding of recurrent costs has differential impacts on the economy. The lack of supplies has an immediate effect on the efficiency of public-sector employees. Without stationery, government correspondence lapses, taxes cannot be collected nor memos written, bills delivered, and information shared. Without books and writing materials, schools become ineffective as institutions of learning. Without fuel, power cannot be generated, water cannot be pumped, garbage cannot be collected, and border customs posts cannot be staffed. And without medical supplies, basic health services cannot be provided.

During the latter part of 1984 and throughout 1985, The Gambia experienced many of these problems. Fuel, in particular, was regularly unavailable. Rice shortages occurred periodically. The government often ran short of office supplies, spare parts for vehicles, and medicine. But, again, the shortages were not universal. The State House always had electricity, and many senior civil servants could find the resources necessary to travel abroad.

Over the longer term the deteriorating capital stock began to impose costs on a wide front. Vehicles depreciated more rapidly because they had to travel over rutted roads, business and personal interaction took more time and effort because transportation services and telecommunications had broken down, medical risks increased because the hospital system had deteriorated, and electrical equipment wore out more frequently because of brownouts and blackouts. Some of the costs associated with these difficulties could have been defrayed with appropriate adjustments. For example, backup electricity generators could have been installed. But all such adjustments entailed dead-weight losses: they would have been unnecessary had recurrent costs been funded adequately.

The main economic effect of these factors was to reduce the overall level of economic productivity, which in turn lowered the rate of economic growth. A detailed model would be necessary to disentangle the various effects of recurrent costs from other influences. But it cannot be argued that the recurrent cost problem was not an important factor in the dramatic reduction in the productivity of capital in The Gambia from the mid-1970s onward. To illustrate, the aggregate capital/output ratio was 2.8 between 1965–1966 and 1975–1976 but increased to 7.6 in the period from 1975–1976 to 1985–1986.

Reasons for the Recurrent Cost Problem

The recurrent cost problem may be due to one of several factors. First, the government may attach a low priority to funding O&M. When budgetary pressures emerge, O&M expenditures are often the first to be cut. Since newly built roads and bridges take time to wear out, it is tempting to postpone routine maintenance. One reason for this tendency is that the costs of lack of maintenance are not always immediately obvious to decisionmakers. But even when the long-term costs are known, other concerns may be perceived as more pressing. For example, the GUC postponed routine maintenance on its main generator in 1987 out of high-level concern that electricity shortages could harm the ruling party in the impending elections.

Second, although some changes have occurred in the past decade, donors still focus on capital expenditures. Despite overwhelming evidence to the contrary, donors continue to assume that the normal operating costs of development activities will be met by the government—if not during the early phases of a project, then ultimately.

Third, donor assistance to the government significantly distorts the relative costs of resources. Because it is poor, The Gambia receives grants from most bilateral donors, as well as highly concessional loans from the multilateral agencies. These resources typically cover the cost of capital equipment and imported commodities. Their opportunity cost for the government is low, and often zero. In contrast, when a government wishes to augment its recurrent resources, it must increase taxes and/or borrow and/or cut its other expenditures. All of these options are unattractive and have high opportunity costs. Viewed from the government's perspective, it is perfectly rational not to fund the recurrent costs of donor-supported investment.

Fourth, because donors regularly cycle their staff and change the focus of their support, they have limited leverage to make the government comply with agreements to fund recurrent costs. By the time the agreements become operational, the donor staff have departed, and their replacements often have different priorities. The outcome is that the capital invested in development projects is rarely maintained adequately.

Fifth, given political pressures to promote development projects actively, governments substitute quantity for quality. In The Gambia, for instance, the commitment to education has often been framed in terms of the number of schools built and teachers hired. That the schools have been short of furniture, supplies, and books and have had to use unqualified teachers has been of secondary importance.

Sixth, as highlighted by the economic crisis of the 1980s in The Gambia, a shortage of foreign exchange can preclude meeting the foreign component of recurrent expenditures. With the dramatic depreciation of the dalasi after the float, expenditures on "other charges" increased sharply. In 1987–1988, for example, this component of the budget was overspent by 18 percent, although the budgeted allocation had been increased by 25 percent in the previous year.

Finally, a recurrent cost problem may arise even when a government has made adequate funds available if recurrent resources are diverted to other uses. For example, drivers might sell petrol or substitute used parts for new ones on vehicles; medical workers might divert government drugs to the local market; office assistants can supplement their incomes by selling office supplies; office phones can be used for private purposes; and so on. These problems often go unchecked and are exacerbated because recurrent costs are not funded adequately in other areas of the government. For instance, diversion of supplies may increase in the knowledge that government auditors do not have the resources (typically vehicles and fuel) to make spot checks.

Public Expenditure Programming

The Objectives

Public expenditure programming is the latest in a series of initiatives by the donor community to encourage the Gambian government to improve the allocation of public resources. (Chapter 19 discusses the expenditure programming matrix adopted by the IMF.) The first such initiative, which emerged in the late 1970s, called for adopting a sector-by-sector approach to the recurrent cost problem. That approach had been worked out as part of a broader study of recurrent costs in the Sahel (CILSS, 1982; Gray and Martens, 1983).

The effort failed, leaving little impression on those involved in budgeting or planning of the nature of the recurrent cost problem. Neither the second five-year plan nor the midterm review of the second plan dealt with the recurrent cost issue in any detail (see, respectively, GOTG, 1981 and 1984). The essence of the midterm review was a major expansion in public-sector investment to reverse The Gambia's poor growth performance.

In view of the acute nature of the recurrent cost problem at the time, such a massive expansion in public expenditures (D1.15 billion over four years) would simply have compounded the problem.

The World Bank also attempted to deal with the recurrent cost problem in its 1985 country economic memorandum. The study highlighted the main dimensions of the problem and urged a complete overhaul of The Gambia's public investment program.[5] It recommended several measures for improving the productivity of public investment:

- to revise the PIP in light of existing economic realities and to initiate a series of three-year rolling plans as a substitute for the national development plan;
- to focus on a core program of activities for rehabilitating existing capital, refurbishing essential public services, and supporting the production of tradable goods;
- to develop plans for rehabilitating key sectors of the economy in an effort to mobilize donor support for the "full nonsalary recurrent cost financing and foreign exchange requirements of a particular sector";
- to ensure closer cooperation between the Ministry of Finance and the Ministry of Economic Planning in an effort to improve planning, screen investments, monitor implementation, and coordinate the recurrent and capital budgets.

Lacking better alternatives for improving the performance of public investment, the ERP task force adopted these recommendations. The World Bank included them as part of its conditions for its Structural Adjustment Credit (SAC-I). One of the conditions was that analyses of the recurrent cost implications of development projects in health, education, agriculture, and transport and communications be undertaken. Those conditions were never met.

Implementation
By implementing the ERP and agreeing to the World Bank's conditions, the government indicated its commitment to the recommended strategy. Operationalizing its commitment was difficult. In effect, the World Bank required that the government abandon the idea of national planning by institutionalizing a system of accounting and accountability into capital and recurrent budgeting that had not existed previously. Those changes

struck at the core of the system of discretionary control over spending and lack of accountability for funds that had emerged in both the planning ministry and the MoF. Not surprisingly, none of the senior staff in the respective ministries was enthusiastic about the modifications. Bureaucratic resistance to the proposals was inevitable.

Everyone verbally agreed that the changes were necessary, some modifications in the choice of projects were made, studies were undertaken, and the appearance of forward motion was created. Yet with the exception of specific provisions that were implemented when continued support from donors was vital, nothing substantive was achieved during the ERP.

To illustrate, public investment projects were classified into "A," "B," and "C" groups; the "A" group projects had the highest social returns and most immediacy. The classifications were reviewed annually with the World Bank. Nonetheless, the parallel commitment to conduct a full-scale evaluation of each project, including its recurrent cost implications, was ignored. Moreover, the government proceeded with some "C" list projects despite agreements with the donors to the contrary.[6]

The recurrent cost implications of development projects were never estimated. In 1987 both the recurrent and development budgets were computerized in an effort to link them so that the recurrent cost implications of public investment could be analyzed during the three-year rolling plan. However, the effort stalled after the computerization exercise was completed. Senior members of both the planning ministry and the MoF were unwilling to move in a direction that threatened their control over budgetary allocations. More important, however, the computer link was perceived to be a mechanism for enabling the Ministry of Finance to gain influence over budgetary items that the Ministry of Economic Planning considered its prerogative.

Thus few improvements were made in public investment appraisal, monitoring, financing, and implementation beyond the changes that were mandated by the donor community. Indeed, to enable The Gambia to comply with the Structural Adjustment Loan II conditions in 1991, the World Bank had to provide additional consultants to undertake sectoral reviews of public expenditures so that the government could fulfill a condition that it agreed to as part of the SAC in 1986.

The integration of the Ministry of Finance and the Ministry of Economic Planning could potentially remove some of these obstacles. But the concept of forward budgeting still faces strong resistance, and the government continues to be reluctant to devote its own resources to fund the recurrent costs of donor-supported projects.

Allocations for Recurrent Costs and Public Investment During the ERP

Notwithstanding the resistance to budget reform and the reluctance to devote local resources to recurrent costs, some restructuring of the budget occurred under the ERP. The IMF program in 1986 carried several specific requirements. They included a freeze on the wage bill, full funding for debt service, reduced public investment, and increased allocations to "other charges" (primarily inputs). The wage freeze requirement was part of an effort to reduce the size of the civil service. Debt service had to be funded fully if The Gambia was to repair its international creditworthiness. Public investment was to be confined to activities that offered a high social return (a lower limit of 15 percent was set by the World Bank) and for which the donor community would provide concessionary finance. Finally, the increase in "other charges" explicitly recognized that a major reason for the low productivity in the public sector was the lack of complementary inputs. In this regard and despite the pressure to cut the budget deficit, the IMF was prepared to admit that additional government expenditures were essential in some key areas.

As shown in Table 10-2, some dramatic reallocations occurred within the budget under the IMF program. The table compares expenditures in 1984–1985 (prior to the ERP) with those in 1986–1987, the first year of the IMF program. The shares of spending for wages and salaries and for public investment declined substantially. Allocations increased sharply for subsidies (mainly groundnuts) and for net lending (to finance the managed fund, as discussed in Chapter 12). Debt service also rose significantly, partly for interest, but mainly for amortization and arrears payments. The latter two are shown as a memorandum item in Table 10-2 because, according to standard conventions, they are technically (negative) financing items rather than expenditures.

With respect to public investment, the 1986–1987 budget allocation of D153 million represented a decline in government investment of 32 percent in dollar terms. The public investment budget (shown in detail earlier in the top section of Table 10-1) continued to be dominated by expenditures for transport and communications. Agriculture continued to receive much less than its relative contribution to GDP and employment (although it received a higher share of public investment than before the ERP). Expenditures on health and education increased primarily because of increased donor interest.

The Program for Sustained Development, introduced in 1990, did not change the government's basic focus for public investment. The PSD

Table 10-2. Government Expenditures, 1984–1985 to 1986–1987 (Millions of Dalasis)

	1984–85	1985–86	1986–87	Share of Total (%) 1984–85	1986–87
Wages and Salaries	59	63	65	22	13
Interest	29	38	76	11	14
Internal	18	16	27	7	5
External	11	22	49	4	9
Other charges	64	62	88	23	16
Subsidies	10	16	91	4	17
Public investment	109	91	153	40	28
Net lending	0	4	69	0	13
Unallocated	2	8	–2	1	0
Total expenditures	273	282	540	100	100
Memorandum Items					
Amortization and change in arrears	–1	65	78		
Revenue and grants	180	272	485		
Budget deficit after grants	57	51	76		
Deficit as % of GDP	8.5	4.7	5.1		

Source: Ministry of Finance and Economic Affairs.

confirmed the principles to which the government committed itself under the ERP, but it offered no new insights. Coordinated effort in developing such key areas as trade, industry, and financial development has been absent. The result is a patchwork of development projects that depend heavily on the persuasiveness of the personalities who promote them.

One area in which the government has devoted considerable effort is petroleum. It appears that The Gambia, as with Senegal and Guinea Bissau, has petroleum deposits offshore. (There is the possibility of gas on shore as well.) But developing the deposits, if they are found, is decades away. In the meantime considerable official effort is being devoted to encouraging firms to become involved. Expectations have been raised, but unfortunately they have diverted attention from dealing with more pressing current issues, such as health and education.

This experience provides a very potent message about the possibility of fundamentally changing the allocation of recurrent and capital resources in The Gambia. Under pressure from the IMF, the government significantly altered the allocation of the recurrent budget. But it did not take full advantage of the opportunity to restructure its investment program toward more productive investments. Instead, for many projects, it returned to the earlier practice of developing—without thorough appraisal—a list of activities for donor consideration. Many of these projects undoubtedly have low or even negative rates of return and will retard The Gambia's future economic development.

Concluding Observations about Recurrent Costs and Public Investment

The severity of the recurrent cost problem and the low productivity of public-sector investment when the ERP was introduced required immediate action by the government to reorient the public investment program. The backlog of maintenance and rehabilitation seriously strained the entire budget (recurrent and capital) during the ERP.

Donor pressure and funding played a major role in beginning to reorder expenditure priorities. Local initiatives to deal with the recurrent cost problem and to rationalize public investment have not been successful. Indeed, the delay in public expenditure programming suggests that the government is unlikely to deal with the recurrent cost problem in the absence of donor pressure.

In this respect, the donors are locked in. They have generally shown more concern about maintaining an adequate level of recurrent cost funding than have government officials. But this situation exists to a large degree because government officials continue to believe (with good reason) that the donors will fund recurrent costs either directly or indirectly by recapitalizing defunct development projects and will provide balance-of-payments support to pay off debts on projects that did not pay for themselves.

The donors will have difficulty extracting themselves from this bind. Government officials see little point in devoting their efforts and political capital to the task of raising resources that one or more of the donors will eventually provide. As long as the donors continue to fill the funding gap, as well as to pick up the pieces from run-down development projects, there is little incentive for the government to mobilize additional resources or to reallocate existing resources to more productive projects.

NOTES

1. Heller (1974, 1979) theorizes that a recurrent cost problem exists whenever the O&M components of capital projects are not funded at levels consistent with their designed output. Although this notion has widely been used (Gray and Martens, 1983, pp. 103–104; CILSS, 1982, p. 17),

it lacks an economic rationale. For a start, it ignores sunk costs. As economic circumstances change, the decision of capital owners to underfund the recurrent costs of particular projects may be perfectly rational. In The Gambia, for example, it would be a mistake for public resources to be devoted to maintaining the river wharves, even though this project was finished only in the last several years. The only river boat that consistently used the wharves, the *Lady Chilel*, sank in 1985, and there is no prospect of a replacement.

2. Heller, 1979; McPherson, 1979; Club du Sahel, 1982; Gray and Martens, 1983; World Bank, 1984, pp. 24-25; Anderson, 1987; World Bank/UNDP, 1989, pp. 23-26; World Bank, 1989a, pp. 166-168; Singh, 1990, pp. 24-26; Premchand, 1990; Pradhan and Swaroop, 1993.

3. The dual nature of the recurrent cost problem is regularly overlooked. Given how the problem has traditionally been defined, the recurrent cost literature has focused almost exclusively on recurrent expenditures. When recurrent costs are underfunded due to revenue shortfalls, it stems as much from inadequate recurrent revenue as it does from inadequate recurrent expenditures (McPherson, 1979).

4. The capital stock (the middle of the table) was derived with the perpetual inventory approach, based on current investment (the top part of the table) deflated by the GDP deflator. A uniform rate of depreciation of 10 percent was assumed.

5. World Bank (1985b, Chapters 3 and 4, and Annex I) contains a detailed review of the PIP that the government had presented at the November 1984 donors' conference. According to the Bank staff, the PIP was too large and unfocused, and had not addressed the recurrent cost implications of the proposed investment.

6. Two such projects, related to fish processing and livestock ranching, created major difficulties between the Bank and the government. Strong lobbies for both projects existed within the government. Despite its commitment not to proceed, government officials made preparations to implement the projects. When World Bank officials eventually found out, they insisted that the projects be canceled. The president did as the Bank required.

11

External Debt Management

Steven C. Radelet, Clive S. Gray, and Paul E. McNamara

The Gambia's external debt began to mount rapidly in the late 1970s when the government implemented the first five-year plan (which included large increases in public expenditures) and groundnut exports collapsed. Debt-servicing difficulties became serious as The Gambia fell into arrears with several creditors in the early 1980s, and culminated when the government could not remain current with its IMF obligations in early 1985.

The country faced suspension of drawings on both IMF and World Bank loans as well as a loss of access to credit from other multilateral and bilateral institutions accustomed to following the IMF's lead. In 1984 the World Bank classified The Gambia among twelve SSA countries as "IDA-eligible countries with prolonged debt problems"; two years later, The Gambia still ranked among twenty-two "debt distressed" SSA countries in bank reporting (World Bank, 1986; 1988b).

Starting in 1987, the level of debt began to stabilize. By 1990 The Gambia had fully extinguished its outstanding arrears. Both debt relative to GDP and debt service relative to exports declined sharply. Indeed, the World Bank reclassified The Gambia in 1987 and 1988 as one of nine "moderately indebted low-income countries" (World Bank, 1989b; 1990b).

The improvement in The Gambia's external debt situation in the late 1980s corresponded with the overall economic turnaround and followed several changes in both debt *administration* and debt *management*. This chapter discusses the most important of these reforms.

The Gambia's relatively successful experience with external debt provides several insights relevant for other SSA countries that are struggling with external debt difficulties. Much of the discussion about external debt in Africa has focused on who should ultimately pay—the country, by reducing consumption and investment, or the creditors, through debt rescheduling or debt forgiveness. The Gambia's experience indicates the importance of using a *combination* of these strategies. The government reduced the budget deficit and took several other steps to reduce the amount and soften the terms of new borrowing. At the same time, donors rescheduled a large amount of debt and provided a sufficient amount of new funds to enable the government to pay both its current and its overdue debt service obligations without unduly compressing domestic investment. Neither strategy alone would have significantly reduced the debt. The Gambian case also illustrates some of the difficulties encountered in introducing a computerized debt-monitoring system, as has been attempted in several other countries in the region.

This chapter begins by reviewing the buildup in Gambian debt and external arrears. It then examines the major change undertaken in debt administration: the introduction of a computerized debt-monitoring and -reporting system, which tracked debt levels, loan disbursements, debt service payments, and arrears. It also analyzes several debt management initiatives, including debt refinancing and rescheduling, policies to restrict the amount and terms of new borrowing by both the central government and parastatals, and the systematic elimination of outstanding debt service arrears. The chapter concludes with some observations about external debt management in The Gambia.

Buildup in The Gambia's External Debt

At the end of 1975, The Gambia's public and publicly guaranteed external debt amounted to 10 percent of gross national product (GNP). However, external debt began to grow rapidly as the government introduced the first five-year plan, which included a large number of public-sector investment projects financed with external loans. At the same time, public enterprise managers became aware of the availability of petrodollars to finance their investments. Chief among these PEs was the Gambia Produce Marketing Board, which borrowed heavily (on commercial terms) to invest in tourist hotels and other enterprises. A third factor was the decline in world groundnut prices and the drought of the early 1980s, both of which reduced Gambian foreign exchange receipts. Finally, the overvalued exchange rate and low real interest rates encouraged private consumption, adding to the current account deficits and increasing the need for external financing.

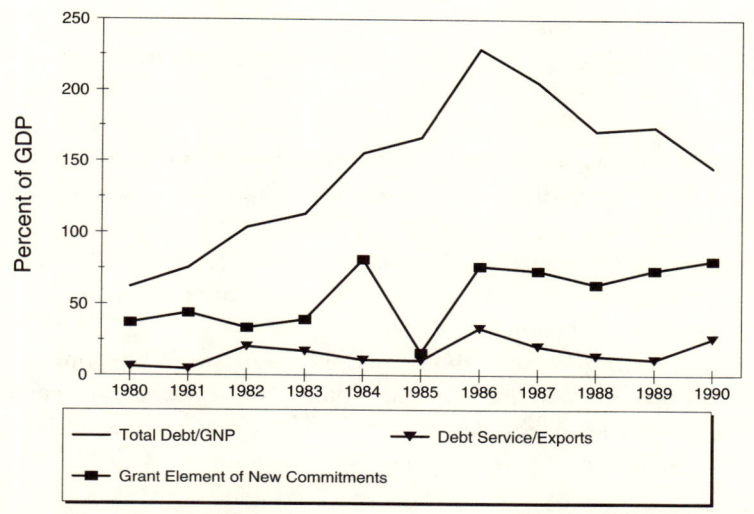

Figure 11-1.   Foreign Debt Indicators.   Source: World Bank 1991c.

The Gambia's foreign debt surged in the early 1980s, peaking at 229 percent of GNP in 1986 (Figure 11-1). Commercial borrowing from banks and suppliers was substantial during the four-year period from 1979 to 1982. These funds were devoted primarily to the construction of tourist hotels. Due mainly to these loans, the grant element in total annual commitments to The Gambia, after averaging 71 percent from 1975 to 1978, dropped to 34 percent in 1979 and averaged 38 percent during the five years ending with 1983.[1]

By the end of 1979, The Gambia's international reserves had practically evaporated, dropping from the equivalent of three months of imports in December 1978 to less than a week's worth. By 1982 external arrears were attracting widespread concern. In 1983 the stock of arrears amounted to US$32 million, or 15 percent of GDP; three years later, they had reached US$105 million, or 53 percent of GDP, and, as noted earlier, The Gambia had fallen into arrears with the IMF.

The Strategy to Improve Debt Administration

As the external debt mounted, concern about the government's loss of control of its foreign borrowing grew. The government and the donors began to focus attention on policies that might curtail the escalating debt (as discussed in the next section) as well as institutional changes in the MoF to improve its administrative capabilities.

The MoF Loans Division

Ideally, the external debt unit of a ministry of finance should serve three functions:

- *Administrative*: The debt unit should participate in loan negotiations, transmit disbursement requests, and process donor invoices for interest and principal payments.
- *Statistical*: The unit should tabulate and summarize all debt trans-actions and stock figures periodically, including both disbursed and undisbursed balances.
- *Analytical*: The unit should monitor and assess the buildup of external debt in light of the country's debt-servicing capacity, advise policymakers on the impacts of proposed loans, and design the government's debt-rescheduling strategy.

In 1985 the Loans Division of the MoF was engaged only in the administrative function to any meaningful extent. It participated fully in most loan negotiations and transmitted disbursement requests from throughout the government to the lending agency. In initiating requests to the accountant general for the payment of debt service obligations, it relied almost exclusively on telexes received from the donors, because it had little capacity to anticipate and verify amounts due independently.

On the statistical side, the unit did not have any systematic method for tabulating and summarizing important debt data. Information on individual loans was kept in files in the unit's cramped office. The ability to access information on a particular loan depended on the memory of the one person who knew the location of (almost) every loan file. The only summary statistics generated by the unit—the annual projections of debt service obligations—were grossly inaccurate.

The Loans Division also lacked the capacity to analyze external debt. The unit had not been designed with this function in mind and was rarely asked to analyze the debt situation.

Computerizing Debt Statistics

As a first step toward enhancing the ability of the Loans Division to carry out its statistical and reporting function, the ministry decided to try to establish what at first appeared to be a simple routine for using a personal computer to track external debt movements. An earlier effort to launch such an exercise with World Bank assistance was stillborn. As testimonial of this short-lived effort, an old NCR computer lay in a corner, gathering dust. The computer had never become fully operational and was awaiting an NCR-trained technician from elsewhere in West Africa. The technician never arrived, because the foreign exchange necessary to pay for his services was not available.

Bearing in mind this earlier failure, the MoF gave careful thought to the most appropriate software for the new system. By 1985 several private consultant groups and multilateral organizations had designed integrated external debt packages that were being advertised as though their mere introduction would ensure sound debt management. In June 1985 the World Bank convened a Debt Systems Conference in Paris, at which ten public and private organizations presented their systems.[2] All of the systems were based on database programs and were protected against user modification. Most purported to facilitate accounting precision by attributing transactions to a given day and then automatically computing interest, commitment charges, and debt outstanding on a daily basis from that point. In this way, their promoters sought to have the packages accepted by central banks, treasuries, and other offices responsible for precise cash management.

Had any of the systems been adopted, the MoF Loans Division staff would have been attempting to use computerized debt-reporting software whose algorithms they could not analyze and that essentially would have been a "black box" to them. This option might have made sense in earlier days of electronic data processing, when the only option was to use mainframes or minicomputers that allowed little interaction with the operator. However, given that The Gambia's debt-reporting system was to function on personal computers, looking for a transparent software that the local staff could interpret and eventually modify as appropriate seemed to be the most sensible action.

Moreover, the focus on accounting precision in these commercial packages added unnecessary complexity. The primary goal was to establish a simple reporting system that would enable ministry management to acquaint itself quickly with correct orders of magnitude and alert it to impending payment obligations. The objective was to provide basic data on broad debt indicators on a regular basis, and not to provide precise amounts due on specific dates. The accounting function could be left to the accountant general's staff, working on an ex post basis with creditors' disbursement notices, invoices, payment receipts, and statements of outstanding balances.[3]

Ultimately, the ministry decided to design a new system using the spreadsheet software Lotus 1-2-3. The system was named GEDRES (Gambia External Debt Reporting System). Its format was modeled closely on printouts issued at the time by the World Bank under its Debt Reporting System (DRS).

The risk of entering data directly onto spreadsheets and then manipulating them to analyze the data was that the data could have been lost or distorted. Moreover, customized database programs such as those offered by the vendors at the World Bank conference could have performed the desired operations much more rapidly than a multipurpose commercial package such as Lotus 1-2-3. Staff from the World Bank's External Debt Division called attention to these issues when they were invited to comment on the initial design of GEDRES in early 1986.

In the end, however, ministry staff believed that the transparency of GEDRES to its operators offset these shortcomings. Moreover, it seemed that The Gambia's external debt portfolio—thought to be less than one hundred loans in 1986—was too small to warrant investing in an outside package. And the opportunity cost of the additional seconds of computer processing time required for GEDRES to produce a report seemed negligible.

Installation of GEDRES

The Loans Division staff began to install The Gambia's loan portfolio on GEDRES in November 1986. Initially, they relied on data from the ministry's files and printouts from the World Bank's DRS system, which in some cases (such as IDA and African Development Bank debt) were based on data supplied by creditors. When large gaps in the data remained, the Loans Division requested updated information from each creditor on the status of every loan.

For the junior Gambian staff members who assisted with the data entry, this task was painstaking, primarily because they had no previous experience in working on any type of keyboard, typewriter, or computer. Indeed, one of the difficulties encountered was that few women had had the opportunity to receive the basic training necessary to work in the office; and very few men had the desire to learn to type, since they considered it to be "women's work." The additional burden of mastering simple Lotus commands unquestionably delayed some stages of data entry beyond the time required with a special debt package. The process required that the ministry dedicate a significant amount of Loans Division staff time for several months. Yet the transparency of the Lotus-based system more than compensated for the delays, and no significant data loss or distortion was observed. Moreover, after the unit staff learned the Lotus 1-2-3 software package, they then used it for many other purposes.

By June 1987 the system was complete enough to produce summary statements of The Gambia's external debt position. In the ensuing months the system was refined and the quality of the data improved, so that summary statements could be produced on a quarterly basis. For the next three years, Loans Division staff entered new or corrected data regularly. GEDRES statements became the most complete and accurate information available on Gambian external debt. They were used extensively in discussions with the World Bank, IMF, and other donors, and became the source for The Gambia's annual submission for the World Bank's debt reporting system.

Other Administrative Improvements: The Lost Payments Problem
GEDRES did not resolve all debt administration problems. Administrative weaknesses sometimes caused payments to be delayed or missed entirely. The external loan payment process began with the Loans Division, when it prepared a request for payment and forwarded it to the accountant general (AG) for approval. The AG had sole authority for requesting that the Central Bank make a payment on the government's behalf. Normally, the entire process took less than two weeks; however, occasionally it could take several months. An investigation in mid-1987 revealed that the required paperwork for executing and recording each payment went through more than thirty-five pairs of hands (including line staff, typists, and messengers). Some payment requests were physically lost in desk drawers; others were not typed accurately and were not approved by the AG or the Central Bank. Rather than following up immediately, the AG or Central Bank staff would often set the paperwork aside and wait for the Loans Division to rectify the situation; in turn, the division rarely knew about such problems until it was notified by the creditor that the payment was in arrears.

The MoF and the Central Bank developed two responses to this problem. First, the Loans Division used GEDRES to prepare a master schedule for monitoring all payments in process. Second, the MoF and the Central Bank established a debt-monitoring committee that met on a biweekly basis to track payments. The committee reviewed the status of each scheduled payment on the master list to ensure that all payments were made promptly. These responses helped reduce missing payments, and The Gambia managed never to breach a target for reducing arrears during the ERP.

GEDRES's Failure to Become a Tool of Policy Formulation
Despite these improvements it would be inaccurate to claim that GEDRES became an integral part of the management information system on which the MoF leadership relied to formulate external borrowing policy. Throughout the period when GEDRES was producing reliable data on

Gambian external debt, MoF management reacted passively to its reports. The impetus for producing reports came from either the World Bank, which required annual debt reports from all member countries, or from the IMF, which set a quarterly debt service arrears target as one of the conditions for its stand-by agreement and Enhanced Structural Adjustment Facility arrangement. Successive ministers and permanent secretaries rarely took the initiative to request the reports, except when they were required to do so by the Bank or the IMF. Perhaps one reason for their lukewarm interest was that while the debt data were useful for long-term economic planning, they were less so for the daily issues facing the ministry. Given the dearth of well-trained ministry staff, it is perhaps not surprising that more effort was devoted to addressing issues that required immediate resolution than to monitoring long-term debt data. The lack of interest may also have stemmed from the inability of senior staff to grasp fully the relationship among and the dynamics of external debt, the balance of payments, and the government budget.

As the economic crisis passed and The Gambia paid off its debt service arrears, the donor community exerted less pressure for accurate debt reporting (although some pressure continued from the World Bank). As the internal and external pressure on the Loans Division to update the GEDRES files relaxed, the reports produced from late 1990 on became progressively less complete, and the system was rarely used.[4]

Debt Management Initiatives

Although the GEDRES system helped The Gambia monitor its external debt more accurately (for a time), it had little direct impact on the size of the debt. Toward this end, the government began to take steps in 1985 to manage its debt portfolio more actively. The government took three major steps:

- It introduced policies to manage the rate at which external debt was growing as well as the quality of projects financed by external debt.
- It rescheduled and refinanced overdue obligations with the Paris and London Clubs and other creditors.
- It systematically reduced its debt service arrears between 1986 and 1990.

External Borrowing Policies

To begin managing the growth and the quality of its external debt, the government introduced four policy changes in 1985 as part of the ERP. First, public-sector agencies (including the government) were no longer allowed to contract foreign debt on commercial terms. Although most commercial creditors and private suppliers had stopped lending to The Gambia as the economic crisis became more severe in 1984 and 1985, several were willing to begin lending again after 1987, when the economy recovered and foreign exchange reserves began to grow. The ban on commercial borrowing—which was an IMF performance criterion—forced government agencies to seek soft-term financing from multilateral and bilateral agencies.

The second policy change was to restrict public enterprises (except the Central Bank) from contracting debt directly from overseas creditors. All public-sector foreign debt had to be channeled through the government, and then on-lent to various state agencies. This change gave the government much more control over investment projects and the financing of government parastatals.

The third new policy was the abolition of government guarantees on private-sector projects. Much of the debt rescheduled with the Paris Club was originally borrowed by private entities in The Gambia and guaranteed by the government. These amounts were lent by commercial creditors in Organization for Economic Cooperation and Development (OECD) countries, with corresponding guarantees from their governments. When the Gambian borrower defaulted, both guarantees were called, and the obligation became a claim against the Gambian government. The IMF stand-by agreements that supported the ERP prohibited further government guarantees.

The importance of these changes was illustrated in 1987, when the Gambia Utilities Corporation (with the support of the Ministry of Public Works) reached preliminary agreement with an external company to purchase a new electricity generator, financed with a supplier's credit. Although the need for new generation facilities was not disputed, the proposed generator was unusually expensive, and the terms of the loan were unfavorable. When the project was brought to Cabinet for approval, the minister of finance reminded Cabinet of the government's policy com-mitments and maintained that the proposed project threatened the IMF agreement. The proposal was rejected. A less expensive generator, financed on concessional terms, was installed later. Similarly, the government rejected loan guarantees on several private-sector projects, most of which (including a large new tourist hotel) proceeded without the guarantee.

The fourth change focused on the quality of the projects financed by external debt. At the insistence of the World Bank, only projects whose internal rate of return was greater than 15 percent were included in the public investment program as of 1985. Although this criterion was not particularly stringent, it forced the government to evaluate its proposed projects more carefully and to reject the poorest ones.

In addition to these debt-specific policies, the macroeconomic policies introduced under the ERP helped curtail the growth in external debt. The most important policy was reducing the government budget deficit, so that less had to be borrowed to finance government recurrent expen-ditures. In addition, the depreciation of the exchange rate and the increase in real interest rates helped dampen private consumption and the current account deficit, further reducing the need for external borrowing.

Together, these policy changes—some of which required continuous support by Cabinet—helped curtail the growth of external debt during the late 1980s. These decisions were one important reason for the decline in The Gambia's debt service ratios in the early 1990s. The extent to which the government continues to follow these policies will have a major impact on both economic growth and the burden of external debt during the remainder of the 1990s.

Debt Rescheduling and Refinancing

The second of the government's debt management initiatives was to refinance and reschedule some of its overdue obligations. The Gambia's debt service arrears reached US$105 million in 1986, and it was clear that it would be impossible for the government to repay these obligations quickly (IMF, 1986). The IMF stand-by agreement in 1986 enabled the government to initiate negotiations with both the Paris Club (the group of OECD-member bilateral creditors) and the London Club (the group of commercial bank creditors).

A total of US$17.7 million in obligations was rescheduled with members of the Paris Club. The Gambia was given a five-year grace period (1987 to 1992), with five years to repay (1992 to 1997). Interest rates differed across creditor countries but averaged 7.2 percent. Of the amount rescheduled, US$6.7 million (38 percent) was for overdue obliga-tions on a government-owned (and technically bankrupt) hotel; another US$6.1 million (34 percent) was originally private-sector debt that either had been guaranteed by the government or had become a government obligation when sufficient foreign exchange was not available for the debtor to make scheduled payments.

A total of US$21 million was refinanced with the members of the London Club. Of this amount, US$2 million was paid up front as a "goodwill" gesture during the negotiations; US$1 million was due in each of the first three years (1988 to 1990), and US$4 million was due each year between 1991 and 1994. Of the total, US$18 million (86 percent) was owed to Standard Chartered Bank (London); US$10.6 million (50 percent) was due on the same government hotel whose debts had been rescheduled under the Paris Club. Thus, this single hotel accounted for US$17.3 million (45 percent) of the amounts rescheduled with the Paris and London Clubs.

The government also rescheduled its arrears of US$6 million with the Islamic Development Bank (IDB). These amounts were overdue on loans to the state-owned Gambia Utilities Corporation and the National Trading Corporation (NTC). Although the IDB did not provide a grace period for repaying the loans, it did not charge late interest on the overdue amounts. Moreover, only 35 percent of the arrears was repayable in foreign exchange; the remainder was repaid in dalasis to finance the local cost of IDB-sponsored projects in The Gambia.

The Central Bank also reached an *unofficial* rescheduling agreement in 1988 on its overdue obligations of US$20 million with the West African Clearing House (WACH). The agreement called for eight quarterly payments of US$2.5 million between 1988 and 1990. The agreement was never formally signed because it gave more favorable terms (a higher interest rate and more rapid repayment) to the WACH than the government had given to the members of the London Club. Rather than sign the WACH agreement and violate the London Club accord, the Central Bank verbally agreed to repay the WACH by the terms of the unsigned agreement.

Thus, US$65 million in debt—30 percent of The Gambia's total foreign debt—was rescheduled between 1986 and 1988. These reschedulings rationalized the debt portfolio and provided immediate balance-of-payments relief during the ERP. However, the rescheduled amounts created a bulge in debt service due between 1992 and 1994. The government began to prepare for the bulge in payments with a structured program to build up foreign exchange reserves between 1986 and 1992. In 1990 the bulge in debt service obligations and the overall debt burden were eased further when the government of France canceled its remaining official bilateral claims against The Gambia as part of its program to forgive debt throughout SSA.

Repayment of Arrears

After the reschedulings the government had remaining arrears of approximately US$41 million. These were repaid steadily between 1986 and 1990.

The Gambia was obliged to make the repayments because the IMF had imposed quarterly ceilings on arrears as part of its stand-by agreement and ESAF arrangement. In the last few days of each quarter, the Central Bank would make a flurry of payments to the creditor whose requests had been most vocal, that had an upcoming important meeting with the government, or from which the government wished to borrow additional funds.

The government was able to repay these arrears mainly because it had received large foreign exchange grants and soft loans from the donor community in support of the ERP (see Chapter 4). While some aid flows were used to finance current consumption and investment (that is, to finance the current account deficit), a large amount, including the World Bank's Structural Adjustment Loans, was used to pay current and overdue debt service obligations and to replenish the government's foreign exchange reserves. Thus, The Gambia's experience illustrates that although the World Bank and other multilateral agencies never explicitly refinance or reschedule their existing loans, their loans can be an important source of implicit refinancing. Given the concessional terms of the World Bank loans (a forty-year repayment period, a ten-year grace period, and a .75 percent service charge), this approach was very favorable to The Gambia.

Concluding Observations about External Debt Management

By the end of the ERP, The Gambia's external debt situation had eased considerably. The ratio of external debt to GDP fell from 229 percent in 1986 to 146 percent in 1990, and its arrears were extinguished completely. Moreover, the terms of the debt had softened significantly. The grant element in new commitments undertaken between 1986 and 1990 averaged 74 percent, and no new loans had been contracted with private creditors. The ratio of debt service to exports fell from 33 percent to 11 percent between 1986 and 1989. It surged again to 26 percent in 1990 when the first rescheduled payments fell due, then declined sharply again in 1991.

Perhaps the most important lesson from the Gambian experience is that a *combination* of changes in economic policies and donor support is crucial to reducing external debt. The commitment to stop new nonconcessional borrowing, parastatal borrowing, and government guarantees, together with more effective macroeconomic policies, helped reduce the growth in and improve the terms of new borrowing. A significant amount of donor financing went to repaying debt service arrears, paying current debt service payments, and building up foreign exchange reserves.

Neither strategy alone would have led to a sustainable reduction in The Gambia's debt service burden.

Despite this turnaround not all aspects of The Gambia's debt administration and management during the ERP were successful. The unsuccessful attempt to install the GEDRES debt-monitoring system as a more permanent tool for economic management highlights the difficulties of introducing institutional changes. As with other aspects of the ERP, policy changes that required a one-time decision (such as the ban on new nonconcessional borrowing) were much easier to implement than were changes that required long-term institutional changes. For GEDRES this was due at least partially to the necessity of devoting most of the available administrative talent to short-term issues. This example provides an important lesson for structural adjustment programs worldwide—that institutional changes, even apparently small ones, are likely to require far more time, effort, and commitment than is often anticipated.

While the overall situation has improved, the amount of debt outstanding is still large. The major question surrounding The Gambia's foreign debt is whether the progress achieved during the ERP can be maintained. The key to meeting this objective is to avoid the major problems that created the debt burden in the first place. Toward this end, several of the policies introduced during the ERP must be strengthened and sustained. First, debt-financed development projects must be appraised more carefully than in the past. Second, the government should continue its moratoria on contracting commercial debt and providing government guarantees. Finally, the government should continue to implement policies that mobilize domestic savings to finance investment projects, primarily by reducing the government budget deficit further but also by encouraging private savings.

NOTES

1. This includes the grant element of commitments from all creditors, according to various issues of the World Bank's *World Debt Tables*.
2. After the presentations one participant remarked from the floor that anyone who was not confused had not been listening.
3. In making this judgment, the staff had the advantage of a comment tabled by one of the software vendors at the June 1985 IBRD-sponsored conference. Noting the discrepancies between initial entries and creditor records of transaction dates and amounts—due to exchange

rate fluctuations, the passage of each payment through several agents, and uncertainty about the purpose of a drawing—the vendor, Interafricaine de Conseils d'Assistance, stated: "To achieve precise figures for dates and amounts on each transaction, ten times more work is required than for the simple capture of loan balances." It urged users of its system to begin with a statistical rather than an accounting approach (World Bank, 1985a).

4. The *World Debt Tables'* annual rating of data submitted to the Bank's External Debt Division by reporting countries lifted The Gambia from the lowest of three categories in 1986–1987 to the highest in 1987–1988, and then in two steps back to the bottom in 1990–1991.

12

Rationalizing Domestic Debt

Catherine J. McAuliffe and Malcolm F. McPherson

Starting in the mid-1970s, the government and the public enterprises were unable to generate the revenue necessary to cover their expenditures. Borrowing—and thus public-sector domestic debt—mounted rapidly. Over time the resulting debt service and other obligations were not discharged fully. The government and the PEs had undischarged interlocking obligations. Loan guarantees provided by the government to the Gambia Commercial and Development Bank on behalf of private individuals and the PEs were not honored. In turn, those defaults prevented the GCDB from repaying its loans to the Central Bank. Government payments to local contractors and suppliers were overdue. And some government expenditures were being financed through suspense accounts at the Central Bank; in effect, the Central Bank allowed the treasury to run up arrears as well.

The rapid accumulation of domestic debt and arrears was largely a product of the overall economic deterioration. The basic cause was a breakdown in financial discipline throughout the public sector. The government did not retire the arrears in a regular manner until the donor community made the elimination of arrears a specific condition of that support.

In The Gambia and other countries, domestic debt problems typically arise between a government and its parastatals when normal budgeting and financial management procedures break down.[1] Under these circumstances the close association between the government and the parastatals makes it easy for either party to avoid payments in order to ease cash flow problems. The government might fail to pay its electricity, telephone, or medical bills on time; the parastatals might fail to transfer taxes collected on behalf of the government or to service debts owed to the government.

The literature contains numerous references to the problems of domestic debt and interlocking arrears.[2] However, detailed analyses of the financial and budgetary implications of interlocking arrears and unserviced debt are rare (Reisen, 1989). Indeed, textbook treatments of budgeting and public finance (Premchand, 1983) generally do not mention the problem.

The work that has been done on the subject generally concludes that the key issues are (1) determining how to unravel the interlocking arrears without creating additional macroeconomic instability and (2) developing procedures to prevent their recurrence. There are several possible ways to unravel the debt. For example, mutual arrears can be offset; debt owed to the government can be written off, written down, converted to equity, refinanced, or rescheduled; and debts owed by the government can be paid in cash or through some long-dated instruments such as a treasury bill or bond.

Preventing interlocking arrears from recurring requires reestablishing budget and financial discipline. The problem usually does not require new regulations; better enforcement of existing rules and conventions will usually suffice. In this respect, an important objective is to develop procedures for improved monitoring of and stronger penalties for domestic arrears.

This chapter explores the nature of the arrears problem, how it arose in The Gambia, its economic effects, and how it has been rationalized. The concluding section discusses some lessons from the experience. Annex A reviews common options for dealing with arrears.

Debt and Arrears

Background

As part of its normal operations, any government incurs debt—that is, it commits itself to a future stream of payments in return for current access to real resources. Short-term debt such as "ways and means" advances from the central bank cover temporary shortfalls in government receipts; long-term borrowing with bonds permits the government to support the expansion of public infrastructure or to invest in long-lived assets. When government expenditures grow at about the same rate as government revenue, the debt can be serviced without difficulty. However, when expenditure growth exceeds revenue growth over a long period of time, debt service begins to absorb a larger share of the government budget.

Only a limited amount of debt can be incurred without creating major macroeconomic distortions. Literature on industrialized countries has focused heavily on the notion of "crowding out" (that is, the extent to which government borrowing restricts the access of the private sector to financing). The ultimate threshold is whether savers (local and foreign) will voluntarily release their surplus resources. Beyond that, arrears accumulate. As with the "forced savings" associated with inflationary finance, arrears involve the involuntary post hoc release of resources to the government. They tend to emerge after the government has exhausted other forms of finance or is unwilling to continue financing its deficit with additional borrowing from domestic banks.[3]

Domestic Debt and Arrears in The Gambia

The rapid expansion of the government after the mid-1970s sharply increased the budget deficit. During the initial stages the deficit was financed with foreign and domestic borrowing. In 1974–1975, at the beginning of the first five-year plan, the government had a cash surplus of US$1.7 million with the local banking system and an external debt of US$11.7 million (approximately 10 percent of GDP). By 1980–1981 it owed the local banking system the equivalent of US$25.7 million and its external creditors US$77.6 million. At that stage the government could no longer fully service its debts, and arrears emerged on both domestic and foreign debt.

Table 12-1 provides an overview of the government budget and the role of arrears in financing that deficit.[4] From 1975–1976 the budget deficit increased as expenditures rose more rapidly than revenue. At the start of the first five-year plan in 1974–1975, government expenditures were 19 percent of GDP; a decade later, in 1984–1985, they were 38 percent of GDP. Corresponding data for revenue were 16 percent and 27 percent, respectively. Budget arrears began to accumulate in 1983–1984. They declined in 1985–1986 as the ERP policies took effect.

As with the government, PE expenditures increased dramatically from the mid-1970s onward. Due to mismanagement, poor planning, malfeasance,

Table 12-1. Arrears and the Government Budget, 1983–1984 to 1987–1988 (Millions of Dalasis)

	Pre-ERP		ERP			
	1983–84	1984–85	1985–86	1986–87	1987–88	1988–89
Government revenue	153	180	275	480	495	576
Government expenditures	211	262	258	542	607	516
Change in arrears	21	26	−35	−14	−5	−25
Deficit (including grants)	−37	−57	−18	−76	−118	34
Arrears as % of GDP	3.5	13.9	−4.1	−1.3	0.4	−1.7

Source: Ministry of Finance and Economic Affairs

and pricing policies that prevented the PEs from covering their costs, a large number of activities undertaken by the PEs were unproductive. Their losses mounted, and arrears emerged (see Chapter 16). Many enterprises did not pay their government obligations, such as taxes, levies, debt service, and revenues collected on behalf of the government.

The interlocking arrears between the government and the PEs were large. Tables 12-2 and 12-3 give data for 1985 and 1986, respectively. In 1985 the government failed to make D6.3 million in current payments to the PEs, which was equivalent to 3.8 percent of current government expenditures and 11.5 percent of the total financing requirement for the year. In 1986 the government accumulated an additional D9.6 million in arrears (3.9 percent of its current expenditures and 13.1 percent of its total financing requirement). At the same time, PEs missed payments of D7.9 million in 1985 and an additional D7 million in 1986. On a net basis the arrears were D1.5 million in favor of the government in 1985 and D2.6 million in favor of the PEs in 1986.

Table 12-2. Arrears Between Parastatals and the Government (Thousands of Dalasis) as of December 31, 1985

Public Enterprise	Owed to Government Current-Year Arrears	Owed to Government Accumulated Arrears	Owed to PEs Current-Year Arrears	Owed to PEs Accumulated Arrears	Net Position Current-Year Arrears	Net Position Accumulated Arrears
GNIC	1,101		36		1,065	
GPMB	257			12,797	257	−12,797
GUC	4,128	64,640	4,008	10,970	120	53,670
GPA	14	10,046	1,844	5,859	−1,830	4,187
GAMTEL			191		−191	
GPTC	311			142	311	−142
GCU		34,006				34,006
NTC			53		−53	
LMB	101				101	
SSHFC						
Atlantic Hotel	1,431		104		1,327	
Senegambia Hotel	541		94		447	
Gambia Airways			4		−4	
Total	7,884	108,692	6,335	29,769	1,549	78,922

Note: A negative entry is a net debit (−).
GNIC = Gambia National Insurance Corporation; GPMB = Gambia Produce Marketing Board; GUC = Gambia Utilities Corporation; GPA = Gambia Ports Authority; GAMTEL = Gambia Telecommunications Company; GPTC = Gambia Public Transport Corporation; GCU = Gambia Cooperatives Union; NTC = National Trading Corporation; LMB = Livestock Marketing Board; SSHFC = Social Security and Housing Finance Corporation.

Table 12-3. Arrears Between Parastatals and the Government (Thousands of Dalasis) as of December 31, 1986

	Owed to Government		Owed to PEs		Net Position	
Public Enterprise	Current-Year Arrears	Accumulated Arrears	Current-Year Arrears	Accumulated Arrears	Current-Year Arrears	Accumulated Arrears
GNIC	286		34		252	
GPMB	257			12,797	257	−12,797
GUC	4,971	67,780	5,217	10,200	−244	57,580
GPA	14	9,613	2,188	6,344	−2,173	3,270
GAMTEL			800		−800	
GPTC	486		276	142	210	−142
GCU		34,006				34,006
NTC			60		−60	
LMB	44		56		−12	
SSHFC	37				37	
Atlantic Hotel	155		330		−175	
Senegambia Hotel	726		83		642	
Gambia Airways			570		−570	
Total	6,977	111,399	9,613	29,484	−2,636	81,914

Note: A negative entry is a net debit (−).
GNIC = Gambia National Insurance Corporation; GPMB = Gambia Produce Marketing Board; GUC = Gambia Utilities Corporation; GPA = Gambia Ports Authority; GAMTEL = Gambia Telecommunications Company; GPTC = Gambia Public Transport Corporation; GCU = Gambia Cooperatives Union; NTC =

Government arrears also emerged indirectly through government bank guarantees and PE ownership. Government guarantees to domestic banks were minimal in the mid-1970s, but they reached major proportions by the early 1980s. Some projects failed, and the borrowers could not repay. In the majority of cases, the borrowers (both individuals and PEs) *refused* to pay. The volume of outstanding unserviced debt on government-guaranteed loans became so large that they threatened the viability of the entire financial system (Wing, 1983; World Bank, 1985c). In 1987 the GCDB held D72.6 million in government guarantees on loans, equivalent to 35 percent of its asset base and 19 percent of all commercial bank assets. One reason for the insolvency of the GCDB was that the government had not honored its guarantees.

Government ownership of PEs increased its contingent liabilities. For example, in 1977–1978 the PEs had operating profits of D18.8 million; by 1982–1983 their operating losses were D47.7 million (World Bank, 1985c, Table 7.1). Bank borrowing funded those losses. By mid-1986 the PEs owed the local banks (primarily the GCDB and the Central Bank) D217 million (approximately US$32 million). A considerable proportion of this debt (for example, the Gambia Cooperatives Union's debt to the GCDB) was overdue. Thus indirectly through its equity, the government was in arrears. It had other arrears as well, most of which became evident only as efforts to straighten out the public-sector accounts unfolded. Examples include the D12.5 million in rent owed by the government to the Central Bank in 1990, which had been accruing since 1979; charges incurred by the Central Bank for operating and eventually liquidating the defunct Agricultural Development Bank; and unserviced advances from the Central Bank to the government to finance emergency generating equipment for the Gambia Utilities Corporation and to pay for the extension of Yundum airport. In addition to its other debts, the GUC was accumulating arrears to the government on its fuel purchases. Finally, the Gambia Cooperatives Union had not recapitalized several revolving funds that had been set up by donors.

Why Did the Government Allow Arrears to Emerge?

The government could have prevented arrears simply by requiring that the Central Bank finance all of its domestic expenditures in full and on time (by using "ways and means" advances or treasury bills, *not* suspended accounts). Why did it not do so? There were two reasons. First, allowing arrears to accumulate helped the government meet the credit targets agreed to with the IMF, at least for a while.[5] That response has been common in developing countries (Diamond and Schiller, 1987). Second, for strategic and/or political reasons, the government was not prepared to pay PEs that were not discharging their obligations. This created a cycle in which the PEs would not pay the government because the government would not pay them, and vice versa.

Despite being a large net creditor to the PEs, the government was in a weak position to force payment. Financial monitoring in any meaningful sense did not exist. Estimates of current revenue and expenditures were often several months out-of-date, and the government's debt records were incomplete (see Chapter 11). Lacking reliable data, the government could not force PEs to pay, because the PEs could challenge the amounts.[6] Furthermore, the PEs could make the valid argument that their arrears arose because the government had failed to pay for the services they had provided or had interfered in their output and/or pricing decisions.

As the economy continued to deteriorate, the government and the PEs alike had few incentives to pay their mutual obligations. The immediate financial benefits of not paying were large, and there were no associated costs. As the interlocking arrears mounted, it became increasingly more rational for both sides simply not to pay current obligations.

The Consequences of Arrears

At one level, mutual arrears between the PEs and the government are economically and financially innocuous. On a consolidated basis the net worth of the public sector is unaffected by such indebtedness. What is the financial harm of having the government owe itself resources that, through one of its agents, it does not repay? Vertically integrated private enterprises often have a large amount of interlocking debt without apparent adverse effects.[7]

On a strict accounting basis, it is difficult to make the case that mutually offsetting arrears between the government and the PEs have any relevance. It is also difficult to argue that arrears have adverse effects if they occur irregularly. All enterprises, public and private, experience cash flow disruptions that may cause them to delay some payments. But arrears do have economically and financially adverse effects when they persist or are used strategically.[8] The persistence of arrears is evidence that established financial and accounting practices have broken down. The strategic use of arrears is an explicit change in the behavior of the debtor, which uses the arrears to gain access to additional interest-free resources. When the government is in arrears, the resources are not only interest-free but are equivalent to a tax.

The distortions created in both instances have real resource costs (Fye and McPherson, 1987). Current payment arrears, for example, imply that a creditor has made an additional loan to the debtor. Debt service arrears imply that a debtor has unilaterally rescheduled the debt with a creditor that involuntarily provides the debt relief. If the creditor already has equity in a debtor's operations (as with the government and PEs), the grants or debt relief are equivalent to providing additional equity unintentionally.[9] Enterprises that benefit the most from the unintended equity are typically those that incur the largest losses—a clearly nonoptimal way to use any nation's resources.

The involuntary transfers distort the allocation of resources in the economy by giving organizations access to resources that, on efficiency grounds, they would normally be denied. By accumulating arrears, debtors are able to maintain levels of output that cannot be justified by their debt-servicing capacity. Conversely, creditors experience an unanticipated loss of resources. Unless they also accumulate arrears (as occurred in The Gambia) or raise additional resources, their output will fall. Economic efficiency declines because the economically inefficient individuals and firms increase their share of overall economic activity. Efficient enterprises are at a further disadvantage because they are crowded out of access to resources. Moreover, the resources they can get come at a higher cost.

The accumulation of arrears erodes the asset base of creditors and reduces their profitability, thereby preventing them from expanding further. For the government, the nonpayment of current payments by debtors increases the budget deficit, which, if not offset by expenditure cuts, nonbank borrowing, tax receipts, or grants, increases government arrears or forces it to borrow further from the banking system. Any increase in the volume of bank credit will have potentially adverse effects on domestic prices, the balance of payments, and/or the exchange rate.

The accumulation of arrears distorts the structure of assets and liabilities. The debtor has a liability that it does not service; the creditor has an asset that is not being serviced. When the assets of both organizations are revalued regularly—for example, through a stock market—the consequent decline in asset quality would be reflected in the market value of the creditor firm. If the debt were traded in secondary markets, its rate of discount would increase.

In the absence of regular market revaluations of assets and corresponding debt, or when accounting procedures do not reflect the eroding quality of assets, third parties may unwittingly incur arrears. The third party (often a state-owned bank) may also face political pressure to lend to organizations whose asset positions are distorted. In The Gambia the financial viability of the GCDB was undermined, in part, because of government requests to make loans to many nonviable organizations.

Persistent arrears, as in The Gambia, can also have an impact on costs and prices in the economy. For creditors arrears imply forced financing. Anticipating the further accumulation of arrears, suppliers adjust prices to allow for payment delays. Creditors will often require higher interest rates on future loans, especially if they anticipate that the loans will not be repaid as scheduled.

Resolving the Arrears Situation

The ERP incorporated several measures for alleviating the arrears problem. It used expenditure controls and revenue-enhancing actions to reimpose fiscal discipline and thus reduce the budget deficit. The parastatal reform program began to improve the financial management of PEs, with beneficial effects on their profitability (see Chapter 16). The performance contracts between the government and the PEs included specific agreements to eliminate the arrears. The government also created a managed fund of nonperforming government-guaranteed debts in order to remove the debts from the GCDB's portfolio. The special deposit account for the local counterpart of external debt service payments was brought up-to-date and administered properly. The government and the Central Bank also sought to unravel the more than 250 suspense accounts on the Central Bank's books.

The IMF and World Bank imposed conditions to initiate the process of eliminating the arrears. Under the 1986–1987 stand-by agreement, the government agreed to prevent further arrears. The National Investment Board was required to monitor the arrears and report on them on a quarterly basis. The World Bank was instrumental in establishing the managed fund (World Bank, 1985c) and enforcing the implementation of the performance contract system.

The magnitude and complexity of arrears necessitated a structured program for eliminating them. Some debts could be resolved by offsetting mutual obligations. Other debts required a combination of write-offs, write-downs, refinancing, rescheduling, and/or the conversion of the debt to equity (see Annex A). The real resource costs of these measures were greatly eased by the government's access to counterpart funds. Those funds, which had been sterilized under the IMF program so as to avoid pressure on the foreign exchange market, allowed the government to straighten out the books without incurring major charges against current or future budgets.

Government/PE Interlocking Arrears

Performance contracts sought to formalize the responsibilities and obligations of both the government and the PEs. Under the contracts the financial operations of the PEs were to be disentangled from those of the government, and procedures were established for keeping them separate. Eliminating interlocking arrears was an important first step in that process.

The government also made a commitment to budget its taxes and subsidies explicitly and to force the parastatals to operate on commercial terms. Those changes sought to ensure full disclosure of the financial interrelationships between the government and the PEs and to ensure that the financial costs borne by the public sector approximated the social opportunity cost of the resources being used.

The first three performance contracts were negotiated with the GPMB, the Gambia Ports Authority, and the GUC (see Chapter 16). The GPA was financially sound. Eliminating its arrears was straightforward. After offsetting mutual debts, the GPA paid off its net balance to the government in quarterly installments in 1986–1987. For the GUC, the task was more complicated, given its long-term and chronic arrears (some of which had been outstanding since 1978) and their value (D72.8 million at the end of 1986). As already noted, the GUC disputed some of the debt. Eventually, an agreement was reached to (1) cancel mutual debts of D14.6 million, (2) convert D26 million of debt into equity, and (3) reschedule the remaining D29.9 million over twenty years, with a ten-year grace period, at 9 percent interest. That interest rate was half the prevailing bank rate at the time.[10]

For the GPMB, government officials recognized that the board's accumulated marketing losses were a major obstacle to restoring its financial viability. The agreement with the GPMB was expanded beyond the objective of eliminating interlocking arrears. The government used its creditor position with the Central Bank to retire the GPMB's pre-1986–1987 debts of D95.8 million. For its part the GPMB wrote off the D12.8 million that was owed by the government.

Government-Guaranteed Debt

The managed fund of government-guaranteed debt was established in January 1987. The fund was suggested by the World Bank Financial Sector Review mission in 1983 as a way to deal with the precarious financial state of the GCDB (World Bank, 1985c).

The managed fund consisted of twenty-four loans with an outstanding value of D74 million owed to the GCDB and guaranteed by the government. Some of the loans, including several to the GCU, had not been serviced at all. Others, such as the loan to a local manufacturer, were being serviced irregularly. The managed fund was established to ensure that the government honored its guarantees. To establish the fund, the government borrowed from the Central Bank at the prevailing bank rate. The interest bill on the debt alone for 1987–1988 was D14 million.[11]

By creating the managed fund, the government demonstrated that it would honor its guarantees. It also strengthened the finances of the GCDB and provided a mechanism for attempting to collect the outstanding debt. An interministerial committee was charged with pursuing the debtors to work out mutually acceptable repayment schedules.[12] The collection of outstanding debt was slow. Only D9.5 million (13 percent of the original amount) was collected between 1987 and 1991. The committee responsible for collecting the debts classified D58.6 million (or 79 percent of the original balance) as nonrecoverable, and these loans effectively were written off.

Other Arrears

The government paid off its debt to the Central Bank for the GUC (the emergency loans for generators) and the extensions to the Yundum airport in 1988. Central Bank expenses incurred in operating and liquidating the Agriculture Development Bank were paid in 1989. The back rent owed by the government was discharged in 1990. And the net amount of the miscellaneous items outstanding in Central Bank suspense accounts was dealt with in 1990.

Despite several agreements to pay, the GUC did not discharge the arrears to the government for payments for fuel. By June 1989 they exceeded D20 million. They increased by another D20 million in 1989–1990. After the GUC repeatedly failed to honor its commitment to reduce the arrears, the IMF made their reduction an explicit performance criterion.

Revaluation losses from the depreciation of the dalasi incurred by the Central Bank on the government's behalf exceeded D450 million by December 1987. In effect, since no formal arrangement had been made for these losses, the Central Bank had allowed another government account to move into arrears. The amounts were eventually covered in 1988, when the Parliament approved the issuance of non–interest-bearing, nonredeemable notes to the Central Bank.

Summary

The most economically debilitating aspects of the arrears situation in The Gambia were brought under control during the ERP. Difficulties still arose from time to time. For instance, the hotels did not always promptly turn over revenue collected for the government. That situation changed after the government enacted the National Sales Tax Act in 1988 and the MoF improved tax collection procedures. Due to pressure on its travel budget, the government often delayed payments to Gambia Airways in order to deflect the attention of donors away from this expenditure item. And arrears on customs duties, particularly for items taken on direct delivery, reached levels that prompted an official inquiry (see Chapter 17).[13]

The Gambia made significant progress in reducing its arrears. This change helped enhance accountability, reduce the accumulation of new arrears, and improve resource allocation. But it did not eliminate them, and the government continued to incur additional arrears (albeit on a smaller scale) when it was expedient to do so, both during and after the ERP.

Concluding Observations about Rationalizing Domestic Debt

Persistent public-sector arrears are an index of financial indiscipline. The practical requirement for avoiding arrears is simple: the government and its agencies must ensure that their expenditures and revenue grow at rates that allow their obligations to be discharged on time and in full.

The emergence of payment difficulties and especially payment arrears should be a signal to debtors that the current financial situation is unsustainable and that adjustments must be made. One strategy would be to reach a mutually acceptable agreement between the creditor(s) and debtor(s) to resolve the arrears systematically. Another would be to have debtors avoid using arrears as a means of gaining access to additional resources.

In The Gambia poor accounting, the absence of accountability, a lack of financial responsibility, and strategic considerations allowed domestic arrears to escalate. The ERP made progress toward unraveling the interlocking arrears between the government and the PEs and developing procedures to prevent them from recurring. Essential to this effort was the oversight provided by donor agencies.

Although the exercise was time-consuming and difficult, its real (resource) costs were minimized by the availability of counterpart funds. Domestic savings have not been absorbed to reduce the arrears. That strategy was convenient; whether it was wise is unclear. The apparent low cost of dealing with the arrears may tempt the government to allow arrears to accumulate in the future, especially if it is no longer under strict donor surveillance. Because both the government and the PEs continue to use arrears strategically, that is a real possibility.

Annex A: Debt Write-Offs and Other Options

Many options to reduce the debt burden on an organization are available. They include write-offs, write-downs, refinancing, rescheduling, and the conversion of the debt to equity. The relative merits of these options differ.

A *debt write-off* grants the debtor a waiver of both the principal and accumulated interest. The creditor absorbs the loss. Write-offs have several disadvantages. They:

- do not involve a penalty for debtors who fail to honor the original loan agreement;
- improve the debtor's balance sheet by (involuntarily) adding resources that could not be obtained by the debtor's productive efforts;
- do not ensure that the conditions that created the arrears have been dealt with;

- adversely affect managerial incentives by creating the expectation that the creditor (particularly if it is the government) will forgive other debts when they become a burden;
- have high opportunity costs for the creditor, since they divert resources from more productive investments.

An additional complication for the Gambian government is that many of the debts involved were loans from external creditors that were on-lent. Write-offs do not extinguish the original obligations.

In general, debt write-offs are counterproductive; they should be used only as a last resort and (possibly) only to rescue an important PE from liquidation. They should never be provided without explicit action to remove the original cause of the arrears. However, a debt write-off would be justified if the debt had been incurred at the government's direction or if the government imposed controls that directly prevented the PE from covering its costs.

A *debt write-down* involves the partial forgiveness of the debt. The creditor may agree to this action in order to prevent the debtor from failing. By forgoing a part of the debt, the creditor may be able to recover the remainder.

Refinancing is typically expensive for the creditor. He or she provides additional resources in exchange for the debtor's commitment to be more diligent about repayments in the future. For governments that are cutting their expenditures, refinancing is unattractive.

Debt rescheduling is common. It involves having the creditor accept the principle that responsible asset management requires flexibility. Debt rescheduling entails some losses to the creditor, because the terms of the original debt will not be met. But it is often the least-cost method for ensuring that the debtor will repay. From the debtor's perspective rescheduling provides an additional period of relief from principal payments that can be used to improve financial performance.

The *conversion of debt* to equity favors the debtor by effectively formalizing the situation that began with the buildup of arrears. For most creditors, including the government, this option is undesirable because it means taking a larger stake in an organization that has already demonstrated its unreliability. Another unattractive feature is that it increases the government's equity in PEs at a time when most are attempting to divest. The advantage of debt conversions is that they reduce the financial burden on the organization.

NOTES

1. The analysis presented here focuses on long-term systemic domestic debt problems. It does not consider temporary payment difficulties as part of the problem.
2. World Bank, 1986, pp. 21–24; Lacey, 1989, p. 29; Shirley, 1989, p. 12; Lee and Nellis, 1990; McKinnon, 1991, p. 6.
3. Few governments legislate against the opportunity to borrow domestically (Indonesia is a notable exception).
4. The magnitude of the arrears problem is difficult to identify and quantify. In practice, considerable discretion exists in classifying overdue payments as arrears. Yet even if a consistent classification were used, measurement would remain a problem. Many data in The Gambia were reported only after long delays and were subject to large inaccuracies.
5. As soon as the IMF staff discovered the arrears, they began to monitor the budget deficit on a commitment basis. The government then relied more heavily on suspense accounts at the Central Bank until the IMF discovered unexplained movements in "other items (net)" in the monetary survey and therefore began to monitor movements in aggregate "domestic assets" in the monetary survey. Another outlet through which the government diverted pressure from its budget—having the public enterprises fund particular items—was cut off when performance contracts were introduced (see Chapter 16).
6. The GUC and the GCU used that tactic regularly to deflect attention from their debts. For instance, GUC staff continually referred to a 1983 Cabinet decision that they maintained had converted their debt to equity, and claimed that one of their earlier debts had been paid. To dispense with the disputes, the MoF finally accepted the GUC's own data.
7. Indeed, as students of transfer pricing among transnational corporations point out, interlocking debt works to the advantage of vertically integrated firms. One local manufacturing company in The Gambia has made a loss each year since it began operations in 1976. Its major shareholder, which is also its main foreign supplier, has given no indication that it will close the firm.
8. The distinction is a fine one. All managers understand that when they have established a reputation for honoring their debts in full and on time their creditors will show forbearance if some payments are inadvertently delayed. Their reputation collapses, however, when they begin regularly to let payments slide. In the first case, the arrears are unintentional; in the second, they are intentional. Only the second case has lasting economic and financial consequences.

9. Recent financial literature has focused on the breakdown of the distinction between equity and debt (Kopcke and Rosengren, 1989). For instance, questions have arisen about whether holders of junk bonds provide loans that would be serviced regularly or equity upon which dividends may eventually be paid. But this distinction views the situation only from the debtor's perspective. Asset holders had a different expectation when they purchased the debt. Had they wanted equity, they could have used other markets more productively. Asset holders have different expectations about the security, liquidity, and yield of debt instruments relative to equity claims.

10. The total in the agreement was D70.5 million, in contrast to the amount of D72.8 million in Table 12-3. The former was taken from the GUC's records; the latter from the government's (see note 6 herein).

11. Having established the principle that it would honor its guarantees (as well as demonstrating to the politicians that guarantees often involve substantial costs), the government cut its interest bill in 1988–1989 by using its accumulated cash balances to retire the Central Bank loan.

12. One of the first issues raised when the committee began its work was the location of the relevant documents. None of the loans had been documented properly. The mortgages either were missing or had been released prematurely, and the loan guarantees had been completely ad hoc.

13. Reports by the auditor general and an external investigation of customs by two experts (see Dunlop and Livings, 1992) indicate that the practice continues.

Part III

Sectoral and Institutional Reform

13

Macroeconomic Reform and Agriculture

Malcolm F. McPherson

The deteriorating economic performance in The Gambia in the early 1980s directed attention to the problems with agriculture. The agricultural sector was the country's largest employer and primary source of export revenue. Obvious difficulties were drought and low world prices for groundnuts. The latter was particularly evident in 1982–1983, when despite the sharp recovery of groundnut production from its drought-affected levels of a year earlier, world groundnut prices fell by more than 40 percent.

Yet drought and fluctuating foreign prices were recurrent phenomena with which producers had been dealing for many years. The problems confronting agriculture were more basic—low farmgate prices, a shortage of inputs, an overvalued exchange rate, disintegrating rural infrastructure, and predatory policies by agriculture-related public enterprises.

Intensifying the general concern was the decline in food availability in 1983 and 1984, when the local harvest failed and the government could not find adequate foreign exchange to import additional food. Thus by the time the ERP was formulated, all parties agreed that a major effort was needed to revitalize agriculture. Indeed, many believed that the ERP could not succeed unless the performance of agriculture improved dramatically.

In The Gambia, as in other developing countries, long-term results in agriculture arise from concrete policy choices about the rate and pattern of technological innovation, the supply of agricultural inputs, incentives for farmers, and rural infrastructure. A successful broad-based agricultural strategy provides cash income and a pattern of demand that promotes growth in the rural nonfarm economy. Furthermore, appropriate rural infrastructure to serve agriculture (roads, electric power, communications, and marketplaces in rural towns) also lowers costs and expands opportunities for rural nonfarm enterprises. Finally, investments in human capital—especially rural primary education, but also selective public health interventions—are essential elements of successful strategies for agricultural development.

The agricultural crisis in The Gambia and the rest of SSA indicated that macroeconomic policies have a more powerful influence on agricultural incentives than do sectoral policies. If the exchange rate is overvalued, if interest rates are kept artificially low, and if other key prices that guide decisionmakers are distorted—all of which are characteristics of The Gambia prior to the ERP and of many SSA countries—the transfer of inappropriate agricultural technology is the likely outcome. Moreover, sound macroeconomic management, particularly control over the government budget, is a prerequisite for adequate funding for government spending on essential public goods and services such as rural infrastructure, agricultural research institutions, primary education, and public health.

Many of these issues were central to the problems faced by the Gambian agricultural sector prior to the ERP. While the ERP has made a start toward revitalizing the agricultural sector, much still must be done. This chapter examines the impact of the ERP policies on agriculture. It begins by reviewing the performance of agriculture prior to the ERP. It then considers how the ERP measures sought to revive the sector and how farmers responded to the ERP. The concluding section offers observations and lessons about the Gambian experience.

The Performance of Agriculture prior to the ERP

In the first decade after independence, 1965–1966 to 1975–1976, Gambian agriculture grew at the same rate as the population (2.6 percent annually), which was slightly more than half the growth rate of total GDP (4.9 percent annually) (see Table 13-1). Agriculture contributed about 38 percent to GDP, sustained largely by high levels of groundnut sales, which, due to a string of good seasons, averaged 123,000 tonnes a year. When combined with rising world export prices, groundnut production contributed significantly to The Gambia's relatively robust balance-of-payments situation. The current account deficit for the decade averaged 8.3 percent of GDP, which was covered more than adequately by capital inflow. By 1975 foreign reserves had accumulated to the equivalent of ten months of imports. During the next decade, 1975–1976 to 1985–1986, the situation unraveled. Agricultural output per capita declined at an annual rate of 1.2 percent. Aggregate output per capita declined as well but at a slower rate than in agriculture (0.3 percent annually). The contribution of

Table 13-1. Basic Economic and Agricultural Data, The Gambia

	1965–66 to 1975–76	1975–76 to 1985–86	1985–86 to 1988–89
Real GDP per capita (% per annum)	2.3	−0.3	0.6
Growth in agriculture (% per annum)	2.6	1.8	3.6
Agriculture growth per capita (% per annum)	0	−1.2	0.4
Agricultural output (% of GDP)	37.8	29.2	29.1
Government recurrent expenditures (% of GDP)	13.6	20.7	29.1[a]
Government budget deficit (% of GDP)	2.6	13.2	13.8[a]
Development expenditures (% of GDP)	3.9	12.8	12.6
Food imports (% GDP)	7.1	15.2	18.6
Balance of payments current account deficit (% of GDP)	8.3	35.9	25.5
Groundnut sales (1000 metric tons per annum)	122.9	88.5	51.3
Harvested area (1000 hectares per annum)			
Grain	—	64.7	83.2
Groundnut	—	88.9	78.0
Grain production (1000 metric tons per annum)	—	75.7	103.6
Groundnut production (1000 metric tons per annum)	—	102.1	101.1
Average groundnut price per tonne (1976–1977 US$)	556	491	287
GPMB's reserves (annual change, millions of dalasis)	7.8	−10.9	7.1
Groundnut producer price (current US$)	105	200	226
Fertilizer price (current US$ prices)			
Compound	—	76.7	156.4
Single super phosphate	—	62.4	127.3
Rainfall (millimeters per annum)			
Yundum (West Gambia)	1,049	870	841
Georgetown	843	708	843
Basse (East Gambia)	919	822	867

[a]These data are inflated by extraordinary transfers to parastatals of 5.1% of GDP.
Source: Ministry of Finance and Economic Affairs, Macro Policy Analysis Unit.

agriculture to GDP continued to decline, averaging 29 percent for the decade as a whole. Since agricultural employment had continued to increase, the poor growth performance increased the prevalence of rural poverty. Moreover, lower groundnut harvests combined with fluctuating export prices to reduce the contribution of groundnut production to GDP and the balance of payments. Annual sales averaged 89,000 tonnes, a 39 percent decline from the previous decade.

Agriculture's contribution to per capita domestic food supplies also fell, sharply increasing food imports. These developments in agriculture added to the economy's balance-of-payments problems, which, as shown elsewhere, were already severe (see Chapter 5).

Thus by the mid-1980s agriculture had deteriorated due to several factors. Detailed analyses of longer-term trends in output and yields pointed to three in particular: heavy taxation, underfunding of recurrent costs and investment, and weather.

Inappropriate output pricing and exchange rate policies resulted in *heavy taxation* on Gambian farmers. For twenty years prior to the ERP, the Gambia Produce Marketing Board had fixed groundnut producer prices at levels that generated average tax revenue of 25.8 percent on groundnut production at the farmgate (World Bank, 1975; Haughton, 1986). The overvalued exchange rate from the mid-1970s onward compounded the effects of the tax (see Chapter 5). By reducing the GPMB's operating margins, the exchange rate kept downward pressure on the groundnut producer price. And by reducing the local costs of imported food, it discouraged farmers from expanding the output of food grain.

Agricultural growth was also undermined by the *underfunding of recurrent costs* (see Chapter 10). Recurrent expenditures on agriculture were equivalent to 60 percent of capital expenditures in 1975, but dropped to 27 percent in 1980 and then to only 14 percent in the year before the ERP. Moreover, since the *share of public resources* devoted to agriculture was significantly below the sector's contribution to both GDP and employment, resources were persistently being transferred from the rural economy to urban areas.

Changes in the weather were important. Between 1974 and 1987 average rainfall declined by 36 percent in western Gambia and 24 percent in eastern Gambia from its level in the period from 1950 to 1965. Seasonal patterns of rainfall also changed: average rainfall in August declined by 50 percent (Wright, 1988). At the farm level this change led to drought stress in the middle of the cropping season; it limited the extent of water recharge in upland soils that affected the yields of late-season crops; and it reduced the freshwater run-off into the rice fields.

Despite numerous adjustments by farmers, the changing rainfall pattern severely affected the production of food, cash crops, and livestock. The grain equivalent of agricultural output in the three good rainfall years (1974 to 1976) was 233,000 tonnes; for the three poor years (1979 to 1981), it was only 172,000 tonnes. The adverse trends in rainfall were accentuated by declining soil fertility, suggesting that farmers themselves could not or would not make the necessary investments in fertility maintenance (OTA, 1988).

Agriculture and the Economic Recovery Program

Many of the ERP policy measures—exchange rate reform, civil service and parastatal reform, changes in monetary and fiscal policies, the reorientation of public investment, and the rationalization of the country's external debt—were expected to help revitalize agriculture. In turn, improvements in agriculture were expected to reinforce the effects of these other measures.

The ERP sought to influence agriculture at both the macro and micro levels. Traditional approaches to agricultural development had tended to concentrate on improvements at the farm and village levels. However, in the early 1980s agricultural specialists began to highlight a point that had been confirmed by the Gambian experience—that inappropriate macro policies can adversely affect agricultural performance (Timmer, Falcon, and Pearson, 1983). The macroeconomic policies in the ERP sought to initiate relative and absolute price changes in an effort to improve incentives. Exchange rate reform and price decontrol were the first steps. Combined with the liberalization of the grain market, devaluation substantially raised the local price of rice and coarse grain. The groundnut subsidies provided further impetus (see Chapter 14). The consequent changes in relative and absolute prices raised farm income and markedly increased the returns to labor. For example, real returns to millet farmers increased nearly 20 percent between 1982–1983 and 1988–1989, due primarily to macroeconomic policy changes (McPherson and Posner, 1991, Table 2). Because the ERP effectively fixed urban nominal wages, the rural–urban terms of trade improved considerably.

Other policy changes also sought to help farmers. Improving the efficiency of the civil service was meant to free up resources for development activities. Particularly relevant in this regard was the Ministry of Agriculture, which had become overstaffed and largely dysfunctional. Parastatal reform was meant to improve the efficiency of the state-owned organizations associated with agriculture, the GPMB, the Gambia Cooperatives Union, and the Livestock Marketing Board (LMB). Farmers were expected to benefit from higher returns for their output and cheaper inputs.

Two major monetary policy changes affected agriculture: the decontrol of interest rates and tighter credit controls. Although higher interest rates adversely affected those who had preferential access to credit, they also helped improve equity. And in the medium term, monetary reform would make the credit market less fragmented and improve the access of all borrowers to credit (Shipton, 1987; 1991). Fiscal reform—especially efforts to reduce the public-sector deficit—was meant to supplement monetary actions so as to lower the rate of inflation permanently.

To reduce farmers' costs, the government sought to rehabilitate infrastructure (roads, ferries, telecommunications, the port, and airport). Transport costs would become more moderate, and the exchange of technical and market information would improve. Finally, by rationalizing its external debt, The Gambia would reestablish its international credibility, thus increasing commodity aid, technical assistance, and financial support. In turn, this enhanced stream of support would ease the burden of structural adjustment on all Gambians, farmers and nonfarmers alike. Moreover, restoring external balance was The Gambia's best option for avoiding another food or fertilizer crisis (von Braun and Puetz, 1987), because the availability of foreign exchange would enable the country to import its necessary inputs.

All of these measures did in fact produce a favorable outcome, as agricultural output began to increase. Indeed, the ERP generated the first general increase in per capita agricultural output since independence. This improved agricultural environment has been maintained under the Program for Sustained Development (see Chapter 19).

Notwithstanding these positive developments, the agricultural recovery depended heavily on improved weather conditions. Fundamental problems still remain, casting serious doubt on the sector's future prospects. The next section discusses the responses of farmers to the ERP and the types of constraints and opportunities they face as they attempt to raise agricultural output to a sustainable basis over the longer term.

The Concerns of Farmers about the ERP and Their Responses

When the ERP was formulated, Gambian farmers were facing a period of intense uncertainty. Concerns focused on food security, government action, changes in regional markets, and constraints on local farming systems.

Food Security

Food security concerns were heightened by food shortages during the period from 1983 to 1985. The 1983 crop season was disastrous for many rural families. After a food grain harvest of 105,000 tonnes in 1982, the 1983 harvest of 70,000 tonnes was a major setback. Food aid and official imports provided a buffer, but the poor grain harvest in 1984 (86,000 tonnes) created serious problems in early 1985, made worse by the inability of the government to purchase additional food supplies due to the lack of foreign exchange.

The crop failure and the government's inability to compensate for the shortfall distressed farmers deeply. Many of them adopted a survival strategy by reallocating land from groundnuts toward cereals (World Bank, 1986). Farmers had reacted similarly after the 1971–1973 drought for food security purposes (CRED, 1977); but at that time, once the weather improved, farmers reduced millet production because of its limited market opportunities. In the mid-1980s the situation was different. The harvested area of cereals increased from 60,000 hectares in 1984–1985 to 87,000 hectares in 1985–1986 as millet production became more attractive. The shift was entirely at the expense of groundnuts, whose area fell from 91,000 hectares to 59,000 hectares.

When groundnut production was subsidized in 1986–1987, the returns to groundnuts increased more than the returns to cereals. The area planted to groundnuts increased, reaching its pre-ERP level in 1987–1988. It has not increased further. The coarse grain area expanded to levels approximately 50 percent higher than prior to the ERP.

Government Action

Despite the relatively coherent and comprehensive policy reforms to support agriculture, several government actions provided mixed signals to farmers. The ERP took several years to implement. Although administrative measures were implemented early in the program (such as the civil service wage freeze, exchange rate reform, and price decontrol), many institutional changes that sought to improve efficiency were delayed. Several changes proved to be time-consuming, expensive, highly political, and only marginally useful. They included efforts to reduce the role of the GPMB in groundnut marketing, improve the management of the GCU, and reorganize the Ministry of Agriculture. Six years after the initiation of the ERP, the formal rural credit system run by the GCU was still disruptive (see Chapter 7), and the Ministry of Agriculture continued to be ineffective at supporting the agricultural sector.

The disarray was compounded by other administrative inconsistencies. An example is fertilizer distribution. The tardy delivery of imports, below-market liquidation prices for old stock, and free distribution by some organizations undermined efforts to privatize the activity. The sharp increase and then decrease in groundnut prices (see Chapter 14) simply deepened producers' mistrust of the GPMB and cast doubt on the government's capacity to maintain its commitment to other policy changes. Efforts to liberalize the credit system were compromised by continued subsidies to selected groups. Overall, farmers developed a deep-seated cynicism about government-supported activities in agriculture.

Market Stimulus for Millet Production

Price decontrol and devaluation increased the prices for all agricultural commodities. For example, since 1986 local prices for coarse grains, meat, and groundnut hay have been high both in relative and absolute terms.

Millet production became particularly attractive. As noted earlier, when farmers were forced to cope with food security concerns, they turned to millet production as a way to increase the degree of cereal self-sufficiency. On the demand side the market for coarse grains in Senegal (and other parts of the western Sahel) has expanded, due to population pressure, the high relative cost of rice production, and dietary substitution as per capita real income has declined. Moreover, millet production represented a rational reallocation of resources away from maize, which has higher cash requirements, especially for fertilizer. Finally, millet is better adapted than either maize or sorghum to the declining rainfall in the western Sahel.

The shift to coarse grains from groundnuts appears to represent an underlying transition in Gambian agriculture. Survey data show that farmers are now applying relatively large amounts of fertilizer to millet. As recently as 1982, that practice was rare.[1]

Pressures on Gambian Farming Systems

To respond to the higher market prices for groundnuts and cereals, Gambian farmers had the option of using additional land or of cultivating their existing land more intensively. At the aggregate level little additional land is available.[2] At the village level studies have shown that land pressure is often acute, with annual cropping on 70 to 90 percent of all crop land (Mills, Kabay, and Boughton, 1988; DOA, 1990).

Given the current pattern of cash crop, food grain, and livestock production in The Gambia, the "land frontier" has effectively closed. Without such inputs as fertilizer, farmers continue to shorten the rotation of crops at great risk. With manpower depleted through outmigration, the destumping of distant fallow fields to permit rapid rainy season cultivation is too difficult for households consisting predominantly of older men, women, and young children.[3]

In the absence of additional land, output can be increased on a sustained basis only by increasing productivity. For many years the Gambian Extension Service has been promoting the use of fertilizer, early-maturation varieties of groundnuts and cereals, and methods for improving crop stands, such as early planting, improved seed, seed dressing, thinning, and timely weeding. Nevertheless, intensifying agriculture on the low-organic matter, sandy-loam soils of the semiarid tropics is difficult. Applying fertilizer and planting improved varieties have little effect unless conservation of the soil itself is practiced carefully. Organic matter management, critical to the nutrient cycling and the water-holding capacities of Gambian soils, is indispensable to developing more productive agricultural systems.

New technologies are available, but farmers have been highly selective in what they adopt. According to the 1990 National Agricultural Sample Survey (NADC, 1991, Section 8), crop-planting dates are widely dispersed, seed treatment is not practiced much (7 percent of the area for coarse grains, 28 percent for groundnuts, and 1 percent for upland and swamp rice), and virtually no improved seed is used (2 percent of the area for coarse grains, 1 percent for groundnuts, and none for upland and swamp rice). However, the majority of farmers thin their cereal crops (67 percent of the area for coarse grains, 11 percent for groundnuts, and 27 percent for upland and swamp rice), use fertilizer/manure on approximately half the cropped area, and use animal traction in most of the upland fields for planting and weeding (95 percent of the area for coarse grains and groundnuts and 4 percent for upland and swamp rice).

The uneven rate at which farmers have adopted improved technologies has several explanations. Some technologies are simply not profitable. For example, the on-farm response of improved technologies for early millet was low (Diallo, O'Neil, and Mannch, 1988). Other technologies have not been adopted because farmers lack capital or because they are preoccupied with food security and are not willing to take additional risks. Another reason for the low adoption rates is the considerable decapitalization of Gambian agriculture before the ERP.[4] Constraints on working capital have been severe. The smaller area sown to a fertilizer-demanding crop such as maize when fertilizer subsidies were eliminated is only one of several examples of this point.[5]

Furthermore, efforts to intensify agriculture have been impeded by the limited role of women in agriculture in general and lowland cropping in particular. Female farmers have few capital resources, and their access to land is tenuous (Dey, 1982; Bastone, 1988; von Braun, Puetz, and Webb, 1989, Table 18; NADC, 1991, Section 6). Recent research on inland valley rice, the major agricultural enterprise for women, has shown that several stand-alone technologies—such as improved varieties, animal traction for land preparation, seeding and weeding, and the use of fertilizer and herbicides—can significantly improve yields. Yet under current circumstances women lack the resources to take advantage of these technologies.

One technology that has increasingly been adopted by Gambian farmers is animal traction, despite its significant cost. High population growth rates and the departure of young rural workers to urban centers has created an anomaly: a large increase in the total population but an on-farm labor pool that is too small to support intensive production systems. Together with the demands of the shorter growing season due to changing rainfall patterns, the labor constraint has prompted farmers to invest in traction. In the decade before the ERP, the number of donkeys and horses used for traction increased at the rate of 25 percent annually (Sumberg and Gilbert, 1986). Their numbers then stabilized at about 45,000, due partly to the heavy replacement requirements (put at 25 percent annually) that are the result of high mortality rates. Additional investment has been directed into oxen.[6]

Without more agricultural labor (to destump the uplands and weed the lowlands) and capital (for fertilizer, improved seed, implements, and traction), the Gambian farming system can neither expand nor intensify markedly. Millet has thus become the crop of choice: it can be grown where fallowing is less frequent, and compared with groundnuts, it requires fewer inputs (the seed costs, for example, are negligible) and less labor (because it can be harvested easily).

Some new enterprises have promise. Improved varieties and modified cropping systems for such crops as cassava, sweet potato, cowpea, disease-resistant cultivars of citrus, and mango provide alternative income sources. Seasonal sheep fattening and localized milk production provide an additional dimension to farmers' livestock activities. The production of horticulture for export has limited possibilities for expansion.[7]

How might farmers take advantage of the potential value of these and other improvements? With price liberalization under the ERP, input prices have increased sharply. Both donors and the government have difficulty seeing beyond subsidized credit as a solution. But experience has shown that when farmers consider inputs to be essential they will, in fact, acquire them even when credit is priced at market-clearing rates.

Concluding Observations and Lessons about the Relationship Between Macroeconomic Reform and the Agricultural Sector

In The Gambia structural adjustment has become the crucial first step toward economic recovery. Sustaining the recovery, however, requires revitalizing agriculture. That task is not easy. Local farming systems are under pressure as farmers shift from extensive to intensive methods of production. The physical and biological constraints are severe, exacerbated by the financial difficulties experienced by farmers in recent years. These difficulties have been compounded by the inability of the public sector to become reengaged constructively in agricultural development.

At the macro level the ERP removed product price and exchange rate distortions, and farmers now receive higher net returns for their produce. These changes have helped reverse the decline in per capita income. Nonetheless, the anticipated revitalization of agriculture has not occurred. Indeed, the Gambian experience shows that, at best, macro policy changes can only create the conditions for expanding agricultural output. For sustained agricultural growth, farm-level productivity must be improved. In The Gambia doing so will require special efforts in at least four areas: the organization of production, access to inputs, the marketing of output, and economic policy.

First, Gambian farming systems are largely in a transition phase, moving from extensive to intensive farming practices. Innovations in technology must be specialized. Some technologies that can have long-term effects can be adopted now. For instance, improved equine health would have an immediate payoff, as would reductions in handling and crop storage losses. And the use of improved quality seed would raise yields and lower the costs of groundnut production (GOTG, 1990a). But changes in relative prices that have favored millet and livestock in the past several years indicate that agricultural research should focus on cereals and fodder rather than on groundnuts. In The Gambia the upland soils and low rainfall are conducive to millet production and fodder crops, while the riverine ecology in the eastern region makes fresh water and pasture available all year.

Second, many farmers have limited or, at best, intermittent access to inputs. Rural credit systems are weak, and fertilizer and seed distribution systems are still underdeveloped. These constraints are especially severe for female farmers, who have received little access to fertilizer, credit, and technical assistance. Attempts to intensify agricultural production will fail unless substantive changes in these areas are made (Gladwin and McMillan, 1989).

Third, despite grudging adjustment efforts and numerous delays, the dominance of state-owned organizations in agricultural marketing and the distortions they have created are being eliminated. Thus far, the restructuring that has occurred has not provided The Gambia with a set of institutions that can market, process, and finance agricultural output effectively. Farmers have avoided some of the problems by marketing their output through alternative channels. Although a solution ultimately may be found, the outcome is unsatisfactory—inefficient public enterprises continue to operate while farmers devote additional effort to finding low-cost alternative outlets for their produce.

Finally, if the government remains committed to the ERP policies, many of the beneficial effects of macroeconomic policy changes will persist. Long-term development can be sustained only if the government ensures that major distortions do not reemerge. But improved macroeconomic policies are a start. Future agricultural growth and development will require sustained improvements in productivity. In The Gambia that farm-level challenge is only just being addressed.

NOTES

1. The surveys were conducted in 1981 and 1982 (Haydu et al., 1986). Five years later, 70 to 85 percent of the millet fields were being fertilized in several villages whose fallow land was limited (Posner and Jallow, 1987). Farmers who could have applied fertilizer to their groundnuts just as easily found it more rewarding to use it on millet (Mills, Kabay, and Boughton, 1988).
2. In 1948, 58 percent of The Gambia was covered by forest; by 1968 forest cover was 8 percent (Mann, 1975), but since then only a minimal amount of primary forest has been cleared (Posner and Gilbert, 1989a; 1989b).
3. Another indication of the shortage of good agricultural land is the recent absence of "strange farmers" (see Chapter 7). In the mid-1970s there were 12,000 to 17,000 strange farmers in The Gambia (World Bank, 1975, p. 16; Dunsmore et al., 1976, pp. 286–287). In 1990 strange farmers cultivated only 1 percent of the area under coarse grains, 4 percent under groundnuts, and 6 percent under swamp and upland rice (NADC, 1991,

Table 8.3). This represents a total of only 5,000 hectares involving fewer than 2,000 individuals.

4. A 1982 study of forty-six "production-consumption units" from nine villages showed that the average value of fixed capital for each farming unit had declined substantially (Haydu et al., 1986, Table IV-13).

5. Farm-level data have shown consistently that farmers spend only a small proportion (significantly less than 10 percent) of their cash on inputs (Dunsmore et al., 1976, Table VI.4; von Braun, Puetz, and Webb, 1989, Tables 23 and 32). Moreover, studies in 1986 showed that 50 percent of farmers did not have enough capital to buy more seednuts to increase their groundnut area (Posner and Jallow, 1987, p. 28).

6. Their number increased from 22,000 to 31,000 between 1987 and 1989 (NADC, 1991, Table 4.2).

7. The main constraints on agro-industrial expansion are capital, energy, management, transport costs, and disease. Some niche producers are doing relatively well. They have all had large amounts of support from the government in the form of subsidies and tax breaks (Gray et al., 1992). The social value of these activities is debatable. Their longer-term impact on agriculture and local employment is still unclear.

14

The Groundnut Sector

Christine Jones and Steven C. Radelet

Groundnuts have long been the backbone of the Gambian economy. Until the late 1970s groundnut production and marketing contributed more than 20 percent to GDP, occupied the majority of the work force, and accounted for 90 percent of export earnings. But during the late 1970s and early 1980s, the groundnut sector deteriorated markedly. Production fell sharply, exports plummeted, and the Gambia Produce Marketing Board (the government agency that until 1989 held a monopoly on groundnut trading, processing, and marketing) approached financial ruin. In many ways the decline of the Gambian economy in the early 1980s was directly related to the collapse of the groundnut sector.

The Gambia's problems with the GPMB and the groundnut sector were typical of the problems facing many African governments in the 1980s with respect to marketing boards. Marketing boards had been established in many African countries by colonial governments in order to procure exportable commodities, stabilize commodity prices, and collect tax revenues. After independence governments retained the marketing boards for these same purposes and also as a means of providing political patronage. Governments established export monopolies to achieve their revenue and price stabilization objectives; many extended the monopolies to cover domestic procurement and marketing as well.[1]

In the immediate post-independence period, most African marketing boards seemed to perform fairly well, aided in many cases by relatively high world prices and favorable climate. But in the late 1970s and early 1980s, the financial and economic performance of many of the boards deteriorated sharply in line with weak commodity prices, overvalued exchange rates, and poor management, which diverted resources away from the central responsibilities of the boards. Instead of adding to tax revenues, many marketing boards began to drain resources from the central government budget, absorb scarce domestic credit, and accumulate foreign debt to finance their losses. The combination of these external and internal problems significantly undermined farmer incomes.[2]

Because of the economic importance of the commodities involved and the size of the financial losses, marketing boards have become a central focus of reform programs in many African countries. Almost all observers agree that improving the macroeconomic environment, especially by introducing a more competitive exchange rate, is the key first step in strengthening the agricultural sector in general, and specifically the export commodities controlled by the marketing boards. Moreover, macroeconomic policy changes should be complemented with sectoral policies aimed at the farm level (see Chapter 13).

But in addition, governments must address the institutional problems within the marketing boards themselves. There is less agreement on this issue, both in terms of the most appropriate marketing and export arrangements, and on the optimal transition path to reach that outcome. Broadly speaking, the options range from attempting to improve marketing board performance without changing the basic institutional structure (for example, with performance contracts), to introducing competition for at least some of the marketing board's activities, to complete divestiture of the marketing board and its assets.[3] The Gambian government attempted each of these strategies to differing degrees with respect to the GPMB. Its experiences provide a number of useful insights for other African countries faced with similar issues. Chapter 16 examines some of these issues with respect to parastatal reform in The Gambia in general; the discussion here focuses on the specific case of the groundnut marketing board.

This chapter reviews the deterioration of the groundnut sector and analyzes three sets of reforms introduced by the government under the ERP. First, in 1986–1987, at the insistence of the IMF, the government raised the farmgate price of groundnuts to 50 percent above the export parity price. The high price required a subsidy for the GPMB equivalent to 8 percent of GDP. The subsidy was subsequently reduced and then eliminated in 1988–1989. Second, the government introduced a series of measures to reform the groundnut trading and marketing system. Third, in 1990 the government began to dismantle the GPMB's monopoly on groundnut processing by allowing private businesses to process and export groundnuts.

The Performance of the Groundnut Sector Prior to the ERP: 1975 to 1985

In the mid- and late 1970s, the world price of groundnuts more than doubled from its level of the early 1970s. The GPMB's profits soared, and by 1977–1978 its reserves reached D106 million (equivalent to 30 percent of GDP), triple the level of only five years earlier. Due largely to groundnut prices, the economy was booming in the mid-1970s. Yet within five years the GPMB's reserves had disappeared, and it was in debt to the Central Bank. The entire groundnut sector essentially collapsed along with the GPMB—groundnut production was 45 percent lower in 1985 than in 1976, and groundnut exports had fallen by 60 percent.

Many factors contributed to the decline of the groundnut sector. Prolonged drought and parasite infestation severely undermined production. At the same time, world prices fell sharply, almost to the level of the early 1970s. The GPMB attempted to maintain nominal producer prices at their previous levels, and in several years it actually increased them. Gambian prices remained at 30 percent or more above the price in neighboring Senegal, propelling imports of Senegalese groundnuts and adding to the GPMB's losses. Only in 1983 did the GPMB finally lower farmgate prices—a year in which world prices rebounded somewhat. But at that point the organization was already insolvent.

The GPMB's financial difficulties stemmed only partially from declining world prices. The GPMB provided generous subsidies for rice, fertilizer, and groundnut oil. It also invested in a series of nongroundnut enterprises that suffered significant financial losses. Central government policies further aggravated the situation. The overvalued exchange rate seriously affected the GPMB's dalasi revenue base and limited the extent to which it could raise producer prices. Moreover, the government extracted more than D40 million from the GPMB's reserves in the late 1970s to cover mounting government budget deficits. By 1984 the GPMB's reserves had disappeared, and it owed the Central Bank D110 million.

The groundnut sector was hurt further by the performance of the second major agricultural parastatal, the Gambia Cooperatives Union. The GCU purchases groundnuts from farmers for delivery to the GPMB and provides farmers with fertilizer, seed, and credit. But in the late 1970s and early 1980s, its inadequate storage facilities led to crop losses as high as 30 percent. Moreover, the GCU often failed to provide inputs promptly. In 1985 an estimated 19,000 hectares (21 percent of the area harvested) were prepared for groundnut cultivation but could not be planted because seeds were not delivered on time (World Bank, 1985b).

The collapse of the groundnut sector fed directly into The Gambia's balance-of-payments crisis. Nominal dollar exports in 1984–1985 were 30 percent less than in 1979–1980—due almost completely to declining groundnut production. Declining export receipts were a major determinant of the erosion of the government's foreign exchange reserves and the rapid escalation in debt service arrears. The crisis intensified as the country fell into arrears with the IMF, and the IMF threatened to declare The Gambia ineligible for further borrowing. The government introduced reforms in three areas to address the problems in the groundnut sector: the groundnut subsidy, groundnut marketing and processing, and the role of the GPMB and the GCU.

The Groundnut Subsidy

Exchange rate reform was the first, and in many ways the most important, step in rationalizing the groundnut sector (see Chapter 5). The 100 percent nominal depreciation over the first seven months of 1986 immediately increased the GPMB's dalasi revenues from its export sales. It removed the bias against farmers that had been inherent in the overvalued exchange rate, and provided the GPMB scope for increasing farmgate prices. The float of the dalasi, coupled with other macroeconomic measures that helped stabilize the economy, provided the foundation for a recovery of the groundnut sector.

But the macroeconomic changes alone would have been insufficient to bring about a groundnut recovery. Therefore, the IMF missions in 1985 and 1986 focused much of their attention on sector-specific groundnut policies. Their thinking on the subject was beguilingly simple. To increase official foreign exchange receipts, the GPMB would have to raise its producer prices in order to attract more nuts and maximize its export sales. Moreover, since Senegal had dramatically raised its prices in 1985, the GPMB would have to raise prices by nearly as much to ensure that Gambian nuts would not flow across the border and reduce the GPMB's foreign exchange earnings. The IMF wanted The Gambia to maximize its official export receipts, since The Gambia would use the foreign exchange to pay its arrears to the IMF. Thus in 1986 the IMF proposed that the GPMB raise the producer price to D1,800 per tonne, roughly equivalent to the Senegalese producer price (CFAF 90,000 per tonne).

The proposed price was three times the 1984 price and 50 percent more than the export parity price. It would require a massive subsidy—D83 million, or the equivalent of 8 percent of GDP. The IMF had never before advocated that such a large subsidy be made to a parastatal. The IMF envisioned that donor support would cover the subsidy fully. Yet as the issue was debated in early 1986, donors did not make any significant commitments to support the ERP or the groundnut subsidy.

Minister of Finance Sisay felt that the subsidy proposed by the IMF was too large and that it could not be financed or sustained fully over time. Thus he proposed a price of D1,400 per tonne (17 percent higher than the export parity price), which would provide farmers a significant increase in the farmgate price but would still be below the Senegalese price. Minister Sisay reasoned that an outflow of groundnuts to Senegal would be advantageous: farmers would be paid in CFA francs (a fully convertible currency) and would be paid much more foreign exchange than the GPMB would receive for its exports on the world market, because Senegal was also subsidizing groundnuts. He believed the government could rely on the newly established interbank market for foreign exchange to induce farmers to convert the CFA francs into dalasis. The strategy entailed obvious risks, since the government had just introduced the interbank market, and it was only beginning to function smoothly. Nevertheless, Minister Sisay believed that it was less risky than the huge, still unfinanced subsidy.

Election-year politics became an important piece of the puzzle. The political appeal of providing farmers with a huge IMF-approved subsidy just before presidential and parliamentary elections was obvious, particularly given the long list of economic reforms being introduced by the government. Farmers were the ruling party's most important political constituency (see Chapter 3). President Jawara decided to follow the IMF's advice, and the government raised the farmgate price to D1,800 per tonne.

Fortunately, financing for the subsidy eventually became available. In mid-1986 donors began to provide financial support to the ERP (see Chapter 4). Helping to finance the groundnut subsidy were structural adjustment loans from the World Bank, counterpart funds from fuel grants from the United Kingdom and the Netherlands, commodity stabilization grants from the European Community (which were committed before the ERP), and (later) grants from the United States. Thus the government was able to finance its large budget deficit fully without borrowing from the Central Bank; indeed, the government reduced its deficit position with the Central Bank in 1986–1987. In effect, much of this aid was transferred directly to farmers—some of the poorest Gambians whom the economic decline of the early 1980s had affected most severely.

Together with the end of the drought, the high price led to a groundnut boom in 1986–1987. Groundnut production jumped by 45 percent from the depressed level of 1985–1986, and the GPMB's purchases increased by 35 percent. Gross farm receipts from groundnuts more than doubled in nominal terms over the previous year, providing farmers with a much needed income boost. Yet even with the high Gambian price, some farmers went to Senegal to sell their groundnuts, because they did not wish to sell through the GCU—either because they wanted to avoid repaying their loans or because the GCU sometimes paid them with promissory chits rather than cash. Even with this unofficial outflow, Gambian groundnut export receipts grew by 15 percent, despite a softening in world prices.

Although the subsidy worked well in 1986–1987, it was clear that it could not be sustained over time. The farmgate price had to be reduced in 1987–1988; the only question was, by how much. The IMF took the opposite position from the previous year, arguing that a large subsidy could not be financed and that in the long run the farmgate price should approximate the world price. It argued further that a lower price would induce exports to Senegal, thus reducing the budget subsidy, and would increase total foreign exchange earnings given the now well-functioning market for foreign exchange. In short, the IMF adopted the position that Minister Sisay had taken in the previous year. It advocated a price of D1,300 per tonne, a 27 percent decline from the 1986–1987 price.

But the government saw things differently. While recognizing that a lower price was necessary, it argued that, given an existing price of D1,800 per tonne, lowering the price by as much as the IMF suggested would be unfair and confusing to farmers. Bolstered by commitments from several donors to provide ongoing financial support, the government pushed for a price of D1,500 per tonne.

The World Bank also wanted the government to reduce the subsidy. In fact, one of the conditions for the first World Bank structural adjustment loan was that the Gambian government eliminate the subsidy completely by 1988–1989. But the bank agreed with the government that the IMF's proposed 27 percent cut was too sharp. After prolonged discussions the government's position prevailed.

Despite a reduction in the farmgate price, groundnut production grew by an additional 9 percent in 1987–1988. However, GPMB purchases fell by about 7 percent, indicating that farmers were exporting a significant amount of groundnuts directly to Senegal. The cross-border sales led to a dramatic increase in Central Bank purchases of CFA francs during the harvest season.

In 1988–1989 the producer price was again reduced, to D1,100 per tonne, completely eliminating the subsidy as required by the World Bank.

Production fell by 18 percent. Even more striking, GPMB purchases fell by 60 percent, indicating even more clearly that large quantities of groundnuts were being sold in Senegal.

The following year, buoyed by an increase in world prices, the GPMB raised the producer price to D1,650 per tonne, and, without a subsidy, was able to post a financial surplus for only the second time since 1977–1978.

The subsidy had several benefits. The most important was that it provided a large, much needed boost to rural income. Real GDP in agriculture grew by 20 percent between 1985 and 1988, due largely to the groundnut subsidy and the end of the drought. The results of the model simulations reported in Chapter 18 suggest that the subsidy led to a 7 percent increase in real rural wages. Groundnut production had temporarily become an attractive employment opportunity for displaced urban workers, particularly civil servants who had been retrenched in early 1986. The subsidy was thus an important income supplement to the poorest Gambians during the period of adjustment.

The subsidy was also critical to the political acceptance of the ERP, helping the ruling People's Progressive Party retain its rural support during the 1987 election (see Chapter 3). Moreover, the subsidy forced the GPMB to begin rationalizing its finances, both because the MoF and the IMF began to scrutinize its costs more closely and because the budget subsidy meant that the GPMB did not have to rely on Central Bank financing for its operations.

The major disadvantage of the subsidy was the erratic producer price for farmers over time. The dramatic increase, then fall, then increase in prices over four years caused much confusion, which in all likelihood affected planting decisions adversely, thus leading to a loss of efficiency. Farmers' confidence in the government's role in supporting agriculture suffered as well (McPherson and Posner, 1991). In retrospect, the original position of Minister Sisay should have prevailed: a constant nominal price of D1,400 per tonne over the period would have been preferable to the sharp oscillations in the producer price.

The Groundnut Marketing System

The subsidy was not the only major ERP policy change that affected the groundnut sector directly. Beginning in 1986, the government took several steps to decontrol groundnut marketing and processing in an effort to increase competition and efficiency.

Unlike many marketing boards in Africa, the GPMB did not actually buy groundnuts at the farm level. Rather, it licensed traders to buy on its behalf and paid them buying and freight allowances. Thus its marketing costs consisted of the total allowances that it paid per tonne delivered. In theory, all risks were borne by the traders: if they could not make a profit from the GPMB allowance, they would go out of business. If the allowance were set too low, traders would have no incentive to enter the market, increasing the likelihood of cross-border sales and reducing the amount of groundnuts delivered to the GPMB.

In practice, the system worked somewhat differently because the GCU was involved in the process. The GPMB licensed two categories of buying agents: cooperatives (coops) and private traders. The GCU was the apex organization for the eighty-two local cooperatives that were directly responsible for purchasing groundnuts. The GCU and its cooperative members received a higher allowance than did private traders; nevertheless, it operated at a loss, financed largely with loans from the state-owned Gambia Commercial and Development Bank. Thus the GPMB could run the risk of squeezing the marketing margins, knowing that the losses would be covered by the banking system. Without pressure to contain its costs, the GCU expanded its operations and crowded out some of the private traders. Between 1974–1975 and 1984–1985, the GCU's market share doubled to 80 percent.

The GCU also had other advantages over private traders. In principle, because private traders and the GCU were required to pay farmers the official price, they could not compete on that basis. However, in many cases it was more advantageous for farmers to sell to the coops, because doing so ensured their access to subsidized credit and fertilizer. From 1981 through 1985 the GCU had a monopoly on the distribution of fertilizer.[4] It was also the sole distributor of seednuts (in the years when the government provided them). Furthermore, the GCU provided inputs to coop members on concessional terms; many of these inputs were supplied by donor agencies. Finally neither the GCDB, the government, nor the donors exerted much pressure on recovering their loans to the GCU.

In 1985–1986 private traders found it particularly difficult to show a profit. The total volume purchased in 1985–1986 was one of the poorest on record, leading to large losses.[5] Furthermore, the allowance had eroded by about one-third in real terms between 1981–1982 and 1985–1986, making it increasingly difficult to break even. The result was that the number of private traders declined each year as the old traders retired, with more and more locations served only by the cooperatives.

The decline in the number of private traders translated into higher overall marketing costs. It was estimated that the GCU's marketing costs were about 60 percent greater than those of private traders, and about 60 percent more than the allowance it received from the GPMB. Thus the GCU was not in a position to pay back the crop purchase credit it received from the GCDB. However, private traders were strictly monitored by the local banks. Credit was advanced to private traders to cover two weeks; only when traders delivered the groundnuts to the depot were they then able to replenish their purchasing fund. The implication of these arrangements was that the increase in the GCU's market share over time led to an increase in average marketing costs without any corresponding gain in efficiency.

In 1986 USAID financed a study to examine how the marketing system could be made more efficient (Jones, 1986). The study was based on a survey that compared traders' costs (both private traders and the cooperatives) with the allowances paid by the GPMB. The survey found that the private traders' marketing costs averaged about D61 per tonne, about 10 percent more than the 1985–1986 GPMB marketing allowance of D55 per tonne. In addition to the buying allowance, the GPMB paid a freight allowance to cover the cost of transporting groundnuts from the buying stations to the nearest GPMB depot; the survey found that the freight allowance was about half of what was necessary for a private trader to break even, given the low volumes purchased in 1985–1986.

Under such circumstances it is perhaps surprising that private traders were able to obtain any clients at all. But private traders did offer competitive advantages—better weighing, screening, and rebagging services; transportation from the village to the weighing station; gifts or tips to good customers after the groundnuts were sold; and interest-free loans during the growing season. For those farmers who did not belong to coops or who wanted to avoid selling their groundnuts to the coops in order to avoid repaying loans, private traders were an attractive alternative.

Pressure to reform the groundnut marketing system came from the donors, the government, and the banking system. All three saw marketing reform as a way to reduce the GCU's financial losses and therefore relieve some of the pressure on the banking system. In addition, the government wanted the GPMB to minimize its financial losses, in order to limit the government subsidy, and believed that marketing reform would reduce the GPMB's costs. Also, the donor community had a strong interest in promoting private-sector development in general.

Thus the primary objective in reforming the groundnut marketing system was to put private traders on an equal footing with the cooperative system because their marketing costs were so much lower. This change required several steps. First, the GCDB had to reduce the amount of credit it extended to the GCU, thus forcing the GCU to reduce its costs. Second, the government had to overhaul the input distribution system. Accordingly, in 1986 it liberalized fertilizer marketing, theoretically putting traders and the GCU on the same footing with respect to fertilizer. Third, the GCU's recovery rate on loans to farmers would have to be raised. The GCU had unfair access to cheap loans for inputs, which allowed the coops to be lax about recovering loans. But private traders who did not recover their loans would be forced out of business, giving them a large incentive to recover the loans; in fact, their recovery rate was very high. Finally, the marketing and transport allowances paid to private traders had to be raised to those made to the GCU.

Even with these changes the problem of setting marketing allowances remained. The higher the allowance, the greater the likelihood that buying agents who were competing for customers would pay some of the allowance to farmers and/or the cooperative administration as a premium. But the higher the allowance, the lower the GPMB's profits. The alternative was to move to a system that allowed marketing margins to be determined competitively by having the GPMB set depot prices rather than farmgate prices. The depot prices would vary according to how far upriver the depots were located, to account for the cost of transporting groundnuts from the depots to the point of final processing. If combined with a system that forced the GCU to recover its costs and therefore set relatively low farmgate prices, private traders could compete effectively. Farmers would have three options for protecting themselves from predatory pricing by private traders: they could sell across the border to Senegal, sell to the coop network, or band together and avoid the traders altogether by selling directly to the GPMB at the depots.

In 1986 these changes began to be implemented gradually, as the GPMB equalized the marketing margins it paid to private traders and the GCU. Also, the amount of bank credit extended to the GCU was reduced and came under much closer scrutiny by Cabinet and the IMF. Then, at the beginning of the 1989–1990 crop season, the GPMB moved to the depot pricing scheme. This change eased the administrative responsibilities of the GPMB, since it no longer had to set the marketing and transport allowances. It also allowed private traders to compete more effectively with the GCU to buy groundnuts at the farmgate: the traders whose costs were the lowest could pay the farmer the highest price. Since then, private traders have taken a much more active role in groundnut trading.

Groundnut Processing

The third set of reforms in the groundnut sector focused on the GPMB's monopoly on processing and exports. The GPMB's facilities were designed for a much larger volume of groundnuts than it was processing in the mid-1980s; thus its unit processing costs were high. The GPMB had the option of exporting either decorticated groundnuts or processed oil and meal. The GPMB management continued to choose to process oil, despite losing money in the process (Biggs et al., 1985, Chapter 3).

In 1987 USAID began to push for a complete liberalization of processing activities, arguing that private agents would have lower processing costs and would choose a more profitable mix of export products than the GPMB had in the past. USAID suggested that private entrepreneurs be allowed to decorticate nuts, process nuts into oil and meal, and export groundnuts and derivative products. To move the government in this direction, USAID attached these conditions to one of its grant programs.

In February 1990 the government responded by removing the GPMB's monopoly on the export of groundnut products, allowing private agencies to participate in the entire chain of groundnut activities. They could now purchase from the farmers, decorticate the nuts, and sell them overseas. Moreover, the government has since begun moving toward a system that gives private traders access (for a fee) to the GPMB's processing facilities. The rationale was that, given the relatively small size of the Gambian crop, traders would not be able to build a second processing mill to compete against the GPMB. The government will probably privatize the GPMB fully in the future; since late 1991 it has been managed by expatriate consultants under a management contract.

Concluding Observations and Lessons about Reforming the Groundnut Sector

The marketing and processing reforms substantially reduced the economic and financial losses incurred by the GPMB and the GCU. Increased competition among domestic traders increased farmgate prices, because farmers had the option of choosing among traders who sold directly to exporters, to domestic processors, or across the border in Senegal.

While substantial progress has been made toward reforming trading and processing, more actions are necessary if the groundnut sector is to regain its former dynamism. The measures taken thus far have had little lasting impact at the farm level. The government must focus on policies that will improve farm productivity. In this regard, the groundnut subsidy in 1986 provided a useful one-shot injection of capital into the rural community. Indeed, it was a reasonably efficient way to direct aid resources to the poorest segment of the population, since it was effectively a transfer of income. However, the fact that groundnut prices subsequently fell generated confusion within the farming community and distrust of the government's intentions. A principal lesson of the groundnut subsidy in The Gambia is that reform programs should avoid policies that cannot be sustained.[6] There are enough uncertainties associated with economic reform without compounding them with unsustainable policies.

The subsidy episode also highlights the importance of considering the operation of parallel markets when designing policy changes. When the potential benefits of unofficial sales in Senegal were ignored in 1986, both the producer price and the government subsidy were set at unnecessarily high levels. In subsequent years government policy took advantage of cross-border sales, leading to a more rational pricing policy and more sustainable outcomes.

With respect to reforming marketing arrangements and the GPMB itself, the government took a more gradual approach than the donors advocated. This was a sensible strategy, given the plethora of reforms the government was trying to implement at the outset of the ERP. The four-year time span over which the institutional reforms were introduced provided adequate transition time and gave the reforms a stronger sense of permanence. Nevertheless, donor pressure was useful in ensuring that the reforms were not unduly delayed.

Finally, The Gambia's experience shows that government policies that distort incentives to the extent that highly inefficient public-sector organizations can out-compete private entrepreneurs are ultimately very costly. Both the GPMB and the GCU contributed significantly to the deterioration of private-sector groundnut activities. The cost to farmers was high, and the process of recovery has been difficult.

NOTES

1. See Timmer (1991) for a discussion of these issues.
2. See Bates (1981) for an early description of the financial, economic, and political issues associated with African marketing boards.

3. See World Bank, 1991b; Galal, 1991; and Swanson and Wolde-Semait, 1989.
4. The GCU had a special line of low-interest credit from the World Bank for fertilizer purchases.
5. Since the allowances were paid on a per tonne basis, the smaller the volume purchased, the larger the potential losses, as fixed costs were covered by smaller volumes.
6. See Rodrick (1990) for a discussion of the importance of sustainability of reform measures.

15

Capacity Improvement in the Ministry of Finance

Clive S. Gray and Deborah A. Hoover

Many of the other chapters in this volume have described the obstacles that inappropriate macroeconomic policies, external shocks, and political factors imposed on The Gambia's economic growth. This chapter examines the institutional context within which the ERP was carried out and assesses the efforts made to revamp the bureaucracy into a more effective tool for promoting growth. It focuses on administrative change within the Ministry of Finance, which was the most central organization in the economic reform process. Formulating and implementing the ERP would have been impossible without improving the performance of the MoF.

As with its counterparts in most developing countries, the Gambian government assumed responsibility for many tasks to promote economic growth. Yet the government administration was unable to carry out many of these tasks successfully. The ERP attempted to deal with this shortfall by changing institutional policies and procedures. Although macroeconomic policy changes proved to be a relatively straightforward process, overcoming institutional constraints was far more difficult (GOTG, 1987).

In this respect The Gambia is, of course, no exception to the broader African scene. The difficulties in capacity building in Africa in general, and more specifically the failure of countless foreign aid initiatives to strengthen African institutions, were dramatized in a speech on "Capacity Building: The Missing Link in African Development" by World Bank vice-president Edward Jaycox.[1] Jaycox refers to the "rush of donors to go in and try and work around lack of capacity by substituting for what capacity exists or attracting that little bit of capacity that exists to their own cause rather than the general one." The result, according to Jaycox, is that the donors are "systematically destroying the capacity that does exist."

This chapter examines the efforts made to improve professional capacity within the MoF. It focuses on the role of one technical assistance project in the ministry, providing a case study of Jaycox's thesis in The Gambia. It concludes by posing the counterfactual of what development of human resources and institutions would likely have taken place in the absence of that technical assistance project, and seeks to answer the question whether technical assistance left the MoF's capacity weaker than it would otherwise have been.

The Ministry of Finance prior to the Economic Recovery Program

Responsibilities and Structure of the MoF

The responsibilities of the minister of finance and his parliamentary secretary ranged from loans to civil servants to oversight of statutory corporations, and they ran three semiautonomous departments in addition to the central ministry: the accountant general, central revenue, and customs and excise. Figure 15-1 shows the organizational structure of the MoF[2] as of 1987. It had changed little since the mid-1970s, when economic planning was split off into the Ministry of Economic Planning and Industrial Development. The most significant change occurred in 1984, when the Central Revenue Department was established.

The MoF's structural stability should have been an advantage, as departmental responsibilities were familiar to the staff, much of the ministry's work was routine, and extensive institutional memory had been developed. Yet in practice these advantages were lost because many procedures had broken down and functions were being neglected. In fact, the ministry's stable structure had become a handicap, as the economic circumstances facing MoF staff began to change rapidly and as its institutional position started to unravel.

First, in the mid-1970s the rapid expansion of the Gambian public sector diluted MoF control over capital spending and public debt (see Chapter 11). Other ministries and the public enterprises started to contract foreign loans on the government's behalf. Second, government transactions began to expand rapidly. The civil service expanded from 5,500 in 1975 to 10,210 in 1977, and public enterprises proliferated during the late 1970s. As a result, the MoF's accounting services and monitoring ability were overwhelmed. Delays in computerizing several departments compounded the problem. Third, by the mid-1980s very few MoF staff had training in the type of policy analysis necessary to address the economy's macroeconomic problems. Even as of mid-1992 none of the ministry members held a Ph.D. in economics, and fewer than thirty out of a staff

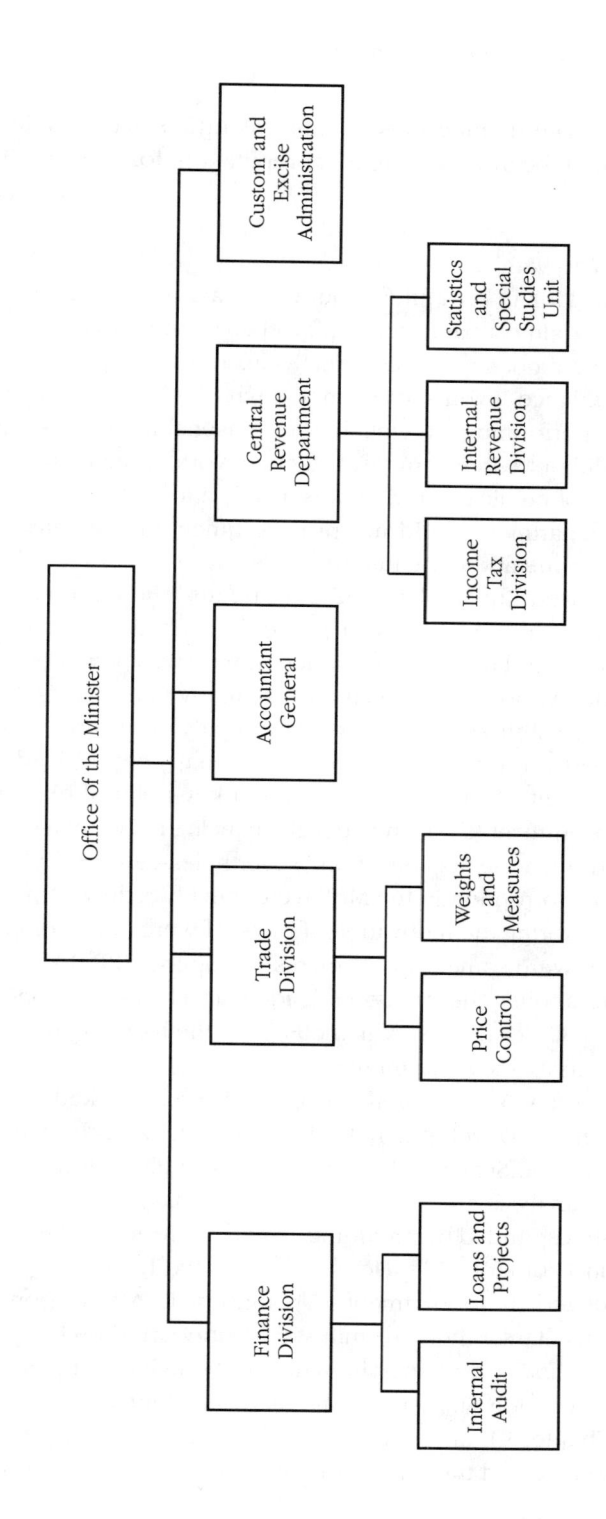

Figure 15.1. Organizational Structure of the Ministry of Finance

of 640 had graduate training in economics. Fourth, since the mid-1970s the ministry had begun to acquire a reputation for corruption and inefficiency.

The Situation in 1982

Returning to the MoF in 1982 after a fourteen-year absence, Minister Sisay found the agency almost paralyzed. Staff lacked the necessary skills, were unmotivated, were not supervised effectively, and were rarely subject to disciplinary guidance. Even staff members who had some postgraduate training were performing at well below reasonable work standards. Ministry staff did not conduct any substantive work on economic policy, and supervision of public enterprises was merely a formality. The accountant general's department could not provide timely or accurate data on government revenue and expenditures. The external debt records of the Loans Division were incomplete and out-of-date. The customs administration allowed many importers to pay only a fraction of the import duties they owed. And the income tax department was powerless to deal with large-scale evasion of personal and company taxes.

The MoF's weakness and its adverse impact on sound economic management did not overly concern the national political leadership.[3] Indeed, a compliant finance ministry served a key political objective—it allowed the government to continue deficit financing rather than to control expenditures or increase tax collection. Nevertheless, after Sisay's arrival, indiscipline and corruption in the MoF were quickly reduced. Improving the skills and restoring the motivation of the staff were more complicated tasks. But there were some improvements during the ERP. How did this progress come about? The minister's leadership clearly was one factor (see Chapter 3). Other factors, which comprise the focus of this chapter, were technical assistance and training.

After only a few months on the job, Minister Sisay asked the British Ministry of Overseas Development for help in revitalizing the accountant general's department. Similarly, he approached USAID for technical assistance in policy analysis.

The British responded by providing an expatriate accountant general, who arrived in February 1984. He was later joined by a data specialist, who computerized the department's operations. USAID responded by providing a consultant to help the minister identify priorities for technical assistance.[4] The first consultancy in March 1983 reviewed the skills and training needs of MoF staff, recommended guidelines on income tax reform (see Chapter 9), and outlined the initial design of a program of technical assistance and training that ultimately led to the Economic and

Financial Policy Analyses project. Not surprisingly, segments of the Gambian administration resisted Minister Sisay's use of foreign advisers. For instance, Cabinet opposed the appointment of the accountant general, only to be overruled by the president, and some senior civil servants strongly objected to the EFPA project.

The Government's Administrative Reform Program

Recognizing that the MoF's institutional weaknesses were common to the Gambian public sector as a whole, those who designed the ERP stressed civil service and parastatal reform. This initiative developed into the Administrative Reform Program (ARP), a broad program that called for overhauling civil service operating procedures, the salary structure, and hiring and firing practices. One of the first issues addressed was the problem of redundant staff. By 1987 more than 3,000 positions, or roughly 25 percent of the pre-ERP civil service establishment, had been eliminated. A personnel management office was later established in the office of the president, and a program was drawn up to review and reorganize key ministries. The MoF itself was reorganized only in 1990.

During the initial stages of the ERP, the absence of attention to the organization of the MoF was due largely to the general disarray and operational inefficiency of other ministries. But Minister Sisay was also concerned that reorganization would divert the attention of MoF staff from the urgent task of implementing the ERP. Moreover, the minister was aware that powerful public-sector interests were opposed to his economic reforms, and he was concerned that these interests might disrupt the organizational reform of the ministry.[5]

Capacity Improvement

Efforts to improve the skills and ability of MoF staff faced several constraints. To begin with, the skill shortage was widespread. Nearly everyone in the ministry, from the minister on down, needed additional training to carry out his or her assigned tasks effectively.[6] But a large-scale training program would disrupt the ministry's work, and so other options had to be found. But even selective overseas training would be difficult because the skill level of some units was so low that staff required basic training simply to meet the admissions requirements.[7] And given the limited number of skilled Gambians in all fields, any training effort risked a high rate of attrition, since trained personnel would then have an opportunity to shift to more lucrative positions in public enterprises, the

National Investment Board, the Central Bank, donor agencies, and the private sector.

These difficulties were compounded by the immediacy of The Gambia's economic problems. Because existing staff did not have the skills to tackle many of the issues, technical assistance was necessary. Although this solution risked compounding The Gambia's dependence on foreign aid, the minister saw no alternative.

The Concept and Elements of Capacity Improvement

The success of structural adjustment and economic reform depends on whether both policies and institutions can be changed. Implementing the changes and sustaining them over the long run require improved capacity. A large body of literature discusses how this goal can be achieved, and efforts are made regularly to formalize the idea. One example is a program currently led by the World Bank, known as the Africa Capacity Building Initiative (ACBI).

The point of departure for the initiators of the ACBI was the definition of capacity in *Webster's Collegiate Dictionary*: "the power to grasp and analyze ideas and cope with problems." This definition has several implications.

The first is that capacity has two dimensions—the ability to recognize key features of a situation and to deal with them in the most relevant manner. For instance, many noneconomists believe that overvalued exchange rates can best be addressed by implementing exchange controls. An economist, however, understands that controls do not eliminate the source of the overvaluation: the excess demand for foreign exchange. Controls simply suppress or divert that excess demand; they do not eliminate it.

Second, beyond analysis, the key features of a situation must be dealt with competently. Improving capacity means enhancing the *power* to "analyze ideas and cope with problems." Obvious vehicles for doing so include on-the-job training, short lecture courses, seminar series, formal degree training, and internships.

The third implication is that capacity is not static, but rather dynamic, and must be responsive to change. For instance, when the dalasi was floated in 1986, price controls were abolished. The result was that the skills and procedures necessary for regulating prices became irrelevant.

Fourth, capacity improvement is not a generic matter. The "power to grasp and analyze ideas" is relevant to specific contexts. For example, a well-trained macroeconomist may be able to review the key economic aggregates and assess the proximate causes of a country's economic problems.

But he or she might generally lack the skills necessary for determining how and whether, say, tax reform or public enterprise reform will help overcome the macro problems. Although he or she could ultimately acquire those skills (through "capacity deepening"), the usual solution is to turn the task over to a specialist in taxes and public enterprise reform.

Four distinct sets of skills are associated with these various abilities—strategic, administrative, technical, and communication (Mann and McPherson, 1981).

- Strategic capacity enables an individual to *recognize* economic problems and place them in their appropriate context.
- Administrative (or managerial) capacity is the ability to *organize* the activities of diverse groups of individuals and institutions to deal with particular economic problems.
- Technical (or analytical) capacity is the ability to *analyze* these problems in depth.
- Communication capacity is the ability to *impart* the skills required by individuals and groups to respond effectively to specific economic problems.

No one individual develops all of these skills with equal depth. Thus the resolution of policy issues typically requires the cooperation of individuals with different skills.

Capacity Within the Ministry of Finance
Only a few MoF staff had developed these skills to any significant degree. It was unusual that anyone would think of economic issues in strategic terms. Models of the economy had never been developed; monetary programming was used only by IMF staff; the government had not developed a rolling plan; and the annual budget was passed without in-depth discussion of government priorities. Indeed, until Minister Sisay appointed the ERP task force, a group of officials had never been assembled to discuss The Gambia's economic problems so comprehensively.[8]

Several studies of the ministry revealed that its administration and management were inadequate (see, for example, MDI, 1989). A highly personalized system of administration had evolved, centered around the permanent secretary. Moreover, despite a commitment to training and much effort in this area, the average skills of the ministry staff had not improved. Many of those who had been trained became discouraged and left.

A more fundamental problem was an erosion of public trust in the ministry. Many senior ministry officials found that the public was skeptical about their attempts to engender reform. Ironically, one reason that the ERP measures met little public resistance was that many Gambians simply doubted that the government was sincere about reform.

Although most of the original and administrative deficiencies can be attributed to the absence of skills, political considerations and opportunism were also culprits. The agenda pursued by some senior ministry officials was at times unrelated to national development. One obvious example is that the ministry and the government failed repeatedly to deal decisively with customs fraud—a failure that was not due to technical or administrative considerations (as discussed in Chapter 17).

Improving the Capacity of the Ministry of Finance

Training offered much potential for achieving marked and sustained improvements in the productivity of ministerial staff. Training can enhance productivity either by improving an individual's facility with his or her existing tasks ("skill deepening") or by increasing the range of tasks in which the employee can excel ("skill broadening"). Both types of training occurred in the ministry through computerization and substantive instruction.

Before September 1985 the only computer in the ministry was a minicomputer used by the accountant general for payroll processing. The EFPA technical assistance project introduced personal computers to the ministry with a view toward achieving two objectives: (1) increasing the efficiency of many MoF operations and (2) attracting the interest of alert MoF staff members and motivating them to work alongside the foreign advisers, absorb some applied economics, and qualify themselves for foreign training.

Computerization affected almost every aspect of the ministry's operations—the budget, World Bank/IMF program monitoring, balance of payments and national accounts, debt reporting, income tax, trade and customs data analysis, and public utility rate making. Over time local staff were trained to operate the computers, and in some areas they began to use them in their analytic work. In other areas, such as income tax, the technical advisers demonstrated potential uses of computers in policy analysis but did not succeed in convincing managers to assign staff to learn the routines and continue the work.

On-the-job training was offered both at the ministry and at the Management Development Institute (MDI) on topics such as budgeting, fiscal policy, micro- and macroeconomic analysis, regression analysis, and accounting procedures (among other subjects). The local training effort was supplemented with training abroad, in the form of conferences, summer workshops, summer schools, remedial and refresher courses, short-term professional training, conventional undergraduate training, and specialized master's-level training. Trainees took courses in a wide range of economic, financial, management, and administrative topics.

Training was an important issue for the staffing of the newly established Statistics and Special Studies Unit in the MoF, to which the EFPA project was attached. The permanent secretary decided that the ministry would not attempt to build up the SSSU with staff drawn from other parts of the government, so as not to weaken the other governmental departments. Instead, he decided that the staff of the SSSU would be promoted from within the ministry and that appropriate on-the-job training, local courses, and training abroad would be used to enhance their skills.

SSSU staff development raised several issues. First, creating a coherent, well-functioning, and self-sustaining policy unit was likely to take many years. Most of the MoF staff first had to be brought up to standards that enabled them to gain entry into graduate and specialized training in the United States and Europe. Second, on-the-job training was a time-consuming activity for the foreign advisers, who, by linking their technical analysis directly to training, conducted what was in effect a continuous tutorial with selected members of the ministry. Third, overseas training courses made the shortage of trained personnel even more severe in the short run while the trainees were away, leading to a heavier dependence on the foreign advisers. Fourth, once key staff had upgraded their skills, they were more likely to leave their jobs for other positions. This exodus occurred either when staff who had been specifically trained for particular positions in the MoF were given different, less attractive assignments or when they took better-paying jobs outside the government.

One case may be cited to illustrate these issues. In 1986 a former member of the Weights and Measures Unit was assigned by the permanent secretary to work in the SSSU as a trainee statistician/economist. At the time she knew practically no economics, was unfamiliar with com-puters, and had only rudimentary typing skills. With time, on-the-job training, individual coaching in basic economics, and selected short courses (a project appraisal course, a budget workshop, and special courses at the Economics Institute in Boulder, Colorado), she became one of the most productive members of the ministry. Yet she has since moved on to work for an international aid agency.

Of course, from a national welfare perspective, the exodus of trained staff from the government to the private sector is not a problem. Indeed, it could be beneficial if the new skills help the person to be even more productive in the private sector. Nevertheless, it creates a management problem for the original agency that has a particular scope of work, a limited budget, and poorly trained staff.

Selecting trainees raised another set of issues. Training confers unique advantages on those selected by enhancing their personal skills and their wage potential and by providing opportunities for travel and cultural interchange. When abroad, many trainees experienced a significantly higher standard of living. Graduate-level training, especially in business or financial management, gave individuals greater opportunities to enter the international job market.

In other words, training generated economic rents. Thus controlling the access to training was an important part of the spoils system in the MoF—illustrated by the frequency with which heads of departments nominated themselves for training. Pressure also was routinely exerted on project staff to send particular individuals for training. But most officials who were more interested in travel than in training were screened out.

Overall, the allocation of training worked out well. Summer workshops lasting five to six weeks proved to be ideal for department heads, as they were short enough not to tie up senior officials for too long, and they occurred at a generally slack time in The Gambia (July and August). These workshops offered sufficient material to challenge the trainees without overwhelming them. And because the heads of departments were sent abroad for training, on-the-job training efforts could focus on more junior staff.

Upon their return trainees expected to be promoted and to be used more effectively. Some trainees indeed were promoted; moreover, because the work load on the ministry was so pressing, many had to assume additional responsibilities. However, because the ministry had not been reorganized substantively, the trainees were still subject to the disarray and disincentives that had hindered their productivity before their training.[9]

By failing to reorganize, the ministry lost an important opportunity to reduce duplication of effort, target employees' skills more effectively, and improve staff supervision. Performance appraisal also suffered, because it was difficult to discern whether an individual's poor performance was due to his or her lack of effort or to the general disarray of the ministry. Much of the benefit of the training was lost.

Some of the more highly motivated trainees encountered other difficulties when they resumed work in the ministry. They often became impatient with the inefficiency and organizational problems in the ministry that hindered their work. Some found their opportunities for promotion blocked on criteria besides merit; others found that they had no desire to accommodate the spoils system. For some of these trainees, seeking employment outside the ministry became more appealing. As discussed earlier, that occurred frequently, especially among the trainees whose performance was above average.

Notwithstanding these potential drawbacks, the training opportunities that were provided to ministry staff had several positive effects. The standard of economic discourse within the ministry improved; arguments made for and against particular positions were more cogent; criticisms of long-established ideas became more insightful; individual staff members were more willing to take positions on economic issues and to defend them; and many of the lower-level staff came to understand the reasons for the economy's difficulties, the types of changes that would have to be made, and why. Perhaps the most encouraging development was that the type of work undertaken regularly by the technical assistance staff changed substantially over time. Initially, all data collection and collation were undertaken by the technical advisers; over time responsibility for that function shifted. Similarly, drafting memoranda and analyses of policy issues had been a basic function left to the expatriate advisers; with the general improvement in staff capacity, much of that work was taken over by regular staff.

The Counterfactual: Did Foreign Technical Assistance Undermine Capacity Building?

A hypothesis suggested by the Jaycox thesis cited earlier is that the foreign technical assistance in the MoF, by "substituting for what capacity exist[ed]" in the MoF, "systematically destroy[ed]" that capacity. This might have happened in one of two ways: (1) the foreigners' presence reduced MoF management's concerns about engaging or retaining competent staff, thereby "pushing away professional (local) talent," and/or (2) competent staff members became discouraged by the extent to which management and the multilateral missions relied on the expatriates, and therefore neglected analytical tasks they otherwise would have performed, and gave up the associated opportunities to gain experience, skill, and job satisfaction.

As an alternative to supplying expatriates, Jaycox suggests three options: (1) "changing the salary structure so that it reflects the salary range that you are trying to keep in the government, which means raises for people in upper skill categories"; (2) contracting work out to the private sector, where professionals earn their opportunity cost; and (3) training, to be conducted primarily in local institutions. Jaycox commits the World Bank to financing all three approaches.

In the Gambian context, it would have been impossible for a USAID-funded project to offer salary supplements to attract senior Gambian professionals from abroad. And there was general agreement that no qualified economists were available locally in the private sector. Such an arrangement would have been contrary to both Gambian civil service regulations and USAID policy and would have aroused resentment on the part of other public officials. Thus the first two options given by Jaycox were not possible in The Gambia.

Instead, as Sisay and USAID developed the EFPA project, they stuck to the traditional model of using project funds to train Gambian counterparts to replace the expatriates. As long as Sisay was in office, he took an active interest in personnel matters, including recruitment, training, and job assignments. He was well aware of which staff members had professional potential and which did not, and on several occasions he discussed with EFPA advisers possible patterns of ministry staffing that would remove weaker middle managers and replace them with more junior staff on their return from training. One of his last official acts was to request his permanent secretary, with EFPA assistance, to prepare a plan for restructuring the ministry.

Sisay's illness removed him from active leadership before the first staff member returned from long-term training. The ministers who eventually succeeded him had less interest in personnel issues or, indeed, in institutional development generally. The permanent secretaries occasionally spoke about their responsibility for personnel management but appeared to be unwilling or unable to deal with nonperforming staff or to use abler staff effectively. As a result, by mid-1992 nearly all the MoF staff trained under the EFPA project who had professional potential had left the ministry.

By the early 1990s most donors (and many host country governments) had learned that technical assistance projects are rarely successful in training counterpart staff to replace expatriate advisers, since most high-quality trainees soon leave the agency. However, as discussed previously, at a macro level the model still can be beneficial for the host country if the staff in question remain in the country and generate sufficient value added in their new jobs.

The impact of a technical assistance project (like the EFPA) on MoF capacity building has to be evaluated in light of the counterfactual: where would the MoF capacity be now in the absence of the project? One scenario, as implied by Jaycox, would be that without the technical assistance project: (1) the higher-potential local staff would have remained in the ministry, doing better work than the present staff; (2) the present staff would be producing higher-quality work because they would not have been alienated by the activities and high profile of the foreign advisers; and (3) MoF management, responding to donor and IMF pressure, would have worked harder to find qualified Gambians and offer them incentives to work in the ministry, even on a short-term contract basis.

A second scenario might be the following: that without the technical assistance project, (1) the better local staff would have remained mired in functions with minimal professional content or else left the ministry in any case; (2) the present staff would be producing lower-quality work, because they did not benefit from working with and learning from the advisers; and (3) the government would have found it was unable to offer sufficient incentives to attract Gambian professionals from overseas and, without trained staff or advisers, would have left more of the formulating and monitoring of reform packages to the donors.

It is not easy to prove or disprove either of these scenarios or an intermediate one. There is some evidence that MoF staff performance in monitoring and analyzing the economy remains (as of early 1994) better than it was before the EFPA project. Moreover, there are strong reasons to believe that had Sisay survived and retained his post, the ministry's current performance would be even better. Time and again during his tenure, Sisay took concrete steps toward building capacity in the MoF. As early as March 1983, he asked a foreign consultant to interview his staff and assess training potential. He later arranged for many recommendations of the ensuing report to be implemented, and consulted repeatedly with project advisers on staff development.

Sisay also frequently expressed his intention to promote successful long-term trainees once they returned. During his tenure the question of designing adequate incentives to retain competent staff never arose, but there was reason to believe that he would have taken the problem seriously and approached it in an imaginative way. Up to the time Sisay's tenure was cut short by illness, it appeared that the MoF might be on the road to strengthening its capacity. Unfortunately, since that time there has been little progress in this direction.

Therefore, an important aspect of the problem is the capability of The Gambia's present political system to provide the type of leadership that can take advantage of opportunities offered by foreign technical assistance, while avoiding the most serious pitfalls. Sisay provided that kind of leadership and therefore was able to make the most of the technical assistance that was provided to him to enhance the capacity of the MoF.

Concluding Observations about Institutional Reform

Structural adjustment depends on both policy and institutional changes. Institutional weaknesses can be offset initially with technical assistance. Ultimately, however, a cadre of motivated, skilled, and competent staff must be developed. Doing so in a ministry that is implementing a structural adjustment program for a government that is itself in the process of undergoing reform is demanding.

Sustaining the effort after the most urgent need for adjustment has passed is even more demanding. One of the unfortunate costs of the type of organizational disarray that occurred in The Gambia is that it ruined the work habits and morale of many officials. Under these circumstances, training was only part of the process of improving productivity and reviving a sense of responsibility.

One lesson that emerges from the Gambian experience is that training and institutional reform must occur simultaneously. Despite the potential political consequences and the internal resistance, it is a mistake to assume that the institutional reform of a ministry can be delayed. In retrospect, the MoF should have been one of the first ministries reorganized under the Administrative Reform Program. The delay compromised much of the benefit of the training that was subsequently provided.

Another lesson is that, paradoxically, the availability of technical assistance can be an obstacle to institutional reform. While the donors continued to fund technical advisers and consultants who could and would do most of the critical analyses and monitoring within The Gambia's MoF, some local staff became less motivated and productive. Others, however, took advantage of the opportunities to learn new skills, and became more productive over time.

The economic advisers did not work themselves out of their jobs, which is the standard criterion by which such efforts are judged. However, they *did* work themselves out of many parts of their jobs. Additional training will help address the continuing problem of low skill levels. Moreover, ongoing enhancement of the strategic and technical capacities of Gambian staff will help improve the dynamics of policy analysis. Ultimately, the combination of reorganization, better management, and training will leave the ministry's work entirely in Gambian hands.

NOTES

1. Transcript of an address to a conference of the African-American Institute in Reston, Virginia, May 20, 1993. World Bank, processed.
2. In September 1990 the Ministry of Finance and Trade and the Ministry of Economic Planning and Industrial Development were combined into the Ministry of Finance and Economic Affairs. The trade division was transferred to the newly formed Ministry of Industry, Trade, and Employment. For the sake of simplicity, we refer to the Ministry of Finance, or MoF.
3. Obviously, by recalling Sisay to the ministry, the president had come to recognize that the ministry's performance was a problem and that he had run out of options. Although both Minister Sisay and President Jawara had helped establish the PPP and both were members of the pre-independence government, their rivalry had intensified as the 1960s unfolded, leading to a widely publicized falling-out.
4. The consultant was Clive S. Gray, one of the authors of this chapter.
5. For example, the appointment of a new permanent secretary dragged out for thirteen months, due to resistance within the civil service. The process normally takes slightly more than six months.
6. Minister Sisay took advantage of his annual leave in 1984 to become a visiting scholar at Harvard University, where he attended lectures and seminars on institutional reorganization and worked on a paper on structural adjustment that he later presented at Vanderbilt University.
7. Most MoF technical staff had only high school diplomas (O levels and A levels), supplemented by on-the-job experience. None of the staff could qualify for overseas training without first taking remedial courses in economics or accounting.
8. Teams of economists and planners had been assembled to formulate the first and second five-year plans and the midterm review of the second plan. Although their task had been to derive a plan through the aggregation of sectoral activities, they had stopped short of determining whether the individual sectoral initiatives were consistent.
9. The reorganization of the ministry in September 1990 did not address that issue.

16

Parastatal Reform, Performance Contracts, and Privatization

Richard M. Hook, Richard D. Mallon, and Malcolm F. McPherson

During the late 1970s and early 1980s, public enterprises represented an important part of the economy in most SSA countries. In countries where data are available, PEs contributed an average of 15 percent to GDP, accounted for 25 to 30 percent of gross domestic investment, and comprised 25 to 30 percent of total formal-sector employment (Swanson and Wolde-Semait, 1989). Since the late 1970s the economic and financial performance of the majority of PEs has been poor, draining financial resources from government budgets, creating economic inefficiencies, and crowding out private-sector activities.

As with most countries in sub-Saharan Africa, The Gambia created PEs to serve several economic and social purposes. Some were created in order to allow the state to control certain strategic sectors of the economy, usually including utilities, transportation, and major agricultural and export commodities. Others were created primarily to expand employment and encourage industrial development. At independence The Gambia had four such enterprises; by 1985 it had twenty.

PEs in The Gambia, as in the rest of SSA, were required to engage in commercial activities and provide public services, such as retail trade and drought relief. They were frequently subject to restrictions on the prices they could charge, the wages they could pay, and their hiring practices. Creating PEs and directing them to perform specific functions were trivial tasks compared to efforts to manage them effectively, meet basic standards of accountability, and ensure acceptable levels of operating efficiency and cost recovery.

Initially, the PEs made a positive net contribution to national income and domestic savings. But toward the end of the 1970s, they became a net financial drain on the economy. The PEs consumed a growing portion of domestic credit and required larger subsidies from the central government.

At the same time, the quality of the services they delivered deteriorated. Thus they quickly became a focus of attention as the ERP was being formulated. Some government officials and virtually all of the donor community saw a direct connection between the poor performance of the PEs and the economy's difficulties, and began to consider how the performance of the PEs could be improved. Yet despite the poor performance of the PEs and the general economic decline, some government officials strongly resisted parastatal reform and even exerted pressure to create additional PEs.[1]

PE reform has been an integral part of structural adjustment programs across SSA, with at best mixed results (see World Bank, 1991b; Galal, 1991; Swanson and Wolde-Semait, 1989). Reform strategies begin at the macroeconomic level; almost all analysts agree that appropriate exchange rate, interest rate, and other pricing policies are crucial to successful PE performance. Most reform programs also call for some combination of divestiture, asset liquidation, and performance contracts. But of these three strategies, analysts, donors, and government officials disagree about which ones are most appropriate for different firms, how the reforms should be implemented, and how long it should take to implement them. In some cases these disagreements reflect different notions about the appropriate role of the state; in other cases they reflect different opinions about how much change can realistically be expected in a relatively short period of time.

The Gambian experience provides insights into some of these issues. After introducing the major macroeconomic reforms, The Gambia relied primarily on performance contracts to reform its most important PEs. It also privatized several PEs. The experience highlights the difficulties associated with choosing the appropriate strategy for different firms, the problems encountered in implementing performance contracts, and the reasons for continued resistance to reform efforts.

This chapter analyzes The Gambia's experiences with PE reform. It begins by reviewing the main elements of the reform program (the performance contract system and divestiture). It then highlights some of the problems encountered in implementing the reforms and considers issues associated with monitoring the performance of the PEs. The chapter concludes with some of the lessons from the Gambian experience.

The Role of Public Enterprises

The first Gambian PE, the Gambia Savings Bank—better known as the Post Office Savings Bank—was established in 1922. The Gambia Oil

Seeds Marketing Board, which later became the Gambia Produce Marketing Board, was formed in 1948, and the Gambia Central Cooperative Banking and Marketing Union Ltd. (the forerunner to the Gambia Cooperatives Union) was created in 1955. Some organizations, such as the Gambia Ports Authority and the Gambia Utilities Corporation, were once operating departments of the Ministry of Works and Services (later the Ministry of Works and Communications). Some PEs were created when the government took over the assets of foreign-owned organizations. For example, the National Trading Corporation emerged when the government bought the assets of the United Africa Corporation. Finally, other PEs were simply created. The Gambia Commercial and Development Bank was formed in 1972 by an act of Parliament (see Table 16-1).

Table 16-1. The Gambia's Public Enterprises: 1985 and 1990

	Government Ownership (%)	
	1985	1990
Financial		
Central Bank of The Gambia (CBG)	100	100
Gambia Commercial and Development Bank (GCDB)	100	100
Gambia National Insurance Corporation (GNIC)	100	0
Government Savings Bank (Post Office)	100	100
Agricultural Development Bank (ADB)	100	0
Social Security and Housing Financing Corporation (SSHFC)	100	100
Nonfinancial		
Gambia Produce Marketing Board (GPMB)	100	100
Gambia Utility Corporation (GUC)	100	100
Gambia Ports Authority (GPA)	100	100
Gambia Telecommunication Company (GAMTEL)	100	99
Gambia River Transport Corporation (GRTC)	100	100
Livestock Marketing Board (LMB)	100	100
Fish Processing and Marketing Corporation (FPMC)	100	0
Atlantic Hotel	100	100
Citrus Products Company Ltd.	100	100
Partially Government-Owned		
Gambia Tannery Company (GAMTAN)	50	50
Seagull Coldstores Ltd.	61	61
Wing Africa Ltd.	50	0
African Hotels (Sunwing)	33	0
Kombo Beach Hotel (Novotel)	20	20
Senegambia Beach Hotel	40	40
Banjul Breweries Ltd.	10	10
CFAO Supermarket Ltd.	9	0
National Trading Corporation	51	40
Standard Chartered Bank (Gambia) Ltd.	10	0

Source: Ministry of Finance and Economic Affairs.

The PEs have played an important role in the Gambian economy. Until the mid-1970s GPMB operations were larger in absolute terms than those of the government itself. The PEs became especially significant after the government introduced the first five-year plan in 1975, because they were an integral part of the government's attempt to accelerate economic growth and promote development.[2]

From 1971 to 1981 twenty PEs were created. Their activities covered all major aspects of the economy—from fishing and tourism to retail trade and insurance. Due to the general economic expansion, the buoyancy of world markets, and the sharp rise in foreign aid, the PEs made a positive net contribution to formal-sector employment, domestic value added, domestic savings, and net foreign exchange earnings. That contribution diminished as the limits of the domestic market were reached, and the profitability of the GPMB was undermined by an increasingly overvalued exchange rate, low output due to drought, and declining foreign prices for groundnuts. During the period from 1979 to 1982, the PEs experienced net losses of D112 million (World Bank, 1985a, Table 7-1).

The GPMB was particularly hard hit. By 1978 it had accumulated reserves of D106 million, equivalent to US$54.6 million, or 30 percent of GDP. Its reserves were exhausted by 1982. By June 1983 the GPMB was in debt by more than D100 million (approximately US$37 million) to the Central Bank. The reversal in the GPMB's fortunes was due to the large transfers from its reserves to the government budget, declining world prices, large losses in domestic groundnut trading, an inability to control costs, and the diversion of resources to peripheral activities. The GPMB's losses and those of other parastatals were financed with bank credit, adding pressure to the already overextended financial system (see Chapter 6).

By the time the ERP was formulated, the PEs were a major financial drain on the entire economy. Fundamental reform of their operations was overdue.

Parastatal Reform

Even before the ERP, the World Bank and USAID had begun to press for the reform of key PEs. Studies of the financial system and the groundnut sector highlighted the precarious financial state of both the GCDB and the GPMB (Wing, 1983; World Bank, 1985b; Biggs et al., 1985). The studies showed that government interference in the operations of both organizations had adversely affected their economic performance.

A key conclusion was that the relationship between the government and the PEs had to change. Privatization (divestiture) and performance contracts were considered to be the most effective ways to achieve that objective.

Privatization would allow the government to disengage from activities that it could not manage properly and for which there was no compelling *public* reason to be involved. Performance contracts were a potentially effective way to improve the management of enterprises that the government would not or could not divest. The World Bank pushed hard for both initiatives; they were subsequently included in the ERP. Performance contracts were to be introduced for strategic PEs, while privatization would be aimed at nonstrategic PEs.

Some MoF officials recognized that parastatal reform had to be part of any effort to revive the economy, but most government officials expressed no enthusiasm for privatization, for several reasons. First, some PEs (such as the GPA and the GUC) were monopolies. The creation and subsequent regulation of private monopolies to provide port services and utilities (electricity and water) were not considered positive steps. Second, many officials believed that all the PEs were strategic to the country's development and that the government had a public duty to maintain control of them. Third, the PE managers formed an influential lobby. Both types of reforms threatened their position. Fourth, some PEs served political purposes. They operated in controlled markets, generating rents that were used to obtain or retain political support. The government was particularly sensitive to suggestions that the agricultural PEs be reformed. Finally, the PEs provided a convenient way to transfer public resources to favored groups and individuals through inflated salaries and perquisites, opportunities for foreign travel, cheap loans that rarely had to be repaid, overstaffing, nepotism, and outright corruption. For all of these reasons, resistance to parastatal reform was potent.[3] It has been overcome only with pressure from donors. For the GCDB and the GPMB, the process dragged out from 1986 to 1992.

Moreover, the actual implementation of the reforms took much longer than anticipated. The original schedule for implementing the performance contracts included in the ERP—namely, to have the GPMB, the GUC, the Gambia Public Transport Corporation, and the Gambia Telecommunication Company (GAMTEL) under contract in the first year—was too ambitious. Designing and negotiating the specifics of each of these contracts took much longer, and officials did not foresee the time and effort necessary to collect and monitor all of the information required by the contracts.

Performance Contracts

After several delays, the basic approach for introducing performance contracts was outlined by the National Investment Board in October 1986, in a document entitled the "Divestiture Strategy Action Plan." Six PEs—the GPMB, the GPA, the GUC, the Livestock Marketing Board, the GAMTEL, and the Social Security and Housing Finance Corporation—were classified as strategic. Although some of their peripheral activities would be sold, the core of their operations would be retained by the government and reorganized under performance contracts.

The purpose of performance contracts was to give the PEs greater autonomy while holding their managers accountable for results. Greater autonomy from bureaucratic regulations was justified on the grounds that parastatals should behave as businesses with primarily commercial objectives. Their managers should thus be treated as businesspersons and be held accountable for the results they achieve, not for how well they comply with procedural regulations. This "arm's length" relationship between government and the PEs was spelled out in contractual obligations that stipulated enterprise performance targets, government financial and regulatory commitments, and specific rewards and penalties linked to contract compliance. To facilitate performance monitoring, the contracts required implicitly that all transactions between the parties be transparent. For example, government transfers or subsidies to parastatals were to be based on the cost of performing noncommercial services and to be included as explicit line items in the government budget.

Three contracts were initiated in 1987 with the GPMB, the GUC, and the GPA.[4] The NIB was given responsibility for monitoring PE performance under the contracts.

Privatization

Privatization sought to improve overall economic efficiency, reduce fiscal losses, broaden the ownership of economic enterprises, and provide access to additional sources of private savings. Economic efficiency was expected to result from the cost-cutting and revenue-enhancing behavior of the private entrepreneurs who acquired the PEs. For most PEs in The Gambia, costs could readily be cut with better work practices, better inventory control, and the retrenchment of labor. Revenue could be increased with improved cash management, the collection of overdue bills, and appropriate pricing decisions. The crucial elements were reorganization and improved management. These were expected of private entrepreneurs whose direct stake in ownership gave them an incentive to focus more intently on net returns. This incentive structure differed from the one for public-sector managers, many of whom were political appointees. For many public-sector managers, profitability was not a primary objective, but rather a constraint on such other objectives as generating employment, rents, or political patronage.

Privatization was expected to reduce fiscal losses in four ways. First, the privatized enterprise would be subject to income tax,[5] from which all PEs in The Gambia had historically been exempt. Second, the operating losses (including debt obligations) of the PEs would no longer be a contingent liability on the government. Third, to the extent that the sale of the PEs reflected greater confidence by the private sector, government revenue would benefit from increased income. Finally, the proceeds from the sale of the PEs would add (albeit marginally) to government revenue (Vickers and Yarrow, 1991).

Broadening the ownership base was an explicit government objective. The NIB Action Plan sought to create the conditions that would encourage a broad-based Gambian entrepreneurial class while avoiding major concentrations of ownership. Employee participation in ownership was stressed.

The Divestiture Strategy Action Plan proposed an ambitious timetable for the sale of government shares. For instance, the hope was that the shares of Banjul Breweries would be sold by October 1986, and those of Africa Hotels (Sunwing) by March 1987. Neither of these targets was met. The first sale of government shares was for CFAO Ltd. and Standard Bank in 1987. The NTC was offered for sale in 1988 and was eventually sold in 1992; the Nyambai sawmill was sold in 1988 (for D4 million); and Gamtours was sold in 1989 (for D1.4 million). By 1992 more than 60 percent of the Gambian PEs had been sold (Rumbaugh, 1992).

Parastatal Reform: Issues, Concerns, and Problems

Numerous issues had to be resolved as the parastatal reform program was implemented: the effective regulation of the PEs, the imposition of hard budget constraints on both the government and the PEs, the design of the performance contracts, the availability of domestic savings to support the privatization effort, and the institutional capacity to monitor the reform process.

Regulatory issues go hand in hand with rationalizing the ownership and control of the PEs. In The Gambia complications arose because it was unclear whether regulatory responsibility rested with the relevant line ministry or with the NIB.[6] The confusion provided the GUC and

GCDB managements numerous opportunities to obstruct the reform process. For example, when the government attempted to restructure the GUC's finances, a long debate ensued about the extent of the debt and whether the government had previously forgiven some portion of it. To make progress, the government accepted the GUC's estimates (see Chapter 12).

In theory, a strong case can be made for deregulating PEs before they are sold; however, for enterprises that face limited competition, complete deregulation seems less likely. In practice, the government adopted a rather ad hoc approach to deregulation. For example, the government liberalized the domestic rice market in the hopes of getting the public sector out of the commercial importation of rice. But while the GPMB was excluded from importing rice, the GCU was not. Another example is the Nyambai sawmill, which was sold in 1988. It faces virtually no domestic competition and has access to a public resource (the Nyambai forest). The necessary regulation of the monopoly did not accompany the privatization. If the government wants the forest replanted, as agreed to at the time of the sale, marked improvements in public oversight are required.

It was recognized at the outset that some detailed preliminary work would be necessary to prepare the PEs for divestiture and/or performance contracts. The three enterprises targeted initially had different characteristics: the GUC was in deep financial trouble, the GPMB was too large to ignore, and the GPA was in a fairly strong financial position. The expectation was that the monitoring procedures, the supply of trained staff, and the general buildup of experience accompanying the reform program would save time and effort. But the cost savings have proved to be illusory. Indeed, the process has been more complex and time-consuming than either the government or the donors imagined. The preparation and implementation of the second round of performance contracts—for the SSHFC, the GAMTEL, and the GPTC—were so delayed that much of the initial learning experience was lost. Staff were reassigned, new consultants adopted different approaches, and the economic circumstances changed. Moreover, so much time had been absorbed in dealing with the problems of the GPMB and the GUC that the follow-on contracts received less attention than was anticipated or than they deserved.

Another problem was that the scope and timing of the performance contracts were overambitious. The proposal in the ERP to implement performance contracts for four major PEs in the first year of the program (including the giant GPMB) was unrealistic. Similarly, the attempted timing of the reforms was too ambitious. In October 1986 the NIB reminded the first group of targeted PEs that the trial run for performance contracts would begin in December. The PEs received preconditions to operating the contracts: clear ministerial statements of policies and objectives for each PE; the settlement of liabilities with other PEs; government agreement to provide financial support for noncommercial PE activities; and agreements on the reorganization of boards of directors and on capital restructuring.

Another issue was the system of rewards and sanctions necessary to make the performance contracts effective. The rewards and sanctions had to be clear, reasonably simple, and enforceable. Even after the first round of performance contracts had been signed, an acceptable approach to calculating performance had not been found. For example, the proposal forwarded in 1988 included sixteen separate indicators, some quantitatively measurable and others a matter of judgment. Such complex scoring schemes with many criteria make pinpointing responsibility difficult and can lead to manipulation by management. Under the system of scoring suggested in 1989, GPMB management would have been able to sustain a massive net loss, fail to service its debt, allow its groundnut evacuation rate to worsen, and fail to maintain its fixed assets, and still collect a bonus of one year's salary. That complex, unwieldy system did not focus on the basic criterion of operating results. Moreover, no punishments were specified for egregious failure to meet targets, other than an investigation if the PE scored 45 percent of total possible marks or lower.

In that event, the main sanction used was the replacement of the PE's managers. The president fired the managing directors of the GPMB and the GUC twice. While these actions indicated that some form of sanctions did indeed exist, their usefulness as a signal of the government's commitment to reform was problematic. The changes occurred only after the donor community made its concerns known about mismanagement and malfeasance in both organizations.

Interestingly, it appeared that the initiation of the performance contract system, on its own, may have boosted the performance of several of the other PEs. The threat of divestiture and the managerial scrutiny involved in negotiating a performance contract were strong signals to the managements of PEs in general that the government (supported by the donors) would be less indulgent of inefficiency than they had been previously.

With respect to privatization, several technical issues arose. For instance, how would the assets be valued given that their book value was entirely unrealistic and no effective market existed? The sale of the

NTC was delayed for more than a year because the NIB had valued its shares at book value *plus* the debt to the government. Only the SSHFC, under pressure from the government, took up shares at that price. What would be done with the accumulated debts and arrears? Would potential purchasers be provided with credit to purchase the shares? On what terms? Would the system of taxation of income and capital gains be changed? Some analysts believed that the rate of company tax (50 percent) would be a deterrent to investment. Would the newly privatized entities be given preferential tax or financial treatment under the Development Act? What supporting measures would be necessary to enhance the liquidity and transferability of the shares? One possibility was to establish a stock exchange, but the size of the Gambian market was too small to support an exchange (Ladd, 1989).

Finally, the success of privatization depended on the existence of individuals or firms with access to sufficient resources to buy the offered shares. Initially, there was some concern that the domestic savings needed to enable individuals and firms to purchase the PEs were not available. The largest portfolio of liquid assets in The Gambia was held by the SSHFC—but it was 100 percent government-owned. The issue, however, was not as clear cut as it first appeared. Many people were willing to buy shares in profitable, well-managed enterprises, such as Standard Bank (Ladd, 1989). Indeed, judging from overseas deposits of US$80 million held by Gambian residents in 1985 (37 percent of GDP), resources were not a problem. The lack of confidence in the economy, and specifically the lack of confidence in the government's commitment to privatization, were far more important.

Monitoring PE Performance: The National Investment Board[7]

The limited capacity of the existing government institutions to support the PE reforms was a major weakness confronting the government. A key organization in this regard was the NIB. From its inception one of the NIB's responsibilities has been to represent the government's interests relative to the PEs. In this capacity the NIB provided commentary on the economic and financial affairs of the PEs. But in its early years, neither the government nor the PEs took much notice of the NIB's views.

As the performance of the PEs continued to degenerate, it became increasingly evident that neither the line ministries nor Cabinet could or would exercise the leadership necessary to rectify the situation. As an alternative, the NIB had several attractive features. First, its chief executive reported directly to the president and thus was well placed to gain high-level support for parastatal reform. Second, the NIB staff were young, energetic, and relatively well trained. Moreover, they generally showed some appreciation of the basic problems confronting the PEs. Third, because the NIB had a separate budget, its salaries were attractive enough to retain its better-trained staff. Finally, the NIB already had statutory responsibility for overseeing government interests. Thus, creating an additional institution was unnecessary.

But there were disadvantages as well. First, the NIB had almost no authority. The capacity to monitor performance meant little if the PEs and line ministries would not cooperate. Second, many of the problems with the PEs were political. The technical recommendations of the NIB might be overruled by political considerations. Third, the risk existed that the NIB itself might become another interest group. Thrusting the NIB into such a prominent position meant that it could become part of the problem rather than part of the solution.

Despite these drawbacks the government and the donors believed that the NIB should become the lead organization in the parastatal reform program. But strengthening the NIB so that it could fulfill that expanded role would take a major effort. The introduction of performance contracts clearly required major organizational and procedural changes in the supervision of parastatals, in government financial controls, and in the flow and use of information.

Responsibility for supervising parastatals has traditionally been entrusted to sectoral ministries, acting both directly and through boards of directors over which they exercise considerable influence. Performance contracts, which are negotiated between parastatal managers and the NIB acting on behalf of the president, constitute a parallel system of supervision, since the roles of sectoral ministries and parastatal boards of directors have not yet been redefined.

The government's financial controls over the parastatals have traditionally been lax: expenditures have been subsidized after the fact, no penalties have been exacted for bills not paid on time or for the accumulation of arrears, and bank credit has regularly been used to finance parastatal deficits.[8]

The flow of information within parastatals and between them and government has traditionally been input–output oriented. Information on cash flow, profit margins, sales-to-inventory ratios, and other financial variables monitored regularly in business firms is largely ignored if gathered at all; and annual financial statements are frequently submitted a year or more late. Indeed, parastatal managers themselves seldom have any precise idea of how the performance of their separate divisions is affecting the commercial success of the business.[9]

But what progress has been made in these areas? It is clear that none of these organizational and procedural deficiencies can be overcome independently of the others. Technical assistance to improve management information systems is ineffective unless parastatal managers are motivated to want more relevant and timely information. For example, why would they want to supply the NIB with more information than they give to their sectoral ministers when they are not sure whose supervision really counts? Why would they want to provide more detailed financial information to the government if they are not subject to stricter financial discipline? Why should they become more commercially oriented when existing budgetary and regulatory processes focus on inputs (primarily personnel and salaries) rather than on outputs?

Under such circumstances parastatal managers could have been expected to adopt a "counterimplementation" strategy toward the performance contract system: lay low; rely on inertia; keep the system complex, hard to coordinate, and vaguely defined; minimize the implementers' legitimacy and influence; and exploit their lack of inside knowledge (Keen, 1981). There is evidence that parastatal managers followed this strategy: the delays in compliance with parastatal reporting requirements, the unwillingness of parastatal managers to assume responsibility for correcting problems identified in the NIB's quarterly performance reports, and the negotiations of the performance contracts were protracted.

One of the greatest threats to implementing the performance contract system successfully was inappropriate and excessive requests for information. For instance, the principal consultant study recommended, and the contracts included, the following reporting requirements for PEs: (1) three-year corporate plans, revised annually, including annual projected profit and loss statements, quarterly cash flows, capital expenditure programs, and a wide range of performance targets and other key indicators; (2) annual budgets with quarterly projections of revenue and expenses for each major good and service produced; and (3) indicative twenty-four-month forecasts, prepared annually, covering borrowing and capital expenditure needs. All of these were to be provided quarterly to the NIB.

Reporting requirements of this magnitude might strain the accounting and management information system capabilities of many major corporations. In the Gambian context in the mid-1980s, they were simply unreasonable. The information requested did not distinguish between the necessity of holding parastatal managers accountable for results and regulating the activities of the PEs and the requirements for instituting and monitoring long-term structural change. The result was that the performance contracts imposed impossible reporting demands on managements and were far beyond the NIB's capacity to monitor.

Most of the information provided by parastatals to the NIB was not critical and therefore was uninformative. NIB staff spent valuable time checking the plausibility and consistency of the data, a regulatory responsibility that should have been left to external auditors. The NIB had neither the personnel nor the knowledge to second-guess management's operating decisions or to audit their accounts. A better approach would have been to focus attention on the difficulties encountered by parastatals in achieving expected results and the measures adopted by managers to correct the problems. The focus should have been helping to improve performance, not simply policing the PEs.

Concluding Lessons about Parastatal Reform

The basic problem with the PEs in The Gambia was not the poor performance of any one parastatal, but the collective financial and economic drain of the PEs as a group. The main issue was the government's failure to recognize that the operations of the PEs as a group were unsustainable. Although some economic inefficiency can be tolerated in any economy, no economy can withstand widespread underperformance and nonperformance by the majority of its key organizations over a long period of time. Unfortunately, no one in the government recognized the negative macroeconomic effects of the collective impact of the PEs. As the adverse effects accumulated, parastatal reform became essential.

The Gambian reform experience illustrates several points, many of which are relevant to other SSA countries considering PE reform. First, given the interest groups involved, parastatal reform faces considerable resistance. In The Gambia even getting the problem on the government's agenda proved to be difficult and was not achieved without pressure from the donors. Some of this resistance stems from the legitimate debate over the proper role of the state in the economy, but much of it derives from the role of the PEs in generating rents and political patronage. Thus PE reform that comes about primarily at the initiative of the donors and without broad government support is unlikely to succeed.

Second, the macroeconomic environment is critical to PE performance. Much of the poor financial performance of PEs in The Gambia and elsewhere in SSA in the late 1970s and early 1980s was due to poor macroeconomic policies, especially overvalued exchange rates and price controls. In turn, PE performance cannot improve appreciably in the absence of stronger macroeconomic policies. The GPMB is perhaps the clearest case in The Gambia. It would have been impossible for the GPMB to make a financial profit had the exchange rate continued to be overvalued, except by offering extremely low farmgate prices to farmers. Performance contracts and privatization will not succeed in the midst of continued macroeconomic imbalances.

Third, in principle, performance contracts and privatization are highly desirable vehicles for reforming PEs. The performance of enterprises that, for whatever reason, must remain under public control can be enhanced. The government can rid itself of the administrative and financial commitments of organizations that are better suited to the private sector. The relevant issues are to determine which type of reform is appropriate for each PE and to decide how each performance contract or divestiture should be delineated. Each PE must be treated separately. Consequently, the preparations involved in implementing performance contracts and privatization are lengthy, complex, and skill-intensive. In The Gambia these were exacerbated by the unreasonable information demands on the organizations involved.

Fourth, the agencies given responsibility for promoting parastatal reform require special assistance. The authority and capability of the oversight agency must be commensurate with its responsibilities. The objective should be to develop the capacities to facilitate privatization and monitor PE performance. The temptation to police the PEs has to be resisted. The pressure on the oversight agency can be relieved by strengthening the government's audit capabilities or by allowing private companies to audit the PEs, so that the oversight agency can focus more heavily on improving performance.

Fifth, the role of the donors is critical to overcoming local resistance to the idea of parastatal reform, providing technical assistance to generate the performance contracts and monitor them, and supporting the government's efforts to value and sell selected PEs. Donor assistance in The Gambia was critical for providing the financing necessary to straighten out the books of bankrupt PEs and enabling managers to strengthen the operations of selected PEs. An issue for the future that has been bypassed in dealing with the problems of the present is how the donors will extricate themselves.

Finally, the problem of parastatal reform raises a broader issue of the role of the government in the economy. Although many Gambians would agree that the government has been overextended, no mechanism exists independently of donor conditionality (which restricts the creation of

PEs, limits external borrowing, and contains the growth of domestic credit) for determining the dividing line between public- and private-sector activity. It should be of some concern that this issue has not been debated in The Gambia. This debate is necessary if the government is to confront the limits of its financial and administrative capacities.

NOTES

1. For instance, the Gambia Telecommunication Company was established when Cable & Wireless Ltd. was taken over in 1985. At the same time, the government attempted to set up the Fish Processing and Marketing Corporation, causing serious problems with the World Bank. At one point, continued World Bank support for The Gambia's adjustment pro-gram hinged on whether the government would cancel plans to establish the organization.
2. The plan noted that "where it is deemed to be in the public interest, activities will be taken into public ownership or Government controlled institutions will be set up" (GOTG, 1975b, p. 168).
3. The minister of finance discovered just how potent when, in 1984, he attempted to use his authority under the GPMB Act to implement an efficiency audit of the GPMB. The GPMB board instructed the managing director to take leave during the process. He refused. Lacking support from the president, the minister abandoned the effort.
4. The firms differ from those noted in the ERP. The GPTC was in the process of being rehabilitated, and the GAMTEL was operating profitably. The GPA had few problems and a well-established management system. It was included because few difficulties were anticipated.
5. An increase in tax revenue presumed that the organization would be privatized without offering its new owners tax incentives and that the new owners will in fact pay the taxes they owe. As several studies of the tax system have shown, that cannot be taken for granted (see Chapter 9).
6. There was a hiatus in changing the law. A Public Enterprises Act, specifically designed to legitimize performance contracts, was not drafted until 1988.
7. This section draws on McPherson and Mallon (1990).
8. At least one PE even earned interest arbitrage by financing the purchase of treasury bills with cheaper Central Bank credit.
9. This was clearly demonstrated for the GUC (Murthy, 1989).

17

Customs Reform

Paul E. McNamara and Malcolm F. McPherson

Much of the credit for the recovery of the Gambian economy rests with the policies included in the ERP. Yet the recovery was also bolstered by actions that were not explicitly part of the ERP. Customs reform is an example.

In framing the ERP, Gambian officials focused on the most evident causes of the economic imbalances—an overvalued exchange rate, negative real interest rates, excessive credit expansion, a bloated civil service, inefficient public enterprises, and unproductive public investment. The distortions created by these factors were obvious, clear, and public. Other distortions, such as customs fraud, which proved to be equally disruptive, were not so obvious.

Customs provided fertile conditions for fraudulent behavior because of its poor control and accountability systems and the high degree of discretion exercised by customs officials. These problems, and the broader problem of corruption in government agencies, occur in many countries. The economic and social costs of corruption can be high. Revenue losses force governments to choose among reducing expenditures, raising other taxes, or financing a larger deficit. Corruption rewards illegal activity instead of productive work and transfers income away from the general population toward the perpetrators. The results are a misallocation of resources, worsening income distribution, and perhaps higher inflation and foreign debt.

Social scientists identify several possible origins of government corruption. Some point to a breakdown in the agency relationship between the central government and its tax collectors (Klitgaard, 1988). Others suggest that poverty and inequity can fuel corruption, as can social norms (such as kinship loyalty) when they conflict with stated bureaucratic objectives. Still others observe that bureaucratic corruption occurs more often when government economic intervention is significant, and a weak or "soft" state exists. If organizational characteristics, including institutional structure, decision-making processes, personnel management practices, and administrative control and accountability systems, are designed and managed without explicitly considering the potential for fraud, bureaucratic corruption is likely to appear (Gould and Amaro-Reyes, 1988). Also, a climate of secrecy can add to corruption and create much higher welfare losses than would result if the bribes and gains from corruption were simply transfers (Shleifer and Vishny, 1993).

Proposed prescriptions for policymakers seeking to minimize fraud tend to focus on greater individual incentives to avoid corruption, reduce discretion, and improve information flows. One approach emphasizes the need for incentives (such as financial bonuses for the achievement of tax collection targets) to ensure that state revenues are collected (Bird, 1989). The "tax farming" school proposes using private parties such as the Swiss surveying firm Société Générale de Surveillance to reduce discretion and increase the tax yield. Another strategy is to develop computer information systems within customs agencies in order to provide greater accountability and improve administrative efficiency (Jenkins, 1992).

In The Gambia, however, the minister of finance did not have the luxury of time to develop and evaluate complicated new information systems. Moreover, providing financial bonuses to customs officials would have created difficulties with other bureaucrats who routinely handled large sums of money. Thus the government tried an ad hoc combination of increased oversight, reduced discretion, and the threat of removal as its main tools to limit customs fraud.

This chapter discusses the problems posed by customs fraud and the numerous, and only partly successful, efforts that were made to deal with the problem. It begins by examining the importance of customs revenue in the economy. It then discusses the dimensions of customs fraud in 1986 and reviews the customs problems that reemerged in 1988. It also examines why customs fraud has proved to be such a difficult problem. The concluding section draws lessons from The Gambia's experiences with customs reform.

Customs Revenue in the Gambian Economy

The government of The Gambia has always derived the bulk of its revenue from customs receipts. In 1965–1966, customs revenue was 59 percent of government revenue; in 1970–1971 it fell to 45 percent; and in 1988–1989 it was 74 percent. The degree of dependence began to fall after the introduction of the national sales tax in 1989–1990; customs revenue fell to 44 percent of government revenue in 1990–1991 (see Table 17-1).

Administrative, economic, and geographic factors contributed to the government's dependence on customs revenue. The absence of appropriate records among private entrepreneurs was given as a reason for not introducing a broad-based sales tax until 1989–1990. Economically, the country's small industrial base, low levels of agricultural and industrial productivity, small labor force, and slow rate of economic growth yield few opportunities to increase the contribution from direct taxes. Geographically, The Gambia is ideally located to provide entrepôt services for West Africa. Thus customs duties continue to be one of the easiest and cheapest ways to raise revenue.

Evident risks are associated with relying so heavily on one revenue source. The government's budget deficit, borrowing requirements, and domestic credit creation are tied directly to the buoyancy of international trade, which is largely beyond the government's control. In turn, the deficit and government borrowing affect inflation and the balance of payments, implying that macroeconomic aggregates are sensitive to changes in customs revenue.

Customs Fraud I: 1985-1986

The IMF mission in December 1985 noted that government revenue had performed poorly in the first half of the year. Without remedial action the government would not meet its deficit target. The mission pressed

Table 17-1. Customs Revenue in The Gambia: Selected Years (Millions of Dalasis)

Year	Imports (cif)	Import Duty	GDP	Government Revenue	Duties/ Government Revenue (percent)
1965–1966	29	8	100	14	59
1970–1971	43	12	133	87	45
1980–1981	263	48	409	80	60
1984–1985	359	89	673	148	60
1985–1986	494	138	859	216	64
1986–1987	860	234	1,078	318	74
1987–1988	869	226	1,251	329	69
1988–1989	1,056	220	1,512	451	74
1989–1990	1,507	217	1,793	508	43
1990–1991	1,805	234	2,057	533	44

Source: Ministry of Finance and Economic Affairs, GDATA file.

Minister of Finance Sisay to take extraordinary measures to cut expenditures and raise revenue by preparing a "minibudget." This action would have been unprecedented in The Gambia and was resisted because it posed serious administrative and political problems.

The government had some room to cut expenditures, but raising additional revenue by imposing higher taxes would have been almost impossible. Import duties had already been increased several times in the recent past. Moreover, because the revenue response from those increases had been limited, higher taxes would not have the desired effect.

The minister directed his staff to explore the reasons for the revenue shortfall. Given the importance of customs, the examination began there.

According to the senior staff of customs and excise who were interviewed at the time, the revenue performance reflected normal seasonal factors and a sluggish traditional reexport trade. They were confident, however, that a major improvement would occur in the second half of the fiscal year. The data they presented seemed to provide some support for their views. Yet the data were inconsistent with other evidence available to the ministry. Trading activity was high, the port was clogged, and the airport had been busy. Ministry officials (including the minister) also received information from several sources that indicated that customs fraud was widespread.

Some evidence that something serious was wrong came from a local businessman, who provided photocopies of false invoices to the minister's staff. He had obtained the material from a disaffected customs officer. Although the evidence was suggestive, the minister required additional information to take significant action.[1] So as not to alert senior customs and senior ministry officials of the investigation, the minister's staff obtained records through the trade division of the ministry, which normally received separate copies of all customs entries. The entries provided a complete summary of the declarations that importers and exporters had made to customs. The records showed clearly that customs fraud was rampant—particularly the practice of undervaluing dutiable commodities.

Determining the extent of undervaluation was problematic. Few reliable data on values and quantities existed, since customs fraud had become well entrenched by late 1985. The data provided by the few traders who were not involved in the fraud were useful but inadequate. The minister's staff turned to the diplomatic community for assistance. Their sources proved to be highly valuable.

The entire import record for 1985 was reworked. Undervaluation was extensive and covered every dutiable commodity imported into The

Gambia, except petroleum.[2] Estimates showed that, at a minimum, D35 million, or approximately 40 percent of customs revenue in 1985, had been lost through undervaluation.

A report was delivered to the minister in January 1986, detailing the importers and commodities involved, the dates, the amount of duties actually paid, and an estimate of the duties that should have been paid. The minister sent a copy of the report to the president.

The minister then instructed the comptroller and the permanent secretary to take action to end the fraud immediately, and to collect all outstanding revenue from 1985. The minister also contacted the attorney general to inquire about his powers in the matter. He was informed that the law contained adequate provisions. Only later did it become apparent that enforcing these laws would become problematic.

A major uncertainty at the time was how the president would react to pressure from traders about the crackdown. Many of the traders were well-connected, politically prominent, and generous supporters of the main political party. However, the president's options were narrowed considerably when the British minister for overseas development, who was visiting The Gambia for independence day celebrations, offered technical assistance to deal with the fraud.[3]

Minister Sisay took advantage of the offer; within weeks a British customs officer arrived in The Gambia. He confirmed that undervaluation was the major problem. His report to the minister found numerous other problems with the customs administration (Kellaway, 1986). He recommended that extensive changes be made and suggested that a British customs officer be given responsibility for customs valuation and investigations. (Annex A lists the main findings of the Kellaway report.) Cabinet endorsed the report, and preparations were made to select the technical assistant.

Because fraud had become so entrenched in customs and the senior customs management would not deal with it, the trade division of the MoF assumed responsibility for customs valuation. It immediately compiled a list of indicative values, derived from a variety of local and external sources. The list was updated regularly. The arrangement persisted from March 1986 until the British customs officer arrived in November 1986. At that point the ministry allowed customs to assume responsibility for monitoring import entries and compiling indicative values.

With these arrangements in place, Minister Sisay fully expected that customs fraud would be kept in check. With the crackdown on undervaluation, revenue increased dramatically, and the budget deficit narrowed (as detailed in Table 17-1). Indeed, customs revenue grew so impressively that most customs duties were reduced by an average of one-third in the 1986–1987 budget. Even with this change, real customs revenue was higher in 1986–1987 than in 1985–1986.

These revenue improvements were generated entirely from the reduction in fraud from February and March 1986 onward. No attempt was made to recover the revenue that was lost previously. In retrospect, this decision was unwise. Not penalizing anyone for their earlier transgressions removed the incentive to resist fraud if opportunities arose again. The lack of sanctions simply set the stage for more fraudulent activity.

Customs Fraud II: 1988

From November 1986 to early 1988, senior ministry officials were not involved directly in customs operations. Revenue collection remained high, and there were no obvious signs or reports that anything was amiss.

Problems emerged in March 1988. Several local traders began protesting to the ministry that an importer was engaging in reexport trade under the pretext that the goods were being transited. The importer would store sugar, textiles, cigarettes, and other commodities in a bonded warehouse and apply periodically to the comptroller of customs to release some of the goods for transit to neighboring countries. Some of the goods supposedly in transit were also being sold locally.

After much vacillation by senior ministry officials, the minister instructed that the importer who was running the phony transit trade be allowed to transit the goods he already had in storage (worth several million dalasis) but that he stop the practice thereafter.

Annoyed that the curtailment of his activities had been initiated by complaints from his competitors, the importer began to expose their fraudulent practices. His allegations, most of which were subsequently verified, were extensive. The most serious was that several traders were removing portions of ships' manifests, with the complicity of customs officials and shipping agents. That practice erased the most important evidence that the goods had actually been delivered to The Gambia. This method of smuggling had been occurring on a large scale.[4]

Numerous other stories of customs fraud, including misspecification, undervaluation, short-landing, and underquantification, began to emerge. Some of these reached the president, who summoned Minister Sisay for an explanation.

In response, the minister, whose staff had informed him that their preliminary investigations revealed serious problems in customs, established a special team to review the allegations and report back within a month. The team, which was headed by the British customs adviser, also included two ministry officials and one expatriate adviser. It was instructed to

- verify declarations of imports against shipping records;
- document cases of import undervaluation, underdeclaration, and nondeclaration;
- update the list of indicative values for goods commonly imported into The Gambia;
- recommend solutions sufficient to address the problems uncovered.

The team concentrated its investigation on three areas: undervaluation, problems with the transit facility, and abuse in the direct delivery facility for bulk commodities.[5] Team members assembled and compared data from customs, shipping agencies, and the port authority. They also interviewed businesspersons and customs agents.

The investigation yielded quick results. Revenue for September 1988 was 40 percent higher than its level in July and August. Some of the improvement came from the collection of outstanding amounts owed on goods taken on direct delivery, but some came from a reduction in fraud. Within a week after embarking on the investigation, the team found cases of undervaluation and abuses of the transit and direct delivery facilities. The team recommended that the direct delivery facility be withdrawn, that several customs officials be reassigned, and that key duties be reallocated. Customs valuation was turned over to an officer with a reputation for honesty.

At the end of the monthlong investigation, the team presented its report (Homan et al., 1988) to the president, who was acting minister in the absence of Minister Sisay due to illness. The team found that the customs administration had failed to collect a total of D32 million in fiscal year 1987–1988 revenue, that smuggling at the Amdalai border post had cost D11 million, and that the abuse of the direct delivery facility accounted for an additional D14.6 million. Further losses came from cases of undervaluation, representing 15.5 percent of customs revenue for that fiscal year.

In response to the report and its recommendations, the president fired the top four customs officers. He placed an MoF official in charge of customs on an interim basis and directed him to collect the missing revenue. But the president decided not to push for legal action or apply punitive sanctions against those listed in the report.

Although the special team covered a lot of material in a short time, its handling of undervaluation was incomplete, and it was unable to update the list of indicative values. When Minister Sisay returned to duty in November 1988, he reviewed the report and made note of these points. He ordered that another review be conducted examining all areas of customs abuse.

A team began work immediately. They documented undervaluation and other fraudulent practices that between January 1987 and June 1988 had cost the government more than D45 million (approximately 13 percent of customs revenue). The report covered more than 200 pages and identified many cases of fraud beyond undervaluation (McPherson, Jabai, and McNamara, 1989). It took five months to complete.[6] In the interim, Minister Sisay had resigned due to ill health. The report was delivered to his successor.

The report implicitly criticized the British customs adviser, creating a diplomatic flap. The British high commissioner complained to the U.S. ambassador and USAID representative. Unfortunately, this issue diverted attention from the central point of the report—that customs fraud had again become massive.

The government took no action on the report. In June 1990, fifteen months after the report had been submitted, Cabinet endorsed a memorandum by the new minister of finance that suggested that the director general of customs be left to determine how to proceed.

Customs fraud did not cease. At the insistence of the World Bank, the government eventually agreed to another investigation. The U.K. government supplied two customs auditors, whose report was delivered in early 1992 (Dunlop and Livings, 1992). It recounts in detail—yet again—major areas of fraud. The revenue losses were again millions of dalasis.

Reform Measures

The various investigations of customs produced some concrete actions and temporary remedies. The 1985–1986 episode led to actions to compile the list of indicative values, provide technical assistance to customs, and give customs officers some additional training. The September 1988 report provoked a quick response by the president. The four most senior customs officials were fired. Both investigations had a positive impact on revenue.

These actions were positive, undoubtedly politically difficult, and instrumental in helping reduce the budget deficit and stabilizing the economy. But they did little to address the underlying sources of fraud and to discourage traders from future fraud. There was little fundamental customs *reform* despite the obvious and overwhelming need for it. Indeed, the 1992 report made the point that almost none of the substantive recommendations of previous investigations had been implemented.

Perhaps the major reason for the lack of reform was that no one in any position to make a difference had an incentive to deal with the problem, especially after the budget crisis had begun to ease. The 1985–1986 customs investigation had been initiated because of the need to reduce the budget deficit and address IMF pressure to make drastic changes in fiscal policy. Because expenditure cuts or tax increases would have been difficult and unpopular, revenue collection had to improve. And with the crackdown on fraud in February 1986, it did—dramatically. But ironically, the revenue gain eased the pressure to introduce further reforms and to punish the perpetrators. The minister of finance stopped short of taking legal action. He did not want to divert attention from more pressing ERP policy changes, and he hoped that by exposing the fraud and bringing in technical assistance, traders and customs officials would mend their ways. Although his response was pragmatic, it was overly optimistic.

The situation in 1988 was more complicated. Senior ministry staff were rumored to have abetted the phony transit trade. Those who believed the rumors doubted that the ministry would take any action; others who had confidence in the expatriate customs adviser were com-placent. Moreover, the somewhat easier budget situation removed the ministry's most direct incentive for reform. The September 1988 investigation was ordered only when political pressure on the minister could no longer be deflected. Under these circumstances it is not surprising that less forceful action was taken than had been the case in earlier years. The lack of action on the March 1989 report indicated that customs reform was no longer a priority. The 1992 report made clear how costly that change had been.

Concluding Observations and Lessons about Customs Reform

The Gambia's experience shows both the potential and the pitfalls of customs reform. The initial actions to reduce customs fraud in early 1986 had a major impact on the success of the ERP. Increased government revenue reduced the budget deficit, slowed monetary growth, and helped stabilize the exchange rate. In 1988 the increase in customs receipts substantially increased official foreign exchange reserves. In both cases the government acted forcefully, first by taking some responsibilities away from customs, and later by firing the top four customs officials.

But fundamental customs reform did not occur. The problem was addressed only periodically when revenue loss seriously affected overall macroeconomic performance. When action *was* taken, it was driven by objectives not directly related to customs. In 1985 it was to reduce the fiscal deficit; in 1988 it was to deflect political pressure; in 1991 it was to meet a World Bank condition.

For policymakers interested in administrative reform, several lessons can be drawn from the episodic crackdown on fraud.

First, the revenue gains from reducing fraud can benefit the macroeconomy substantially. Indeed, the size of the revenue gain clarified the cost to the economy of continued fraud. Without customs reform the government would have had to either sharply reduce expenditures, steeply increase taxes, or breach the IMF agreement. All of these options would have further hurt the welfare of the general population. The ERP would have been in deep trouble in early 1986 without the revenue increase associated with the reduction in customs fraud.

Second, the effects of actions taken to expose and reduce fraud are diminished when improved valuation and monitoring procedures are not institutionalized. In The Gambia, allowing the indicative values to become out-of-date seriously eroded the effectiveness of the original reform.

Third, failing to penalize traders and customs officials for fraudulent actions undermines the sustainability of reforms. The financial gains from customs fraud in The Gambia were huge. The absence of sanctions made the relative reward for honest work very small. Without sanctions those who promote reform should be prepared for limited progress and frequent setbacks.

Fourth, technical assistance is not a cure-all, especially in dealing with such problems as corruption. More fundamental institutional changes are necessary, and these are difficult to bring about on a sustained basis without direct oversight and strong commitment at very senior levels.

Fifth, while donor pressure can help push reforms, lack of pressure can help sustain and even enlarge the problem. Gambian policymakers could ignore the potential revenue gains from the collection of unpaid customs duties because they knew that the donors would compensate for any losses with additional aid. If donors seriously want governments to address customs fraud, they should make their aid contingent on the government's revenue performance. Thus far, donors have been prepared to finance all of the revenue shortfall in The Gambia.

Sixth, in The Gambia the recurrence of problems in customs (and elsewhere in the revenue agencies) indicates that the government lacks an internal mechanism for detecting and correcting major abuses. Until the government establishes some internal mechanism, donor pressure will remain the most effective remedy.

Annex A: The Kellaway Report (April 1986)

The report highlighted the major weaknesses in the customs administration, indicated where performance was satisfactory, and offered suggestions for constructive change.

Weaknesses with the Customs Administration
- The system of direct delivery offered no scope for verifying and detecting fraud.
- The valuation section was dysfunctional—no effective check of values was being made.
- Some customs outposts had no real purpose.
- Customs lacked a system for regular checks of shipments along the Trans-Gambia Highway.
- The mobility of customs officers at outpost stations was severely restricted by the absence of transportation (cars and bikes).
- While numerous customs officers were sent for training, the skills they acquired were not being used effectively.
- Customs officials lacked basic aids for measuring and verification; their communication equipment was poor and inadequate.
- Little scope existed for broader cooperation on customs issues because The Gambia was not a member of the Customs Cooperation Council.
- Most customs watchers were illiterate, and many were innumerate.
- Customs lacked a formal scheme for rotating staff to minimize opportunities for fraud and malfeasance.

Satisfactory Performance of the Customs Administration
- The level of staffing was not excessive, and major redundancies were not evident.
- Despite its limited staff the jerquing section functioned creditably.
- The mobile unit, although small, was effective when deployed.
- The manufacturing industries (the brewery and the bottling factory) seemed to be covered properly.

Recommendations for Changing and Improving the Customs Administration

- The direct delivery of goods should be suspended, and a system based on appropriate valuation and bonds should be introduced.
- The valuation unit should be restructured, and procedures implemented for verifying declared values properly.
- The Gambia should join the Customs Cooperation Council; to avoid arbitrariness and potential fraud, the values of all vehicles imported into The Gambia should be derived from *Glass's Guide*.
- The activities of various customs units should be inspected regularly.
- Selective rummage of ships and aircraft should be undertaken.
- The supply of equipment used by customs staff (vehicles, bikes, and measuring and communication devices) should be increased and upgraded.
- Senior staff should receive management training, and other staff who have been trained should be deployed more effectively.
- A second mobile unit should be established and based in the provinces.
- Penalties for underdeclaration and customs fraud should be strengthened with the addition of jail sentences.
- An expatriate customs expert with direct line responsibility for valuation and investigation should be appointed as soon as possible, reporting directly to the minister of finance and trade.

NOTES

1. Soon after his arrival in mid-1982, the minister had asked his senior staff to review and report on the activities and performance of customs. The report took several months to prepare. It showed that, aside from minor difficulties, the customs administration was sound and productive. The minister knew that the report was a whitewash but, at the time, had no means of dealing with the problem.

2. Petroleum had been imported by the major companies (Shell, Texaco, and British Petroleum) or through special arrangements from Senegal. Fraud in this area occurred *after* the petroleum had been imported through the duty waiver system. Dealing with this issue required a separate inquiry.

3. The possibility of this assistance had been raised by the British high commissioner, who had been aware of the investigation and had been

briefed on its progress by Minister Sisay. In effect, the offer informed the president that the U.K. government believed that The Gambia, while justifiably expecting assistance from the United Kingdom and other donors, could take its own measures to improve its revenue performance.

4. Smuggling of goods being transited from Senegal was also occurring at the border posts. For a small payment to customs officials, the number of containers and their contents would not be entered in the official log book.

5. Direct delivery refers to the practice of allowing importers to take delivery of commodities, typically those that are bulky or perishable, without paying duty. The customs formalities and payments are completed after the importer has possession of the goods (and almost invariably has sold them). The system is a direct subsidy by the government to importers, amounting to the value of interest earnings on outstanding duties that are eventually paid. For those who fail to pay, the subsidy is the total duty owed. The system was widely abused.

6. Updating the indicative values proved to be a major operation. They had not been revised since they were turned over to customs in November 1986.

Part IV

What Can Be Learned?

18

Accounting for Growth under the Economic Recovery Program: Results from a CGE Model

Steven C. Radelet

How much did the ERP policy reforms actually contribute to The Gambia's economic turnaround? The reforms were comprehensive, affecting almost all areas of economic activity. But did they stimulate the renewed growth? Or can the turnaround be explained by the massive inflow of foreign financing and the end of the drought?

In this chapter a computable general equilibrium (CGE) model is used to analyze these questions. The model compares economic conditions after the reforms with a simulation of what the economy would have been in the absence of the adjustment measures and other concurrent changes. The model then disaggregates the effects of individual policy reforms, the policy package, foreign aid, and increased rainfall.

The analysis is only partial, in the sense that it does not capture certain important institutional and microeconomic reforms. These limitations arise partly because institutional changes cannot be captured easily in a macroeconomic model and partly because one model cannot address all of the interesting questions about economic reform. Moreover, it does not attempt to answer questions about what might have been if certain policies were implemented differently or more fully. Instead, the focus is on what actually took place and the relative contributions that policy changes, foreign aid, and the end of the drought made to the economic turnaround.

The analysis suggests that all three factors—but especially the policy reforms and foreign aid—contributed to The Gambia's economic recovery. It indicates further that none of these three influences on its own would have been sufficient to increase per capita income. The results highlight the importance of the *combination* of comprehensive reforms and adequate foreign financing for successful economic adjustment. They also illuminate the different effects that individual policy reforms and foreign aid can have on economic growth and income distribution.

A Computable General Equilibrium Model of the Gambian Economy

This section describes the most important characteristics of the Gambian CGE model.[1] Output in each of the eight sectors in the model is determined by a constant-returns-to-scale Cobb-Douglas production function. The model contains three labor categories: rural, urban formal, and urban informal. Informal and rural labor are fully employed with flexible wages; formal-sector nominal wages are fixed (leading to some unemployment), reflecting the influence of government employment and wage policies. Intertemporal rural–urban migration is specified with a modified Harris-Todaro formulation (Harris and Todaro, 1970). Capital is assumed to be sector-specific and in fixed supply in the short run. Real government expenditures are fixed exogenously.

The model includes both an official and a parallel market exchange rate. All imports, exports (except groundnuts), and private capital transactions are based on the parallel rate. Groundnut exports from the state marketing board and public capital flows are based on the official rate. The parallel exchange rate acts as the numeraire in the model; the official rate is defined as 67 percent of the parallel rate in the base year (1985).

The model is closed by assuming that the level of foreign savings is exogenous and that total foreign and domestic savings determine the level of investment. This closure rule reflects the fact that foreign savings in The Gambia are predominantly aid flows, which are determined primarily by administrative decision rather than by economic signals. This specification also facilitates analyzing the effects of changing the level of foreign aid.

Model Simulations

The model simulations show the impacts of seven major ERP policy changes and external events that affected the Gambian economy between 1985 and 1988:

1. the float of the dalasi
2. a decline in government recurrent expenditures

3. an increase in the groundnut subsidy
4. an increase in the inflow of private capital
5. a reduction in the import tariff on reexport products
6. an increase in rainfall
7. changes in foreign aid

Simulations of items 1 to 5 represent the major *policy* changes of the ERP that contributed to the economic turnaround. Simulations of items 6 and 7 represent exogenous *nonpolicy* changes that affected economic performance during the period. Analyzing the various combinations allows an evaluation of the impacts of individual policies, the synergistic effects of the *package* of reforms, and the interaction between the policy reforms and external changes.

The impacts of these changes are measured against a simulation of the economy in the absence of reform. This methodology captures the full impact of the reforms by incorporating the economic deterioration that would have ensued had the ERP not been implemented.

Simulation of 1988 in the Absence of the ERP (the Base Scenario)

Had there been no reforms in The Gambia, the amount of capital inflow would have fallen sharply: donors had already stopped disbursing funds, and the government's foreign exchange reserves were nearly exhausted. Thus the base scenario assumes that the level of public foreign capital inflow would have fallen from US$28 million in 1985 to US$10 million each year thereafter.[2] The results of this simulation are shown in Table 18-1.

Table 18-1. Model Simulation Results: Aggregate Change in Output (1985 to 1988) from a Reduction in Public Foreign Savings to US$10 million (Base Scenario)

Sector	Change in Aggregate Output, 1985 to 1988 (%)
Agriculture	−3.2
Groundnut production	5.9
Groundnut processing	5.3
Industry	−12.1
Construction	−49.5
Public services	0.0
Services	2.2
Reexports	7.2
GDP	−2.7

The sharp decline in foreign savings, and thus investment, would have reduced output in both industry and construction. Labor would have shifted away from these activities into groundnut processing, reexports, and, to a lesser degree, services—all tradables sectors. Thus exports would have increased and imports declined, reducing the current account deficit, as necessitated by the fall in foreign financing. Agricultural output would have declined, but groundnut production would have increased with the movement of rural labor into relatively more profitable groundnut cultivation. Overall, GDP would have fallen by 2.7 percent over the three years. Real wages in both the rural and informal sectors would have fallen, while the number of employees in the fixed-wage formal sector would have declined sharply.

These results indicate the extent to which the Gambian economy would have deteriorated in the absence of both the ERP and the accompanying aid flow. Indeed, the deterioration had already begun in 1985: shortages were widespread, much urban labor was idle, public investment projects had been interrupted, and a general malaise was evident (see Chapter 2).

Update to 1988 with All Changes

As simulated, the seven policy reforms and external changes combined would increase total output by 14.9 percent over the base scenario (column 1 of Table 18-2). Construction and industry would benefit from the sharp expansion in investment, financed with greater savings in each category: household (as income rises), government (as the recurrent budget moves from a deficit to a surplus), and foreign (as both aid and private capital inflow increase). Higher levels of rainfall and the float of the dalasi would stimulate both agricultural and groundnut production; the subsidy would encourage groundnut production even further. Real wages in both the rural and informal sectors would increase sharply, and formal-sector employment would expand as the real wage falls. These results indicate that the changes had a net positive impact on poorer Gambians, thereby improving the distribution of income. The higher incomes and increased aggregate demand (relative to the base scenario) would lead to price increases in each sector and hence to a decline in international competitiveness. Thus, despite the float, exports would be smaller than under the base scenario (although they would still be larger than before the reforms), and imports would rise. As expected with larger foreign borrowing, these changes would lead to a larger current account deficit.

The next set of experiments simulates each of the seven policy changes and external events individually.

Table 18-2. Simulation Results: Change in Output from Policy Reforms, Increased Rainfall, and Foreign Services (Percentage Change from Base Scenario)

Sector	All Changes (1)	Float (2)	Government Expenditure (3)	Groundnut Subsidy (4)	Private Capital Flows (5)	Import Tariff in Reexport Sector (6)	Entire Policy Package (7)	Increased Rainfall (8)	Foreign Savings (9)
Agriculture	16.6	2.2	0.0	−1.5	1.5	−0.6	1.4	8.6	4.1
Groundnut production	23.5	7.5	1.3	9.0	−2.4	0.5	16.1	6.1	−0.4
Groundnut processing	28.2	10.4	1.5	11.5	−2.4	0.5	21.5	4.1	0.0
Industry	32.8	15.0	0.9	−2.4	4.5	−3.2	14.1	1.1	12.8
Construction	176.7	88.5	21.5	−10.3	17.0	−24.9	87.3	0.0	69.0
Public services	−7.8	0.0	−7.8	0.0	0.0	0.0	−7.8	0.0	0.0
Services	3.6	−0.2	0.2	−2.7	0.5	−0.4	−3.8	2.3	3.0
Reexports	3.7	−16.6	0.7	−1.5	−1.8	15.0	−2.3	1.3	−2.0
Total	14.9	2.8	0.8	−1.0	1.3	1.6	5.1	2.9	4.7

The Policy Changes

The Float. In this simulation the official and parallel rates are merged so that all foreign exchange transactions take place at a unified, higher rate. This specification highlights the expenditure-switching effects of the change in relative prices from the depreciation of the official rate. The results are shown in column 2 of Table 18-2. The simulation indicates that the policy change would raise the dalasi value of groundnut export receipts, foreign aid flows, and debt service payments by 50 percent. Domestic prices for imported goods would also rise (even though importers would still be using the same exchange rate), because customs officials would be valuing imports for tariff purposes at the new exchange rate.

The combination of higher government revenue and the increased dalasi value of public foreign borrowing would increase the supply of investable funds. Output in industry and construction would grow, driving up wages and prices in each sector. Higher domestic prices would adversely affect international competitiveness, and production would shift away from exports toward the domestic market. Exports would decline, except in groundnut processing, the one sector that previously used the official rate. Although import prices would rise slightly, import volumes would increase because domestic demand would be higher. On the whole, production would grow by 2.8 percent.

The stimulus to groundnut production and the investment sectors would increase real wages in both rural and informal sectors. The real wage in the formal sector would fall, so that formal-sector employment would expand, reducing urban unemployment.

In this simulation the float would not improve the current account deficit because of the closure rule assumption—that foreign borrowing is fixed and that investment adjusts in response to total savings. In effect, the simulation assumes that the government would use the increase in domestic savings to expand investment rather than to reduce foreign borrowing, which would have been the case had donors been willing to continue providing finance. In a separate simulation with an alternative closure assumption—that investment is fixed and foreign borrowing is endogenous to the model—groundnut exports would expand and imports would fall, reducing the current account deficit by US$10 million. With the decline in imports, and lacking the stimulus to the investment sectors, output would fall by 1.4 percent. Real wages in the rural sector would rise, although not by as much as in the first simulation, and real wages in the informal sector would fall slightly. Thus the impact of the float depends critically on the corresponding level of foreign financing.

Reduction in Government Expenditures. Government spending in the three years after the ERP was introduced was 15 percent, 19 percent, and 8 percent lower (in real terms) than in 1985. A large component of this reduction was the government's retrenchment of nearly 3,000 employees in 1986. Accordingly, this model simulation reduces aggregate government spending and adjusts the input–output coefficients in the public-service sector to reflect the relative decline in the wage bill (column 3 of Table 18-2).

The reduction in recurrent spending would be offset by an increase in investment, as government savings increase. In effect, government spending would shift from current consumption to public investment. The net impact on output would be minimal. Industry and services would lose from the decline in government spending but would gain (along with construction) from the growth in investment. Formal-sector employment would fall with an increase in the real wage, and real wages in the rural and informal sectors would change little.

With the alternative closure assumption of fixed investment and endogenous foreign borrowing, the reduction in government spending would reduce the current account deficit. Output in public services would fall. It would also fall in the three sectors that receive government spending (industry, construction, and services), and overall production would decline by 1.3 percent. A greater number of formal-sector workers would lose their jobs than under the exogenous investment assumption, and real wages in the rural and informal sectors would fall sharply. Thus when the reduction in government spending is used to reduce the current account deficit rather than expand investment, output would decline, and much of the burden would fall on the poor.

The Groundnut Subsidy. In one of the most remarkable policy thrusts of the ERP, the government raised the farmgate price of groundnuts in 1986–1987 from D1,100 to D1,800 per tonne, 50 percent above the export parity price of approximately D1,200 per tonne (see Chapter 14). The government lowered the price to D1,500 per tonne in 1987–1988 and eliminated the subsidy completely in 1988–1989.

The model simulates the subsidy by changing the export tax on groundnuts from 12 percent in 1984–1985 and 1985–1986 to –50 percent and –25 percent in 1986–1987 and 1987–1988, respectively (column 4 of Table 18-2). Output in the groundnut production and groundnut processing sectors would grow by 9 percent and 11.5 percent, respectively, over the three years. The subsidy would sharply increase the government budget deficit, reducing total savings and investment. Overall output would decline by 1 percent.

An important effect of the groundnut subsidy was to provide financial relief to rural dwellers, whose incomes had shrunk markedly during the late 1970s and early 1980s. The 7 percent increase in real wages in the rural sector and the increase in agricultural and groundnut production indicate significant growth in rural income. Although the subsidy was temporary, it was crucial to supporting the poorest Gambians during the adjustment period.

In this simulation, the closure assumption of fixed foreign borrowing implies that the subsidy would be funded by a reduction in public investment, reducing output in the capital goods sectors. The alternative, more realistic assumption is that the subsidy was financed with foreign aid, with investment remaining constant. Under this assumption, output in the construction and industrial sectors would not decline as sharply, and total output would increase slightly. Real wages in the rural sector would increase, and wages in the informal sector would also rise. Formal-sector employment would increase as the real wage falls. Thus under the fixed-investment assumption, the positive impact of the groundnut subsidy on poorer Gambians would be even larger.

Private Capital Inflows. In late 1985 and early 1986, the Central Bank first raised, then decontrolled, interest rates with a treasury bill tender (see Chapter 6). The depreciation of the dalasi, combined with the increase in real returns on dalasi-denominated assets, led to a turnaround in private capital inflows. Between 1985 and 1988 the private capital component of the balance of payments changed from US$–2.5 million to US$2.3 million—an increase of about one-sixth of the 1988 current account deficit. Assuming (consistent with most observers) that the major stimuli to private capital inflows were the dalasi float and higher interest rates, the increase in private capital inflow can be regarded as a policy change rather than an external change. The results of a simulation that combines the float with a change in private capital inflows (compared with the float alone) are shown in column 5 of Table 18-2.

The increase in total savings and investment would stimulate the industrial and construction sectors. The real exchange rate would appreciate as the price of nontradables (especially construction) increases relative to tradables (especially groundnut processing and reexports). Exports would fall and imports would grow as production shifts to meet domestic demand. Although output in the tradables sectors would fall, growth in the capital goods sectors would more than compensate. Higher real income would raise the demand for food, and agricultural output would expand slightly. The stimulus to the investment and agricultural sectors would increase real wages in the rural and informal sectors. Formal-sector wages would fall, with a corresponding increase in formal employment. Overall GDP would grow by 1.3 percent. Thus the float and increased private capital inflows would combine for GDP growth of 4.1 percent.

Reduction of the Import Tariff in the Reexport Sector. The Gambia has been an active entrepôt for trade in the subregion for generations. The reexport trade expanded rapidly in the 1970s as The Gambia kept its tariffs relatively low, while neighboring Senegal, Mali, and Guinea-Bissau raised import barriers. In 1987 The Gambia lowered the import tariff on most reexport goods. The model simulates this change by reducing the tariff rate in the reexport sector from 33 percent to 17 percent (column 6 of Table 18-2).

The reexport sector would expand rapidly, but the loss of government revenue would reduce total savings and investment. Labor would move away from construction and industry toward the reexport sector. The reduction in the demand for investment goods would reduce prices, increasing international competitiveness and stimulating exports. Imports in each sector except reexports would fall. The growth in the reexport sector would cover losses in the other sectors, and overall output would increase slightly. The simulation shows little impact on real wages or aggregate employment.

The Policy Package. Column 7 of Table 18-2 shows the results of a simulation of the *combination* of the five policy reforms without the changes in rainfall and foreign borrowing. Output would grow strongly in four sectors—groundnut production, groundnut processing, industry, and construction. The combination of the float and the groundnut subsidy would promote growth in groundnut production and processing. The float, private capital inflows, and the reduction in government expenditures would increase savings and investment (more than offsetting the declines from the groundnut subsidy and the lower import tariffs on reexports), stimulating industry and construction.

Due primarily to an increase in demand for investment goods, domestic prices would rise, and the international terms of trade would deteriorate. Thus imports would increase. Groundnut exports would also expand, but other exports (which used the parallel exchange rate before the ERP) would decline as their relative prices fall. Although the net producer price in each sector except public services would rise, the largest increase would be in the groundnut sectors, industry, and construction. Because these activities draw labor from the other sectors, production in services and reexports would fall. Real wages in the rural and informal sectors would increase, while formal-sector wages would fall, reducing urban unemployment.

Overall, the policy package would generate an increase in GDP of 5.1 percent over the three years, accounting for approximately 34 percent of the difference in GDP between the simulation with all seven changes and the base scenario (14.9 percent, as shown in column 1 of Table 18-2). Although this growth is significant, the Gambian population grew by more than 9 percent during the period. Thus, on their own, the policy reforms would have been insufficient to increase per capita income.

External Events: Rainfall and Foreign Aid

Rainfall. The Gambia's recovery efforts were helped by the return of more normal rainfall levels after the drought of the early 1980s. Rainfall levels between 1985 and 1988 were 30 percent higher than between 1980 and 1984. The end of the drought was the major determinant of the 14.7 percent increase in grain yields over the period. The model simulates this change by increasing the shift parameter in the production function for both the agricultural and groundnut production sectors by a similar amount (column 8 of Table 18-2).

The consequent strong growth in the agricultural and groundnut sectors would drive prices down, improving the international terms of trade. Exports would expand in each sector. Overall, output would increase by 2.9 percent, accounting for about 20 percent of the difference in growth between the simulation with all seven changes and the base scenario (column 1 of Table 18-2).

Foreign Aid. In the first year of the ERP, most donors were unwilling to provide financial support until they were convinced that the government was serious about implementing the reforms. After the government floated the dalasi, raised interest rates, and retrenched nearly 3,000 employees, donors provided substantial support (see Chapter 4). In 1987 and 1988 the government received aid flows that averaged the equivalent of 62 percent and 36 percent of GDP, respectively. By almost any measure these resources were huge. However, the numbers give a somewhat misleading impression of the impact of aid flow on economic growth. Less than one-third of the resources were used to finance current consumption and investment—a dollar amount similar to historical trends for the country. The bulk of the aid went toward paying current and overdue debt service and increasing the government's foreign reserves. In effect, these resources began to rationalize the implicit borrowing undertaken by The Gambia in the early 1980s.

For example, the deficit on the current account of the balance of payments rose from SDR35 million in 1985 to SDR39 million in 1987, then fell to SDR29 million in 1988. The total aid flow in 1988 was nearly SDR20 million larger than in 1985—a 50 percent increase—yet the current account deficit was SDR5.7 million smaller. Despite the narrowing of the current account deficit (by 25 percent in one year), GDP grew by 5.5 percent in 1988, indicating further that factors other than aid were supporting growth.

The model includes only the portion of aid flow that was used to finance current consumption and investment. Although the aid that was used to build up reserves and pay debt service arrears was crucial to restoring confidence in the economy and strengthening the foundation for long-term growth, it did not contribute directly to the economic growth between 1985 and 1988. Of course, in the absence of this aid flow, it would have been necessary to divert domestic resources away from current consumption and investment—an effect captured under the base scenario.

The sharp expansion in savings and investment would stimulate the capital goods sectors (particularly construction), while most other sectors would stagnate or contract (column 9 of Table 18-2). Prices in each sector would rise, as would real wages (except in the fixed-wage formal-sector category), reducing international competitiveness. Exports would fall in each sector, while imports would increase sharply. Higher real income would increase the demand for food, and agricultural output would rise by 4.1 percent. Overall, the increased demand for capital goods would more than compensate for the decline in exports, and GDP would grow by 4.7 percent.[3]

Thus foreign aid accounted for about 32 percent of the difference in growth between the simulation with all seven changes and the base scenario (column 1 of Table 18-2). As with the policy package, the stimulus from aid flows was clearly important, but not sufficient on its own to ensure growth in per capita income.

Concluding Observations from the CGE Model

The model results show that no single factor was responsible for the economic turnaround. A *combination* of comprehensive reforms, adequate foreign financing, and a little luck with rainfall and world prices—all were important in the recovery. As far-reaching as the policy reforms were, they would have been insufficient on their own to ensure a return to growth in per capita income. Similarly, despite the massive amount of donor support, it alone would have done little more than to allow the country to pay its debt service arrears and build up reserves.

A significant portion of the observed growth stemmed from the mutually reinforcing nature of the changes. For example, the float was supported by higher interest rates, improved fiscal discipline, and aid flows. The model reflects those positive interactions. When simulated individually, the GDP-related effects from the all-policy package (5.1 percent), foreign aid (4.7 percent), and rainfall (2.9 percent) would account for a total of 12.7 percent growth in GDP. Yet when the same changes are modeled simultaneously from the same base, output would grow by 14.9 percent. The difference is accounted for by the synergistic effects of the various changes. These interactions contributed to both renewed economic growth and the acceptance of the austerity measures by the public.

Most of the policy reforms improved the distribution of income, as indicated by higher real wages in the rural and informal sectors, increased agricultural output, and a decline in urban unemployment. The float and the groundnut subsidy were especially beneficial to the poor. Yet the reduction in government expenditures was detrimental to the poor, under the assumption that the increased domestic savings were used to reduce foreign borrowing. The alternative assumption that aid flow remained constant and that the increased domestic savings added to investment largely ameliorates the negative impact of reduced government spending on the poor.

This analysis captures the effects of the major macroeconomic reforms of the ERP. It does not address what the impacts *might* have been of more complete institutional reforms in the budget process, customs administration, parastatal management, the civil service, and agricultural support systems. These issues cannot be adequately examined by this type of model. But this omission suggests the possibility that the economic recovery could have been even stronger had the institutional reforms been implemented more fully.

Many of the characteristics of the ERP that are highlighted in this chapter can be found in the adjustment programs of other countries. What made The Gambia different was the presence of *all* of them: a comprehensive program, minimal slippage during implementation, sufficient foreign financing, fortuitous external circumstances, and a conducive political environment. The Gambia's experience suggests that economic reforms can succeed if they are well designed and conscientiously implemented, and receive sufficient domestic and international support.

NOTES

1. This chapter is largely a condensed version of Radelet (1993). The substance of that article is reprinted by permission of Elsevier Science, Inc., from "The Gambia's Economic Recovery: Policy Reforms, Foreign Aid, or Rain?", by Steven C. Radelet, *Journal of Policy Modeling*, vol. 15 No. 3, pp. 251–276. Copyright 1993 by the Society for Policy Modeling. The article provides a more complete description of the model, including a list of the equations and a social accounting matrix for The Gambia. The model draws on a model for Cameroon, developed by Benjamin, Devarajan, and Weiner (1989).

2. The US$10 million is approximately equal to the amount of interest due on foreign debt. Continued foreign financing of that amount implies that debt service simply would not have been paid.

3. Note the classic "Dutch disease" effects from both the aid and private capital inflows, which stimulate the recipient sectors (primarily industry and construction), while undermining the competitiveness of other sectors.

19

The Program for Sustained Development

Brendan M. Walsh

The ERP was introduced in 1985 in response to a national economic crisis. It called for many sacrifices that were perceived as necessary to save the economy, indeed the nation, from collapse. The crisis-laden overtones of the ERP created the presumption that when the country had weathered the storm, there would be scope for the austerity measures to be relaxed.

As the ERP drew to a close in 1989, the economy indeed had stabilized. Inflation had declined, the fiscal deficit had narrowed sharply, external debt service arrears had been eliminated, the foreign exchange system was functioning smoothly, and the level of external reserves was adequate. With the success of the ERP, the government could simply have let the program expire without fanfare and without using it as a foundation for future programs. But in 1990 it launched a successor to the ERP—the Program for Sustained Development.

This chapter examines the PSD in the context of the achievements and the unfinished business of the ERP. After reviewing those achievements, the chapter outlines the PSD and considers the challenges for the future. The concluding section contains observations about the transition from the ERP to the PSD.

Achievements under the ERP

Restoring Economic Discipline
Unlike the previous five-year development plans, the ERP was not an exercise in detailed economic planning. It did not contain sectoral blueprints, nor did it specify detailed targets for growth in output, employment, or other macroeconomic variables. As was described in other chapters, it consisted of a package of policy reforms that called for liberalizing the

markets for credit, essential commodities, and foreign exchange; curtailing the size and scope of the public sector's role in the economy; increasing the efficiency of the civil service; and concentrating public-sector spending on creating a favorable environment for private-sector investment. The program was linked directly to the government's agreements with the IMF and the World Bank that formed the basis for the credits made available to The Gambia during the ERP.

As the ERP drew to a close, there was little pressure to abandon the policies that had been introduced under it. The recovery program had worked well in the sense that markets were functioning smoothly and that shortages and rationing were no longer common, as they had been in the mid-1980s. However, the ERP measures to retrench civil servants and to impose tight controls on public expenditures were unpopular and viewed widely as restrictions that would be rescinded with the end of the public finance crisis. An important rationale for the PSD was to reaffirm The Gambia's commitment to the market-oriented reforms called for in the ERP and to dispel the notion that fiscal discipline was merely a temporary expedient. Furthermore, the wide-ranging structural reforms to which the country was committed were by no means complete by 1989. A start had been made, but more work remained.

Moreover, the goal of 4.5 percent real GDP growth in the ERP implied only a 1 percent annual improvement in real income per capita. The new program set a target of 5.5 percent annual growth, doubling the targeted rate of growth in income per capita.

The IMF Programs

Throughout the ERP, macroeconomic policy was formulated within the framework of IMF stand-by agreements, Structural Adjustment and Enhanced Structural Adjustment Facility arrangements, and World Bank Structural Adjustment Loans (SAL), all provided under conditionality. Bilateral donors, notably USAID, also agreed to provide conditional financing. It is important to realize the scope of these agreements and the constraints they put on Gambian economic policy. Under the IMF programs the government was committed not to incur any new debts except on highly concessional terms; it pledged to eliminate the stock of external payments arrears by mid-1990; and it halted lending to state-owned enterprises except in IMF-specified cases. The agreements limited the growth of domestic bank credit and specified targets for the accumulation of external reserves and the government's balances with the Central Bank. They also specified indicative figures for government revenue and recurrent expenditures and hence for the fiscal deficit. In 1990–1991 the agreements placed a ceiling on current expenditures (excluding debt service).

At the core of the IMF programs is a monetary programming framework in which the growth of the money supply is constrained to equal the predicted growth of money GDP. The foreign reserves component of the money supply is programmed to increase, while the domestic asset component is programmed to decline. Net credit to the government is programmed to contract more rapidly than total domestic credit, leaving room for an expansion in private-sector borrowing. The programmed increase in reserves stems from a projected inflow of nonproject external financing (including monetized commodity aid), growth in export receipts, and Central Bank purchases of foreign exchange from the interbank market. The government builds up its balances with the Central Bank from the inflow of nonproject financing and the balance between domestic revenue and expenditures over the year.

The thrust of this macroeconomic adjustment package is to use nonproject (balance of payments or budgetary) external assistance to build up the country's external reserves and to reduce the public sector's net credit from the banking system. As such, financial resources are freed up for the private sector within an overall ceiling on credit expansion.

Several factors explain the emphasis of the IMF programs on building up foreign exchange reserves and sterilizing foreign exchange inflow in The Gambia. As of 1986 the country's foreign exchange reserves had been completely depleted, and a sizeable stock of external debt service arrears had accumulated. The IMF arrangements and concurrent financing provided an inflow of balance-of-payments support, enabling the country to eliminate its arrears and build up its external reserves.

By mid-1991, at the end of the third annual ESAF arrangement with the IMF, reserves had increased to the equivalent of five months of import coverage. (If imports for reexport are excluded, the reserves represented eight months of coverage.) This amount had been targeted to meet the growing interest and principal repayments that would fall due in the early 1990s under the Paris Club and London Club reschedulings. But in fact, as the Caisse Centrale and other creditors canceled their debts, the bulge in The Gambia's debt service was less dramatic than had been forecast. Having attained the target for official reserves, The Gambia will not have to run them down as sharply as had been anticipated. However, although The Gambia is operating a floating exchange rate system, the extreme openness of its economy and its vulnerability to external shocks mandate that an adequate level of reserves be retained if confidence in the currency is to be maintained and the foreign exchange market is to continue to function smoothly. Although the flexible exchange rate will help the economy adjust to external shocks, it will not insulate the economy from those shocks, so adequate reserves are absolutely necessary. But the commitment to amassing reserves and the necessity of offsetting the growth in liquidity generated by purchases of foreign exchange forced the Central Bank to increase the stock of treasury bills held by the nonbank public. This action exerted upward pressure on interest rates and increased the burden of internal debt service. By the end of 1991–1992, the targeted level of reserves was reached, and thus sterilizing further net inflows of foreign exchange and allowing them to affect the exchange rate became unnecessary.

Meeting the precise revenue, expenditure, and credit targets specified in the IMF programs would have been daunting in an economy in which international trade was relatively unimportant. In a small open economy such as The Gambia, the difficulty of adhering to targets is magnified by the impact of external shocks. Revenue is affected by the level of activity in the tourism sector and the reexport trade, as well as by the level of domestic spending, which in turn is affected by the groundnut harvest and world groundnut prices. Recurrent expenditures are affected by world interest rates, the exchange rate, and import prices.

Despite the shocks to the economy from such events as the breakup of the Senegambia Confederation in 1989, the Gulf War in 1990–1991, and the deep recession in the United Kingdom from 1989 to 1992, it is remarkable that the government met the 1989–1990 and 1990–1991 targets for both revenue and expenditures *within 1 percent*. That the budget adhered so closely to the targets indicates the degree of control exercised by the IMF programs over the daily management of the Gambian economy. Furthermore, during the last year of the ESAF arrangement, the IMF ruled that the targets that had been negotiated under the assumption of a certain level of nonproject aid inflows would be adjusted only by 25 percent of the net shortfall in these inflows. In 1990–1991 a net shortfall of D125 million occurred, due primarily to the nondisbursement of the second tranche of the World Bank SAL-II and related financing. To meet the adjusted targets, The Gambia had to fill a gap of D94 million, equivalent to 17 percent of budgeted expenditures.

It clearly was unreasonable to expect the country to adjust expenditures and/or revenue on such a large scale in the course of the fiscal year. Yet the IMF wanted to ensure that the country was doing all that it could to meet the conditions attached to the nonproject financing.

The IMF based the disbursement of the last tranche of the ESAF on the end-March outturn but programmed the SAL-II disbursement for the quarter ending in June. In this way, the funding could be disbursed even if, as became increasingly clear in the course of the year, the World Bank's conditions were not going to be met.

Other Donors

In addition to macroeconomic targets, the IMF and World Bank programs specified a wide range of structural reforms. A major thrust of the programs was to reform state-owned enterprises. These PEs operated in all sectors of the economy—public utilities, crop marketing, banking, and ferries, and in a shipyard, a mechanical workshop, and a cotton ginnery. The immediate goal of the structural reform conditions was to break the intimate links between the enterprises and the government that in the prereform era had led to widespread inefficiencies and mutual indebtedness. In most instances, the ultimate end envisaged was privatization. Structural reform also sought to phase out subsidies to agriculture, replacing them either with preferential credit or with supplies of below-cost fertilizers or seed. Moreover, projects in the public investment program were to demonstrate an economic rate of return ("where calculable") of 15 percent, "while projects in the social sectors, where economic rates of return cannot be determined, were to be selected on the basis of least-cost alternatives" (World Bank 1985b).

The World Bank matrix of policy reform conditions overlapped considerably with the IMF's conditions, although its range was wider and the terms of its conditions specified less precisely. The main condition of the USAID African Economic Policy Reform Program grant agreements was to make all domestic lending at market-determined rates, while PL 480 food aid was conditional on agreeing to a schedule for privatizing the Gambia Produce Marketing Board. Other donors (the United Kingdom, the European Community, and the African Development Bank) attached additional conditions to their grants and loans. Interpreting the individual structural conditions often involved protracted exchanges between Banjul and Washington.[1]

Furthermore, the process of designing, supervising, and reviewing the multiplicity of projects contained in the PIP absorbed much of the attention of local officials. Most of these projects involved considerable overseas travel, which tended to disrupt administration.[2] Local capacity to implement projects deteriorated considerably in the late 1980s, provoking serious concern at the World Bank about the lack of success in improving productive infrastructure during the ERP.

The Program for Sustained Development

The reason for dwelling on the details of the ERP in the context of the transition to the PSD is to highlight the extent to which the Gambian economy had been guided externally during the ERP. One of the achievements of the ERP was that, by implementing a comprehensive package of reforms, the government restored the donors' confidence in the country, greatly increasing the inflow of external project and program assistance. Within a year after the ERP ended, the country's program with the IMF came to an end. The IMF Staff Review, discussed by the board in mid-July 1991, was based on performance to the end of March, so that in effect the targets for March 1991 were the last on which disbursement of a credit depended. While it was agreed that a close policy dialogue would be highly desirable after the conclusion of the ESAF arrangement, and while economic and financial targets for 1991–1992 were agreed to, no further disbursements of IMF credits depend on meeting these targets.

Furthermore, despite the difficulty in convincing the World Bank that the country had met the conditions for the disbursement of the second tranche of SAL-II, the final tranche of SAL-II was disbursed early in 1991–1992. There are no immediate plans for a third SAL. Thus, beginning in 1991–1992, the country faced a future free from the heavy burden of conditionality for the first time since 1986.[3]

Against this background, the launching of the PSD was a clear statement that although the crisis conditions that spurred the ERP were over and the tight conditionality imposed by the IMF was nearing its end, the government did not intend to abandon the commitment to the prudent fiscal and monetary policies and structural reforms that guided the economy for the previous five years. The document introducing the PSD was brief, dealing with the direction of macroeconomic policy and structural reform only at a general level (GOTG, 1990b).

The PSD clearly stated the intention of maintaining continuity with the ERP and emphasized the necessity of accelerating the rate of economic growth. It pointed out that the rapid population growth would require a 3.5 percent annual GDP growth rate just to prevent a decline in living standards. It drew attention to the widening gap between The Gambia and the rapidly growing countries of Southeast Asia. Even if a growth rate of 5.5 percent were achieved, living standards would improve only at 2 percent annually, and by the year 2000 the standard of living would still be extremely low.

The PSD also acknowledged that the program of structural reform that was linked to the ERP had by no means been implemented fully by

1989. Unforeseen problems, the absence of administrative capacity, and in some areas the absence of commitment to unpalatable actions had seriously delayed some of the reforms. The wide-ranging divestiture program was far from complete in 1989. Although the government sold its minority shareholdings in several companies and privatized several small enterprises, it still owned all the major institutions—the Gambia Produce Marketing Board, the Gambia Commercial and Development Bank, and the Gambia Utilities Corporation. Many thorny issues had to be tackled in 1990 and 1991 before visible progress was made in these areas.[4]

The PSD spelled out the strategy that would achieve faster growth. The main components were that

- the private sector would be the primary source of the investment necessary to generate employment and raise income;
- the public sector would be relatively small but efficient, concentrating on providing essential public services and productive infrastructure and creating an environment conducive to private-sector investment;
- market-oriented policies would continue to apply to the key prices in the economy.

In particular, the PSD called for maintaining the liberalized exchange rate system, keeping credit markets unregulated, determining interest rates according to the supply and demand of funds in the interbank market, abolishing restrictions on imports, and maintaining or lowering existing duty rates in the interest of improving The Gambia's price competitiveness in the subregional market. The program looked forward to continued support from the country's traditional donors and increased assistance from new sources.

Challenges for the Future

The declared commitment of both the ERP and the PSD to the role of private-sector investment as the locomotive of growth in The Gambia is not entirely convincing, for two reasons. First, private-sector savings and development investment have contributed relatively little to growth since the start of the ERP. Although gross domestic savings increased from an estimated 4.7 percent of GDP in 1986–1987 to 8.5 percent in 1990–1991, they still constitute less than half of gross national savings, which equaled an estimated 20.7 percent of GDP in 1990–1991. The public sector still makes the bulk of investment. Second, as noted earlier, part of the rationale for the PSD was an appeal to the international donor community for increased assistance.

After the PSD was launched, a Round Table Conference was held in Geneva under the auspices of the United Nations Development Program in December 1990, at which The Gambia presented its case for increased assistance from donors. Conference participants did not broach the inconsistency between the government's appeal for more assistance to be channeled through the budget (even if most of it is to be for infrastructure) and the rhetoric of the private sector as the engine for growth. The inconsistency remains an anomaly in the government's thinking about the development of the economy.

Yet allocating additional resources to social "overhead" and productive infrastructure is fully consistent with a policy to rely on private-sector investment in the commercial areas of the economy. Notwithstanding decades of exceptionally generous external developmental assistance, glaring deficiencies in training and skills, educational levels, public utilities, and transport services in The Gambia are seriously inhibiting private-sector investment. It is not entirely coincidental that some of the language in the PSD echoes the wording in the World Bank (1989a) publication *Sub-Saharan Africa: From Crisis to Sustainable Growth*. The strategy described in the PSD was in keeping with the renewed emphasis of the international donor community on "strengthening the enabling environment" by reorienting incentives and improving the infrastructure. The World Bank stated that:

> An enabling environment creates the conditions for higher productivity, but growth rates will only be raised and sustained if African capacities are much enhanced.[5]

The necessary capacity building encompasses three components:

- human development, especially improved health and education standards;
- incentives for skilled workers and managers to perform effectively;
- political leadership and good governance.

The PSD adverted to all three of these areas, recognizing the urgency of enhancing the ability of the population to participate effectively in the wealth-creating process. It acknowledged that the poor health status of the population and the absence of technical, craft, and managerial skills in the work force were major obstacles to promoting sustained economic growth and development. In response, the 1991–1992 budget proposed a 10.7 percent increase in the recurrent budget devoted to health and a 21 percent increase devoted to education. The government planned to continue to increase the allocations to these ministries throughout the PSD. However, these resource allocations are very modest for the daunting task of raising health and education standards to a level that enables the population to participate effectively in the process of development. Moreover, larger budgetary allocations are clearly not sufficient for achieving that goal. Problems have emerged in the absorption and management of the available resources, and raising the *quality* of the services being provided is as urgent a mandate as the need for additional resources, if not more so.

The Gambia is a particularly challenging test of the philosophy of development that seeks primarily to create an enabling environment, in the hope that private domestic and foreign investment will be the locomotive for economic growth. The country's small size, its limited natural resource endowment and peripheral location, its low level of human capital, and the legacy of the shocks and mistakes of the 1970s and early 1980s—all render a private-sector investment boom improbable. The financial reforms of the ERP created market-determined exchange rates, removed exchange controls, and led to high positive real interest rates.[6] But combined, these effects led to a return of only a small portion of the capital that fled the country under less favorable circumstances or to an inflow of new private funds.

In the competition for the limited amount of footloose direct investment from the industrialized world, The Gambia does not have an edge over numerous alternative locations. Local funding and expertise are limited and highly concentrated in a minority group whose comparative advantage lies in trading and services rather than production. However, several sectors have clear development potential. The most promising are tourism and tropical horticulture. But problems with quality control and price competitiveness must first be overcome, and the relevant infrastructure (the airport and power supplies in particular) must first be rehabilitated substantially. The commitment to creating a favorable environment for private-sector investment should concentrate on rapid and tangible improvements in these areas.

Maintaining the discipline of the tight conditionality formerly imposed by the donor community on The Gambia's internal priorities will be crucial to sustaining growth in the future. When the country was under donor conditionality, the penalties for not meeting targets were significant. The threat that a tranche of a loan or grant would not be disbursed was real, and the potential embarrassment to the government considerable. There are now fewer conditions to be met, and less depends on meeting them, and the supervisory role of the IMF and the World Bank is being curtailed. The MoF and the spending ministries must continue the restraint engendered by tight conditionality, simply because good economic management demands it.

The British legacy to The Gambia extended to the design and financing of the country's public-sector capital spending during the early years of independence. As time passed, the sources for this support were broadened to include a wide range of donors and international agencies. More than 80 percent of the country's development budget is still financed by external grants and loans. The extent to which the priorities reflected in this budget are those of the donor community or of the host country is unclear, but the fact that even projects that reflect local priorities are financed from external sources influences their implementation. The generosity of the international donor community toward The Gambia has reinforced the notion that identifying a need or bottleneck progresses naturally to searching for an external source of funds and expertise for its solution. Aid may not only replace local sources of investment funding but may also reduce the local capacity for economic management. Nowhere is this syndrome more evident than with technical assistance.

Diagnostic studies of parastatals and ministries invariably conclude that additional technical assistance is a necessity. The willingness of the donors to meet the identified needs has made the country increasingly dependent on them.[7] The PSD may be faulted for failing to address this issue. In fact, its plea for intensifying external assistance could be viewed as a further manifestation of aid dependency.

Concluding Observations about the Transition from the ERP to the PSD

The Gambia is among the poorest countries in the world. The 1990 UNDP Human Development Index, which captures health and educational indicators in addition to income per person, placed The Gambia second from last in a total of 164 countries. The growth in real income per capita has averaged only about 1.5 percent annually since the mid-1980s. Raising the living standards of the population is thus urgent.

Under the ERP, prudent macroeconomic policies halted the decline of the economy and restored the preconditions for economic growth. A central element of the PSD is the call for additional assistance in order to accelerate the rate of growth. However, the level of foreign assistance to The Gambia is already among the highest in the world relative to GNP; in

1988 per capita aid was US$103, equivalent to 47 percent of GNP per capita (IMF, 1990). A comprehensive evaluation of the effectiveness of existing aid has not been carried out, and there are grounds for skepticism about the claim that a lack of aid is a constraint on growth. The greatest challenge facing the economy as the PSD unfolds is to demonstrate that the lessons of the previous five years have been internalized and to reverse the trend toward relying increasingly on aid and external economic management by enhancing the effectiveness of resource use. Failing to do so will postpone the day when the country will be able to meet the challenge of providing an acceptable standard of living for its rapidly growing population.

NOTES

1. For example, the SAL-II agreement that was concluded with the World Bank in 1989 contained a commitment to "preparing a medium-term public expenditure programme (PEP)." This was the latest expression of a series of commitments to budget reform. However, the interpretation of this condition became a bone of contention between the Bank and Gambian officials in 1991, contributing to the delay in the disbursement of the second tranche of the loan.
2. In 1990 The Gambia had ten active projects with the World Bank alone, involving a total of US$100 million. The local professional capacity in such areas as financial control and engineering was hardly adequate to deal competently with the administrative demands of these projects. Furthermore, some of the projects were poorly designed. Due to these factors The Gambia's rating on the implementation of its World Bank project portfolio deteriorated sharply in 1989–1990.
3. However, USAID grants continue to be tied to several conditions relating to further financial sector reform.
4. The GPMB has been managed by expatriate consultants under a management contract since late 1991; the Gambia Commercial and Development Bank has been offered for sale; and the first steps have been taken in preparing a management lease for the Gambia Utility Corporation.
5. World Bank, 1989a, p. 53.
6. From 1986 to 1990 the exchange-rate-adjusted returns to investment in three-month treasury bills in The Gambia matched those on compa-

rable investments in the United Kingdom and far exceeded those in the United States (see Walsh, 1991).

7. According to the 1989 *Development Coordination Report* released by the United Nations Development Program (UNDP), more than 300 full-time technical assistants were working in the Gambian public sector. Several recent examples of the tendency for donors to increase the country's reliance on external technical assistance can be cited. Disagreement with the World Bank over what was entailed in a public expenditure program led to UNDP funding of short-term consultancies in four ministries. In 1990–1991 the UNDP mounted a major exercise to enhance indigenous capacity for economic management, the immediate result of which was a sizeable influx of short-term technical assistants, whose report in turn recommended a significant increase in the level of long-term assistance! In mid-1991 the local management of the GPMB was replaced by an expatriate team, and plans are to tackle the long-standing problems in the GUC by leasing the company to an expatriate management team.

20

Insights from the Economic Recovery Program for Sub-Saharan Africa

Merilee S. Grindle and Michael Roemer

Much has been written about the necessity for fundamental policy reform if the economies of sub-Saharan Africa are to grow out of the stagnation and decline of the past two decades.[1] Yet economic and political conditions facing many African countries make this task herculean.

Some of Africa's economic malaise stems from external causes. Beginning in the 1970s but especially in the 1980s, the world economy became a less stable, less nurturing climate for developing countries. Fluctuating exchange rates after the collapse of the Bretton Woods system in 1971, the first oil shock, rising inflation and interest rates in the late 1970s, the second oil shock, the worldwide recession of the early 1980s, a decade-long disinflation that carried commodity prices down, and the requirement for stabilization and structural adjustment—all these made the task of managing any economy more difficult in the 1980s than it had been in the 1960s. To compound these problems, much of Africa suffered a severe and extended drought during the 1980s.

Both Africa and Latin America suffered badly from a more hostile world climate. But not all of Africa's woes can be blamed on external causes. In the wake of independence in the 1960s, many African countries adopted development strategies unsuited to their human and natural resources and relied on centralized controls that overtaxed the ability of governments to make wise and consistent policy choices. Overvalued exchange rates and inefficient marketing boards discouraged farmers and destroyed the agricultural base of some economies. High protection and excessive regulation fostered inefficient industries. Unprofitable state-owned enterprises fed larger fiscal deficits. Swollen, mismanaged bureaucracies lost the capacity to respond to changed conditions. Confronted by repeated external shocks, economies debilitated by inappropriate policies were unable to adjust. Without economic growth many African countries could not find the resources to respond to health and educational needs and the welfare of their populations. By the end of the 1980s, average real income in Africa was back to the level of the mid-1960s.

Political factors have created or exacerbated many of Africa's economic problems. Most African states have been weak, unable to gain sufficient power or legitimacy to realize national policy goals. In many countries, economic policy has become a commodity to politicians and bureaucrats, and politicians have sold policy favors to private rent-seekers in exchange for wealth and the tenuous right to continue in power. Corruption has been exacerbated by economic decline, making it difficult even to subsist by following formal rules of employment and career advancement. A stagnant or shrinking economy has increased ethnic and regional tensions, making it difficult to pursue, or even to define, a national interest. Centralized one-party and patrimonial regimes, lacking popular legitimacy, have been unable to exert control, despite harsh, authoritarian methods. And in a few countries, political contention led to long wars.[2]

In recent years economic analysts have reached broad consensus about the reforms necessary to halt the decline of African economies and move them toward sustained growth.[3] The task of reform is daunting, however, and the recommended policy changes would impose high costs on politically powerful groups in most African societies. Few political observers see much reason to believe that decisive local action will be taken to design and implement the recommended reforms.

Yet a few countries in Africa have belied this bleak assessment. Botswana, rich in mineral resources, has sustained one of the world's highest growth rates for twenty-five years. Countries such as Cameroon, Kenya, Mali, Nigeria, and Zimbabwe have achieved modest growth rates. Ghana, after a disastrous fifteen years of decline, has implemented a comprehensive set of reforms. And, as this book has related, The Gambia began a series of reforms in 1985 that have substantially reversed its economic fortunes. Among the debris of failed African development since independence, only a very few countries may emerge as models for other countries. The Gambia should be one. This chapter seeks to draw on earlier chapters to provide lessons about the experience of Gambian policy reform that can be applied to other African countries.

It is tempting to dismiss the remarkable performance of The Gambia after 1985. It is, after all, one of the world's smallest and poorest countries, a microstate with less than a million inhabitants, a land area about the size of Puerto Rico, and an economy no larger than an average American town of 10,000 people. The Gambia has little choice of development strategy: it is forced to manage an economy completely open to world trade and financial markets, with little scope to deviate from its comparative advantages as an agricultural exporter, a tourist destination, and an entrepôt trader within West Africa. As a small enclave within Senegal, its very existence as a nation encourages The Gambia to manage its affairs with concern about maintaining political stability and economic balance. Because relatively small flows of foreign aid loom large in its economy, The Gambia is influenced heavily by the advice of the international aid community. Thus constrained in so many ways, The Gambia was a logical candidate for a reform program adhering closely to the tenets of the neoclassical economic model.

It would be a mistake to dismiss The Gambia as an example for Africa, however. The region contains many states that, though larger than The Gambia, are nevertheless small and equally poor, with similar resource endowments. As in other countries of the region, The Gambia was able to avoid adjustment for several years despite the Sahelian drought, deteriorating world market conditions, and the political turmoil that led to military support from Senegal in 1981. Similar to The Gambia, aid flows to many African countries loom far larger in their economies than they do in the portfolios of the major donors. The problems and limited choices of other African countries differ in degree, but not always in kind, from those faced in The Gambia.

The policy reforms undertaken in The Gambia closely resemble those recommended for other countries in Africa and elsewhere. Just as in other countries, those reforms imposed costs on virtually all segments of society. The Gambian story provides insights into the economic context for which reforms are designed, the political context in which they are introduced, and requirements for their implementation.

Designing Policy Reforms: The Economic Context

The ERP sought to encourage economic recovery and growth in a small, open economy whose base is in agriculture. In this, The Gambia shares much in common with many other countries of sub-Saharan Africa. With very few if any exceptions, African economies are small and open in the sense that:

- They cannot affect world prices for their exports and imports.
- Their domestic economies are too small to sustain inward-looking, import-substituting development strategies.

- Despite official controls over capital flows, investment will be determined by the relative attractiveness of returns in the domestic economy compared to those in world financial markets.
- Consequently, income and welfare depend totally on the international competitiveness of domestic producers in all sectors.

The Gambian reforms were designed in full recognition of these constraints and provide a model for other countries with similar characteristics. Distinctive accomplishment was made in three areas: gaining and maintaining macroeconomic balance, establishing an open trade and payments regime, and supporting smallholder agriculture.

Macroeconomic Balance

After a decade of economic reform around the world, economists are virtually unanimous that sustained growth in open economies depends upon a stable macroeconomy, with sustainable balances in foreign payments and the government budget, and acceptable rates of inflation. These goals in turn require maintaining an appropriate exchange rate, adhering to a restrained monetary policy, generating greater tax revenue, and reducing government expenditures.

Gambian reformers moved decisively in 1985 to restore external balance. The dalasi was permitted to float, and its exchange rate is now determined in the free market.[4] From a fixed rate of 5.00 dalasi to the pound sterling in 1983–1984, the rate floated to an average of 13.3 dalasi per pound by the end of 1991.

In the initial years of reform, the large groundnut subsidy actually made monetary and fiscal performance worse until a greater measure of austerity was imposed after 1987–1988.[5] Money supply growth, which averaged 30 percent annually from 1983–1984 to 1987–1988, was restricted to only 14 percent annually in the following three fiscal years. Bank discount rates were doubled to 21 percent by 1987, then fell back to 15.5 percent by 1991, with concomitant changes in other rates. The government budget deficit, measured in the absence of proceeds from foreign grants, initially rose from 13 percent of GDP in the year before the ERP to 22 percent by 1987–1988, then fell to 8 percent of GDP by the end of the following three fiscal years. When foreign grants are included, the budget was close to balance during this latter period. These measures eventually cooled down inflation, which had flared to an average 29 percent a year from 1983 to 1987, but fell to only 10 percent a year from 1987 to 1991.

An Open Trade Regime

Beyond macroeconomic stability, neoclassical prescriptions for sustained growth suggest a trade regime that treats producers of exports on a par with producers of import substitutes, or even a regime that favors exporters. Outside of East Asia, however, most developing countries have protected their import-competing producers more than they have subsidized their exporters. The Gambia, as with Hong Kong and Singapore, is a classic entrepôt economy, earning much of its foreign exchange by trading. The reexport business depends crucially on traders' ability to import goods through Banjul at low cost and to resell them to neighboring countries where they are largely smuggled past high protective barriers. Little scope for protection exists to promote the production of the tiny Gambian market, so most tariffs are designed for revenue collection rather than protection and are kept at moderate rates. Thus in The Gambia, export industries are relatively free of the high costs due to import substitution that plague most African countries.

In one respect the Gambians went beyond conventional wisdom in opening their economy. With virtually no controls over foreign capital flows, the dalasi became fully convertible in 1986. Only a few developing countries, such as Hong Kong, Singapore, Indonesia, Malaysia, Thailand, and the CFA franc zone countries of West Africa, have convertible currencies. Convertibility has been a controversial issue in the literature on reform. When Chile opened its economy to foreign capital flows in the 1970s, it led to the desired inflow of private capital. However, this inflow caused currency appreciation that damaged export growth, a concentration of assets in the hands of those with access to foreign loans, and a marked rise in private foreign debt, all of which inhibited Chilean recovery. Based on this and other examples, many economists have argued that capital movements should be freed late in the reform process, after domestic financial markets have been deregulated and developed more fully.[6]

Yet the countries of Southeast Asia have maintained open capital accounts to advantage for many years, even when domestic financial markets were repressed. Convertibility reassures foreign investors, who flocked to Indonesia, Malaysia, and Thailand in the 1980s. It also imposes strict discipline on the government to maintain macroeconomic balance in all respects; otherwise the country would lose its reserves or face a rapidly depreciating currency. The Gambia's ability to manage its economy with a convertible currency should encourage other African countries to move in the same direction. Until recently, most countries have doggedly maintained capital controls in the fear that liberalization would lead to capital flight. It is doubtful that these controls were ever very effective. Recently, the governments of Kenya and Ghana have been easing their regulations over currency transactions, and other countries are being encouraged to follow these examples.

Support for Smallholder Agriculture

Most countries of sub-Saharan Africa are agrarian. Agriculture accounts for the largest share of GDP, the most important exports, the majority of the work force, and most of the poor. African agriculture is dominated by smallholding farmers who gain from some reforms and lose from others. When smallholders are also exporters, as is true in The Gambia and much of Africa, devaluation raises their incomes, sometimes substantially. Deregulation of domestic grain markets raises farmgate prices. However, budget cuts—especially reduced subsidies for food consumption—are borne partly by small farmers, both the producers of net grain surpluses who face declining demand for grain and especially farmers who are net consumers of grain. Smallholders are affected much less by increases in the price of fuel, electricity, public transportation, and imports. The balance between costs and benefits depends on the structure of the rural economy, with a presumption in favor of net benefits if exports are a major source of income to smallholders.

In The Gambia, where small farmers are the ruling party's most important constituency, the government was not willing to leave this balance of costs and benefits to the play of structural characteristics and market forces. In one of the most curious episodes in the recent annals of stabilization (described by Jones and Radelet in Chapter 14), the IMF encouraged the Gambian government to raise the domestic price of groundnuts to 50 percent above world prices. The ostensible purpose was to ensure that produce would not escape across the border to Senegal, which maintained a high domestic price. The groundnut subsidy placed an additional 8 percent of GDP into the hands of this important constituency of poor farmers, improving the incomes of the poorest Gambians and making reform far more acceptable.

Yet the groundnut subsidy had potentially dire macroeconomic consequences. The budget deficit soared to 22 percent of GDP in 1986–1987 and 1987–1988, and the money supply expanded by an inflationary 74 percent in those two fiscal years. True fiscal and monetary austerity, essential for continued stabilization, did not begin in earnest until the groundnut subsidy was eliminated in 1988–1989. In the interim, donor grants, which averaged 14 percent of GDP, effectively paid the subsidy. This measure was a particularly dramatic and effective, if implicit, use of aid to alleviate poverty during economic stabilization. The donor community now promotes poverty-focused aid as an explicit part of stabilization and reform programs. The Gambian experience shows how well it can work. However, it is hard to imagine that aid resources will be available to address poverty on such an extensive scale in countries much larger than The Gambia.

Stabilization in agrarian countries is also affected seriously by weather. Rains ended the Sahelian drought in 1985, contributing to a 14 percent increase in grain yields and a 45 percent surge in groundnut production. Increased output of staple commodities is essential to helping reduce inflationary pressures and establish the credibility of a reform program. The timing of economic adjustment between good and bad rainy seasons may not be a choice open to governments, but evidence of a good growing year should be taken as an opportunity to accelerate stabilization and reform programs.

Introducing Reforms

The economic reforms introduced in The Gambia were no different from those recommended for many other countries in sub-Saharan Africa, in that they imposed costs on virtually all sectors of the population. As pointed out by McPherson and Radelet in Chapter 2:

> The devaluation of the dalasi eroded the incomes of civil servants and those on fixed incomes; high interest rates raised the cost of institutional finance for individuals and enterprises; the contraction in government employment and the retargeting of government expenditures required some painful adjustments, particularly among the urban population; the reorganization of the parastatal sector increased the costs of . . . basic services; and higher user charges and commodity prices, particularly for petrol, raised costs for businesses and individuals.

Given the potential political reaction to such measures, the success of even well-designed policy reforms cannot be assumed. The next subsections discuss four dimensions of the process of introducing reforms in The Gambia: the speed and pace of implementation; the role played by economic crisis; the importance of political leadership; and the contributions of donor support. All four factors contributed significantly to overcoming the potential political hazards of strong reform measures.

Sequencing and Pace
The scope and speed of the Gambian reforms were breathtaking. Within an eighteen-month period after mid-1985, the government floated the

dalasi and made it fully convertible; first raised interest rates and later established a treasury bill tender system to determine market interest rates; raised taxes on petroleum and rice while lowering many import duties; cracked down on customs fraud; rescheduled external debt with the creditor countries; reduced the civil service by 18 percent; adopted stricter public investment criteria; sharply increased the producer price of groundnuts; increased public transportation fares, water charges, electricity rates, and petroleum prices; liberalized the fertilizer market; and privatized a government bank and a trading company.

In the literature on stabilization and structural reforms, the Gambian program would be called *shock treatment*; its alternative is called *gradualism*.[7] The two principal arguments in favor of shock treatment are the converse of the two main drawbacks of gradualism. First, in a highly unbalanced or distorted economy, gradual or partial reforms can make things worse, because improved efficiency in one market can increase the costs of the remaining distortions in other markets. If foreign capital flows are decontrolled, for example, more investment is likely to move into the still protected and thus inefficient industries.

Second, when reforms are gradual, the benefits of reform take longer, while the impending costs may be anticipated by the potential losers. Thus constituencies have greater time and scope to coalesce against reform. Gambian reforms were swift and comprehensive enough to turn the economy around: after three years of a slight decline in GDP, the ERP contributed to a growth rate of 4.3 percent annually from 1985–1986 to 1990–1991.[8]

But the main argument against shock treatment seems equally compelling in the Gambian case: only the strongest, best-disciplined governments seem capable of instituting comprehensive reforms in a short period. How was the Gambian government able to manage so much in just eighteen months? Most of the reforms instituted from late 1985 through early 1987 were changes in macroeconomic policies that required self-implementing decisions (as discussed later in this chapter). A price was raised, such as the exchange rate or electricity charges, or controls were suspended—for example, on currency flows and fertilizer marketing. These reforms did not require focused, extended administrative efforts. Two crucial policies that were sustained for several years—monetary restraint and reduced budget deficits—were backed by the concentrated leverage of the donors, particularly the IMF. Other reforms that required sustained implementation were less successful, including the crackdown on customs fraud, the improvement in investment criteria, performance contracts for public enterprises, and tax reform.

The Gambian experience suggests that a limited shock treatment is both workable and effective in Africa. The crucial macroeconomic prices should be moved immediately to their long-run equilibrium rates. Deregulation and privatization, which reduce the government's need for sustained management, should be pursued vigorously. And the limited potential for sustained effort should go into pivotal macroeconomic adjustments, especially reducing budget deficits and restraining money supply growth. Other reforms that require extended government involvement, such as performance contracts for public enterprises and the creation of new financial markets, may have to be left to the longer term.

National Crisis and Economic Reform

The problems of The Gambia's economy were evident as early as 1979. In Chapter 2, McPherson and Radelet suggest that the country's adjustment would have been much easier had policymakers acted then rather than wait until mid-1985 to introduce the ERP. By 1985 the economy was in the midst of a major economic crisis, exacerbated by the widespread perception that economic collapse might be followed by the absorption of the country into surrounding Senegal. This dire situation limited the choices available to policymakers.

From the perspective of a country's political economy, however, a crisis can facilitate reform. The Gambian crisis predisposed political leaders to blame existing policies for their predicament and to believe that drastic measures were required to deal with the economy.[9] In addition, the public's acceptance of change, or even the demand for it, grows in the face of a widespread sense that current conditions are intolerable. In The Gambia this popular perception helped overcome the equally obvious costs of reform to major groups in the population. Thus the dual perception that existing policies were at fault and that existing conditions were insupportable helped move policymakers and citizens toward willingness to accept the need for change.

Political Leadership

Crisis alone cannot explain the introduction of major policy reforms. Much of sub-Saharan Africa has experienced economic trauma since the mid-1970s, but only a few countries have embarked on the perilous journey taken by The Gambia. The Gambia's political leadership, and how it managed the introduction of the reforms, were crucial to the success of the ERP.

As emphasized throughout this book, President Jawara placed economic policy reform squarely on the government's agenda and advocated decisive action in the face of a major crisis. He made the important decision to call Sheriff Sisay to the MoF, a choice that could not have been easy, given the historic political rivalries between the two men. When Minister Sisay was in office, President Jawara accorded him the room and support necessary to take the lead in designing the policy reform package. In turn, the minister demonstrated strong leadership in convincing colleagues in Cabinet to support the measures and in negotiating with donor agencies for advice and economic support.[10]

The nature of The Gambia's leading political party, and its regular recourse to elections, also eased the introduction of reform. The party, with a strong base in the country's rural area, provided widespread legitimacy to the president's leadership and helped carry the message about the importance of the reforms to its membership. The elections in 1987 ratified the government's program by returning a substantial majority to the People's Progressive Party just a year and a half after the ERP was introduced. It has been argued that democratic political systems find it more difficult to introduce reform than authoritarian ones,[11] but the case of The Gambia belies this generalization. The openness of the debate about policy reforms, possible only in a relatively free democratic atmosphere, helped build consensus about their importance and provided an opportunity for citizens to assess the costs of current problems against the probable costs of policy change.

The decisiveness of political leaders also encouraged strong and constructive donor support for the reform package. Faced with threats from its own economy, from Senegal, and from the donors, the president and his finance minister took the initiative to design the Economic Reform Program. Authors McPherson and Radelet emphasize in Chapter 2 that because the ERP was not dictated by the donors, but planned by the government, the country's leadership was strongly committed to carrying it out. This contrasts with the more typical case in which donors impose conditions and governments go along reluctantly, doing no more than necessary to satisfy the conditions of loan agreements in an effort to continue drawing program aid.[12] There may be a fine line between donor-imposed conditions and a government's own programs, but the distinction can be crucial: reforms imposed from outside generally do not work as well and are often short-lived.

Donor Support

The Gambia offers a textbook example of how leverage by the donor agencies can support stabilization and reform. On top of the crisis of a deteriorating economy and perceived threats of Senegalese invasion, the donors also made it clear that in the absence of stabilization and reform, the aid agencies might let events take their course. Thus additional aid was effectively tied to stabilization and reform. Moreover, as has been emphasized, donors were able to offer amounts of aid that, though small in their eyes, could make a very great difference to the economic welfare of The Gambia.

The donors also provided technical assistance that enhanced The Gambia's capacity to design and implement reforms and, ironically, provided it with a counterpoint to donor advice and conditionality. In the absence of this increased technical capacity, the program would have been designed primarily by the donors, in which case The Gambia would have been less committed to the ERP. Armed with technical capacity under their own control, the Gambians did not always acquiesce to the positions of the donors. From the agencies' standpoint this may have been an inconvenience or even an annoyance. But it also made the feeling of Gambian ownership of the ERP more concrete and may well have contributed to more effective reform management.

For aid donors seeking the most productive use of their resources, one possible strategy is to "pick winners" simply by putting their money on governments that clearly face the need for economic reform and demonstrate the commitment and capacity to carry it out. That, in essence, is what happened in The Gambia. This strategy suggests less active intervention by the aid agencies in the economic decision making and management of governments, especially in Africa, where such intervention has often been intense. It would also lead to fewer but larger aid programs, targeted at countries with effective economic adjustment programs or with the clear intention and capacity to introduce them.

Implementing Reform

The ERP was successful in the sense that policy reforms were introduced, and within a relatively brief period, the Gambian economy recovered from a decade of stagnation and began to grow effectively. But a closer look at the ERP package shows that while several crucial reforms were implemented successfully, several were not.

Successfully implemented reforms included the float of the dalasi; foreign exchange deregulation; the introduction of market-based interest rates and agricultural prices; a narrowing of the budget deficit; and a reduction in the size of the civil service. In addition, at least in the short term, customs fraud was significantly curtailed, the external debt was managed successfully, and arrears on the domestic debt fell significantly.

Less successful or failed reforms, as judged by the analysts in previous chapters, included the reorganization of the Ministry of Finance; the restructuring of state-owned enterprises; the revamping of financial institutions; the reform of the agricultural credit system; budget reform; tax reform; and attention to the problem of recurrent expenditures.

Characteristics of Success

The characteristics of the reforms themselves contribute much to understanding why some were successful and others were less so. With the exceptions of the retrenchment of the civil service and the clean-up of the customs agency, the successful reforms shared one significant feature: they were all decree-driven measures that did not require a long period of time or a long chain of institutional or bureaucratic compliance in order to be implemented. Once announced by the president, the minister of finance, or the Central Bank, these reforms were effectively self-implementing.

Of course, self-implementing reforms are by no means easy to introduce. As indicated earlier, their success depends on whether they are designed effectively, managed carefully, and sustained long enough to produce benefits that can compensate for the costs to groups and interests. In The Gambia the perception of a national crisis, determined political leadership, and the supportive role of donors made it possible to introduce these decree-driven reforms without major political resistance or upheaval.

National crisis, high-level leadership, and donor support were less crucial to implementing other reforms. The less successful policies in The Gambia also shared one significant feature: each required that institutions be reorganized and reoriented and that public officials adopt new rules of behavior and new attitudes. These changes could be accomplished only with extensive, sustained attention to the characteristics of existing institutions and their implicit or explicit incentive systems.

Earlier chapters related the fate of efforts to reorganize government ministries and parastatals and to alter established forms of providing credit, managing the budget, and collecting revenue. Those authors consistently indicated that time, complexity, commitment, and resistance all significantly affected the reforms. The politics of implementation and resistance to reform were played out within the halls and offices of bureaucratic institutions, as indicated in the following excerpts:

During the initial stages of the ERP, the absence of attention to the organization of the MoF was due largely to the general disarray and operational inefficiency of other ministries. But Minister Sisay was also concerned that reorganization would divert the attention of MoF staff from the urgent task of implementing the ERP. Moreover, the minister was aware that powerful public-sector interests were opposed to his economic reforms, and he was concerned that these interests might disrupt the organizational reform of the ministry. (Gray and Hoover, Chapter 15)

[M]ost government officials expressed no enthusiasm for privatization. . . . [R]esistance to parastatal reform was potent. . . . [T]he preparations involved in implementing performance contracts and privatization are lengthy, complex, and skill intensive. (Hook, Mallon, and McPherson, Chapter 16)

The ERP left a mixed legacy with respect to fiscal policy. On the one hand, the government dramatically reduced the budget deficit, helping to stabilize the economy. On the other hand, it made very little progress in changing the underlying budgeting process, and many chronic budgetary problems were not addressed. Ironically, the success in reducing the deficit may have hampered efforts to reform the budget process. The story of the attempted budget reform during the ERP illustrates how difficult it is to obtain the institutional and policy-making support necessary to improve the quality of the government's expenditure decisions. (McNamara, Chapter 8)

Tax reform aroused significant and concerted resistance from the beneficiaries of tax exemptions, and at times from tax officials themselves. In many areas the pace of reform was sluggish; in others there was essentially no progress. It took several years to introduce the major policy changes on the income tax and the sales tax. The revision of the National Development Act failed to eliminate many wasteful exemptions. Computerization has yet to take hold, despite its promise for improved analysis and increased revenue. (Gray and McPherson, Chapter 9)

Indeed, the 1992 report made the point that almost none of the substantive recommendations of previous investigations had been implemented. Perhaps the major reason for the lack of reform was that no one in any position to make a difference had an incentive to deal with the problem, especially after the budget crisis had begun to ease. (McNamara and McPherson, Chapter 17)

In each of these and other cases, institutional factors slowed or stymied the reforms incorporated in the ERP: the lack of interest among government officials, particularly at high levels; the lack of support or outright opposition by civil servants, particularly at middle levels; and effective bureaucratic lobbying by interest groups.

Leadership and Management

Opposition to change is not enough to explain the difference between the more and less successful reforms. In all cases the opposition was a real or potential aspect of introducing the reforms. For the self-implementing reforms, however, there is clear evidence that political and bureaucratic leaders considered the political impediments and acted to ameliorate opposition from interest groups and the public. High-level officials had at least an implicit strategy for introducing these reforms. We have already emphasized the importance of contextual factors—the Senegalese threat, the government's legitimacy and its rural base, and substantial donor assistance—in making reforms effective. As Radelet and McPherson argue in Chapter 3, it was the interaction of these factors and the political strategy that cleared a path for the macroeconomic reforms-by-decree.

While the self-implementing reforms benefited from attention to the politics of public reaction, they suffered from the fact that the bureaucratic politics of institutional reform was largely ignored. In part this can be explained by the difference between the high drama of public politics and the low drama of bureaucratic resistance.[13] Politicians and analysts are often skilled at anticipating the former and overlooking the latter. Public opposition, protest, and violence can threaten not only the substance of the reform measures but also the life of the regime in power or the tenure of incumbent leadership. These reforms imply hardship for significant groups in the population, and resistance is often anticipated, and feared, by political leaders.[14]

In contrast, bureaucratic resistance, sabotage, and sloth, although they threaten the substance of reforms, do so in quiet, persistent ways that generally escape the notice of political leaders. In The Gambia it is clear that little systematic attention was given to the importance and difficulty of implementing reforms that required slow, protracted, and often conflict-ridden institutional and behavioral changes.

Could political and bureaucratic leadership have made a difference in the outcome of institutional reforms in The Gambia? The country's leaders could have demonstrated high-level commitment to these reforms and emphasized their importance to economic recovery. They could have sent politically compelling messages to public officials about appropriate behavior by those who controlled access to budgetary resources, career mobility, the perquisites of office, and overseas training. Senior leadership could also have tried to garner resources from donor agencies to offset some of the costs of institutional and behavioral adjustments.

High-level commitment to institutional and bureaucratic change is important, but it is not sufficient to encourage success. Managerial skills were also required in The Gambia. These skills could have been used more effectively to build consensus within implementing organizations, to assign supporters of reform to key positions, to create incentives for career advancement and prestige in return for active commitment to carrying out the reforms, and to use training opportunities to reward reformers. Effective managers could have created a greater sense of ownership among subordinates by encouraging them to participate in planning the implementation of reforms. Skillful managers also could have enlisted high-level support at critical moments to ensure that messages about the importance of reform were heard clearly by those who would ignore or resist it.

Similarly, technical skills would have been useful to help convince officials of the rationale for change; to assess how the costs of reorganization or cutbacks could be shared across ministries and departments; to encourage the enhancement of skills with training and participation in efforts to monitor and evaluate important changes; and to assess what problems were delaying the advancement of reform.

The importance of leadership, management, and technical support is obvious in retrospect. Nevertheless, these factors were frequently overlooked in The Gambia and elsewhere in sub-Saharan Africa. The literature on economic policy reform has focused on the issues associated with building public consensus and explaining why groups will resist policy initiatives.[15] Equally important is a political economy that focuses on problems inherent in complex, time-consuming institutional reforms and how they can be overcome. In The Gambia these considerations could have broadened and deepened the impact of the ERP.

Concluding Observations about the Gambian Experience

A significant lesson from the Gambian experience in implementing the ERP is that, at least in the short term, improved economic performance can be achieved by introducing effective macroeconomic policies. This case history suggests that a limited shock treatment is workable and effective in sub-Saharan Africa. The crucial macroeconomic prices can be moved immediately to their long-run equilibrium rates. By its nature, deregulation reduces the demand on the government's capacity to manage the economy. The Gambia's experiment with one critical deregulation—the transition to a convertible currency—should encourage other African countries to move in the same direction. However, both budgetary balance and monetary balance require the sustained vigilance of officials and political leaders.

Ultimately, the fact that The Gambia is a small, poor, resource-poor country may severely limit its possibilities for economic development. Short of this, however, the remaining potential of economic reforms to sustain growth—in The Gambia as in the rest of Africa—hinges on the government's ability to deal more effectively with the institutional changes. Improved management of the agricultural sector, more efficient financial institutions, better revenue collection procedures, and more disciplined public expenditure systems are among the improvements necessary for continued development in The Gambia beyond the initial burst of growth led by improved macroeconomic policy. A similar list applies to many other African countries. While the impediments to institutional reform are considerable and high-level interest in them is often absent, it is possible to think strategically about how they can be supported and furthered, just as it is possible to focus on the strategic management of self-implementing reforms.

The Gambia demonstrates that leadership for a reform shock can come from a democratic government. Because President Jawara's government was elected, its reform program gained legitimacy with the population. Because its constituency was dominated by small farmers, the government skewed the benefits toward the largest group of poor families in the country. President Jawara's trust in and support for his technically qualified finance minister, Sisay, suggest the importance of putting well-qualified, politically insulated officials in charge of macroeconomic policy.

Other countries in Africa have found that economic reforms and elections can be mutually reinforcing. The newly elected Chiluba government in Zambia had a mandate that made it possible to institute and sustain economic reforms that had eluded its predecessor for years. Rawlings's election in Ghana after several years of austerity and economic recovery under his military government echoed another lesson from The Gambia: successful economic reform can in turn enhance political legitimacy.

The Gambia's experience also points out a possible path for aid donors seeking to improve the productivity of their resources in Africa: select a few secure governments with dedicated leadership and well-designed reform programs; support them with a generous amount of financial and technical assistance; and then depend more on the integrity of the country's own program than on donors' proclivities for frequent policy intervention. This approach worked, not only in The Gambia, but in Ghana as well. Massive donor support for the groundnut subsidy also suggests the benefits of targeting aid at the poor and at politically strategic groups during reform shocks. In African countries facing civil service reform, for example, donors might consider funding termination benefits for civil servants.

The Gambia is a small country, but its experience suggests some large lessons for other countries in sub-Saharan Africa and for donor organizations interested in facilitating the process of adjustment. Among the most important lessons are that fundamental policy change can occur despite significant constraints when government is committed to change, good technical analysis is available to government, reforms minimize administrative burdens on government, and donors help cushion the negative impact of adjustment on politically important interests and vulnerable groups. The success of initiatives to introduce and sustain economic policy reforms cannot be ensured, but the case of The Gambia indicates that such facilitating conditions can significantly increase the possibilities for effective policy change.

NOTES

1. Much of the rationale for economic policy reform in sub-Saharan Africa is developed in World Bank (1981a; 1984; 1986; 1989a). In addition, see Ravenhill (1986), Roemer (1982), and Winrock International (1991). The political impediments to policy change are discussed in Herbst (1990), Sandbrook (1986), Rothchild and Chazan (1988), Bratton (1989), Wunsch and Olowu (1990), and Jackson (1987). Policy as a source of economic stagnation is explored in Bates (1981) and Frimpong-Ansah (1991). On the problems of public-sector officials, see Chew (1990).
2. Patrimonial regimes are those in which an authoritarian leader or "strongman" dispenses favors and government largesse in exchange for personal loyalty and political support. See Sandbrook (1986) on patrimonialism and neopatrimonialism.
3. For an overview, see World Bank (1989a) and the items cited in note 1.
4. In floating the dalasi, The Gambia went beyond conventional recommendations, which usually counsel a crawling peg, with the exchange rate managing to retain its real value, given inflation at home and in the markets of major trading partners. Ghana also floated its currency in the early 1980s, and African governments are increasingly being advised by the IMF to take similar actions.
5. The subsidy, which is discussed later in the chapter, was recommended by the IMF and supported implicitly by donor grants.
6. See Edwards (1987) for a summary of this and other issues of reform sequencing.

7. See Roemer and Radelet (1991) for a discussion of gradualism versus shock treatment.
8. Radelet (Chapter 8) attributes one-third of the gain in Gambian GDP to the macroeconomic measures of the ERP.
9. Grindle and Thomas (1991, Chapter 4) discuss the importance of crisis in reform programs.
10. Here is a reflection of the marked tendency in East and Southeast Asia for political leaders to entrust macroeconomic policy to a strong cadre of technically competent senior officials, and to insulate them from political pressures. This arrangement has been one of the keys to rapid economic growth in these countries.
11. Sheahan (1987) applies this argument to Latin America; Haggard and Kaufmann (1989) analyze the experience of different types of regimes with stabilization and structural adjustment.
12. Callaghy (1989, p. 129) has characterized this situation as a "ritual dance" between donors and governments.
13. Grindle and Thomas (1991, Chapter 6) discuss the difference between reforms that encourage reaction in a public arena and those that invite bureaucratic responses.
14. Lindenberg (1989) discusses the winners and losers in adjustment.
15. See, for example, Nelson (1990).

Epilogue: The July 1994 Coup d'État

Steven C. Radelet and Malcolm F. McPherson

The Gambia's economic and political situation took a dramatic turn in July 1994 when four junior military officers led a successful coup d'état against President Jawara. Led by twenty-nine-year-old Lieutenant Yaya Jammeh and three other young lieutenants, the soldiers immediately established a military ruling council, suspended the constitution, and banned all political parties. President Jawara boarded a U.S. navy ship that was in Banjul on a courtesy call and fled to Dakar.

The soldiers apparently were motivated by their unhappiness over late pay, discontent with the Nigerian soldiers who held commanding positions in the Gambian army, and displeasure with a perceived increase in government corruption, especially within the senior ranks of the army. Media reports and discussions with several Gambians suggest that popular reaction to the coup was generally positive. Many citizens expressed discontent with the Jawara regime's long hold on power, its failure to achieve sustained improvements in standards of living, and the apparent increase in corruption. Others, however, decried the dissolution of democratic institutions and were worried about the prospects for either political or economic improvements under a military dictatorship. This epilogue briefly examines the coup, its relationships to the policy reforms of the late 1980s and early 1990s, and its implications for future policy and economic development.

Military Background and the Build-up to the Coup

The Gambia did not have an army until 1984. In the aftermath of the 1981 attempted coup (see Chapter 3), President Jawara created a small army of eight hundred men to complement the existing gendarmerie.

311

Under the mutual defense treaty with Senegal, Senegalese soldiers were brought in to advise the new army and to guard the State House. Their presence suggested that the full Senegalese army stood ready to defend Jawara and The Gambia against armed threats (including any from within the Gambian army). Although there were murmurs at the time that the new army might ultimately be a destabilizing force, the fact that more seasoned Senegalese soldiers would guard the State House partially muted these concerns. However, in 1989, the Senegambia Confederation was dissolved on unfriendly terms, and the Senegalese soldiers left.

Two years later, sixty Gambian soldiers staged a protest at the State House, demanding back pay for their service in the multinational force in Liberia, improved living conditions, and the resignation of the Gambian commander of the army. The soldiers were unhappy about the mishandling of their rations and back pay by senior army officials and the sacking of several officers who had served in Liberia (*West Africa*, July 1, 1991). The protesting soldiers were suspended immediately. Although the army commander resigned a week later, the seeds of discontent clearly had germinated.

The government responded by signing a mutual defense treaty with Nigeria in 1992, under which sixty-eight Nigerian officers were stationed in Banjul, mainly to guard the State House. Perhaps more importantly, a Nigerian officer was given command of the Gambian army. Gambian soldiers strongly resented the presence of the Nigerians. Discontent increased as barracks became overcrowded. In addition, the perception grew that senior officers were taking a cut of the younger troop's rations and allowances.[1] The final straw apparently came the night before the coup, when Lieutenant Jammeh was publicly disarmed (and humiliated) by Nigerian soldiers as he attempted to attend an airport ceremony welcoming Jawara from an overseas trip (*Africa Confidential*, December 2, 1994).

Public Reaction to the Coup

There were several dimensions to the general public support for the coup.[2] Many people simply felt that after thirty years of Jawara in power, a change was needed. There was a sense that while The Gambia had enjoyed relative political stability and had recovered from the depths of the economic crisis of the mid–1980s, little had been done to bring about sustained increases in welfare during the thirty years following independence. Most importantly, many Gambians believed that corruption had risen markedly in the early 1990s as the economy recovered and rent-seeking opportunities became more plentiful (*West Africa*, August 1, 1994). Paradoxically, as the economic crisis eased, a political crisis began to emerge.

Others, however, were much less sanguine about the coup. Correspondence in the media indicated that some people were very concerned about the dissolution of democratic institutions, which had been Jawara's greatest legacy. They were also legitimately worried that both the political and economic situation would grow much worse under a military dictatorship, despite the shortcomings of the Jawara administration.

Public support for Jawara and his government apparently began to fade around the time of the 1992 elections. Jawara had announced in 1990 that he would not seek reelection in 1992, and seemed to be paving the way for a successor. Most observers thought that would be Bakary Dabo, his Vice President at the time, who enjoyed a reputation for honesty and competency both inside The Gambia and abroad, would be that candidate. In late 1991 Jawara changed his mind, and went on to win reelection. Dabo was demoted to Minister of Finance, perhaps because he had been too aggressive in his attempts to position himself as successor. He was replaced by Saihou Sabally, who had been Minister of Agriculture during the ERP and the Minister of Finance after the death of Sheriff Sisay. Sabally's reputation was poor; he had been charged with various counts of alleged corruption by opposition leaders and the local press for years. In a well-known case, he and two other ministers sued a local newspaper reporter for libel after the reporter alleged the ministers' involvement in corruption. The presiding judge eventually acquitted the defendant of all but one minor charge, remarking that Sabally's conduct was such that he can hardly be libeled (*West Africa*, August 1, 1994). Many people interpreted Sabally's promotion to the vice presidency as a selection by Jawara of the next president, and it was not a popular move.

A series of financial scandals further affected public opinion. The process of selling the assets of the GCDB (Chapters 6 and 16) uncovered many large nonperforming loans to high-ranking members and supporters of the ruling party, the PPP. There was a widely held perception that efforts to force repayment of the loans were being frustrated by the president. Similarly, in 1993, a scandal erupted at the Gambia Cooperative Union (GCU), when it was alleged that three top officers had embezzled funds. Sabally was linked to these allegations. The president effectively ignored the results of an audit that seemed to confirm the allegations (*West Africa*, August 1, 1995).

Many citizens were also disenchanted with the apparently poor results of at least parts of the government's privatization program. For example, after management of the Gambia Utilities Corporation was turned over to a private company acting under a management contract, it was commonly claimed that electricity service worsened, even as higher rates were charged. Several weeks before the coup, public demonstrations about the privatization of the municipal water supply led to clashes with police and the arrest of several demonstrators.

Was the Coup Related to the Economic Reforms?

In considering the possible links between these events, the ERP, and PSD, a distinction should be made between the coup itself and public reaction to the coup. There was little direct relationship between the coup itself and the economic policy reforms. The coup was a result of internal problems in the army and the government's security and defense policies. The soldiers' earlier protests to Jawara and the first statements of the new regime had almost nothing to say about economic policy. The soldiers' protests about late pay were not because of budget cuts, but because their pay had been siphoned off before they received it. During the military regime's first year in power, most of the key policy reforms of the ERP remained unchanged, including the floating exchange rate, flexible interest rates, and private management of the GPMB. Some changes were reversed—the management contract of the poorly run GUC was revoked and subsidies for rice were reintroduced—but these policies were not what provoked the coup. Instead, the soldiers apparently were motivated by anger over how they were treated by their superiors and the government, and they grabbed power when the opportunity arose. Perhaps the soldiers behind the coup were emboldened by their experience in Liberia, when they worked with soldiers from military dictatorships in the region. (Indeed, some diplomats fear that the peacekeeping force in Liberia may in the end serve to extend the chain of unstable Anglophone military governments in West Africa—Nigeria, Liberia, Sierra Leone, and now The Gambia (Africa Confidential, 12 Aug 1994). The idea that the coup was a grab for power, rather than a reaction to economic policies, is reinforced by the clear divisions that have emerged and the struggle for power that has taken place among the coup plotters themselves. There have been almost a dozen changes in the new Cabinet, many of the former ministers and soldiers who participated in the coup have been jailed, and an attempted counter coup in November 1994 by senior officers resulted in an estimated 50 casualties within the military. A second attempted counter coup in January 1995 led to the arrest of the vice president of the ruling council, and in October 1995, the spokesman for the council fled and was charged with stealing $3 million and plotting to bring Jawara back to power.

The initial public support for the coup at least partly reflected economic concerns, including the absence of sustained development and the increase in corruption. The chapters in this volume have shown that the ERP successfully stabilized the macroeconomy, although it failed significantly to lay the foundation for sustained economic development. In particular, the reforms did not achieve much long-term institutional change. There were some exceptions, such as the privatization of the GPMB and the management contract with the Gambian Ports Authority, but in many areas—customs reform, tax administration, the public investment program, budget administration, and others—the changes were superficial.

The public was particularly outraged with the perceived increase in corruption, especially because corruption apparently had diminished in the latter half of the 1980s, first as the country ran out of foreign exchange reserves, then later when the government was under the close scrutiny of the IMF. Both Jawara and Sisay had been serious about cutting expenditures and curtailing waste so the country could survive the crisis. But as the economic pressures eased and both Sisay and the IMF passed from the scene, oversight weakened. For example, during the height of the economic crisis, Jawara reacted quickly and forcefully to abate rent-seeking in customs administration when it threatened the budget and the stabilization program. Customs corruption remained under control for several years. When it began to reemerge, Jawara took some action, but not as forcefully as before, and there was little impact. By the early 1990s, with the budget deficit mainly under control, donor support secure, and IMF oversight withdrawn, customs corruption emerged on a wide scale. At this stage, the President failed to take any action to address the problem.

In some cases, the reforms created difficulties for the Jawara government by increasing transparency and uncovering the extent of government corruption. The scandals at GCDB and GCU mentioned earlier are good examples. What seemed to bother the public was not so much the extent of the fraud, but the failure of the Jawara government to do anything about it once it was exposed. This simply increased the public perception that ordinary Gambians were being asked to sacrifice in the name of reform, while Jawara allowed his colleagues to reap the benefits.

This discontent did not contribute directly to the coup, but it meant that most Gambians were not unhappy to see Jawara deposed.

The Future

Will the new regime consolidate the gains made under the ERP and make further changes that will lead to sustained economic development? Or, will it hand over power to a civilian government that can make such changes? The history of military dictatorships in Africa is not reassuring; neither is the new government's first year in power. Its pledges to uphold human rights were the first to be broken, with arbitrary detentions, the banning of political parties, the closure of newspapers, and the reinstatement of the death penalty. Its decision to reintroduce rice subsidies (apparently to curry favor with urban consumer groups) reversed one of the key reforms of the ERP. Most major donors canceled their aid programs after the coup. Tourism fell sharply, especially after the November 1994 attempted counter coup, and up to half of the international hotels in and around Banjul closed (*West Africa*, December 26, 1994). Senegal had already closed its borders with The Gambia in the early 1990s after the Senegambia Confederation collapsed, but its controls tightened after the coup, severely restricting The Gambia's reexports to the rest of the region.

As a result of all of these influences, foreign exchange inflows have plummeted. In December 1994, the new government was forced to slash the 1994/95 budget by 23 percent (*West Africa*, February 13, 1995). In addition, the regime had four different people serve as Minister of Finance in its first year in power, including Dabo, who briefly returned after the coup, only to be replaced and arrested a few weeks later. The third Minister of Finance was found dead in his burned out car in a mysterious crash in June 1995. None of this augers well for economic policy or international credibility. The most likely outcome is a steady decline in foreign exchange reserves (which were the equivalent of nearly six months of imports at the time of the coup), followed by increasing shortages and other economic difficulties. If this occurs, the fragile gains from the ERP will be reversed, and The Gambia will slide into economic retrogression similar to that of the early 1980s.

History will likely remember the Jawara government for its exemplary human rights record, its commitment to democracy, its relatively free and fair elections, and its broad success at stabilizing the Gambian economy and bringing it back from the edge of economic disaster. But it will also likely remember the Jawara government for failing to achieve sustained development and to control widespread corruption. On both counts, there are many lessons for other African countries. In the end, we are left with a sense of the overwhelming challenges—even under the best of circumstances—of the process of economic reform and sustained economic and political development in sub-Saharan Africa.

Notes

1. President Jawara later admitted that some soldiers had to live in nearby villages because of the poor condition of the barracks, and that there was concern within the ranks about the "mishandling" of their rations by senior officers (*West Africa,* October 10, 1994).

2. The information on the public reaction to the coup is drawn from articles and correspondence recorded in *West Africa, Africa Confidential,* and other magazines, and from conversations with several Gambians in the aftermath of the coup.

Select Bibliography

Abdel-Rahman, A. M., M. R. Vaez-Zadeh, and D. S. Frampton. 1982. The Gambia: Survey of the tax system. Washington, D.C.: IMF.

Aghevli, B., M. S. Khan, and P. Monteil. 1991. Exchange rate policy in developing countries: Some analytical issues. International Monetary Fund Occasional Paper, No. 78. Washington, D.C.: IMF.

Allan, B., M. Woolley, and T. Rumbaugh. 1991. Aide-memoire from The Gambia: Improving budgeting and expenditure control. Washington, D.C.: IMF.

Amin, S., C. Atta-Mills, A. Bujra, G. Hamid, and T. Mkandawire. 1978. Social sciences and the development crisis in Africa: Problems and prospects. *Africa Development* 3 (4): 23–45.

Anderson, D. 1987. The public revenue and economic policy of African countries. World Bank Discussion Paper, No. 19. Washington, D.C.: World Bank.

Ayittey, G. B. N. 1991. *Indigenous African institutions.* Ardsley-on-Hudson, NY: Transnational Publishers.

Bajo, M. C. 1978. Special role of a central bank in developing countries. Central Bank of The Gambia. 105–113.

Bastone, S. M. 1988. The impact of agricultural development from an intrahousehold perspective. University of Michigan Center for Research on Economic Development Discussion Paper, No. 120. Ann Arbor, MI: CRED.

Bates, R. H. 1981. *Markets and states in tropical Africa.* Berkeley, CA: University of California Press.

Benjamin, N., S. Devarajan, and R. Weiner. 1989. The "Dutch" disease in a developing country: Oil reserves in Cameroon. *Journal of Development Economics* 30: 71–92.

Biggs, T., et al. 1985. An economic and operational analysis of The Gambia Produce Marketing Board. Cambridge, MA: Harvard Institute for International Development for the United States Agency for International Development/Banjul.

Bird, R. M. 1982. Budgeting and expenditure control in Columbia. *Public Budgeting and Finance* 2(3): 87–89.

———. 1989. The administrative dimension of tax reform in developing countries. In M. Gillis, ed. *Tax reform in developing countries*. Durham, NC: Duke University Press. 315–346.

Bird, R. M., and O. Oldman, eds. 1990. *Taxation in developing countries*, 4th ed. Baltimore: Johns Hopkins University Press.

Brent, R. S. 1990. Aiding Africa. *Foreign Policy* 80 (fall): 121–140.

Caiden, N., and A. Wildavsky. 1974. *Planning and budgeting in poor countries*. New York: John Wiley.

Callier, P., ed. 1991. *Financial systems and development in Africa*. Washington, D.C.: World Bank.

Caprio, G., and P. Honohan, eds. 1991. *Monetary policy instruments for developing countries*. Washington, D.C.: World Bank.

Chand, S. K. 1989. Toward a growth-oriented model of financial programming. *World Development* 17 (4): 473–490.

Clark, R. H. 1987. A study of the agricultural credit operations of the cooperative movement in The Gambia. Report to the United Nations International Labour Office, Cooperative Development Project.

Club du Sahel, 1982. *The recurrent costs in the countries of the Sahel: How to evaluate, finance and control them*. Acts of the Ouagadougou Symposium in Paris, CILSS, OECD.

Club du Sahel, Working Group on Recurrent Costs. 1980. *Recurrent costs of development programs in the countries of the Sahel: Analysis and recommendations*. Ouagadougou: CILSS.

Cnossen, G., H. de Zoysa, and T. Kimaro. 1976. *Fiscal survey of The Gambia*. Washington, D.C.: International Monetary Fund.

Collier, P. 1991. Africa's external economic relations 1960–90. In D. Rimmer, ed. *Africa thirty years on*. London: The Royal African Society.

Conway, P., and J. Greene. 1993. Is Africa different? *World Development* 21 (12): 2017–2028.

Cornia, G. A., R. van der Hoeven, and T. Mkandawire, eds. 1992. *Africa's recovery in the 1990s*. New York: St. John's Press.

Dean, P. N. 1989. *Government budgeting in developing countries*. New York: Routledge.

Deloitte & Touche. 1990. Assessment of the financial sector in The Gambia. Banjul: USAID.

Demissie, A., L. Brenneman, and J. Nash. 1989. Study of the operations and management of The Gambian Cooperative Union. Banjul: Ministry of Finance and Trade.

Dey, J. 1982. Development planning in The Gambia: The gap between planners' and farmers' perceptions, expectations, and objectives. *World Development* 10 (5): 377–396.

Diallo, I., P. O'Neil, and B. Manneh. 1988. Agricultural research achievements in The Gambia and impacts of research on selected farm economies. Banjul: USAID.

Diamond, J., and C. Schiller. 1987. Government arrears in fiscal adjustment programs. International Monetary Fund Working Paper, WP/87/3. Washington, D.C.: IMF.

Dooley, M. P., and D. J. Mathieson. 1987. Financial liberalization and stability in developing countries. International Monetary Fund Working Paper, WP/87/19. Washington, D.C.: IMF.

Dornbusch, R. 1988. The adjustment mechanism: Theory and problems. In N. S. Fieleke, ed. *International payments imbalances in the 1980s*. Federal Reserve Bank of Boston Conference Series, No. 32. Boston: Federal Reserve Bank of Boston.

Duesenberry, J. S. 1986. Fiscal and monetary policy in The Gambia. Banjul: Ministry of Finance and Trade.

Duesenberry, J. S., C. S. Gray, J. D. Lewis, M. F. McPherson, and S. D. Younger. 1994. Improving exchange rate management in Sub-Saharan Africa. CAER Discussion Paper No. 31. Cambridge, MA: Harvard Institute for International Development.

Dumont, R. 1969. *False start in Africa*. New York: Frederick A. Praeger.

Dunlop, M. and M. Livings. 1992. *United Kingdom customs report*. Report for the Ministry of Finance and Trade, Government of The Gambia.

Dunsmore, J. R., A. B. Rains, G. D. N. Lowe, D. J. Moffatt, I. P. Anderson, and J. B. Williams. 1976. The agricultural development of The Gambia: An agricultural, environmental and socioeconomic analysis. Land Resource Study No. 22. London: Ministry of Overseas Development.

Edwards, S. 1988. *Real exchange rates, devaluation and adjustment: exchange rate policy in developing countries*. Cambridge, MA: MIT Press.

Frankel, S. H. 1938. *Capital investment in Africa*. London: Oxford University Press.

Frimpong-Ansah, J. H. 1991. *The vampire state in Africa: The political economy of decline in Ghana*. Trenton, NJ: Africa World Press.

Fye, L. M., and M. F. McPherson. 1987. Government and parastatal interlocking arrears in The Gambia. Economic Note. Banjul: Statistics and Special Studies Unit, Ministry of Finance and Trade.

Gailey, H. A. 1965. *A history of The Gambia*. New York: Frederick A. Praeger.

Galal, A. 1991. Public enterprise reform: Lessons from the past and issues for the future. World Bank Discussion Paper No. 119. Washington, D.C.: World Bank.

Gallagher, M. 1991. A scorecard of African economic reforms. *The Fletcher Forum of World Affairs* 15 (winter): 57–76.

Gamble, D. 1955. *Economic conditions of two Mandinka villages: Kerewan and Keneba*. London: Research Department, Colonial Office.

Gillis, M., ed. 1989. *Tax reform in developing countries*. Durham, NC: Duke University Press.

Gladwin, C. H., and D. McMillan. 1989. Is a turnaround in Africa possible without helping African women to farm? *Economic Development and Cultural Change* 37 (2): 345–369.

Gleske, L. 1987. Monetary policy: Priorities and limitations. In E. Seiler, ed. *International monetary cooperation: Essays in honor of Henry C. Wallich*. Essays in International Finance, No. 169. Princeton, NJ: Princeton University Press.

Gordon, L. E. 1986. *Some lessons from foreign economic assistance*. Tokyo: Japan Economic Research Institute.

Gould, D. J., and J. A. Amaro-Reyes. 1983. The effects of corruption on administrative performance: Illustrations from developing countries. World Bank Working Paper 580 No. 7 (Management and Development Series). Washington, D.C.: World Bank.

Government of The Gambia. 1975a. *Annual plan 1976/77*. Banjul: Republic of The Gambia.

―――. 1975b. *Five-year plan for economic and social development 1975/76 to 1979/80*. Banjul: Republic of The Gambia.

―――. 1979. Preparation report for a rural development programme 1980–1985. Banjul: Ministry of Agriculture and Natural Resources.

―――. 1981. The Commission of Enquiry: Rural development project, summary, and recommendations, vol. 1. Presented to the president of the Republic of The Gambia through the Ministry of Justice. Banjul: Republic of The Gambia.

―――. 1985. *Action programme for economic reform*. Report of Task Force Appointed by the Honorable Minister of Finance and Trade. Banjul: Republic of The Gambia.

———. 1986. Introduction of flexible exchange rate system. Radio broadcast by the honorable minister of finance and trade, January 20.
———. 1987. Memorandum by the Honorable Minister of Finance and Trade on the economic recovery program. Banjul: Republic of The Gambia.
———. 1990a. *Agricultural Research Service annual report 1987.* Banjul: Ministry of Agriculture.
———. 1990b. Budget speech. Sessional Paper, No. 1. Banjul: Republic of The Gambia.
Graham, Douglas H., Richard L. Meyer, and Carlos E. Cuevas, eds. 1993. *Financial Markets in The Gambia, 1981–91.* Report to the USAID Mission in Banjul, The Gambia. Columbus, OH: Dept. of Agricultural Economics and Rural Sociology, Ohio State University.
Gray, C. G. 1983. Issues paper for the Task Force on Tax Reform. Draft, March 28. Banjul: Ministry of Finance and Trade.
———. 1985. Alternatives for income tax reform in The Gambia: Reflections based on computerized analysis of October 1985. Draft, November 18.
Gray, C. G., and A. Martens. 1983. The political economy of the "recurrent cost problem" in the West African Sahel. *World Development* 11 (2): 101–117.
Gray, C. G., M. McPherson, F. Owens, and C. Zinnes. 1992. Taxes and private sector activity in The Gambia: Overview and recommendations for change. Cambridge, MA: Harvard Institute for International Development.
Griffen, K. 1973. Agrarian policy: The political and economic context. *World Development* 1 (11): 1–11.
Grindle, M. S., and J. W. Thomas. 1991. *Public choices and policy change: The political economy of reform in developing countries.* Baltimore: Johns Hopkins University Press.
Haggard, S., and R. Kaufman. 1989. The politics of stabilization and structural adjustment. In J. D. Sachs, ed. *Developing country debt and economic performance.* Chicago and London: University of Chicago Press. 209–254.
Harberger, A. C. 1990. Principles of taxation applied to developing countries: What have we learned? In M. J. Boskin and C. E. McLure, Jr., eds. *World tax reform: Case studies of developed and developing countries.* San Francisco: International Center for Economic Growth.
Harris, J. R., and M. P. Todaro. 1970. Migration, unemployment and development: A two-sector analysis. *American Economic Review* 60 (1): 126–142.

Haswell, M. R. 1975. *The nature of poverty: A case-history of the first quarter-century after World War II*. New York: St. Martin's Press.

Haughton, J. 1986. *Cereals policy in the Sahel: The Gambia*. Paris: Organization for Economic Cooperation and Development, CILSS, Club du Sahel. D(86)285.

Haydu, J., M. Alers-Montalvo, J. B. Eckert, F. Dumbaya, B. Gai, and L. Jabang. 1986. Mixed farming in The Gambia. Gambia Mixed Farming and Resource Management Project, Technical Report, No. 10.

Heller, P. 1974. Public investment in LDC's with recurrent cost constraints: The Kenyan case. *Quarterly Journal of Economics* 88(May): 251–277.

———. 1979. The underfinancing of recurrent development costs. *Finance and Development* 16(1):38–41.

Homan, B. M., et al. 1988. A review of customs practices and procedures in The Gambia. Banjul: Republic of The Gambia.

Hyden, G. 1983. *No shortcuts to progress: African development management in perspective*. Berkeley, CA: University of California Press.

Hyden, G., and M. Barrett. 1991. *Government policies in Africa*. Boulder, CO: Lynn Reinner.

International Monetary Fund. 1982. The Gambia: Request for standby arrangement and approval of multiple currency practice. Washington, D.C.: IMF. EBS/12/17.

———. 1983. The Gambia: Staff report for the 1983 Article IV consultation. Washington, D.C.: IMF. SM/83/165.

———. 1986. Aide memoire of IMF mission. Banjul: IMF.

———. 1991. *International financial statistics yearbook 1991*. Washington, D.C.: IMF.

———. 1992. *Government finance statistics yearbook 1992*. Washington, D.C.: IMF.

Jenkins, G. 1991. Tax reform: Lessons learned. In D. Perkins and M. Roemer, eds. *Reforming economic systems in developing countries*. Cambridge, MA: Harvard Institute for International Development.

———. 1992. Economic reform and institutional innovation. *Bulletin for International Fiscal Documentation* 46 (December): 588–596.

Johnson, H. G. 1967. Planning and the market in economic development. In H. G. Johnson, *Money, trade and economic growth*. Cambridge, MA: Harvard University Press.

Johnson, R. A. 1986. Monetary policy: The changing environment. *Bulletin* (Reserve Bank of Australia) (November): 1–3.

Jones, C. 1986. The domestic groundnut marketing system in The Gambia. Report to the Ministry of Finance of The Gambia, April.

Keen, P. G. W. 1981. Information systems and organizational change. *Communications of the ACM* 28 (1): 24–33.

Kellaway, R. 1986. Report on Gambian customs. Banjul: British High Commission.

Killick, T. 1993. *The adaptive economy: Adjustment policies in low-income countries.* London: Overseas Development Institute.

Klitgaard, R. 1988. *Controlling corruption.* Berkeley, CA: University of California Press.

Lacey, R. M. 1989. Managing public expenditure. World Bank Discussion Paper, No. 56. Washington, D.C.: World Bank.

Ladd, J. 1989. Stock market feasibility in The Gambia. Report submitted to the United States Agency for International Development, June.

Langdell-Mills, P., and I. Serageldin. 1991. Governance and the development process. *Finance and Development* 3 (September): 14–17.

Latham, R. S. 1970. Survey of the income tax system in The Gambia. Banjul: Ministry of Finance and Trade.

Lee, B., and J. Nellis. 1990. Enterprise reform and privatization in socialist economies. World Bank Discussion Paper, No. 104. Washington, D.C.: World Bank.

Lee, R. D. Jr., 1992. Linkages among poverty, development and budget systems. *Public Budgeting and Finance* 12 (1): 48–60.

Long, M., et al. 1990. Financial systems and development. Policy and Research Series, No. 15. Washington, D.C.: World Bank.

Loutfi, M. 1989. Development issues and state policies in Sub-Saharan Africa. *International Labor Review* 128 (2): 137–154.

Management Development Institute. 1989. Review of the Ministry of Finance and Trade. Kanifing: The Gambia: Management Development Institute.

Mann, R. 1975. The Gambia: Land and vegetation degradation survey: The need for land reclamation by comprehensive ecological methods. Report prepared for the Ministry of Agriculture and Natural Resources. Banjul: FAO. No. C/AM/LRP/75.

Mann, C.K. and M.F. McPherson. 1982. Improving food policy. International Agricultural Development Service Report. New York: IADS. 1982: 27–33.

Mazrui, A. 1980. *The African condition: A political diagram.* New York and Cambridge: Cambridge University Press.

McKinnon, R. I. 1991. *The order of economic liberalization: Financial control in the transition to a market economy.* Baltimore: Johns Hopkins University Press.

McPherson, M. F. 1979. An analysis of the recurrent cost problem in The Gambia. Cambridge, MA: Harvard Institute for International Development.

———. 1983. Monetary policy in The Gambia. Paper prepared for the Harvard Institute for International Development, December.

———. 1984. Revenue collection outside the Ministry of Finance and Trade, The Gambia: Review and recommendations for change. Banjul: Ministry of Finance and Trade.

———. 1991. The politics of economic reform in The Gambia. Development Discussion Paper, No. 386. Cambridge, MA: Harvard Institute for International Development. Revised April 1992.

McPherson, M. F., Jabai, S., and P. McNamara. 1989. Report on and review of the customs records (January 1987 to June 1988). Banjul: Ministry of Finance and Trade.

McPherson, M. F., and R. D. Mallon. 1990. The role of information in stabilization and economic recovery: The case of The Gambia. Development Discussion Paper, No. 350. Cambridge, MA: Harvard Institute for International Development.

McPherson, M. F., and J. L. Posner. 1991. Structural adjustment and agriculture in Sub-Saharan Africa: Lessons from The Gambia. Development Discussion Paper, No. 410. Cambridge, MA: Harvard Institute for International Development.

McPherson, M. F., and S. Radelet. 1991. Economic recovery in The Gambia: Policies, politics, foreign aid, and luck. In D. H. Perkins and M. Roemer, eds. *Reforming economic systems in developing countries*. Cambridge, MA: Harvard Institute for International Development.

McPherson, M. F., and C. F. Zinnes. 1991. Economic retrogression in Sub-Saharan Africa. Paper presented to the Northeast Universities Development Conference, October 4–5, at Harvard University, Cambridge, Massachusetts.

———. 1992. Institutional weakness, social norms, and economic retrogression. Harvard Institute for International Development Discussion Paper, No. 423. Cambridge, MA: Harvard Institute for International Development.

Meier, G. H., ed. 1983. *Pricing policy for development management*. Baltimore: Johns Hopkins University Press for the World Bank.

Mills, B. F., M. B. Kabay, and D. Boughton. 1988. Soil fertility management strategies in three villages of Eastern Gambia. Gambia Agricultural Research Papers, No. 2. Banjul: Ministry of Agriculture.

Morrison, D. G. 1992. Organizational re-engineering: Information technology and the search for organizational direction and focus: The example of the customs administration in The Dominican Republic. Paper presented at Conference on Information Technology and Fiscal Compliance, Harvard International Tax Program, November.

Murthy, S. 1989. Gambia Utilities Corporation. Case presented at the NIB/HIID workshop on parastatal reform, October, at the Management Development Institute, Kanifing, The Gambia.

Mwaipaya, P. 1980. *The importance of quality leadership in national development, with special reference to Africa.* New York: Vantage Press.

National Agricultural Data Centre. 1991. *1990/91 national agricultural sample survey statistical yearbook of Gambian agriculture 1990.* Banjul: NADC.

Nelson, J., ed. 1990. *Economic crisis and policy choice.* Princeton, NJ: Princeton University Press.

Niehans, J. 1984. *International monetary economics.* Baltimore: Johns Hopkins University Press.

Obasanjo, O. 1987. *Africa in perspective: Myths and realities.* New York: Council on Foreign Relations.

Office of Technology Assessment. 1988. *Enhancing agriculture in Africa: A role for U.S. development assistance.* Washington, D.C.: OTA, U.S. Congress, OTA–F–365.

Omolehinwa, E., and E. M. Roe. 1989. Boom and bust budgeting: Repetitive budgetary processes in Nigeria, Kenya and Ghana. *Public Budgeting and Finance* 9 (2): 43–65.

Organization for African Unity. 1980. *The Lagos plan of action for the implementation of the Monrovia strategy for the economic development of Africa.* Lagos: OAU.

Parfitt, T. W., and S. P. Riley. 1989. *The African debt crisis.* London: Routledge.

Perry, G. 1985. Taxes in The Gambia. Memo for the Ministry of Finance and Trade, Banjul, June.

Posner, J. L., and E. Gilbert. 1989a. District agricultural profile Central Baddibu, North Bank Division. Gambia Agricultural Research Papers, Working Paper No. 2. Banjul: Ministry of Agriculture, Department of Agricultural Research.

―――. 1989b. District agricultural profile of Foni Berefet and Foni Bintang-Karenai, western division. Gambia Agricultural Research

Papers, Working Paper No. 3. Banjul: Ministry of Agriculture, Department of Agricultural Research.

Posner, J. L., and T. Jallow. 1987. A survey of groundnut and millet farming practices: Implications for agronomic research. Gambia Agricultural Research Papers, 1987, No. 1. Banjul: Ministry of Agriculture, Department of Agricultural Research.

Pradhan, S., and V. Swaroop. 1993. Public spending and adjustment. *Finance and Development* 30 (3): 28–31.

Premchand, A. 1981. Government budget reforms: An overview. *Public Budgeting and Finance* (summer): 74–85.

———. 1983. *Government budgeting and expenditure controls: Theory and practice.* Washington, D.C.: IMF.

Quirk, P. J., B V. Christensen, K. Huh, and T. Sasaki. 1987. Floating exchange rates in developing countries: Experience with auction and interbank markets. International Monetary Fund Occasional Paper, No. 53. Washington, D.C.: IMF.

Radelet, S. 1990. Economic recovery in The Gambia: The anatomy of an economic recovery program. Ph.D. diss., Harvard University.

———. 1992a. Reform without revolt: The political economy of economic reform in The Gambia. *World Development* 20 (8): 1087–1099.

———. 1992b. Stabilization policies and economic performance in Sub-Saharan Africa. Draft report for The Bureau for Africa, United States Agency for International Development, March.

———. 1993. The Gambia's economic recovery: Policy reforms, foreign aid or rain? *Journal of Policy Modeling* 15 (3): 251–276.

Ramamurthy, G. V. 1986. Agricultural credit policy and structure: The Gambia. Report to the United Nations Food and Agricultural Organization, Technical Cooperation Program, Rome, July. TCP/GAM/4503.

Ravenhill, J. 1986. Africa's continuing crises: The elusiveness of development. In J. Ravenhill, ed. *Africa in economic crisis.* New York: Columbia University Press. 1–43.

Reisen, H. 1989. Public debt, external competitiveness, and fiscal discipline in developing countries. Princeton Studies in International Finance, No. 66. Princeton, NJ: Princeton University Press.

Robertson, A. F. 1987. *The dynamics of productive relationships: African share contracts in comparative perspective.* Cambridge: Cambridge University Press.

Rodrick, D. 1990. How should structural adjustment programs be designed? *World Development* 18 (7): 933–947.

Roe, E. M. 1986. The ceiling as base: National budgeting in Kenya. *Public Budgeting and Finance* 6 (2): 87–103.

Roemer, M. 1992. Strategies of industrialization: Lessons for The Gambia. Prepared for the Government of The Gambia at the Harvard Institute for International Development, July 1.

Roemer, M., and S. Radelet. 1991. "Macroeconomic Reform in Developing Countries." In Dwight H. Perkins and Michael Roemer, eds., *Reforming Economic Systems in Developing Countries*, pages 55–80. Cambridge, Mass.: Harvard Institute for International Development.

Rumbaugh, T. 1992. The Gambia sustains economic reforms, significantly improves performance. *IMF Survey* 21 (17): 270.

Sandbrook, R. 1987. *The politics of Africa's economic stagnation*. Cambridge: Cambridge University Press.

———. 1990. Taming the African leviathan. *World Policy Journal* 7(4): 673–701.

Shalizi, Z., and L. Squire. 1988. Tax policy in Sub-Saharan Africa. World Bank Policy and Research Series, No. 2. Washington, D.C.: World Bank.

Shipton, P.M. 1992. "The Rope and the Box: Group Savings in The Gambia." In Dale W. Adams and Delbert A. Fitchett, eds., *Informal Finance in Low-Income Countries*, pages 25–42. Boulder: Westview Press.

———. 1993. "Borrowing and Lending in The Gambia: Local Perspectives on Formal and Informal Finance in Agarian West Africa." In Lawrence H. White, ed., *African Finance: Research and Reform*, pages 133–161 and 429–435. San Francisco: ICS Press.

———. 1994. "Time and Money in the Western Sahel: A Clash of Cultures in Gambian Rural Finance." In James P. Acheson, ed., *Anthropology and Institutional Economics*, pages 283–330. Lanham, MD: University Press of New England, for the Society for Economic Anthropology.

———. 1995. "How Gambians Save: Culture and Economic Strategy at an Ethnic Crossroads." In Jane I. Guyer, ed., *Money Matters: Instability, Values, and Social Payments in the Modern History of West African Communities*, pages 245–276. Portsmouth N.H. and London: Heinemann and James Currey.

Shirley, M. 1989. The reform of state-owned enterprises: Lessons from World Bank lending. Policy and Research Series, No. 4. Washington, D.C.: World Bank.

Shleifer, A., and R. W. Vishny. 1993. Corruption. *Quarterly Journal of Economics* (August): 599–617.

Singh, J. P. 1990. Analysis of project costs in Sub-Saharan Africa in selected sectors. In World Bank. *The long-term perspective study of Sub-Saharan Africa, Vol. 2.* Washington, D.C.: World Bank.

Stiglitz, J. E. 1994. The role of the state in financial markets. *Proceedings of the World Bank Annual Conference on Development Economics 1993.* Washington, D.C.: World Bank.

Sumberg, J. R., and E. Gilbert. 1988. Draft animal and crop production in The Gambia. Paper prepared for the Department of Animal Health and Production, Ministry of Agriculture, The Gambia.

Swanson, D., and T. Wolde-Semait. 1989. Africa's public enterprise sector and evidence of reforms. World Bank Technical Paper, No. 95. Washington, D.C.: World Bank.

Timmer, C. P. 1991. The role of the state in agricultural development. In C. P. Timmer, ed. *Agriculture and the state: Growth, employment, and poverty in developing countries.* Ithaca: Cornell University Press.

Timmer, C. P., W. P. Falcon, and S. R. Pearson. 1983. *Food policy analysis.* Baltimore: Johns Hopkins University Press.

United Nations. 1986. Report on the Preparatory Committee of the Whole for the special session of the General Assembly on the critical economic situation in Africa. UN 13th Special Session Supplement, No 1. New York: United Nations.

United Nations Economic Commission for Africa. 1985. *Survey of economic and social conditions in Africa 1983–1984.* Addis Ababa: UNECA.

———. 1989. *African alternative framework to structural adjustment programmes for socio-economic recovery and transformation.* Addis Ababa: UNECA. E.ECA.CM.15/6/Rev.3.

United States Agency for International Development. 1984. *Economic and financial policy analyses project 635–0225.* The Gambia: USAID.

United States Department of Agriculture. 1990. USDA Economic Research Division statistical bulletin. In *World agriculture trends and indicators 1970–89.* Washington, D.C.: USDA. No. 815.

University of Michigan Center for Research on Economic Development. 1977. *Marketing, price policy and storage of food grains in The Sahel, volume II; Country studies: The Gambia.* Ann Arbor, MI: CRED.

Vickers, J., and G. Yarrow. 1991. Economic perspective on privatization. *Journal of Economic Perspectives* 5 (2): 111–132.

Vincze, J. 1987. A national sales tax for The Gambia. Memo for the Ministry of Finance and Trade, Banjul, May.

von Braun, J., and D. Peutz. 1987. An African fertilizer crisis: Origin and economic effects in The Gambia. *Food Policy* 12(4):337–348.

von Braun, J., D. Peutz, and J. Webb. 1989. Irrigation technology and commercialization of rice in The Gambia: Effect on income and nutrition. Research Report, No. 75. Washington, D.C.: International Food Policy Research Institute.

Walsh, B. 1990. The Gambia's exchange rate system, 1986–1990. Economic Note. Banjul: Gambia Ministry of Finance and Trade.

———. 1991. Interest rates and economic development in The Gambia. Economic Note. Banjul: Gambia Ministry of Finance and Economic Affairs.

Ward, H.G. 1989. *African development reconsidered: New perspectives from the continent.* New York: Phelps-Stokes Institute.

Wing, M. D. 1983. The credit system in The Gambia. Banjul: USAID/Banjul.

World Bank. 1975. The economy of The Gambia. Washington, D.C.: The World Bank/West Africa Region. No. 907–GM.

———. 1981a. *Accelerating development in Sub-Saharan Africa: An agenda for action.* Washington, D.C.: World Bank.

———. 1981b. *Basic needs in The Gambia.* Washington, D.C.: The World Bank.

———. 1984. *Towards sustained development in Sub-Saharan Africa.* Washington, D.C.: World Bank.

———. 1985a. Debt Systems Conference. External Debt Division Economic Analysis and Projections Department. Washington, D.C.: World Bank.

———. 1985b. The Gambia: Development issues and prospects. Washington, D.C.: World Bank/West Africa Region. No. 5693–GM .

———. 1985c. The Gambia: Financial sector review. Washington, D.C.: World Bank/West Africa Region. No. 4766–GM.

———. 1986. *Financing adjustment with growth in Sub-Saharan Africa, 1986–90.* Washington, D.C.: World Bank.

———. 1986. *World debt tables 1985.* Washington, D.C.: World Bank.

———. 1988a. *Report on adjustment lending.* Washington, D.C.: Country Economics Department, World Bank.

———. 1988b. *World debt tables 1987.* Washington, D.C.: World Bank.

———. 1988c. *World development report 1988.* Washington, D.C.: World Bank.

———. 1989a. *Sub-Saharan Africa: From crisis to sustainable growth.* Washington, D.C.: World Bank.

———. 1989b. *World debt tables 1988*. Washington, D.C.: World Bank.

———. 1989c. *World development report 1989*. Washington, D.C.: World Bank.

———. 1990a. *A framework for capacity building in policy analysis and economic management in Sub-Saharan Africa*. Washington, D.C.: World Bank/Africa Region.

———. 1990b. *World debt tables 1989*. Washington, D.C.: World Bank.

———. 1991a. *Lessons of tax reform*. Washington, D.C.: World Bank.

———. 1991b. The reform of public sector management: Lessons from experience. Policy and Research Series, No. 18. Washington, D.C.: Country Economics Department, World Bank.

———. 1991c. *World debt tables 1990*. Washington, D.C.: World Bank.

———. 1991d. *World tables 1991*. Baltimore and London: Johns Hopkins University Press.

———. 1994. *Adjustment in Africa: Reforms, results, and the road ahead*. Oxford: Oxford University Press.

World Bank and United Nations Development Program. 1989. *Africa's adjustment and growth in the 1980s*. Washington, D.C.: World Bank and UNDP.

Wright, J. 1988. Maize/cowpea relay performance as affected by relay time and tied ridges cultivation in The Gambia. Master's thesis, University of Wisconsin.

Index

ACBI, 224
ADB, 237
  insolvency of, 178, 183
Administrative capacity, 225
Administrative Reform Program (ARP), 223, 232
Africa Capacity Building Initiative (ACBI), 224
Africa Development Bank, 52
Africa Hotels (Sunswing), 237, 241
African Economic Policy Reform Program, 117, 285
Agricultural Development Bank (ADB), 237
  insolvency of, 178, 183
Agricultural Development Project II, 103, 104
Agriculture
  and economic reform, 14
  ERP and, 105–109, 195–197
  effect of rainfall on, 194–195, 276
  government regulation of, 197–198
  macroeconomic policies and, 192, 194, 201–202
  performance prior to ERP, 192–195
  pressures on, 198–201
  problems in, 191
  promotion of, 25–26
  rural lending, 96–99, 101–104
  rural saving, 99–101
  smallholder, 298–299
  technologies of, 199–200
Agriculture Ministry, reorganization of, 28

Analytical capacity, 225
Angola
  economic difficulties of, 4
  political upheaval in, 7
ARP (Administrative Reform Program), 223, 232
Arrears, 178
  between parastatals and government, 176
  consequences of, 179–180
  domestic debt, 175–178
  external, 49, 169–170
  resolution of, 180–183
Atlantic Hotel, 237

Banjul Breweries Ltd., 237, 241
BICI (International Bank for Commerce and Industry), 79
Botswana, economic growth in, 4, 294
Bretton Woods system, collapse of, 293
Budget, 114–116
  calculated effect of reduction of, 273–274
  donor input on, 115, 117
  process of, 117
  recurrent expenditures in, 116, 121
Budget deficit, 296, 298
  reduction of, 26, 111, 113–114
Budget reform, 13, 26
  computers in, 119, 120
  in ERP, 112–113, 117–119
  failure of, 121–122
  IMF and, 120

333

Budget reform *(continued)*
  Ministry of Finance proposals for, 118–119
  obstacles to, 119–121
  types of, 111, 112
Bureaucracy
  attempts to cut, 50, 113–114, 121, 309
  growth of, 22–23
  resistance to reform, 306
Burkina Faso, economic recovery of, 4

Caisse Centrale, 283
Cameroon, economic growth in, 294
Capacity improvement, 224–225
  in Ministry of Finance, 225–226
Capital gains tax, 126
Central Bank (CBG), 79, 90, 237
  arrears owed to, 178, 182
  monetary policy enforced by, 86–87
  rate-setting by, 26, 27, 72–73, 85, 274–275
  relation to Ministry of Finance, 80–81
  reserves of, 71–72
  resistance to ERP, 37–38
  role in ERP, 282–283
  treasury bill tender system of, 27, 80, 88
Central revenue department (CRD), 137
CFA zone, 66
CFAO Supermarket Ltd., 237
  sale of, 241
CGE. *See* Computable general equilibrium model
Chad, economic difficulties of, 4
Chile, foreign capital flow in, 297
Citrus Products Company Ltd., 237
Civil service
  growth of, 22–23
  reform of, 50, 113–114, 121, 309
  resistance to reform, 306
Cobb-Douglas production function, 268
Communications capacity, 225
Computable general equilibrium (CGE) model, 267
  of Gambian economy, 268–278
Consumption taxes, 125–126, 138
Convertible currencies, 297–298
Cooperative societies, rural, 106–108

Cost/benefit analysis, 112
Country Economic Memorandum (World Bank), 49–50
CRD, 137
Credit, 13
  and agriculture, 13, 95–108, 196
  controls, 86–87
  cyclic patterns of, 87
Crowding out, 174
Customs
  corruption in, 251, 253–258
  effects of ERP on, 30
  graft in, 10–11
  performance of, 261
  revenue from, 252–253
  weaknesses in, 261
Customs reform, 15–16, 121
  drawbacks to, 260–261
  ERP and, 114
  implementation of, 258–259
  importance of, 251
  in 1986, 255–256, 259
  in 1988, 257–258, 259
  recommendations for, 262

Dalasi
  convertibility of, 297
  devaluation of, 25–26, 27
  effect of floating, 61, 68, 70–73, 272
  floating of, 50, 67–68, 283–284, 296
  refixing of, 89
  value vs. pound sterling, 69
Debt. *See* Domestic debt; External debt
Deregulation, of PEs, 242
Development Act, 128
  revision of, 28, 140
Diouf, prime minister of Senegal, 39
Divestiture. *See* Privatization
Divestiture Strategy Action Plan, 241
Domestic debt
  accumulation of, 173
  in arrears, 174–183
  financing of, 14
  government-guaranteed, 182
  problems of, 173–174
  rationalizing, 183–184

Economic Recovery Program. *See* ERP
Economic reform
  design of, 36, 295–296

Economic reform *(continued)*
  donor role in, 308
  facilitated by crisis, 301
  gradualism in, 300
  guidelines for success of, 304–305
  implementation of, 303–304
  institutional problems with, 6
  introduction of, 299–303
  macroeconomic balance and, 296
  macroeconomic policies and, 307
  mandate for, 40–42
  obstacles to, 306
  politics of, 12, 31, 33–44
  postponement of, 33–35
  resistance to, 37–38
  self-implementing, 304
  shock treatment, 300–301
  See also ERP
EEC, grants to The Gambia, 53
EFPA (Economic and Financial Policy Analyses project), 222–223
  effects of, 231
  rationale for, 230
Eritrea, elections in, 7
ERP
  accomplishments of, 28–29, 290
  agriculture and, 105–109, 195–197
  assessment of, 16, 19, 30–31
  budget reform in, 111, 112–113, 117–119
  CGE model of, 268–278
  computed effects of, 271
  continued by PSD, 286, 290–291
  donor support for, 12, 30, 49–57, 302–303
  effects on institutional policy, 219
  exchange rate reform and, 64–67
  formulation of, 24
  and groundnut industry, 208–216
  hardships imposed by, 29–30
  IMF guidelines for, 282–285
  IMF support of, 50
  impact on financial system, 81, 86
  implementation of, 27–28, 303–305
  investment incentives in, 91
  lessons to be learned from, 295–309
  political leadership and, 41–42, 301–302, 306
  political success of, 33
  relation to coup of 1994, 10
  resistance to, 41
  role of Central Bank in, 282–283
  rural finance under, 105–108
  sequencing and pace of, 299–300
  World Bank and, 282, 285
Ethiopia, economic difficulties of, 4
Exchange rate, 283–284
  and economic performance, 62, 64
  fluctuations in, 15, 71–72
  real, 64
  table of, 69
Exchange rate reform, 12, 25–26
  effects of, 50, 61, 68, 70–73, 272
  ERP and, 64–67
  mechanism of, 67–68
  policies supporting, 69–70
Extended Structural Adjustment Facility (ESAF), 52
External debt, 20, 23, 24, 27, 49, 283
  administration of, 159, 161–166
  borrowing policies, 167–168
  buildup of, 160–161
  management of, 14, 159–160, 166–171
  payment procedures, 165
  refinancing of, 168–169
  relation to agriculture, 196
  repayment of arrears, 169–170
  statistical reporting of, 162–164

Fertilizer market, liberalization of, 27
Financial Institutions Act, 90
Financial reform, 13, 77, 87–93
  alternative instruments, 88
  Central Bank and, 90
  confidence building, 88–89
  contingency plans, 91–92
  ERP and, 81
  legal basis for, 89–90
  new institutions, 89
  price decontrol, 88
Fish Processing and Marketing Corporation (FPMC), 237
Fixed-rate system, 65, 66
Float, 283–284, 296
  consequences of, 68, 70–73, 272
  donor relations and, 50, 61
  vs. fixed rate, 65–66
  justifications for, 67
  mechanism of, 67–68
  supporting policies, 69–70
Food shortages, 24, 191, 197
  US aid to combat, 53–54

Foreign aid, 49–54
  economic effects of, 55–56, 276–277
Foreign exchange, 80
  and recurrent costs, 151
FPMC, 237
France, grants to The Gambia, 54

The Gambia
  agriculture in, 7–8
  as aid recipient, 22
  balance of payments of, 65, 277
  British influence on, 290
  budget deficit of, 296
  budget process of, 117
  budgeting of, 22–23
  capital expenditures in, 147, 148
  CGE model of economy, 268–278
  countercoup of 1994, 10
  coup of 1981, 7, 34–35, 39
  coup of 1994, 7, 10
  currency devaluation in, 23–24
  democracy in, 7, 40
  economic expansion in 1970s, 220
  economic recovery of, 3
  economic stabilization of, 9, 28–29, 30
  economic statistics for, 193
  economy at beginning of study, 8–9
  exchange rate system of, 283–284
  external debt of, 20, 23, 24, 27, 283
  financial indicators of, 63
  financial markets in, 80
  financial system of, 79–80
  foreign aid to, 276–277
  foreign exchange reserves of, 23, 283
  geography of, 7
  government of, 7
  government personnel cuts mandated by ERP, 28
  growth of bureaucracy in, 22–23
  harvest failure in 1983–1984, 24
  leadership problems in, 231–232
  legal system of, 89–90
  as microcosm of SSA, 295
  monetary aggregates in, 82–85
  money supply growth in, 296
  political leadership of, 301–302
  population of, 7
  post-ERP economic condition, 21, 28–29
  pre-ERP economic condition, 20–24
  prognosis for, 9–10, 31, 308
  public sector expansion of, 48–49
  recurrent cost problem in, 147–149
  relations with Senegal, 7, 38–40, 127, 284
  trade relations of, 8
  withdrawal of donor support to, 35, 49
Gambia Central Cooperative Banking and Marketing Union, 237
Gambia Commercial and Development Bank (GCDB), 27, 79, 237
  arrears owed to, 178, 180, 181
  difficulties of, 103–104, 238
  insolvency of, 104, 173, 177
  and monetary policy, 86
  rural activities of, 102–103
Gambia Cooperatives Union (GCU), 237, 242
  counterproductive effects of, 102, 108–109
  economic impact of, 105
  financial services provided by, 79
  function of, 34, 95
  graft in, 10
  groundnut trade by, 207, 210, 212–214
  history of, 103–104
  reform of, 104–105
  relations with GCDB, 102–103
Gambia National Insurance Corporation (GNIC), 237
Gambia Oil Seeds Marketing Board, 236–237
Gambia Ports Authority (GPA), 237
  debt servicing of, 181
  performance contracts of, 181
Gambia Produce Marketing Board (GPMB), 127, 237
  bankruptcy of, 23
  debt restructuring of, 182
  difficulties of, 205, 207–208, 238, 242
  financial services provided by, 79
  groundnut prices fixed by, 194
  management changes in, 211, 243
  performance contracts of, 181
  privatization of, 285

Gambia Produce Marketing Board
  (continued)
  procedures of, 212
  reform of, 239
  revenues of, 34
  See also Groundnut industry
Gambia Public Transport Corporation
  (GPTC)
  ERP and, 27
  reform of, 239, 242
Gambia River Transport Corporation
  (GRTC), 237
Gambia Savings Bank, (POSB), 79,
  236, 237
Gambia Tannery Company
  (GAMTAN), 237
Gambia Telecommunication Company (GAMTEL), 237
  reform of, 239, 242
Gambia Utilities Corporation
  (GUC), 237
  external debt of, 167, 169, 182
  implementation of ERP by, 27
  management changes in, 243
  performance contracts of, 181
  reform of, 239, 242
Gambia Women's Finance Corp., 79
GAMTAN (Gambia Tannery Company), 237
GAMTEL (Gambia Telecommunication Company), 237
  reform of, 239, 242
Gamtours, sale of, 241
GCDB. See Gambia Commercial
  and Development Bank
GCU. See Gambia Cooperatives
  Union
GEDRES (Gambia External Debt Reporting System), 163, 171
  installation of, 164–165
Ghana
  economic difficulties of, 4
  economic recovery of, 4
  economic reforms in, 294, 308
  Rawlings government in, 308
GNIC (Gambia National Insurance
  Corporation), 237
GPA. See Gambia Ports Authority
GPMB. See Gambia Produce Marketing Board
GPTC (Gambia Public Transport
  Corporation)
  implementation of ERP in, 27

  reform of, 239, 242
Gradualism, 300
Groundnut industry, 15
  effect of float on, 272
  effect of rainfall on, 191, 276
  importance of, 205, 208
  marketing system of, 102–103,
    107–108, 211–214
  problems with, 206, 207–208
  processing system of, 215
  reform of, 208–216
  studies of, 213
  subsidy of, 114, 197, 208–211,
    273–274, 296, 298–299, 308
GRTC (Gambia River Transport
  Corporation), 237
GUC. See Gambia Utilities Corporation

Hong Kong
  effects of convertible currency,
    297–298
  trade in, 297

IBAS, 79
IDB (Islamic Development Bank),
  54, 169
IMF
  budget reforms required by, 120
  and PSD, 282–285
  support of ERP, 50–52
Import tax, effect of, 275
Income tax, 127
  corporate, 129–130
  distribution of burden of, 131
  personal, 129
  reforms of, 133–136, 142
  restructuring of, 28, 30
  schedules of, 129–131, 132
Income Tax Act, 129
India, budget reform in, 112
Indigenous Business Advisory
  Service (IBAS), 79
Indonesia, effects of convertible
  currency, 297–298
Infrastructure repair, 147, 149–150,
  196
Institutional reform, importance of,
  232
Interest rates, 26, 27, 50
  and agriculture, 196
  control of, 274–275
  and economic troubles in SSA, 293

Interest rates *(continued)*
    under ERP, 82, 84–85
    and exchange rates, 70
International Bank for Commerce
    and Industry (BICI), 79
International Monetary Fund. *See*
    IMF
Islamic Development Bank (IDB),
    54, 169

Jammeh, Lieutenant Yaya, 10
Jawara, Sir Dawda, 7, 10, 19, 28,
    31, 33, 35, 36, 37–38, 43, 209,
    301–302, 308
Jaycox, Edward, 219, 220, 229, 230,
    231

Kellaway report, 261–262
Kenya
    budget reform in, 112
    economic growth in, 294
Kombo Beach Hotel (Novotel),
    237

Lesotho, economic successes of, 4
Liberia
    economic difficulties of, 4
    political upheaval in, 7
Livestock Marketing Board (LMB),
    237
Loans Division, of Ministry of Finance, 222
London Club, 28, 54, 168, 169, 283

Macroeconomic reform, 14, 296, 307
    and agriculture, 192–203
    budget reform, 111–123
    domestic debt management,
        173–189
    exchange rate reform, 61–75
    external debt management,
        159–171
    monetary policy and financial reform, 77–93
    public expenditures, 145–158
    rural credit and savings, 95–108
    tax reform, 125–143
Malaysia
    budget reform in, 112
    effects of convertible currency,
        297–298
Mali, economic growth in, 294
Managed Fund Agreement, 104

Management Development Institute
    (MDI), 226
Managerial capacity, 225
Mauritius, economic successes of, 4
MEPID, 117, 120
Millet, farming of, 198
MinFin budget program, 119, 120
Ministry of Economic Planning and
    Industrial Development
    (MEPID), budgetary responsibilities of, 117, 120
Ministry of Finance, 15
    budgetary responsibilities of,
        117, 119–120
    capacity improvement in, 219,
        223–229
    computerization of, 226
    in 1982, 222–223
    Loans Division of, 162
    personnel of, 220, 222
    personnel training in, 226–228
    relation to Central Bank, 80–81
    reputation of, 222
    responsibilities of, 220
    shortcomings of, 225–226
    structure of, 220, 221
Ministry of Overseas Development
    (GB), 222
Ministry of Works and Communications, 237
Ministry of Works and Services, 237
Monetary policy, 13, 78–79
    credit controls, 86–87
    intermediate targets, 85–86
    monetary aggregates, 82–85
    monetary management, 82
    problems of, 77

National Investment Board (NIB),
    240
    Action Plan of, 241
    authority of, 245
    financial services of, 79
    methods of, 243–244
    obstacles to, 244–247
    responsibilities of, 244–245
National Trading Corporation
    (NTC), 237
    external debt of, 169
    sale of, 241, 244
Netherlands, grants to The Gambia,
    53, 56
NIB. *See* National Investment Board

NIB Action Plan, 241
Nigeria, economic growth in, 294
Norway, grants to The Gambia, 53
Novotel, 237
NTC. See National Trading Corporation
Nyambai sawmill, 242
  sale of, 241

OAU (Organization of African Unity), 6
Oil price shocks, 20, 22, 293
  effects of, 284
Open economy
  sustained growth in, 296
  trade in, 297–298
Operations and maintenance expenditures, 145–147
  underfunding of, 149–151
Organization of African Unity (OAU), alternative structural adjustment plan, 6

Parallel markets, 89
Parastatal reform, 15, 26, 236, 238
  obstacles to, 245–246
  performance contracts, 239, 240, 245
  privatization, 239–241
  regulatory concerns in, 241–242
  resistance to, 239, 247
Paris Club, 28, 54, 167, 168, 169, 283
People's Progressive Party (PPP), 7, 33, 40
  makeup of, 302
Performance budgeting, 112
Performance contracts, 15, 28, 181–182, 239, 240, 245
  effectiveness of, 248
  implementation of, 243
  purpose of, 240
PEs. See Public enterprises
Philippines, budget reform in, 112
Planning and programming budgeting system (PPBS), 112
Post Office Savings Bank (POSB). See Gambia Savings Bank
PPBS (Planning and programming budgeting system), 112
PPP (People's Progressive Party), 7, 33, 40
  makeup of, 302

Price controls, 23
Privatization, 15, 28, 239
  effectiveness of, 248
  purpose of, 240–241
  technical issues in, 243–244
Program for Sustained Development
  achievements of, 16, 281
  assessment of, 16
  challenges for, 287–290
  continuity with ERP, 286, 290–291
  described, 286–287
  philosophy of, 288–289
Public enterprises (PEs)
  creation of, 238
  debt of, 88, 176–182
  deregulation of, 242
  economic climate and, 247–248
  importance of, 235, 238
  interlocked debt obligations with government, 176–177, 181–182
  monitoring of, 244–247
  monopolies, 239
  performance of, 236, 238
  privatization of, 241
  reform of. See Parastatal reform
  tax status of, 241
Public expenditure program, 14
  and ERP, 154–156
  implementation of, 152–153
  objectives of, 151–152
Public sector, reform of. See Parastatal reform

Rainfall, effect on economy, 42, 194, 276
Recurrent costs
  capital expenditures as substitute for, 147, 148
  donor involvement in management of, 150
  ERP and, 154–156
  foreign exchange and, 151
  problems of, 145–151
  trimming of, 116, 121
  underfunding of, 149–150, 194
Repetitive budgeting, 111
Rice
  grants of, 54
  market for, 69–70
  price of, 42
Rural credit and savings, 13, 95
  analyzed, 105–108
  cooperative societies, 106–108

Rural credit and savings (continued)
    cultural economy of, 96–101
    government-sponsored, 101–104
Rural Development Project I, 103–104
    Socio-Economic Survey and
        Monitoring Unit, 103
Rwanda, political upheaval in, 7

Sahel, drought in, 299
SAL (Structural Adjustment Loans),
    282
Sales tax, 125, 142
    general, 138, 139, 140
    institution of, 28
    reform of, 114
Saudi Arabia, grants to The Gambia,
    52
SBG. *See* Standard Chartered Bank
    Gambia
Seagull Coldstores Ltd, 237
Senegal
    economic difficulties of, 4
    groundnut industry in, 209, 210,
        214
    relations with The Gambia, 7,
        38–40, 127, 284
Senegambia Beach Hotel, 237
Senegambia Confederation, 7, 127
    breakup of, 284
    formation of, 39
Seychelles, economic successes of, 4
Shock treatment, 300–301
Singapore
    budget reform in, 112
    effects of convertible currency,
        297–298
    trade in, 297
Sisay, Sheriff Saikouba, 16, 24, 27,
    31, 36, 37, 38, 39, 42, 43, 44,
    51, 91, 125, 126, 127, 133,
    209, 222, 223, 225, 230, 231,
    254, 255, 257, 258, 302, 308
Skill broadening, 226
Skill deepening, 226
Social Security and Housing Financ-
    ing Corporation (SSHFC), 79,
    237, 242
    sale of, 244
Somalia
    economic difficulties of, 4
    political upheaval in, 7
South Africa, elections in, 7
Sri Lanka, budget reform in, 112

SSHFC. *See* Social Security and
    Housing Financing Corpora-
    tion
SSSU (Statistics and Special Studies
    Unit), 227
STABEX grants to The Gambia, 53
Standard Chartered Bank Gambia
    (SBG), 79, 237
    sale of, 241, 244
Standard Chartered Merchant Bank
    (London), 51, 169
Strategic capacity, 225
Structural Adjustment Credit, 52–53,
    117, 120, 152
Structural Adjustment Loans (SAL), 282
Sub-Saharan Africa
    causes of economic troubles in,
        293
    development strategies in, 293
    economic adjustment in, 5–7
    economic deterioration in, 4–5
    political reform in, 7
    political turmoil in, 294
    problems of, 5
Sudan, economic difficulties of, 4
Sustainable Growth with Equity
    (World Bank), 288
Swaziland, economic successes of, 4
Switzerland, grants to The Gambia, 53

Tanzania
    economic difficulties of, 4
    economic recovery of, 4
Tax reform, 13
    computerization, 141–142
    of direct taxes, 114, 129–136
    elements of, 126
    importance of, 125
    of income taxes, 28, 30, 133–136,
        142
    of indirect taxes, 136–142
    Ministry of Finance involvement
        in, 127–128
    need for, 126–127
    results of, 128
    of sales tax, 114, 138, 139, 140
    success of, 142–143
    tax base broadening, 126
Taxes Act, 137
Technical assistance
    computer-related, 119–120, 226
    importance of institutional re-
        form to, 232

Technical assistance *(continued)*
  training, 226–229
  unanticipated effects of, 229–230, 230–231
Technical capacity, 225
Thailand, effects of convertible currency, 297–298
Trade, in open economy, 297–298
Trade taxes, 125, 127
Training
  in Ministry of Finance, 227–228
  problems pursuant to, 228–229, 230–231
  types of, 226
Treasury bill tender, 27, 80, 88

Uganda
  economic difficulties of, 4
  economic recovery of, 4
United Africa Corporation, 237
United Kingdom (UK), grants to The Gambia, 52, 53, 54, 56
United Nations Economic Commission for Africa, 6
United States, grants to The Gambia, 53–54

USAID
  assistance to Ministry of Finance, 222
  and ERP, 117, 282, 285
Value-added tax, 125, 138

WACH, 54, 169
Weather, effect on economy, 42, 194, 276
West African Clearing House (WACH), 54, 169
Wing Africa Ltd., 237
World Bank, 55
  and ERP, 282, 285
  Structural Adjustment Credit, 52–53, 117, 120, 152
  Structural Adjustment Loans (SAL), 282

Zambia
  Chiluba government of, 308
  economic difficulties of, 4
  elections in, 7, 308
Zimbabwe
  economic growth in, 294
  economic recovery of, 4